Napoleon For Dummies®

Cheat Sheet

Napoleon's Military Career

The often-used term *Napoleonic Wars* implies that Napoleon was the instigator in every military campaign of the period. That's not the whole story. The wars of this period were really about other nations of Europe trying to overthrow first the French Revolution and then Napoleon. Seven coalitions were formed for these purposes:

- **First Coalition (1792–1797):** Austria, Great Britain, Spain, and Prussia variously were in or out of this coalition against Revolutionary France. The coalition collapsed with General Napoleon Bonaparte's success in Italy that led to the Treaty of Campo Formio. The most important battle was probably the Battle of Lodi (May 10, 1796).

- **Second Coalition (1799–1802):** Britain, Austria, and Russia, which were unhappy with French expansion, were the main culprits here. Napoleon was in Egypt for part of this time, winning the Battle of the Pyramids and establishing modern Egyptology, but he hastened back in 1799 and took control of France as First Consul. His campaign in Italy, mostly against the Austrians, was highlighted by the Battle of Marengo (June 14, 1800).

- **Third Coalition (1805):** Fearful of an expanding France, Britain, Austria, and Russia formed the Third Coalition, but the latter two were soundly beaten at the Battle of Austerlitz (December 2, 1805). The ensuing treaty ended hostilities for only a short time.

- **Fourth Coalition (1806–1807):** Russia and Britain were still at war with France, and Prussia jumped into a new coalition. But the Prussians and Russians were soundly drubbed at the Battle of Friedland (June 14, 1807), effectively ending hostilities.

- **Fifth Coalition (1809):** Once again, the Austrians and British (these guys just *don't* give up, do they?) joined hands to try to throw Napoleon out of France. And once again Napoleon thumped the Austrians, this time at the Battle of Wagram (July 5–6, 1809). But the Brits were getting active in Spain, and the handwriting was on the wall.

- **Sixth Coalition (1812–1814):** Russia betrayed Napoleon, and the resulting hostilities led to Napoleon's invasion of Russia and victory at Borodino (September 7, 1812). But Napoleon's withdrawal from Russia opened the floodgates, and one by one his allies became former allies and members of the Sixth Coalition. Napoleon's defeat at the Battle of Leipzig (October 16–19, 1813) sealed his fate, and in 1814 he was exiled from France (as Emperor of Elba).

- **Seventh Coalition (1815):** Napoleon's return to France in M̶ ̶ 1815 for a second reign as emperor (dubbed *the Hundred Days* to i̶n̶d̶i̶ ̶ ̶ ̶ ̶ ̶sed all his old enemies to unite against him, with final de̶f̶ ̶ ̶ ̶ ̶ ̶ That was it for Napoleon, who was exiled to the isl ̶ ̶ ̶ ̶ ̶ ̶5, 1821.

Napoleon For Dummies®

Cheat Sheet

Napoleon's Legacy

When you hear the name Napoleon, you may think first and foremost of a military leader. But as I discuss in this book, Napoleon made many lasting contributions to the institutions of France and to Europe as a whole. Following are just a handful:

- **The *Code Napoléon:*** When Napoleon became the leader of France, one of his top priorities was to reorganize the entire legal structure. By the time he was done, France had a unified, progressive legal system, which Napoleon then gave to other parts of his empire. Today, the *Code Napoléon* is the basis of law in France and a number of other countries, as well as in the state of Louisiana!

- **Economic reforms:** The terrible French economy was one of the key factors leading to the French Revolution. When Napoleon came to power, he turned it around in only a year. Fair taxes, increased trade, the development of French luxury industries, a new commercial code, an improved infrastructure, and a central bank to control monetary policy were keys to his success.

- **Religious freedom:** The Catholic Church had dominated French society, but the French Revolution tossed it out on its ear. Napoleon reached an agreement with the Pope allowing the Church a major role in French society while providing religious freedom for all others. He also abolished slavery and freed the serfs, and today he is seen as a progressive force in European history.

- **Freedom for the Jews:** The previous item might seem to encompass this accomplishment, but the awful discrimination against Jews makes them a special case. In various parts of Europe, they had been forced to wear arm bands, kept from certain professions, made to live in ghettos, and prevented from attending their synagogues. Napoleon put an end to all of those restrictions, made Jews full citizens of France, and even wrote a proclamation that established the idea of a Jewish homeland in Israel.

- **Education reforms:** To create a middle-class cadre of leaders, Napoleon reorganized France's education system. He restarted the primary schools, created a new elite secondary system of schools (called *lycées*), and established many other schools for the general populace. He promoted education for girls and greatly improved teacher training. Literacy levels in France soared under Napoleon's reforms.

- **European unity:** Napoleon's empire, accompanied by his legal and other reforms, helped provide the basis for what is today the European Union. He worked hard to create a unified Italy, Poland, and Germany. Napoleon was also responsible for sweeping away many of the old regimes and promoting the ideals of equality and European solidarity. Sure, the old regimes still had some life in them when Napoleon left the scene, but things were never really the same. For that reason, Napoleon is often considered the father of modern Europe.

For Dummies: Bestselling Book Series for Beginners

by J. David Markham

WILEY

Wiley Publishing, Inc.

Napoleon For Dummies®

Published by
Wiley Publishing, Inc.
111 River St.
Hoboken, NJ 07030-5774
www.wiley.com

WILEY

About the Author

J. David Markham is an internationally acclaimed historian and Napoleonic scholar. His major books include *Napoleon's Road to Glory: Triumphs, Defeats and Immortality* (winner of the 2004 Napoleonic Society of America *Literary Award*); *Imperial Glory: The Bulletins of Napoleon's Grande Armée* (winner of the International Napoleonic Society's 2003 *President's Choice Award*); and *Napoleon and Dr. Verling on St. Helena.* He has been featured on the History Channel International's *Global View* program on Napoleon, the History Channel's *Conquerors* program *(Napoleon's Greatest Victory; Caesar in Gaul)* and *Napoleon: The Man Who Would Conquer Europe,* as well as in programs on the Learning and Discovery channels. He has served as historical consultant to History Channel and National Geographic Society programs. Markham has contributed to four important reference encyclopedias *(Leadership; World History; American Revolution; French Revolution and Napoleon).* He has presented numerous academic papers to conferences in the United States, the UK, France, Italy, Israel, Georgia, and Russia. He is President of the Napoleonic Alliance and Executive Vice-President and Editor-in-Chief of the International Napoleonic Society. David has organized International Napoleonic Congresses in Italy, Israel, the Republic of Georgia, and France. He was the first American scholar to present a paper at the Borodino Conference in Russia. His awards include the *Legion of Merit* from the International Napoleonic Society, the *President's Medal* from the Napoleonic Alliance, and the *Marengo Medal* from the province of Alessandria, Italy.

Dedication

This book is dedicated to my wife, Barbara A. Markham, whose encouragement and help have made all the difference.

Author's Acknowledgments

I owe a deep debt of gratitude to Stacy Kennedy of Wiley for giving me the chance to write this book and to Joan Friedman for serving as the editor. Both of these ladies have been a pleasure to work with. Any number of other people have helped and encouraged me in my work, including Jerry Gallaher, Don Horward, Ben Weider, my dear friend Doug La Follette, and most of all my wife, Barbara.

Publisher's Acknowledgments

We're proud of this book; please send us your comments through our Dummies online registration form located at www.dummies.com/register/.

Some of the people who helped bring this book to market include the following:

Acquisitions, Editorial, and Media Development

Project Editor: Joan Friedman

Acquisitions Editor: Stacy Kennedy

Technical Editor: Alexander Mikaberidze, PhD, INFR, FINS

Editorial Supervisor: Carmen Krikorian

Editorial Manager: Michelle Hacker

Editorial Assistants: Hanna Scott, Nadine Bell

Cover Photos: © J. David Markham

Cartoons: Rich Tennant (www.the5thwave.com)

Composition Services

Project Coordinators: Adrienne Martinez, Nancee Reeves

Layout and Graphics: Carl Byers, Andrea Dahl, Joyce Haughey, Barry Offringa

Interior Photos: The David Markham Collection

Proofreaders: Laura Albert, Leeann Harney, Carl William Pierce, TECHBOOKS Production Services

Indexer: TECHBOOKS Production Services

Publishing and Editorial for Consumer Dummies

> **Diane Graves Steele,** Vice President and Publisher, Consumer Dummies
>
> **Joyce Pepple,** Acquisitions Director, Consumer Dummies
>
> **Kristin A. Cocks,** Product Development Director, Consumer Dummies
>
> **Michael Spring,** Vice President and Publisher, Travel
>
> **Kelly Regan,** Editorial Director, Travel

Publishing for Technology Dummies

> **Andy Cummings,** Vice President and Publisher, Dummies Technology/General User

Composition Services

> **Gerry Fahey,** Vice President of Production Services
>
> **Debbie Stailey,** Director of Composition Services

Contents at a Glance

Table of Contents

Part II: Building an Empire 75

Chapter 6: Improvising an Army in Italy 77

Chapter 7: Mixing Art, Science, and Guns in Egypt 97

Introduction

Few people in human history are more recognizable than Napoleon
Bonaparte. Go anywhere in the world, and you will find an image of him
in a local museum, antiques related to him in the local shops, and maybe
even a men's store or some other retail space carrying the name "Napoleon."
Even the grocery store isn't safe, as there is a brand of canned goods carrying
his name and image. Starbucks, the famous coffee company, uses Napoleon in
some of its advertising, and, of course, there is Courvoisier Cognac, "The
Cognac of Napoleon." As I keep telling my wife, Barbara, "He's everywhere!"
And you know what? I think she's finally starting to believe me!

And then there are the books. More books are written about Napoleon than
about anyone else in history. Amazing, huh?

Okay, so Napoleon is a pretty big deal. But wasn't he just some warmongering
conqueror who was too short for his own good? Absolutely not. Napoleon
was definitely a conqueror, but he was far more complex than that. It turns
out that he was a very progressive force in history and a fascinating man to
get to know "up close and personal."

And that is what this book tries to do: give you a chance to get to know
Napoleon the man. I tell you his life story, to be sure, but I also tell you about
the forces that influenced his development and the forces with which he had
to contend throughout his career. There is stuff on his battles but also on his
many accomplishments and on his importance to our world today.

And I don't forget his loves: I give you the inside story on his love affair and
marriage to Josephine, why they divorced, why Napoleon then married an
Austrian princess, why a beautiful young Polish woman threw herself at
him . . . well, you get the idea.

If you'd like to get past some of the stereotypes and discover the *real* story of
Napoleon, this is the book for you.

About This Book

This book gives you "everything you ever wanted to know about Napoleon
but were afraid to ask." I start from the beginning of his life and go to the end,
giving you what I hope is a pretty exciting ride. Then I turn to a number of

important elements of Napoleon's storied career that are better dealt with by themselves, rather than squished into a chronological tale. His reforms of everything from the military to the law, his political genius, his problems with the British, his promotion of religious liberty, and his moves toward creating a united Europe: All are discussed herein.

Many people like to read the story of a person's life from start to finish, and you can do that with this book. But you don't have to. Fascinated with the Battle of Waterloo? Head straight to Chapter 15. Want to know more about Napoleon's role in providing religious freedom for the Jews? Chapter 23 is for you. Heard that the Rosetta Stone was found by Napoleon's soldiers in Egypt and want to know more? Head directly to Chapter 7. And so it goes. No matter how you choose to read this book, I think you'll find it a very interesting story.

Oh, one more thing. There are lots of pictures in this book. They are all of engravings or other artifacts from the period or shortly thereafter, and all are from my private collection. Too many history books don't *show* as well as *tell,* and I'm grateful to Wiley for making this truly a show-and-tell book.

Conventions Used in This Book

The short answer: not many. This isn't a scientific book. There's not much technical material and little in the way of Web sites. But there are a few things to keep in mind:

- First, just what should we call this guy, anyway? His name in English is spelled *Napoleon Bonaparte.* Some historians call him Bonaparte until they discuss the period when he became emperor; then they call him Napoleon. To keep it simple, I pretty much always call him Napoleon. The original spelling of his last name was *Buonaparte,* but he got rid of that as soon as he really became somebody, so I use the spelling he preferred and that is most well-known.

- I mention the 18th century and 19th century from time to time, so I'll remind you that the 18th century is actually 1700–1799, and the 19th century is 1800–1899. Just subtract one number and you've got it.

- There are some French words and phrases in the book, and the first time I use them I give English translations.

What You're Not to Read

Listen, I wrote this whole book, so of course *I* think you should read and savor each and every word! But, okay, some words *are* more important than others. Some of the less important are

✔ **Sidebars:** I've included a few sidebars that, while useful, are not critical to your understanding of the main points of the text.

✔ **Technical Stuff paragraphs:** This isn't a scientific or computer book, but some items are somewhat technical in nature. If you see a Technical Stuff icon next to a paragraph, you can skip it if you wish.

Foolish Assumptions

I wrote this book for people just like you!

✔ You like history or biography but don't really want to read 450 pages of small print on one person's life.

✔ You have heard of Napoleon but don't know much about him and want to know more.

✔ You may not know a lot about history, but you have heard of people like Alexander the Great or Julius Caesar.

✔ You think that history can sometimes be dry and are hoping that this book will not put you to sleep. Well, I'm hoping that, too!

How This Book Is Organized

Napoleon is a giant in history, far too big to be devoured in one giant gulp. This book chops his life and accomplishments into six parts, allowing you to take it a little or a lot at a time, as you prefer. The first three parts are a more or less chronological look at his life, while the last three parts look at some of his specific accomplishments.

Part I: Beginnings

Anyone's early life is key to his future development, and Napoleon's birth on the island of Corsica was especially important to the directions he ultimately took. In this part, I first look at Napoleon's overall importance, and then I trace how his early life and the French Revolution led to his moving into a position of prominence. And here is where you get the first installment of one of the great love stories (and some of Napoleon's romances that preceded it).

Part II: Building an Empire

You probably already think of Napoleon as a conqueror who controlled much of Europe. But how did he get to that position? Here I take you with Napoleon to Italy and Egypt and then to France, where we watch him take control of the reins of government. Then we join him as he marches across Europe and wins some of history's most famous battles.

Part III: Losing an Empire

Napoleon was a great military commander, but eventually his luck ran out. This part explains the forces and mistakes that led to his ultimate defeat and removal from power. If we followed him to glory, it's only fair that we follow him to defeat and exile, and I conclude this part with his final days of life.

Part IV: A True Revolutionary

Napoleon was a brilliant person who had great dreams for progressive change. And in the few years he was in power, he was able to give many of those ideas a good start, anyway. This part shows his innovations in the military and talks about what he did to keep the French happy with him in charge. And how did he get from general to emperor, and what happened to Josephine, and just who was that Austrian princess? Tune in to this part for all those answers and more.

Part V: Influencing Nations: Diplomacy and Legacy

This part first looks at Napoleon's relations with his greatest nemesis: Great Britain. It also looks at an unintended consequence of his control of Europe, nationalism, and how it both helped and hurt his cause (and the cause of a united Europe). Finally, I discuss one of Napoleon's most important legacies, the concept of religious freedom, especially for the Jews.

Part VI: The Part of Tens

Wiley told me I "had" to put this part in here, but it was one of the most fun parts to do and, I hope, to read. Planning a trip to Europe? Don't miss some of the battlefields and museums I describe in this part. Wish you could give some historical figure a piece of your mind? I do just that here, and it's great fun. Want to know more about Napoleon? Good for you! This part offers some tips on where to look.

Appendixes

It's always good to be able to see a person's life and accomplishments in some sort of timeframe, and that's what I do for you in the first appendix, a timeline of Napoleon's life. Obviously, page limits mean that I can't list *every-thing* he did. Some books out there actually follow his life day by day, hour by hour. Not this one. But I give you a good overview here.

In the second appendix, I provide two maps that offer visual evidence of Napoleon's power as the Emperor of the French. In the first, you can see how much European territory Napoleon controlled at the height of his reign. In the second, I show you where Napoleon's various military campaigns took him through the years.

Icons Used in This Book

I love the concept of icons, which to me are one of the really neat things about books *For Dummies*. I've selected three for this book:

This icon suggests that what you see here will be relevant elsewhere in the book, so you may want to file it away in the not-so-deep recesses of your mind.

The stuff that follows this icon is perhaps less important to your understanding of what is going on than other material may be. You can skip it (though frankly, I suggest you at least skim it).

This is my favorite! Napoleon is often seen as larger than life, as having his very own legend created around him. This icon suggests some of the elements that have become part of that legend — some negative, mostly positive.

Where to Go from Here

You can start anywhere you want, depending on your interests. Clearly, some people prefer to start at the beginning and move forward. If you do that, some of the chapters on Napoleon's specific accomplishments may fall right into place. But maybe you prefer to read about, say, his Russian campaign and then go back and see how he got there and what happened next. Or maybe you want to read my advice to Napoleon in Chapter 25, and then check out the relevant chapters to see if you agree with me.

Whatever your preference, read on!

Part I
Beginnings

The 5th Wave   By Rich Tennant

While studying at Brienne, Napoleon becomes greatly influenced by the life and politics of Caesar, and vows that some day, he too, will have a salad named after him.

In this part . . .

You've probably heard of Napoleon Bonaparte (after all, you picked up this book) and may even recognize that he was a leader of France who conquered a bunch of countries. You've likely heard of his wife, Josephine, as well. But did you know that neither Napoleon nor Josephine was even French? Indeed, they came from two separate islands thousands of miles apart!

This part answers the burning question, "Just where did this guy Napoleon come from, and how was he able to rise to power?" Okay, that's two questions, but go with it.

In this part, you get an idea why Napoleon is worth reading about. Then, you get to read about him! — his early childhood, the influence of the French Revolution on his early career, and Napoleon's first moves toward greatness. And, of course, I tell you all about Josephine!

Chapter 1

Why Remember Napoleon?

He was a man with amazing abilities and a dangerous ambition; by his talents the finest man to have appeared since Caesar, whom in our eyes he would appear to have surpassed.

Stendhal, A Life of Napoleon

More books have been written about Napoleon than about anyone else in history — more than about Christ, Mohammad, Alexander the Great, or Julius Caesar. The last estimate for the number of books written on Napoleon was over 300,000. We're talking separate *titles* here, not just copies!

There are Napoleonic societies all over the world, and he is routinely featured on television shows and in movies. I am convinced that there are more representations of Napoleon in the decorative arts (engravings, miniatures, bronze and porcelain statues, snuffboxes, and so on) than anyone else — see Figure 1-1 for just one example.

Depose a la Bibliotheque Imperiale

Louis Lacoste del. et Sculp.

NAPOLÉON PREMIER

Empereur des N *Français*

Né à Ajaccio le 15 Aout 1769.

A Paris, chez Jean, Rue St Jean de Beauvais, No 10.

Figure 1-1:
A rare
period
engraving of
Napoleon
as Emperor
of the
French.

And yet, it seems the world can't quite make up its collective mind about who Napoleon really was and why he mattered. To some, he was a promoter of the great values represented by the American and French Revolutions. To others, he was little more than a power-hungry conqueror. But everyone seems to agree that Napoleon was important. As the quote from the 19th-century French writer Stendhal indicates, he is remembered as being both brilliant and a little dangerous, much like the two men to whom he is often compared, Alexander the Great and Julius Caesar.

In this chapter, I touch on why Napoleon was important while he lived and why he is seen as important today. Obviously, answering those questions is the point of this entire book, and I get into much more detail in subsequent chapters. But before I dive into the details (which I find pretty fascinating and think you will, too), I want to whet your appetite.

A Legend in His Own Time

Napoleon was without question the most important person of his age. At the peak of his career, he stood like a colossus astride all of Europe. For a short time, he controlled most of western and central Europe. But his importance was not just in his conquests.

Napoleon's importance can be seen in terms of what he did for France, for Europe, and for the rest of the world. Although he was in power for only around 15 years, his influence extended far beyond what might have been expected for a reign that short.

Speaking of short

Okay, folks, it's time to put the short jokes to rest, once and for all. Lots of people, probably including you, think of Napoleon as that short fellow with a *Napoleonic complex,* the term given to people who feel they have to make up for their lack of height. Well, the evidence is in, and it suggests that Napoleon was actually about 5'6" or 5'7", which, as it happens, was about the average height for Frenchmen in those days. So there!

And, while we're at it, he didn't run around with his hand inside his shirt, either. He wasn't dealing with a stomachache or pains from cancer, and he wasn't (as one Starbucks ad would have it) holding a demitasse of coffee under his coat. That was a popular pose of the 18th and 19th centuries when sitting for a portrait; I've even seen George Washington portrayed that way!

Changing France's institutions

Few leaders in French history (or in the history of any other country, for that matter) had as much influence on their nation as Napoleon did. As you discover later in the book, Napoleon completely reorganized his nation's economic, legal, and educational institutions. He brought a level of unity to the nation that it had never experienced before, and he did so largely by centralizing French institutions. In education, for example, he centralized the curriculum and teacher selection process, giving more power to the education bureaucrats in Paris. But he also reorganized, expanded, and greatly improved educational opportunities for French citizens, changing the education system from an elite-oriented institution to one that produced well-educated and productive middle-class citizens (see Chapter 19).

Napoleon did the same for France's economy, forming the Bank of France and restructuring France's finances and budget process, as well as her tax structure (see Chapter 19). While he was at it, he improved France's infrastructure and promoted religious equality (see Chapters 19 and 23, respectively).

His most famous domestic work was his rewriting of the civil code into a document that would eventually become known as the *Code Napoléon.* Napoleon believed that his legal code was his greatest legacy, and I discuss it in Chapter 19.

Influencing Europe and beyond

Napoleon was able to conquer and control much of Europe just long enough to institute some of the reforms that he had implemented in France. He extended the *Code Napoléon,* in part or in whole, to most of western and some of central Europe. He swept away much of the old feudal order that had dominated Europe for so long and put in its place governments based on equality and the other progressive ideals of the French Revolution (which I discuss in Chapter 3).

When Napoleon fell from power (see Chapter 15), some of that feudal order returned for a while. But as the old saying goes, "How are you going to keep 'em down on the farm after they've seen the big city?" Once introduced to progressive liberalism, the people of Europe would not long tolerate the old order.

Napoleon's ability to take his progressive ideas to Europe depended largely on the success of his army, and that success depended largely on Napoleon ushering in what we might call *modern warfare*. No, he didn't have tanks and planes, but he did reorganize the French army to make it more effective. And he also used tactics that completely bamboozled his opponents. As I show in Chapter 17 (as well as in Chapters 9 and 10), Napoleon is often called the *master of war* for good reason. His tactics are still taught in the world's finest military academies.

Napoleon reorganized France's and Europe's social, political, economic, and military systems. Is that enough to make him the most important person of his day? I think so, and I suspect that you'll agree after you read more of this book.

Respecting Napoleon's Legacy

Napoleon was considered extraordinary during his lifetime, and his reputation has only grown in the years since his death in 1821. Here are a few reasons why:

- As I note in the previous section, he is seen as the father of modern warfare, and in Parts II and III of this book, you get a good idea why.

- Napoleon is often described as the father of the European Union because of the various steps toward greater unity that took place while he was in power.

- His sale of the Louisiana territory to the United States is credited as a major contribution to the U.S. rise as a world power.

- Napoleon's rewriting of the civil code, known as the *Code Napoléon,* has survived in France and in numerous other countries that were influenced by France. (I discuss this code in Chapter 19.)

Napoleon literally changed the face of Europe. His name was used in the cause of revolutions throughout Europe during the 19th century. As I explain in Chapter 6, the unification of Italy had its beginnings with Napoleon's actions there as early as 1796. The modern state of Germany owes much to his actions as well, as I discuss in Chapter 22. His support of Polish independence (see Chapter 22) is still fondly remembered by modern Poles; a large equestrian statue of one of Napoleon's marshals, Prince Joseph Poniatowski, stands at the entrance to the Namiestnikowski Palace that is now used as the Polish president's house.

But we remember Napoleon for much more than his accomplishments. We remember him for his brilliance. He was a genius with a breadth of intellect that has seldom been measured. He could, for example, dictate four different letters to four different secretaries at the same time, rotating a paragraph at a time through each of them, without being reminded where he had left off.

We remember him not only for what he took to countries he came to dominate, but for what he brought back. For example, his soldiers discovered the Rosetta Stone in Egypt, which helped bring about modern Egyptology (see Chapter 7).

Napoleon also captures our imagination from the very nature of his story. His life is a classic rags-to-riches tale; he went from obscurity in Corsica to dominance of a continent. Throw into the mix at least two captivating love stories and a healthy measure of pathos, and you have the makings of all those books and movies.

Napoleon was perhaps the last great man of action. He was constantly on the go, sleeping very little, wolfing down his meals. He was determined to do as much as possible in the small amount of time he knew he would have. As it turned out, he had even less time than he imagined, but he accomplished an amazing amount anyway.

I am not alone, of course, in my estimation of Napoleon as one of the most extraordinary men in history. The German philosopher Johann Goethe wrote that Napoleon was "always enlightened by reason, always clear and decisive, and gifted at every moment with enough energy to translate into action whatever he recognized as being advantageous or necessary. . . . He was in a permanent state of enlightenment, which is why his fate was more brilliant than the world has ever seen or is likely to see after him." Charles Maurice de Talleyrand-Périgord, Napoleon's sometimes friend, sometimes enemy, said that Napoleon's career was "the most extraordinary that has occurred for one thousand years."

A Napoleonic Primer

Before we dive into the good stuff, I want to clarify a few terms that you'll see in later chapters or in other books about Napoleon. First, some historical terms you may want to be familiar with:

✔ **Bourbon Dynasty:** No, I'm not referring to the drink. This was the line of kings of France that began with the 16th-century rule of Henry IV (who ruled 1589–1610) and included Louis XIV (1643–1715), Louis XV (1715–1774), Louis XVI (he of French Revolution fame, 1774–1792), Louis XVIII (1814–1824, minus a few months for the Hundred Days, Napoleon's brief return to power in 1815), Charles X (1824–1830), and Louis Philippe (1830–1848).

The Bourbons also ruled Spain for hundreds of years. In fact, the current king of Spain, Juan Carlos (1975–present), is a Bourbon.

✔ **Hapsburg Dynasty:** This dynasty, centered on Austria, was a major competitor to the Bourbon dynasty. It ruled the Holy Roman Empire from 1273 until its final destruction after World War I in 1918. Francis I of Austria, who you meet in this book, was a member of the Hapsburg Dynasty. (He was also called Francis II of the Holy Roman Empire until he abdicated that title in 1806.) Francis was the father of Marie Louise, Napoleon's second wife.

✔ **Napoleonic Wars:** This term, used to describe wars fought under Napoleon's command, seems to lay blame for these conflicts squarely at Napoleon's feet. In fact, most of the wars fought by Napoleon were really extensions of those started during the French Revolution (see Chapter 3). The old political regimes in Europe feared that the progressive ideas of the Revolution, and later of Napoleon, would spread to their people. (They were right, of course.)

As a result, the old regimes of Europe formed a number of coalitions, or alliances, against first Revolutionary and then Napoleonic France. Thus, these wars are often called the War of the First Coalition, the War of the Second Coalition, and so on. On the Cheat Sheet at the beginning of this book, I explain who took part in each coalition.

✔ **French Empire:** French Empire generally means the period from 1804–1815, when Napoleon was Emperor of the French. However, it also is sometimes used to denote a style of furniture and other decorative arts of that period.

✔ **First Empire and Second Empire:** These terms are usually associated with decorative art styles, or they're used to delineate the period of an artifact. *First Empire* refers to the period when Napoleon I was emperor, generally 1804 to 1815. *Second Empire* is the period of Napoleon III, 1851 to 1870.

✔ **Napoleon I and Napoleon III:** When Napoleon became Emperor of the French (see Chapter 20), his title was Napoleon I because he was the first person named Napoleon to ever be king or emperor in that country. Later in the century, his nephew, Louis Napoleon, was also crowned emperor, becoming Napoleon III.

Wait a minute, couldn't the French even count? Where's Napoleon II? Napoleon had a son, and in 1815, when Napoleon was forced to abdicate his throne (see Chapter 15), his supporters briefly declared the son Napoleon II. (Before that time, and since then, Napoleon's son is usually referred to as *The King of Rome*.) Napoleon's son never really became France's emperor, but in deference to his memory, Louis Napoleon took the title of Napoleon III.

Next, some military and political titles you'll run across:

- ✔ **General:** This is the highest military rank in the army. The type of general denoted the level of command. Thus a *general of brigade* (brigadier general) commanded a brigade. A *general of division* commanded — you guessed it — a division.

- ✔ **Marshal:** This term describes a handful of men (26, to be exact) who were granted the title of Marshal of the Empire. The title often brought with it the command of a major military unit, but it was not strictly a military title; it also came with civilian titles of nobility and great wealth. The symbol of the *Marshalate* (as they were collectively known) was the marshal's baton. Marshals were hand-picked by Napoleon himself, based on their military abilities, political considerations, and personal relationships.

- ✔ **Consul:** After Napoleon gained power in 1799, a new constitution established a three-member executive committee to run the country, replacing the inept and corrupt Directory. Each of these three men was called a Consul, and Napoleon was made First Consul, a position that in reality gave him almost all of the executive power. He retained this position until he was crowned emperor on December 2, 1804.

- ✔ **Consulate:** This term denotes the period from 1799–1804 when France was governed by three Consuls, with Napoleon serving as First Consul. The term also is used to describe a particular style of decorative arts popular during that period.

Chapter 2

Raising a Genius

*N*apoleon's birthplace, Corsica, is a small island off the northern coast of Italy in the warm waters of the Mediterranean. Just over 100 miles long, it is blessed with beautiful beaches and picturesque mountains. Its capital city of Ajaccio sits on a beautiful and strategically located bay. The pleasant nature of the island and its friendly people belie its sometimes stormy past.

In this chapter, I offer some insights into the influence that Napoleon's birthplace and its political situation had during his formative years. I also introduce you to Napoleon's family, whose influence on the emerging genius was important, though not always positive. And I explain the role that the French governor of Corsica, Count Charles René Marbeuf, played in his life by helping Napoleon get an education at a French military school.

Fighting for Corsican Independence

The first Punic War (264–221 BCE) was an epic struggle between the early Roman Republic and its primary rival, Carthage, which resulted in a complete Roman victory. Among its spoils of war were three islands: Sardinia, Elba, and Corsica. All three remained Italian long after the fall of Rome.

In the years leading up to Napoleon's birth, Italy was not the unified nation that we know today. What is today modern Italy was actually a collection of republics, kingdoms, and Papal States (governed by the Pope). One of the republics was the Republic of Genoa, which had owned Corsica since 1284. The official language of Corsica (and hence of Napoleon and his family) was Italian. The local rulers of Corsica were appointed by Genoa, and the Corsicans were none too happy about it.

In time, the Corsicans began to demand independence from Genoa. By 1755, they managed to force the local Genoese governors from the island. Led by Pasquale Paoli, the Corsicans were convinced that complete independence lay just around the corner. Paoli took charge of island government and was quite successful, and popular, in his new role.

Battling a new enemy

Unfortunately for the Corsicans, the Genoese decided to cut their losses and make a nice profit in the bargain. At first, they simply transferred their rights to Corsican ports to France. The King of France, Louis XV, was anxious to expand French hegemony in the area, and Corsica was key to his success. A few years later, in 1768, Genoa sold Corsica outright to a grateful King Louis. France had already sent soldiers to occupy the ports, and after the sale, King Louis sent more troops, commanded by Lieutenant General Count Charles René Marbeuf.

Corsican patriots, led by Paoli, were outraged and immediately began to fight for their independence from France. This task was much more difficult than rebelling against Genoa, however, as the French garrison was large and Louis was determined to hold on to his new purchase. Paoli sought help from the British, who were quite willing to give support to anything that might increase their influence in the area.

Stalemate

The British assistance promised was considerably more than the British assistance rendered. Paoli soon found that he was on his own. The Brits sent money but no troops. The French troops, in the meantime, had gained control of most of the cities and ports, while the Corsican nationalists held sway in the interior.

By 1769, a stalemate seemed certain, but Paoli blundered into a confrontation that ultimately cost him much of his fighting force. The French, meanwhile, had gained a new commander, Lieutenant General Comte de Vaux, who was determined to end the stalemate once and for all.

Checkmate

General de Vaux was as good as his word. Slowly and methodically, he pushed Paoli and his soldiers back. At the battle of Ponte Nuovo on May 9, 1769, he administered a deathblow — a *coup de grâce* — to Paoli's forces. Those that survived fled to parts unknown. Paoli and a few of his closest companions managed to get aboard a British ship and flee to London.

The fight for Corsican independence was over, at least for the moment. General de Vaux, realizing that compassion now would reap rewards later, offered a general amnesty, which was gratefully accepted by virtually all Corsicans.

Coming under French rule

Even though the fighting was over, for many Corsicans, the dream of independence would never die. Corsica soon became divided between those who were quite willing to accept French rule, which proved to be fairly enlightened, and those who simply bided their time waiting for Paoli to return. Those Corsicans who lived in the cities did reasonably well under French rule. Poorer folk, mostly in the countryside, were less happy. To them, Paoli took on almost Christ-like imagery as they awaited his return.

Accepting amnesty

One of the families that accepted General de Vaux's amnesty was that of Carlo and Leticia Buonaparte. No, that's not a typo; *Buonaparte* is the Italian way of spelling Bonaparte. (I use the latter spelling throughout this book, but the earlier spelling pops up from time to time.)

Carlo had good reason to accept the offer of amnesty and be glad of the chance. His beautiful, 19-year-old wife was quite pregnant. Fleeing French soldiers in the mountains is not exactly ideal for a pregnant woman, so the family was happy to return to their home in Ajaccio.

Napoleon's birthplace today

Napoleon's home on Corsica is, not surprisingly, a major tourist attraction. The house is an imposing sight, but you must remember that during Napoleon's childhood the family owned only a few rooms. (They gradually expanded their holdings until they owned the entire house.)

If you visit his birthplace, you can see

- ✔ The room and couch where Napoleon is said to have been born

- ✔ A gallery that seems like a miniature hall of mirrors from Versailles

- ✔ A room with a trap door that Napoleon could use to leave the house to avoid his many admirers

- ✔ Leticia's bedroom

- ✔ The room where Napoleon stayed in 1799 on his way home from Egypt, the last time he set foot on the island

In addition, the city of Ajaccio is filled with statues, museums, and historical sites dedicated to Napoleon. Of special interest is the Ajaccio Cathedral, where Leticia first felt the pains of labor for Napoleon's birth. There is also the Imperial Chapel, where Napoleon's parents, his uncle Joseph Fesch, and some of his siblings are buried. The Place de Gaulle has large statues of Napoleon and his brothers. Nearby is the grotto where the young Napoleon is said to have gone to daydream from time to time. In the countryside around the city, you can visit the Bonapartes' country home, with a huge olive press on the ground floor.

Entering the world

There, life settled down to something far more normal. Until August 15, that is. On that day, Leticia was attending Mass in the family church when she felt the onset of labor. She walked the narrow streets back to her home, which consisted of part of a large house in a central part of town. Soon after, she gave birth to her second son, Napoleon. (Today, you can still visit the church, walk down the streets, and see the very bed on which Napoleon Bonaparte was born; see the sidebar "Napoleon's birthplace today.")

Getting to Know Napoleon's Family

Part of the Corsican cultural heritage is a reliance on and loyalty to one's family. The positive aspect of this heritage is that it can provide an emotional and economic support system invaluable to each member of the family. But this family loyalty can also lead to generations-long vendettas; Corsican history can attest to the existence of such family feuds. As Napoleon would learn, loyalty toward family members can also become problematic if those family members are of lesser ability or lesser loyalty than yourself.

Throughout his life, Napoleon experienced both the good and bad consequences of the tradition of family loyalty he was born into. In this section, I introduce you to the members of his immediate family and explain a bit about the role they played in Napoleon's life.

Napoleon's father, Carlo

Napoleon's father was trained in the law. After participating in the failed effort for Corsican independence, Carlo (1746–1785) quickly accepted a position working for the local court. He became active in politics and gained some modest importance. Despite his previous fight for Corsican independence from Genoese rule, Carlo established good relationships, even alliances, with French officials on the island and in Paris. He became especially close to Count Marbeuf, who was then the governor of the island.

Napoleon must have heard stories of his father's bravery during Corsica's struggle for liberation and was no doubt impressed with Carlo's willingness to put his life on the line for a patriotic cause, even exposing his family to danger. At the same time, Carlo's willingness to switch sides when the victor became clear taught Napoleon a valuable lesson in practical politics.

Carlo came from a family of some wealth and importance, even of noble title, but most of the wealth had been dissipated and the title somehow lost. Indeed, one of the things Carlo did that would have the most influence on Napoleon's future — and the entire family's — was to doggedly petition to

Napoleon's fall from power led to a complete reconciliation. Lucien was with Napoleon throughout the Hundred Days (when Napoleon returned from his first exile) and at Waterloo (see Chapter 15). When Napoleon was in exile on the island of St. Helena, Lucien attempted to join him there but was refused this opportunity by the British government. He spent the rest of his life in Italy.

Louis

Louis Bonaparte (1778–1846) began his career in the military. Napoleon had taken him under his wing by supporting him on a meager lieutenant's pay while Louis was in school. Later, in Napoleon's 1796 campaign in Italy (see Chapter 6), Louis was on board as an *aide-de-camp* (chief military aide). Louis also joined Napoleon in Egypt (see Chapter 7) and by 1804 had risen to the position of general of division.

In 1802, Napoleon more or less forced his younger brother to marry Josephine's daughter, Hortense. This marriage made no one happy, least of all the newly married couple. Louis became embittered toward his brother. He had a son with Hortense — a possible successor to Napoleon — but the boy died young.

In 1806, Louis was made King of Holland. While he implemented several reforms, he argued bitterly with Napoleon over various economic issues and abdicated his throne in 1810. He lived most of the rest of his life in Italy.

Louis and Hortense did make one lasting contribution to French — and Napoleonic — history. One of their children, Charles Louis Napoleon, eventually became president and then emperor of France, ruling as Napoleon III.

Jérôme

Like Napoleon's other brothers, Jérôme (1784–1860) would prove to be both good news and bad news for Napoleon. When Napoleon became First Consul (ruler of France) in 1799 (see Chapter 8), Jérôme left school and, at the ripe old age of 15, joined the navy. Not surprisingly, given his older brother's political prominence, he soon rose through the ranks and was an admiral by 1806. While Jérôme was on duty in the West Indies, a British blockade afforded him the opportunity to travel throughout the United States. While there, he fell in love with a young woman named Elizabeth Patterson, and they married in 1803. Napoleon was furious, and nothing Jérôme did persuaded Napoleon to accept the marriage. Elizabeth was not allowed to set foot on French soil. After bearing Jérôme a son while in England, she eventually returned to the United States.

In contrast, Napoleon admired Jérôme's military actions and made him a prince. After his first marriage was annulled by Napoleonic decree, Jérôme married Princess Catherine of Württemberg in 1807. That same year, he became king of a new country, Westphalia, which was created from some of Napoleon's conquests in Germany.

Like Louis, Jérôme ran his country as he saw fit and was rather fond of the perks that came with being king. He spent far too much money on himself and not nearly enough on the kingdom. A furious Napoleon did all he could to turn Jérôme around, but it didn't work. The two grew apart, and in 1813, Westphalia fell to the Sixth Coalition allies.

Upon Napoleon's return from exile in Elba, Jérôme rejoined his brother, who welcomed him back into the fold. Jérôme was given a significant command at Waterloo (see Chapter 15). When Napoleon III took power, Jérôme was made governor of the Invalides (a retired soldier's home in Paris where Napoleon is now buried) and a marshal of France.

Elisa

Napoleon's eldest sister, Elisa (1777–1820), was generally a thorn in Napoleon's side (much like many of her siblings). But Napoleon's devotion to providing for his family naturally extended to her. In 1797, she married a minor Corsican nobleman named Felix Pasquale Bacciochi, despite her family's opposition to the marriage. Napoleon rewarded Elisa's husband the title of Prince of Piombino (a city in Tuscany, Italy), which made his sister the princess.

Like her famous brother, Elisa displayed remarkable administrative talents. She made significant improvements in her territory, which expanded as Napoleon gained greater control over the broader region. In governing, as well as in many affairs, Elisa generally ignored her husband. When Napoleon added Tuscany to her territory, Elisa was given the title of Grand Duchess of Tuscany, which she held from 1809 to 1814.

Elisa began to fancy herself an heir to the famous Medici family of Italy and a great patron of the arts. When Napoleon's fortunes were falling in 1814, Elisa's only real concern was to preserve her own position, but she failed in those efforts. She eventually retired to Trieste, where she lived the rest of her life.

Pauline

Without a doubt, Napoleon's sister Pauline (1780–1825) was the most interesting of the siblings. She was also the only sister who remained truly loyal to and appreciative of her imperial brother. Perhaps because of that, she is generally considered to have been Napoleon's favorite.

After a torrid affair with Louis Marie Stanislas Fréron (see Chapter 3), Pauline married General Victor Leclerc in 1797, but he died in 1802 in Haiti. By then,

Pauline had developed a much-deserved reputation for enjoying a life of, shall we say, pleasure. Napoleon, who was actually something of a prude, did not approve of this sort of behavior, but he would soon learn that there was little to be done about it. Anxious to live a lifestyle of the rich and famous, Pauline married Italian Prince Camillo Borghese in 1803. Between his wealth and a substantial dowry granted by Napoleon, she was set.

The marriage, however, was less than successful. Pauline and the prince each entertained a substantial number of lovers in a lifestyle that some found fascinating and others found scandalous. A well-known seductress, Pauline was fond of posing in the nude. A drinking cup was even molded from her breast. (It would fetch a pretty price on eBay today!)

Of all Napoleon's siblings, Pauline was the most loyal during times of difficulty. She joined him in exile on Elba and used her great wealth to help him out. She followed him to Paris for the Hundred Days (see Chapter 14), but after Waterloo her health deteriorated and she moved to Rome. Reconciled with her husband by none other than the Pope (these people ran in high circles, folks), she managed to recover. Hearing of Napoleon's ill health on St. Helena (see Chapter 16), she petitioned to join him in exile. Her petition was granted, but Napoleon died before she could leave. Her health once again crushed, she lived out her days with her husband in Rome and Florence.

Caroline

If Pauline was the most loyal to Napoleon, Napoleon's youngest sister, Caroline (1782–1839), was the most disloyal and unappreciative of all of the family. Deeply resentful of Josephine and her family, Caroline eventually married Joachim Murat, one of Napoleon's friends and a general in the army. When Murat was stationed in Paris, Caroline began to display an ambition that would eventually spell trouble for Napoleon and even her husband.

In 1804, Murat was made a Marshal of the Empire, and Caroline became increasingly important in the new social order. Jealous of the positions given to Josephine's daughter, Hortense, Caroline sought some level of revenge by arranging for mistresses for Napoleon, all the while lobbying for a title for herself and her husband. They were eventually awarded the Grand Duchy of Berg and Cleves, and later the Kingdom of Naples.

You may think that being Queen of Naples would be a nice life to which one could quickly become accustomed. Not so Caroline. She soon became involved in a struggle for power with her husband, the king! The smart money was on her, and she soon became the dominant force. When Murat, who was still a marshal and had military duties in Napoleon's army, was away on campaign in 1812, Caroline ruled as though he didn't exist.

When Napoleon began to fall from power after 1812, Caroline, with a somewhat reluctant Joachim in tow, tried to negotiate a treaty with the Austrians that would allow them to keep their thrones if they turned on Napoleon. Talk about sibling rivalry! The deal was cut, but when King Murat saw Napoleon return for the Hundred Days, he turned on his Austrian allies and attacked them, hoping to help Napoleon. His actions had the opposite effect; they infuriated the Austrians, who not only drove Murat out of Italy but were unwilling to trust Napoleon and allow him to rule after his return to France (see Chapters 14 and 15).

In the end, Murat was executed by his own people and Caroline sent into exile in Trieste, where she married another Napoleonic figure, General Etienne-Jacques MacDonald. Caroline returned to Paris, where she was granted a nice pension by France. She lived out her days in Florence, Italy.

Educating a Genius

Napoleon's family was not impoverished, but it was by no means wealthy. During Napoleon's childhood, the Bonapartes owned only a few rooms of a large house (which they would eventually own in its entirety).

The Bonapartes were greatly helped when Carlo applied for and received recognition as a member of the noble class. This allowed Carlo to pursue his political career and gave him advantages as a lawyer as well.

Even so, Carlo's salary was never great. Like parents everywhere, Carlo and Leticia wondered how they would afford their children's education. And like people throughout history, they would find that it never hurt to have good connections. Their connection in this case was substantial: Count Marbeuf, the French governor of Corsica.

Getting a helping hand from Marbeuf

By all accounts, Count Marbeuf was an outstanding governor of Corsica. He had been sent at a time when emotions were high and the French were not universally loved. But he worked hard to organize reforms and to improve life for average Corsicans. He lowered taxes and organized numerous building projects. This was made easier by the fact that the French government in Paris recognized the delicate nature of his position and supported him with adequate funds to try to make the Corsicans happy with his rule. He even worked on speaking the Corsican dialect of French so that he could better communicate with the common people on the island. In short, he was about as good as the islanders could have ever hoped to get.

When Marbeuf first arrived on the island, he actually stayed at the Bonaparte home. Carlo and Marbeuf hit it off quite well and developed a mutually useful relationship. Both men had a strong interest in agriculture and worked together on a couple of projects. They were also both interested in politics, and each supported the French presence on the island. Marbeuf might have helped the Bonapartes regardless of any other factors.

But there was another factor, of course. As I mention earlier in the chapter, Marbeuf developed quite a strong interest in Carlo's wife, Leticia. With great beauty and a pleasing personality, she no doubt attracted the eyes and inspired the hopes of more than one man on the island. But Marbeuf, of course, was quite different than other men. At 64, he was much older, but more importantly, he was the governor and could offer favors the others could not.

Leticia was interested only in a friendly relationship, which seems to have been enough for Marbeuf. They took long walks and had nice talks. Marbeuf treated her family as though they were his own. It was Marbeuf who helped Carlo prove his nobility, and it was Marbeuf who told Carlo of the existence of free scholarships for education in France. With the right recommendation, boys could attend the seminary in Aix, France or a military academy, while girls could go to finishing school at Saint-Cyr — all paid for by the king!

This news was almost too good to be true, and Carlo was quick to take advantage of it. In 1777, Marbeuf forwarded his recommendations, and soon Napoleon was accepted to the military academy at Brienne and Joseph was accepted to the seminary at Aix. But Joseph was too young to start seminary, and Napoleon had to await further processing before he could enter the academy. Again Marbeuf stepped in and sent both boys to stay (at his expense) with his nephew at the college of Autun, where they could learn French. (Marbeuf's nephew just happened to be the local bishop.) And just to help out a little more, Marbeuf arranged for Leticia's half-brother, Joseph Fesch, to attend the seminary at Aix.

On December 15, the two boys and Leticia's half-brother left Corsica for the mainland of France. Napoleon was 9 years old and about to enter a world beyond anything he had ever imagined possible. (No one would ever say that these three young men squandered their educations; they would eventually become an emperor, a king, and a cardinal.)

Learning to speak French

While at Autun, Napoleon had to learn French; as of yet, the future Emperor of the French could hardly speak the language. The effort did not go well. Like many of us, Napoleon found memorizing difficult, and his natural inclination to hurry did not do him well in the study of language. Worse yet, his

French had (and always would have) a strong Corsican accent, a fact that did him no favors throughout his schooling. Still, after three months at Autun, Napoleon had learned conversational French and was able to pass his language exams.

By May 1778, Carlo had secured the necessary documents so Napoleon could move to the military school at Brienne. Napoleon and Joseph were unhappy to have to part company for what might be a very long time. But Napoleon's time at Autun had been well spent, and he was ready, at the ripe old age of 9, to move on.

Attending French military school

French military education in the late 18th century was not exactly a model of democracy. The opportunity to be an officer was reserved almost exclusively for the nobility and almost exclusively for native Frenchmen. To say that the system was elitist would be an understatement. Moreover, at least half the young students attended military school on expense accounts provided by their wealthy families. Scholarship recipients like Napoleon were looked down on by most of the students. Napoleon was poor by their standards, and it would show.

Worse yet, Napoleon wasn't even French! True, Corsica had become a French territory, but the French had a very low opinion of Corsicans (noble or otherwise), seeing them as just this side of barbarians. Many of the cadets came from wealthy and powerful families, and they did not necessarily appreciate having to mix with the "rabble," even that which was nobility. On Corsica, Napoleon's family was fairly high on the social scale. At Brienne, he was virtually at the bottom.

Add to that the fact that Napoleon didn't speak great French (and spoke it with a heavy Corsican accent), and it was clear that Napoleon was stepping into a situation that could prove to be very difficult. Young boys can be cruel in any circumstance, and this situation was made to order for bad behavior and bad attitudes.

Napoleon was assigned a small room in a dormitory. It was a Spartan existence, but that didn't seem to bother Napoleon. If nothing else, the dorm situation put all cadets on a somewhat equal footing. All cadets wore a uniform, which was another equalizer.

Napoleon was determined to succeed and immediately settled in to his new routine. As a student, he began to excel. (He wasn't a perfect student, though: His spelling and handwriting were quite bad. While this no doubt caused concern among his teachers, I'm afraid that I am personally in no position to criticize him on either count!) He was serious about his studies and spent much of his free time reading. Of course, with his lack of funds he could do little else.

Napoleon's relations with the other cadets, however, did not go so well. The young boys of the elite nobility bullied Napoleon. Slight of build, he was less able to physically defend himself than he might have liked, though he did develop a reputation for generally holding his own against his larger adversaries. He began to withdraw somewhat, tending to keep to himself rather than socialize or engage in group activities. (He did enjoy gardening — each cadet was given a small plot of land.)

Dealing with poverty

Napoleon's poverty continued to be a problem, isolating him from some of the other cadets and preventing him from buying some things he may have wanted. As the years went on, his poverty bothered him more, and he longed to be either removed from school or given an allowance. In 1781, at the age of 12, he wrote his father asking for an allowance or a withdrawal, saying "I am tired of exhibiting indigence, and of seeing the smiles of insolent scholars who are only superior to me by reason of their fortune."

Carlo was in no position to give Napoleon any further assistance. His financial picture had not improved, and his health was deteriorating. He and Leticia were anxious for Napoleon to graduate as soon as possible to allow his brother Lucien to go to school on the same scholarship.

Condemned to poverty, Napoleon resolved to do all the better in school. Soon he began to excel in history, math, and geography. Math was likely the most important of the three for a military career, but history really captured Napoleon's imagination (a fact that warms the hearts of all historians writing the story of his life!). Like many young men, Napoleon was especially taken with the stories of ancient heroes like Achilles, Alexander the Great, and Julius Caesar. No one could have suspected then that he would eventually join that elite group.

While his poverty was certainly a source of difficulty for Napoleon, it almost certainly influenced his later behavior. For example,

- ✔ Napoleon's poverty may have inspired his later commitment to promoting equality in France and throughout his empire (see Chapter 19).

- ✔ The treatment he received at the hands of the arrogant French noble cadets was also likely a major reason he developed strong feelings for Corsican independence. Notwithstanding the fact that he was receiving an excellent education at French expense, Napoleon began to dream of Corsican independence and to idolize Paoli. These feelings would shape much of his behavior throughout his early career (see Chapters 3 and 4).

Napoleon also began to develop some important friendships. Probably the most important was Louis-Antoine Fauvelet de Bourrienne, who would later serve as Napoleon's secretary. Napoleon also became friends with some of the adult staff. His relations with the other students improved somewhat, perhaps because they could see that he was exceptionally talented. His leadership was often sought for the periodic snowball fights that took place.

Moving to the next level

While Napoleon was at Brienne, Carlo's health continued to get worse. Joseph, who had been very successful at Autun, decided not to enter the seminary and seek a career in the Church. Instead, he wanted to go into the military. (Napoleon opposed this decision and said so, but to no avail.) Lucien, meanwhile, was poised to enter Brienne, which he did in 1784. Unlike Napoleon, however, Lucien had no financial aid, hoping to pick up Napoleon's scholarship upon his older brother's graduation. And Caroline had been enrolled at the exclusive school at Saint Cyr, where Carlo had managed to get her a scholarship.

It was clearly in the family's best interest for Napoleon to graduate as soon as possible. An islander by heritage, Napoleon applied for a position in the navy, but nothing came of that effort. Napoleon was very young, a fact that probably delayed his graduation and may well have prevented positive action on his request for naval service. Another factor was probably the death of the family benefactor, Count Marbeuf, who had been promoting Napoleon's naval aspirations.

With Marbeuf gone, the Bonapartes were on their own, and Napoleon needed to move forward in his education. Fortunately, he passed his exams in October 1784 and was accepted to the Military School of Paris. He was only 15 years old.

Having excelled at math and geometry, Napoleon selected the military branch that made the best use of those subjects: artillery. This was an excellent decision for many reasons, including the fact that artillery was an elite branch that offered excellent career opportunities. Those opportunities would be greatly enhanced by Napoleon's acceptance to his new school, which was essentially the equivalent of West Point in the United States or Sandhurst in the United Kingdom. Napoleon had really arrived: His nomination had been signed by no less than King Louis XVI.

With Napoleon graduated from Brienne, Carlo had hoped that Lucien would receive his scholarship, but that didn't happen. Fortunately, Joseph was able to attend Brienne on a royal scholarship, which certainly helped the family finances.

Wowing them in Paris

In late October 1784, Napoleon arrived in Paris. It was by far the largest city he had ever seen, and he was completely taken by all the sights. He bought a book about the city and was prepared for a grand time. He would soon discover, however, that Paris was a reflection of the state of French society. It was a city of great wealth but with great poverty as well. A large gap between the rich and the poor is always problematic, and the gap in Paris and throughout France was enormous. As I discuss in Chapter 3, those who were poor found the whole situation, well, revolting.

None of that mattered much to Napoleon as he entered his new school. He was among the most elite of all France's military leaders. In keeping with its clientele, the school was luxurious. While the quarters were a bit on the small side, the classrooms were large and elegant. Located at one end of the Champ de Mars (today, the Eiffel Tower is at the other end) and near the Hôtel des Invalides (the home for retired veterans), it was very much in the center of things. (In death, Napoleon would return to the area, with his final resting place being under the gold dome of the Invalides. An adjacent military museum is largely dedicated to his career.)

In Paris, life was in some ways much grander for Napoleon. The cadets ate five-course meals and had the very best teachers available. The student-teacher ratio was very nearly one to one, which was (and is) virtually unheard of in other schools. Napoleon actually objected to the extravagance of the meals and wrote a lengthy letter to that effect to the Minister of War. At the advice of his former director at Brienne, he dropped the matter.

Napoleon continued to be something of a loner. The French nobility at this school were even higher on the social scale than those at Brienne, and they never missed an opportunity to put Napoleon in his place. He had more than one altercation with his comrades. On the other hand, he continued to be a popular selection for snowball fights.

As a student, Napoleon continued to excel, though his grades were not as good as they had been in Brienne. In addition to history and math, he developed a strong interest in literature. Still hoping for a commission in the navy, he nevertheless excelled at artillery. His love of Corsica and dreams of her independence did not lessen, nor did the negative reaction of both his classmates and his teachers, who had to remind him from time to time that he was there courtesy of the *French* king.

Losing his father

Napoleon's father continued to have serious health problems, and shortly after Napoleon entered school in Paris, Carlo went to southern France to seek diagnosis and treatment. He was told by doctors that his condition was terminal stomach cancer. He died in February 1785. As he had been in life, in death Carlo was deep in debt. If Napoleon thought he was poor when Carlo was alive, he was truly destitute with his father gone.

Napoleon was no doubt heartbroken with his father's death, though he likely saw it coming. He showed his strength of character by immediately writing to his mother and even by refusing the usual priestly consolation. As the eldest, it fell to Joseph to return to Corsica to see to family affairs, which allowed Napoleon to remain in school.

Graduating ahead of his class

The normal course of study for artillery at the Military School of Paris was two years. But Napoleon, who worked hard and excelled in much of what he did, was able to graduate after only one year. Detractors love to point out that his score was not that high — he ranked 42nd of the 58 young men who passed their exams that year. But most of those 58 had been in school at least two years. Napoleon was the fourth youngest of his graduating class and the only one for whom French was not his native language.

At 16, Napoleon received his commission as a Second Lieutenant in the Royal Artillery. He was about to step out into the real world — a world that he would soon come to dominate.

Continuing education

One of Napoleon's closest friends in both schools was fellow cadet Alexander des Mazis. Both young men were assigned to the La Fère Regiment in Valence in the south of France, fairly close to Napoleon's family in Corsica. Though he had received his commission, Napoleon was really on probation and receiving what we might call on-the-job training. He worked with gunners who had far more experience than he, learning the ins and outs of what it took to be a successful artillery officer.

Napoleon took the idea of continuing education very seriously. If his days were spent learning his duties and the requirements of his career, his off time was spent reading. The one luxury he allowed himself was the periodic purchase of books. He read widely but with a heavy concentration on history. He also read Jean Jacques Rousseau, whose writings on human liberty led him to be considered the father of the French Revolution. Napoleon took copious notes on everything he read and often made marks and comments in the books. He kept many lists and compiled statistics on a wide range of subjects. Clearly, his quest for education did not end upon graduation.

Napoleon also continued his fascination with Corsica and his support of her independence. He read James Boswell's book on Corsican history and began preliminary work on his own history of Corsica. (That project would consume much of his time and emotion for several years but would never be completed.) Though he was in the French army, he began to see France's role in Corsica as tyrannical.

Heading Home

After Carlo's death, the Bonaparte family fortunes were tenuous at best. Napoleon's mother, Leticia, had lost an agricultural contract for her mulberry nursery, and Napoleon had been unsuccessful in his efforts to have it restored. Leticia's treatment by the French government was clearly unjust and only served to make Napoleon even more determined that Corsica should become independent.

The family had been helped by Napoleon's grand uncle, but his health was failing as well. Napoleon received permission to take leave to visit his family on Corsica. He left in September 1786 and visited his Uncle Fesch and brother Lucien along the way. His mother and siblings, led by Joseph, were elated to see him. His education and career had gone quite well, and Napoleon was pretty clearly the leader of his family and the one most able to provide support.

Napoleon stayed for quite some time, helping his mother with her grape harvest, visiting with family and friends, and exploring the island. He and Joseph spent a great deal of time together, time they both would later recall with great fondness. With Napoleon there to help, Joseph was able to leave to study law in Pisa, Italy.

Napoleon was granted an extension of his leave and was able to stay until September 1787. (Such long leaves, which seem unusual to us, were actually fairly common in those days.) All good things come to an end, however, and Napoleon had to return to duty.

Well, not quite. He actually went to Paris, where he tried to personally intervene in the dispute over Leticia's mulberries. He failed in the effort but managed to get an additional leave to Corsica, returning to continue writing his history and visiting with his fellow islanders.

His leave finally up, Napoleon was required to return to his military duties in 1788. His regiment had been transferred to Auxonne, and as summer approached, he reported there for duty. In Auxonne, his education — and his life — would take a giant step forward.

Chapter 3

The French Revolution: Liberty, Equality, Fraternity

*T*he last half of the 18th century was a period of major turmoil on two continents. Depending on your point of view, it was either a time of tumultuous upheaval that destroyed the stability of civilization, or it was a period of progressive change that swept out ancient, decaying regimes and replaced them with a system that would ultimately lead to the betterment of humankind. Either way, the world was clearly never going to be the same again.

Two events shaped the last half of the 18th century and all that was to follow: the United States War of Independence (or *American Revolution*) and the French Revolution. As I explain in this chapter, the two events were closely linked.

The Declaration of Independence, adopted in 1776, propelled the colonies into war with Great Britain. Based on the ideas of religious liberty and representative government, the Declaration of Independence stunned the old order. But while her ideals were bold, the United States herself remained weak and tentative even after the war was won. Most of her energy was spent in the complex and difficult task of building a nation.

The United States didn't fight her war alone. Her strongest ally was France. King Louis XVI sent soldiers, arms, ammunition, money, and anything else he could to help the Americans defeat the British. King Louis didn't have a sudden conversion to belief in democracy. But anything that would weaken France's old nemesis, Great Britain, was fine with him.

Little did King Louis know that he was laying the groundwork for his own demise. The soldiers and officers who went to America came home with new ideas of freedom and an understanding that it was possible for the people to overthrow a government. As I explain in this chapter, just a few years after the American Revolution, the people of France did just that.

Tension at Versailles

As the 18th century entered its final quarter, the palace of Versailles near Paris symbolized both the glorious past and the perilous future of France. Built by Louis XIII in 1623 as a hunting lodge, it was expanded by Louis XIV starting in 1669 as a statement of both personal and state power. In its new, extravagant form, Versailles reflected an increasingly strong and centralized French state.

But Versailles also exposed the cracks in the social structure of 18th-century France — cracks that would ultimately lead to revolution.

Reflecting disparity

A long-standing conflict existed between kings and nobles in France for two key reasons:

- The nobility constantly struggled with the king for power.
- The nobility refused to pay taxes, even though they accounted for most of the country's wealth.

As I explain in the next section, this second point was a particularly sore spot, because France had racked up quite a debt over the years.

Louis XIV tried to ease the tension by having many of the nobles live in Versailles, where he could keep an eye on them. But Versailles was expensive, and Louis wasn't picking up the nobles' expenses. Low on funds and out of touch with the country, these nobles became even less likely to agree to pay the taxes that were increasingly necessary to run the state.

Versailles also symbolized the yawning gap between the top levels of French society and its mass of people who made up the bottom 98 percent. The poor were unable to purchase anything but the most basic necessities, and their lives were defined by fear, hunger, humiliation, and exhaustion. For them, Versailles increasingly became the symbol of a monarchy completely out of touch with the reality that was France.

Symbolizing massive debt

When Versailles became home to Louis XVI, the latest in a long line of Bourbon kings, it also symbolized the most desperate of French problems of the era: the enormous debt that had been carried forth since the days of Louis XIV. This debt was based on the cost of assorted expensive wars, as well as the cost of the palace itself and the lifestyle of its inhabitants.

The debt was the most basic underlying cause of the French Revolution. Approximately 50 percent of all government revenue went to servicing the debt, with another 25 percent going to current military expenses. That didn't leave much to cover everything else a government needs to do.

One of the major sources of debt was the help France gave to the U.S. War of Independence. Without that help, history may have taken a sharp turn in a different direction. If the American Revolution had failed for lack of French support, the French Revolution may never have occurred. But because France did provide that help, the history of both the United States and Europe moved in progressive directions. The ideals of the United States, combined with those of the Enlightenment (especially Jean Jacques Rousseau), which emphasized individual freedom and the right to determine one's government, ultimately fueled the intellectual engines of the French Revolution.

Convening the Estates General

In the spring of 1789, Louis XVI, besieged with difficulties on all fronts, took desperate measures. Facing crop failures, rising crime, the intransigence of the clergy and nobility regarding taxes, and the refusal of banks to loan additional funds, Louis called a meeting of the Estates General, a sort of congress or parliament.

The Estates General, which had not met since 1614, reflected the deep divisions in French society. The Estates General consisted of 300 representatives of the First Estate (clergy), 300 representatives of the Second Estate (nobility), and 600 representatives of the Third Estate (everyone else, mostly city workers and rural peasants). I explain the three estates in more detail in the sidebar cleverly titled "The three estates." Louis XVI called this body together in 1789 to try to solve the problem that was created largely by the clergy's and nobility's refusal to accept their fair share of taxes.

King Louis hoped that the Estates General would pass some economic reforms, including requiring the nobles to pay some taxes. Instead, the Estates General created a new social and political order in France.

The three estates

Since the early Middle Ages, French society had been divided into three estates. These estates were somewhat like what we would call *social classes,* but they were much more rigidly defined:

✔ The **First Estate** was the clergy. This estate included everyone from the local parish priest (or *cure*) to an archbishop. While the priests often lived simply, the higher clergy were very wealthy and had the lifestyles to show it. The First Estate contained about half of 1 percent of the French population, or some 150,000 people, but most of the estate's wealth was concentrated in the richest 10,000 of them, some of whom lived with the nobles in Versailles. Most of church wealth was gained by a tithe on the common people. Rich as some of them were, members of the First Estate did not pay taxes.

✔ The **Second Estate** was the nobility. About equal in number to the First Estate, the Second Estate had great wealth, largely concentrated in a relative handful of incredibly wealthy nobles. And — surprise — the nobles paid no taxes! Also, the nobility had certain privileges, such as the ability to hunt on anyone's land without liability for damaging crops or other property. These privileges rankled many of the peasants even more than the lack of taxation. The nobles were in constant competition with the king for power and would not accept any reforms that required them to pay taxes.

✔ The **Third Estate** was everyone else. This included about 500,000 middle class people (a few of whom had a fair amount of money), about 2.5 million city workers (often called *sans culottes* because they didn't wear the elegant knee britches favored by the nobility), and more than 22 million very poor peasants. The peasants lived on the edge of despair. They had very little hope for improvement in their lot, and they often turned to highway robbery or other forms of thievery to make ends meet. Oh, and one thing more: Guess who paid pretty much all of the taxes? That's right, and the Third Estate found that fact rather revolting.

Refusing to be dominated by the first two estates, the majority of people (who made up the Third Estate), along with their liberal allies in the other estates, called for sweeping changes. When the king refused to cooperate with their agenda, they took the famous *Tennis Court Oath* on June 20, 1789, in which they declared that they were now the National Assembly and vowed to write a constitution.

Sparking Revolution

The actions of the Third Estate had sweeping effects. Vast changes were underway, and people feared that foreign troops would be called into Paris to help defend the nobility against the reforms and reassert the power of the king. To prepare for such a possibility, a mob seized the Bastille, an old castle that was being used as a prison.

The mob raided the Bastille's gunpowder supplies on July 14, 1789, and the Revolution was underway in full force. (That date is now known as *Bastille Day,* the equivalent of Independence Day in the United States.) In short order, the peasants of the countryside were armed and storming throughout the country, destroying financial records and forcing many nobles to flee for their lives.

On August 4, the nobility agreed to give up its hated privileges, and the National Assembly essentially eliminated the feudal system. The Declaration of the Rights of Man and of the Citizen was passed, along with many other reforms.

Lacking the king's support

Throughout all of this, the people wanted their king to be part of their Revolution. You can clearly see this fact in Figure 3-1, which shows a locket meant to be worn by delegates to the National Assembly. On one side you have Louis, and on the other side a caption that translates as "The Law and the King, National Assembly, 1789." (The portrait of the king was probably meant to be flattering, even if it doesn't look that way to us now.)

Figure 3-1: This locket shows early support for the king as part of the Revolution.

The people may have wanted Louis to join in their Revolution, but the king and queen (Marie Antoinette) were having none of it. Eventually, they fled the capital, hoping to link up with Austrian forces and perhaps retake the country. Unfortunately for them, Louis was recognized in the French village of Varennes and forced to return to Paris. A centuries-old era was about to draw to a close.

Battling the old order

The Revolutionaries preached a message of universal rejection of the old order, and the old order of other nations heard them and reacted. Threats led to war which, in time, led to French victories over Austria and Prussia. Inspired by Georges-Jacques Danton, the new French army, with a little help from a certain officer named Bonaparte, ultimately proved itself a worthy opponent to the combined armies of Europe. (See the sidebar "Who was who in the French Revolution" for more information on Danton and other Revolutionary leaders.)

A nation at war against the established order could hardly continue as a member of that same order. In January 1793, the inevitable happened, and Louis XVI was executed. When that happened, the number of nobles who emigrated increased, and the battle lines both within and without France hardened. (See Chapter 4 for more on Revolutionary conflict.) A few months later, Queen Marie Antoinette was also executed (see Figure 3-2).

Figure 3-2:
This period ivory snuffbox shows Queen Marie Antoinette.

Who was who in the French Revolution

I could write a whole book on this topic. The Revolution had a virtually endless cast of characters. Here are just a few whose activities were important to the development of Napoleon's career:

- **Maximilien Robespierre** (1758–1794): One of the most radical of the Revolutionaries, Maximilien rose to leadership of the radical *Jacobin club,* a group of people who had meetings to plan ways to control the direction of the Revolution. In time, he became the most powerful member of the *Committee of Public Safety,* the dozen or so people who made up the executive branch of government from roughly 1793 to 1795. And in 1793 and 1794, he promoted the use of terror (during a period called, not surprisingly, *the Terror*) to "purify" the Revolution. Responsible for the death of Georges-Jacques Danton and other alleged moderates, his actions provoked a backlash. He was arrested on July 27, 1794 and executed by guillotine the next day.

- **Augustine Robespierre** (1763–1794): A major Revolutionary in his own right, Augustine wasn't hurt any by being Maximilien's brother (unless you count that messy business in 1794!). A lawyer by trade, Augustine was eventually sent to deal with difficulties in the south of France, where several cities, including Toulon, were actively opposing the French Revolution. There, he was instrumental in promoting the fortunes of a young officer named Bonaparte (see Chapter 4). He supported his brother Maximilien through thick and thin, and he joined him at the guillotine, having failed in an attempt to commit suicide.

- **Georges-Jacques Danton** (1759–1794): A lawyer by trade (notice a trend here?), Danton became involved in the early days of the Revolution. He was known for his fiery oratory and, less advantageous to his career, his love of some of the finer things of life (that would be wine, women, and song). Though he had begun as a radical, he was soon seen as a moderate, a big no-no to Robespierre and his followers. He was given a sham trial and guillotined on April 5, 1794. He famously told the executioner to "show the crowd my head: it's worth a look."

- **Antonio Cristoforo Saliceti** (1757–1809): A Corsican by birth and a lawyer by trade, Saliceti worked his way up through the Revolutionary hierarchy, developing a reputation for his radical beliefs along the way. His biggest issue was making Corsica a full part of France, and this interest brought him into contact with Napoleon. He was instrumental in getting Napoleon the command of artillery at Toulon and was involved with Napoleon's arrest and subsequent release after the fall of the Robespierres. (I discuss both topics in Chapter 4.) He remained loyal to Napoleon, serving in several diplomatic posts until his death in Naples in 1809 under somewhat suspicious circumstances.

- **Louis Marie Stanislas Fréron** (1754–1802): Born into a conservative family, Fréron was greatly taken by the French Revolutionary ideals and began publishing a radical newspaper, *The Orator of the People*. A member of the Convention, as the legislature was then called, he was made Representative on Mission to the south of France, where he became involved with the young Napoleon Bonaparte. Radical and rather bloodthirsty, Fréron was largely responsible for bloody retributions against counterrevolutionaries in Marseilles and Toulon (see Chapter 4). After the fall of the Robespierres, his career stagnated. On one mission to the south of France, he had a torrid affair with Napoleon's sister, Pauline, but that relationship went nowhere. His last assignment was with the French expedition to Haiti, where he died of yellow fever.

Resorting to terror

Rather than be intimidated by increased external hostility, the Revolution entered a new and far more dangerous phase. Turning first against the old order and then against the Revolution itself, Maximilien Robespierre, the leader of the most radical group of Revolutionaries, used terror to "purify" the Revolution. This purification cost France first Danton, then Robespierre, and then its Revolution. It also eliminated, by guillotine (a device designed to cut off one's head painlessly) or by flight, many of its military leaders, opening the way for a new cadre of leadership to evolve. I talk much more about this subject in Chapter 4.

The Terror and its aftermath led to retrenchment. Some reforms were abolished, and the middle class government of the *Directory,* a five-man executive committee that pretty much ran things, was established. Assailed from both Revolutionaries and royalists, this government completely failed to solve France's increasing problems. Bankruptcy threatened, and fears of renewed violence spread. The nation, having survived ten years of turmoil, was ready for a leader who could promise both an end — and a beginning. (See Chapter 4 for more on France's government after the fall of Robespierre.)

Supporting Revolution, Winning Support

It is against this backdrop that Napoleon first entered the military and political scene. Napoleon Bonaparte was an officer in the French army, a position that was a decidedly mixed blessing in those days. Officers in the French military had always been nobles, and many nobles had fled or been executed during the Revolution.

On the positive side, the loss of so many officers created numerous vacancies at the top, so to speak, and a bright young man like Napoleon had a good chance for advancement. Opportunities were also increased by the fact that France was at war; war always creates opportunities for advancement, one way or the other.

However, officers were under increasing surveillance and suspicion, and one wrong move or a word from the wrong person could literally cut someone's career short. Political operatives, called Representatives on Mission, were keeping a close eye on the generals and often interjecting themselves into military decisions.

Keeping one foot in Corsica

Napoleon's early military career was marked as much as anything by his extended leaves of absence to visit his birthplace, the island of Corsica. He left on one such leave in February 1787, became involved in political intrigues, and began to write a history of the island (see Chapter 2).

Back in France in June 1788, Napoleon was stationed in Auxonne under the command of General Jean-Pierre du Teil, who also happened to be a baron. Not surprisingly, du Teil was impressed with the brilliant young Napoleon and happy to advance his career. (Later on, du Teil's brother, Jean, would be helpful as well.) Napoleon was learning at a very early stage that it isn't just what you know but who you know that is important to success. As I discuss in Chapter 4, it was a lesson he would learn well.

Respecting the Revolutionary ideal

When the Paris mob stormed the Bastille on July 14, 1789, Napoleon was in Auxonne, far from the action. But Revolutionary fervor swept throughout much of the country, and Napoleon joined many others in developing a support for the ideal it embodied.

If supporting the peasants seems risky (after all, Napoleon was in the *royal* artillery), remember that in the early days of the Revolution there was very little talk of removing the king from power. Most people thought that Louis XVI was at least somewhat supportive of the Revolution and that maybe they'd end up with some kind of a constitutional monarchy.

Working for Corsican rights

Napoleon was never one to let a little thing like a revolution interfere with his plans, and very soon he was back on leave in Corsica. There, he became involved in the movement to make Corsica a part of France, rather than just a territory, which would make Corsicans full French citizens.

Corsica's new leader was a man named Pasquale Paoli, and he and Napoleon became allied in the cause. But duty called, and Napoleon left Corsica to accept a new assignment in Valence. He was there when Louis XVI and Marie Antoinette were caught in the village of Varennes as they tried to flee the country.

The king's attempted escape outraged many people and served to radicalize the Revolution. After this event, there was far less talk of a constitutional monarchy and far more talk of a French Republic. Like many of his countrymen, Napoleon swore allegiance to the Revolution. Letters he wrote at the time seem to confirm that his feelings were quite honest.

His allegiance to the Revolution did not, however, prevent him from going on yet another leave to Corsica. (Let me tell you, when *I* was in the service, leaves were a lot harder to come by! In 18th-century France, long leaves were fairly common, but even then, Napoleon must surely have been pushing the envelope.)

Witnessing change

Back on Corsica in October 1791, Napoleon discovered that change was afoot. His hero, Paoli, had turned on the Revolution and had become a royalist (a supporter of the monarchy). The island was in turmoil, and there was little Napoleon could do. Forced at one point to actually fire on Corsican citizens, Napoleon returned to France in May 1792.

His leave had long been up, and Napoleon was in real danger of losing his military commission. Indeed, his name had already been removed from the military roles, so he hastened off to Paris to deal with the inevitable paperwork necessary for reinstatement.

Paris had certainly changed since his last visit. Revolution was in the air, and the king was in trouble. On June 20, 1792, the Paris mob surrounded the Tuileries Palace, the kings' home when he was in Paris, and they spent much of the day shouting insults at him. On August 10, they returned. This time, they were not satisfied with insults. Members of the Swiss guard that were stationed to protect the king were slaughtered, and the king beat a very hasty retreat, seeking the protection of the National Assembly. It wasn't a great move on his part, but his options were clearly limited. Napoleon actually witnessed the attack by the mob, and it made a clear impression on him. He would forever after fear mob action.

Fleeing home

Napoleon was promoted to captain, and to celebrate he took another — you guessed it! — leave to Corsica, arriving in September 1792. This trip did not go well. Napoleon, his family, and his friend Antonio Cristoforo Saliceti, a native of Corsica and a representative of the Revolutionary government in Paris, soon found themselves in very hot water with Paoli, who had really turned against the Revolution. The Bonapartes were literally in danger of losing their lives, so Napoleon and his family left their family estate and quickly sailed for France in June 1793.

Getting a warm reception in France

While Napoleon was on Corsica, events in France had taken a major turn (for the better or worse, depending on your point of view). On January 21, 1793,

King Louis XVI was executed by the guillotine for treason. The monarchy was over, at least for the time being, and it was replaced by a Revolutionary government run by a legislative body and several committees.

Napoleon's actions in Corsica caused him trouble there, but his pro-Revolutionary stance led to a favorable reception in France. Stationed in Nice, his commander was Jean du Teil, brother of his former commanding officer at Auxonne.

Some of Napoleon's duties caused him to be stationed at Avignon. During his stay there, he wrote a short story called "Le Souper de Beaucaire" ("Supper at Beaucaire"). In this story, Napoleon argued for all French to rally to the cause of the Revolution, and he supported the most radical of the various branches of the Revolution. (If you visit Avignon today, you can still see the building where Napoleon wrote the story.)

Needless to say, the Revolutionary government was pleased. The most powerful organization in the French government, the Committee of Public Safety, gave the story its blessing. At the head of the Committee was the *de facto* ruler of France, Maximilien Robespierre, whose brother, Augustine, had become friendly with Napoleon. The future emperor was already running in some pretty lofty circles.

Showing signs of greatness

Thus far, Napoleon's career had depended on several things. First and foremost was his own brilliance. His commanders and those around him could see that he was a man of extraordinary talent. But Napoleon also gained from his ability to make influential friends and use that friendship to advantage. Doing so was not cynical; it reflected an astute understanding that success is achieved through more than one approach.

Napoleon was also willing to take risks and stand up for what he believed. A cynic may say that in supporting the Revolution he was merely "riding the wave," but his later actions showed that he really did believe in at least some of the ideals of the French Revolution.

One story about Napoleon relates a time when he was being told of the various leadership virtues of a particular officer. Napoleon is said to have commented, "Yes, but is he lucky?" Luck can be defined in many ways, including simply being in the right place at the right time with the right people close at hand. Napoleon had that luck for much of his life, and never more so than in the next stage of his career.

Chapter 4

Moving into the Limelight

- -

In This Chapter

▶ Being governed by Committee

▶ Leading the siege of Toulon

▶ Gaining promotion and fame

▶ Serving time in jail

▶ Saving a reputation — and a career

- -

There is a myth about the American Revolution (more properly called the *U.S. War of Independence*) that says that all Americans rose up as one against the tyranny of King George and the British Parliament. Nothing could be further from the truth.

The American uprising largely was led by a middle class that was protecting its economic interests as much as promoting the lofty ideals expressed so well in the Declaration of Independence and other writings. And for a long time, it was not at all clear that the American insurgents would win.

A large number of American colonialists were quite happy to be His Royal Majesty's Loyal Subjects, hoping only for some reforms in the way the colonies were treated. Had the French not joined the struggle, those whom the United States now venerates as heroic founding fathers may have instead gone down in history as hanged and disemboweled traitors.

The situation in France in the early days of the French Revolution was similar to what the Americans had faced. In this chapter, I discuss why the French Revolution actually horrified many French citizens and caused deep divisions within the country and even within the Revolutionary leadership. I then explain how the French Revolution helped give Napoleon an opportunity to advance very quickly in his military career. I discuss his earliest victory (Toulon) and how it led to Napoleon's early fame. And finally, I tell you how Napoleon saved the French government from a royalist takeover and became a national hero.

Losing Some Revolutionary Fervor

Since the beginning of time, France had had a king, and many French citizens thought that was just the way it was supposed to be. Humans like tradition, and at that time there was nothing more traditional than having a king. Also, kings claimed to rule by *divine right,* meaning that they served as king because God wanted them in that position. That argument was weaker in the 18th century than it had been previously, but many people still believed it.

When the leaders of the Revolution executed King Louis XVI in January 1793 (see Chapter 3) and later executed the queen, many people were horrified. To some, this action went against deeply-held religious beliefs. To others, it was simply cruel and unnecessary; perhaps the king could have still been part of the Revolution despite his early lack of support.

Getting radical

Indeed, the execution of the king helped split the leadership cadre of the Revolution itself. Rather than a monolithic movement, the Revolution soon was comprised of several factions, and the most radical of those factions, a group known as the *Jacobins,* was gaining the upper hand. That would not be good news for anyone who opposed them.

The Committee of Public Safety, a group of 12 "just men" who governed France after the Jacobins took power in 1793, had become increasingly radical. The execution of the king was only the start. Soon, anyone who disagreed with these "just men" was in trouble, a condition generally associated with a one-way trip to the guillotine.

Effectively run by Maximilien Robespierre, one of the most radical Revolutionaries, the Committee consisted of middle class lawyers, some of whom can only be described as violent and bloodthirsty. While the Revolution was based on lofty goals, such as religious freedom, the Committee of Public Safety turned on anyone who failed to exhibit what it considered proper political or religious beliefs. One-time Revolutionaries like Georges-Jacques Danton made that trip to the guillotine as the Revolution turned on itself.

Some of the Committee's other actions included

- Eliminating the traditional calendar in favor of one based on the beginning of the Revolution, with months named after seasons
- Fighting to eliminate Christianity and replace it with a "Cult of the Supreme Being"

As a result, not everyone in France was all that excited about the Revolution. Many were outraged at its excesses.

Recognizing opposition

In the United States, people sometimes talk about *blue states* and *red states,* with blue indicating greater support for the Democratic Party and red indicating support for the Republican Party. We have our liberal cities and our Bible-belt South. France was much the same way in the late 18th century.

A country divided

Support for the Revolution was strongest in Paris and in some other cities, such as Grenoble. Elsewhere, citizens either took a wait-and-see attitude or, as was the case in the city of Lyon, offered outright opposition. Widespread opposition among some segments of French society and in some geographic areas made the Revolution much like a civil war. And citizens who sided with the ultimate losers could find their careers — and their heads — cut off. (We should try to understand Napoleon's moves during this period in this context.)

One area noted for its strong opposition was the Vendée, an area of unusual religious fervor located in western France. The Revolution was anticlerical in nature. Years of excesses by the Roman Catholic Church had led to deep distrust and disillusionment among many people, which even developed into fierce hatred toward the Church for some. But not everyone felt that way. Many French citizens were pious believers who were appalled by the destruction of church property and the murder of some members of the clergy. As a result, the Vendée openly opposed the Revolution.

Another area of opposition to the increasingly radical Revolution was the Mediterranean port city of Toulon. Citizens there were probably okay with some of the ideas of the Revolution, but they wanted nothing to do with executing a king or anyone else.

British interference

As a port city with a population approaching 30,000, Toulon was important for trade and defense. It contained a very large arsenal for the navy. If you look at a map, you will clearly see that it was also an important strategic location for the French presence in the Mediterranean. Control of Toulon was key for any defending French government, as well as any would-be French conqueror.

And guess who was more than willing to foment discord wherever they could? The British government opposed the French Revolution, especially after the execution of Louis XVI, and was pleased to do anything that might ultimately restore the Bourbon monarchy. In this effort, it had the support of Spain and most of the other old monarchies of Europe.

It so happens that the British naval fleet was just sort of hanging around, looking for something to do. Toulon's city fathers decided to take bold action. On August 27, 1793, they declared themselves an independent city, no longer part of Revolutionary France. They further declared the young Louis XVII king, notwithstanding the fact that he was in prison at the time. After the Bourbon monarchy was restored, the city would quickly rejoin French society and all would be forgiven, right? Well, maybe, maybe not.

The city fathers of Toulon were foolish, but they were not fools. They invited the British navy, commanded by Admiral Samuel Hood, to occupy their harbor and British marines to occupy their town. I'm sure you will be shocked to hear that the British, hardly able to conceal their glee, were quick to move in and settle down. In the process, they gained control of a major French port and a number of French ships, and they stuck a very large thorn in the side of the hated Revolutionaries in Paris. From the British point of view, this was a marvelous gift.

Even so, this whole episode raises the question that I'd sure like to ask those city fathers in Toulon: What *were* you thinking? Gee, is there a word for inviting the enemy to come in and take over your city, turning against your own government? Yes, indeed, and the word is *treason*. While I'm at it, I'd ask if they really believed that the French government in Paris was going to just shrug its shoulders and ignore them. Not! Other French cities had tried this — Marseilles and Lyon come to mine, each having tried to declare independence from the Revolutionary government — and other cities had failed.

Moreover, this was an act of war by Great Britain. After all, occupying French territory without the permission of the French government is a big no-no, regardless of what the mayor of Toulon has to say.

Catching a Break

Napoleon was about to step right into this difficult situation. Indeed, he had already had to deal with opposition to the Revolution and the need to oppose French citizens in the name of defending the Revolutionary government. In 1792, as an officer in the French army assigned to Avignon, Napoleon had experienced the unique horror of seeing citizen killing citizen, in this case in trying to acquire the ammunition at Avignon for the government. Shortly after that experience, he wrote his short story "Supper at Beaucaire," which argued for French unity with order restored by the army (see Chapter 3.)

Napoleon was beginning to make his mark, but he still had routine military assignments to fulfill; he was, after all, a relatively low-ranking officer. But not for long.

France had an army in Italy, and in September 1793 Napoleon was assigned to escort an ammunition convoy to re-supply that army. Such a convoy does not move quickly, so along the way Napoleon took the time to stop for a visit in the town of Le Beausset, perhaps a dozen miles from Toulon. Napoleon's uncle, Joseph Fesch, was the storekeeper at the military depot there. As a reward for the Bonapartes' loyalty on Corsica and the difficulties they had encountered as a result of that loyalty, the Revolutionary government had extended its largess to them, including Uncle Fesch's appointment.

Visiting friends in high places

Napoleon's visit wasn't just a family matter. Among other friends in the area was one Antonio Cristoforo Saliceti, a fellow Corsican who had fought for the island's independence. Like the Bonaparte family, Saliceti had left the island when Corsican leader Pasquale Paoli had turned against the Revolution and, thus, against its Corsican supporters.

Saliceti was a member of the Revolutionary government called a *Representative on Mission,* which meant he had enormous power. From that post, he had given a glowing report on the conduct of the Bonapartes to the Committee on Public Safety As a result, not only had Uncle Fesch received his appointment, but Napoleon's brother Joseph was made comptroller of army supplies and his brother Lucien was the military storekeeper at St. Maximin. Something of a firebrand, Lucien had become quite active in Revolutionary politics, rising to become president of the local chapter of the Jacobin club, the most radical of the Revolutionaries at that time. The Jacobins were something like a very radical political party, and each area had its own chapter. The chapter Lucien led was headquartered in Toulon.

In addition to Saliceti, several other important contacts were in the Toulon area as well:

- **Louis-Marie Stanislas Fréron:** Like Saliceti, Fréron was a Representative on Mission. He was especially unhappy with the unrest in Toulon because his sister and niece were trapped in the city and at the mercy of those who opposed the Revolution he was helping to lead. (Fréron would later have an affair with Napoleon's sister Pauline. While that hardly made him unique, the affair stemmed from his relationship with Napoleon forged during the siege of Toulon.)

- **Thomas Gasparin:** Gasparin was another Revolutionary leader who was Corsican.

- **Paul Barras:** A rising star in Revolutionary France, Barras would one day be one of France's most powerful leaders and a mentor to Napoleon.

- **Augustine Robespierre:** His presence was perhaps the most important of all. Augustine was the brother of the revered, and feared, Maximilien Robespierre, the most powerful member of the all-powerful Committee of Public Safety.

If you get the sense that Napoleon was pretty well connected for a junior army officer, you'd be right; he had friends and relatives in pretty high places. He had already gained attention in both military and political circles, and now the two worlds would begin to converge.

Seizing an opportunity

Saliceti needed an artillery officer to replace one who had been wounded. Artillery was key to driving out the British ships. Napoleon was a perfect selection. As an artillery officer, his credentials were impeccable. Moreover, he was a rising star with good political connections. Saliceti could do far worse than give this promising young man a chance to make a name for himself defending the very same Revolution he had already defended with both his pen and his military action. Saliceti offered Napoleon the job.

Napoleon was no fool. He was on a mundane convoy mission to an obscure campaign in Italy. If he went to Toulon instead, he would have the opportunity to defend the Revolution and the French nation against 18,000 foreign troops, mostly the hated British and a few traitors. As long as Toulon held out, the royalists — the people hoping to restore the Bourbon monarchy — would have hope, and the Revolution, with all of its great ideas of liberty and equality, was in danger. The conqueror of Toulon would surely be a great hero to the fledgling French Republic.

Hmmm. Obscurity or glory: Which would *you* choose? The words were probably barely out of Saliceti's mouth before Napoleon said "Yes!" And how could he go wrong? He had just been selected by some of the most powerful men in France to do something that relied on his strong points, leadership and artillery, to protect the nation. It was an assignment made in heaven, and Napoleon was determined to make the most of it.

Napoleon was brilliant, and he had important political backing. Still, he was not a top officer, and he had to convince the commanding general to follow his suggestions. Moreover, the military force drawn up against the insurgents in Toulon was not ideal. Rival Revolutionary factions in Marseilles contended for military recruits, and some of the army was tied down in a siege at Lyon. Plus, desertion in the ranks was a problem. In short, things were not going as well as the Revolutionary government may have hoped.

From Napoleon's point of view, the biggest problem was the commanding general, an undistinguished man named Jean Carteaux, who had been a painter before the Revolutionary government had made him a general. (Petty jealousies and political intrigue combined to inhibit both the political and military command structures from making good decisions.)

General Carteaux insisted on repeated frontal assaults in columns of three, a completely losing proposition. Worse, it became clear to Napoleon that his commanding general had not the slightest clue of anything regarding artillery, either as to its potential or the technicalities of its use. Exasperated, Napoleon wrote to the Committee of Public Safety on October 25, 1793, asking for a new general to command the artillery. As if this wasn't bold enough, he described the current leadership as "a band of fools" guilty of "ignorance," and he practically demanded that a general who could stand up to them be sent to take command of the artillery.

It didn't take much to obtain a one-way trip to the *national razor* (as the guillotine was often called), so this was pretty bold stuff. But Napoleon was not one to pull his punches, and his letter actually worked. An artillery commander was sent, and it turned out to be none other than General Jean du Teil, brother of Napoleon's former commander (see Chapter 3). Napoleon was essentially placed in charge of the artillery, and he began to use the division effectively, including to bombard the British ships.

Ultimately, General Jacques Coquille Dugommier was sent to take overall charge of the army at Toulon. General Dugommier recognized the brilliance of his young artillery commander and the value of his plans. The two men hit it off rather well. By then, additional supplies had begun to arrive, including forces fresh from the successful siege of Lyon, and it was time for decisive action.

Retaking Toulon

To retake Toulon, Napoleon knew it was essential to gain control of a series of forts that controlled the heights overlooking the harbor. If the French were positioned in these heights, a couple miles from the city itself, the British navy would be helpless to resist a bombardment and would have to withdraw. With the British navy gone, along with its marines, Toulon would be ripe for the taking. Meetings took place, the politicians agreed to the plan, and all was in place.

On December 17, 1793, the Revolutionary forces stormed Fort Mulgrave (also called Little Gibraltar), which dominated the heights and controlled access to two smaller fortifications known as l'Eguillette and Balaguier. In a simultaneous action, they stormed Mount Faron. To their credit, the Representatives on Mission helped lead the action, notwithstanding their distinct lack of military experience.

The fighting was fierce, and Napoleon was in the thick of it all. He received a bayonet wound that nearly cost him a leg. After several hours, during which the result was sometimes in doubt, Fort Mulgrave fell. Shortly thereafter, l'Eguillette and Balaguier were deserted.

With control of the high ground theirs, the French began a bombardment of the British and Spanish fleet in the harbor. No fools they, the Brits and

Spanish immediately began to withdraw, taking their marines and quite a few French traitors with them. Unable to adequately staff some of the French ships in the harbor, they sank them. They also set fire to the arsenal. By morning, they were gone. Meanwhile, the streets of Toulon were a scene of chaos and bloodshed, as Revolutionaries began to take their revenge on royalists unable to quickly escape to the ships.

Basking in victory

With the British gone, Toulon quickly fell to the French army and its Revolutionary leaders. More bloodshed followed, as the Revolutionary leaders sought to punish any traitors who remained behind. The definition of *traitor* soon became rather loose. People were summarily executed without trial, often several hundred at a time. Ironically, the worst offenders, the leaders of the insurrection, had escaped with the British fleet. Unhappy with the bloodshed, Napoleon and others tried to limit it but weren't very successful.

In time, things calmed down. Meanwhile, the political and military leaders made their reports to Paris. The action in Toulon had been very important, as it effectively ended the counterrevolutionary movement in the south of France and kicked the British and Spanish off French soil. The action caught the imagination of the French people and was the subject of songs, a play, and engravings.

From all sides, Napoleon Bonaparte received accolades. Naturally, the politicians took much of the credit themselves, but Napoleon was praised by General Dugommier, who called him "a rare officer," and others. For his efforts, Napoleon became a brigadier general at the ripe old age of 24. He received mention in the national newspaper and recognition in the highest councils of government. In his first real combat, Napoleon had shown that he could be a bold and decisive leader who was willing to take chances. One of history's greatest careers was underway.

Toulon was also the beginning of some very long and important friendships. Napoleon's secretary, Sergeant Andoche Junot, was impressed with him and would stay with him for his entire career. Captain Auguste Frédéric Louis Marmont became his best friend and remained close until he finally deserted Napoleon in 1814. Other long-term relationships that came from Toulon included Louis Suchet, Louis Charles Desaix, Geraud Duroc, and Claude-Victor Perrin (generally known as Marshal Victor).

After Toulon, everything seemed to be going Napoleon's way. As a brigadier general, his salary increased substantially. True to his Corsican heritage that stressed the importance of family (see Chapter 2), he made sure that his mother shared in his success. He established the family home near Antibes, a decision that would later prove fortuitous.

In addition to his military promotion, Napoleon received the relatively mundane position of Inspector of Coastal Defenses, which he found interesting. Using his political connections, Napoleon made plans to drive the Austrians out of Italy (though ultimately those plans were abandoned).

Generally, life was pretty good. Still, he did have to be careful. He knew that it was all too easy to run afoul of the Revolutionary government in Paris. He had friends in high places, but some of those friends were competing with each other, and he had to be careful not to get caught in the middle.

Taking a Step Backward

Just as things were looking rosy for Napoleon, disaster struck. The Committee of Public Safety, led by Maximilien Robespierre, had gone too far. Too many good Revolutionaries had been executed in the name of purifying the Revolution. No one trusted anyone, and everyone feared they would be next.

With that atmosphere, the inevitable happened. Maximilien and Augustine Robespierre and other members of the most radical faction of Revolutionary leadership were arrested. The very next day, July 28, 1794, they were sent to the same guillotine to which they had sent so many before them.

France breathed a collective sigh of relief, but the bloodshed was far from over. A national backlash occurred, and anyone associated with the Robespierre brothers was immediately suspect and often just as immediately executed.

Going to jail

Napoleon was on the southern coast of France, a fact that probably saved his life. A friend of the Robespierres and others of their ilk, Napoleon was arrested and thrown into jail at the *Chateau d'Antibes,* which, despite its name, was no luxury hotel! He was charged with planning to build a prison and conducting a treasonous secret mission to Genoa, Italy. The charges were bogus, of course — Napoleon was just doing what he had been told to do — but nevertheless, he was kept in prison for two weeks. The situation was very dangerous for Napoleon. His old friend Saliceti was in charge of the investigation, but he may have been the source of the charges as well!

Napoleon was not one to sit quietly and let events run their course. He prepared his own defense, writing letters to his family and others protesting his innocence. He claimed he would have killed Robespierre himself had he suspected any aspirations to tyranny and pointed out that he had sacrificed much to the cause of the Revolution. His most immediate commanding general wrote in his defense. Junot, his *aide-de-camp,* was willing to help

Napoleon escape, but Napoleon refused. Convinced that he eventually would be released, Napoleon chose to wait it out, keeping himself occupied by drawing up plans for a future Italian campaign.

His optimism was justified: All charges were ultimately dropped — whether in spite of or because of Saliceti is a little hard to determine. Napoleon came out of this situation unscathed, but his career was still very much up in the air.

Floundering in his career

In the spring of 1795, Napoleon was ordered to the Vendée, a *departement* (regional government) in west central France. There, counterrevolutionary forces were gaining the upper hand, and the military was being sent to quell a revolt. Napoleon could clearly see that this was a losing proposition all around. It was one thing to fire upon traitors in Toulon; after all, the British and Spanish were there. But firing on French citizens in the interior of the country was quite another matter, and Napoleon wanted none of it.

Napoleon decided to go to Paris, with his friend Marmont and his loyal secretary Junot in tow, to ask the Minister of War to change his orders. Instead, Napoleon found himself removed from the artillery and assigned to command an infantry unit. This was a serious blow not only to his ego but to his possibilities for advancement, as the artillery was the elite of the army and the infantry was, well, the infantry!

Napoleon could hardly disobey orders, but he could call in sick. Heck, he had previously taken long personal leaves (see Chapter 2), so calling in sick was just another ploy along the same lines. While in Paris, he went to the opera and attended scholarly lectures. He, Junot, and Marmont solidified their relationship.

But times had changed since Napoleon had taken his long leaves to Corsica, and Napoleon knew he could claim to be sick for only so long. Depressed and fearful of being sent to the Vendée, Napoleon requested to be sent to join the Turkish artillery in Constantinople. Napoleon actually had a legitimate chance of getting the request approved (we can only imagine the effect on history if he did), but it seems that the request disappeared into the bureaucracy. Napoleon also applied to serve in the Russian army, but that idea went nowhere.

Napoleon's career floundered, and he became somewhat despondent. With most of his money going to support his family, he moved into more humble quarters. Once full of hope and seemingly at the beginning of a great career, a hero of his nation, Napoleon was down and out in Paris. Things were looking grim, and nothing his friends did could improve his mood.

Getting a new assignment

Just in the nick of time, a new war minister was appointed. Napoleon was right there in Paris with his request for reassignment (but not to Turkey), and this time he had much better luck. Impressed with Napoleon's plans for an Italian campaign, the new Minister of War assigned Napoleon to the Topographical Bureau, Italian section.

Napoleon had hoped to be sent to Italy, but he made the most of his desk job in Paris, spending much of his time hobnobbing with top generals and politicians, both professionally and socially. He began to make the social rounds, attending receptions known as *salons,* where he met a wide range of important people. He probably met his future wife, Josephine, at one of these events (see Chapter 5).

Even so, Napoleon was frustrated at being so far from the action. Maps and planning were fine for a time, but he longed to put his ideas into effect. Moreover, in September 1795, he was placed on half pay, even though he was working full-time in his assigned post. The pay cut was either due to incompetence on the part of some personnel clerk or, possibly, due to someone not trusting a former Jacobin general. (Remember: Napoleon had been very close to the Robespierre brothers.) Whatever the case, it certainly had a major impact on Napoleon's lifestyle and career potential.

To say that Napoleon was frustrated would be a gross understatement. When France decided to send a small group of artillerymen to Turkey to help modernize the Turkish forces, Napoleon managed to get named as head of the delegation. But once again events would intervene and send Napoleon on a far different path.

Securing a Government

With the fall of Robespierre, the French government was controlled by a legislative body known as the *Convention.* This body attempted to reduce the influence of the radical Jacobins. But as I discuss in this section, its security was threatened not just from the radical left, but also from right-wing factions that wanted to bring back the monarchy.

Fearing the left and the right

The French government was now firmly in the hands of the middle class. As such, it was fearful of the working class Parisians who had sustained so many of the radical actions under the Committee of Public Safety.

As I note in Chapter 3, the Revolution had been brought on in part by severe economic difficulties. The gap between rich and poor in France had been enormous and growing, and Louis XVI was unable to find an economic fix for the plight of the poor.

Unfortunately, the Revolution had done little better. The Convention had been unable to adequately deal with France's many economic problems, and inflation was running wild. Bread, that staple of workers everywhere, was expensive and in very short supply. Bread riots in Paris were not uncommon. Anger toward the government was growing, and the streets sometimes approached anarchy.

At first, the government seemed to get support from bands of youth known as the *jeunesse dorée*, or "gilded youth." These gangs would roam the streets in outlandish attire, putting on airs and eating expensive food. (They were so absurd that they gained the nickname of *les Incroyables*, or "the Incredibles.") These youth were not simply fops trying to pretend to be royal and/or British. Though many of them were deserters or were avoiding military service, they were happy to beat up any Jacobins they happened to find. Armed and dangerous, they exerted a fair amount of influence on the Convention that they claimed to support.

But throughout the country, there was a right-wing, or royalist, backlash against the Revolution and, thus, against the government. Initially supportive of the government against the remaining radicals of the left, the *jeunesse dorée* soon became the violent spearhead of those who wanted to bring back a monarchy, even if they needed to get help from the British to do so. Thus, an odd coalition of the poor Parisian left and the gilded youth of the right threatened the peace and stability that most people desired.

Royalist supporters actually controlled many, perhaps most, of the administrative units of Paris, called *sections*. The Convention could not tolerate this situation.

Practicing self-perpetuating politics

To maintain control of the government, the Convention proposed a new constitution. The Convention would be replaced with a two-house legislative body:

- ✔ The Council of Five Hundred would initiate legislation.
- ✔ The smaller Council of Ancients (with 250 members) would have veto power.
- ✔ Executive functions would be controlled by a Directory composed of five directors with a rotating chair.

While this move was rather popular, the Convention's next move was decidedly less so. In one last effort to maintain power, the new constitution decreed that two-thirds of each of the two new legislative bodies would come from — you guessed it — the current membership of the Convention!

The people were not blind; they knew what was happening. So while the constitution passed easily in a September 1795 *plebiscite* (a direct vote of the citizens), there was great unrest in the streets. Not surprisingly, most of this unrest was centered in Paris. Voter turnout had been low, and charges of fraud were heard far and wide.

Preparing for a fight

In June of that year, the young son of Louis XVI had died in prison. Sensing an opportunity, Louis's brother, the Comte d'Artois, had declared himself Louis XVIII. This action outraged some people and delighted others. The streets were alive with tension and outright conflict. Paris was threatened with anarchy, and the government was threatened with overthrow.

On October 4, the Convention sent the elderly General Jacques Menou to quell the disturbances, which were on the verge of getting completely out of hand. Menou faced the insurgents and, upon their agreement to disband, removed his troops from the scene. This was hardly effective action, and the Convention sacked Menou on the spot. (Later, Napoleon would intervene to save Menou's career.)

And — surprise! — the insurgents did not disband. Instead, they quickly armed and mobilized for an all-out attack on the Convention. Now in serious fear for its very survival, the Convention turned to Paul Barras, a leading member of the Convention, to organize its defense. Barras had essentially no military skills, but he knew Napoleon from the siege of Toulon and quickly sought his assistance.

On the evening of October 4, Napoleon had been to see a play. On his way home, he heard the drums of the insurgents and could see something was up. He made his way to the galleries of the Convention and actually observed the Convention as it organized its defense and put Barras in charge. Accounts differ as to how Napoleon was informed of his own appointment. His old acquaintance Louis Marie Stanislas Fréron may have had a hand in it, or Napoleon may have been informed by Barras himself later in the evening. However it happened, Napoleon had very little time to decide if he would take the job. He didn't need much time: The answer was clearly to be yes.

There was good news and bad news in all of this for Napoleon. The good news is that, as with Toulon, he was being given a chance to save the Revolutionary government. The bad news was that he would almost certainly have to fire on French citizens. Even when done in defense of one's government, shooting at citizens is a dicey proposition at best and clearly fraught with danger. But these French citizens were royalists mixed in with a healthy portion of anarchists and some units of the National Guard who had turned against their own government. If ever there was a group of citizens on whom it was pretty safe to fire, this was it. If he succeeded, he would likely be seen as a hero, and Napoleon did not plan to fail.

Taking charge

Paul Barras was technically in command of the defense of the Tuileries, the palace where the Convention held its meetings, but Napoleon was soon the one giving the orders. Not surprisingly, he quickly decided that artillery was key to controlling the streets that led to the Tuileries Palace, especially the streets leading from the church of St. Roch, headquarters for the insurgents. Incredibly, the Convention forces would be far outnumbered by the growing band of insurgents, by a margin of almost six to one. The only hope lay in the effective use of artillery, but the artillery was stored six miles away on the Plain of Sablons.

Napoleon quickly ordered the closest cavalry unit he could find to ride to get the cannon before they fell to the insurgents, who were quite aware of their existence. (By the way, *cannon* is one of those words that is both singular and plural and, of course, means artillery. Cannon is sometimes called "guns" or "heavy guns" as well.) The cavalry, led by the dashing young officer Joachim Murat, just barely got the artillery, arriving mere moments before insurgent forces. There was a brief standoff, but Murat's cavalry, with sabers drawn and a clear intent to use them, was up to the task, and the insurgents fled.

Early in the morning of October 5, the artillery, a total of 40 guns, arrived and was quickly put into place. By afternoon, the two forces faced each other, often within just a few paces. The insurgents attempted to entice the soldiers to desert, even sending some women over to, uh, distract the men. None of it worked.

Napoleon feared that the royalist insurgents might try to infiltrate his defenses under cover of darkness. So as the day wore on, the Convention itself was armed. At 4:00 in the afternoon, the drums were beat, cheers were heard, and thousands of insurgents began to march from the church of St. Roch toward the Tuileries. Push was about to become shove, and Napoleon was ready.

Sweeping the streets (with grapeshot)

Napoleon had filled his cannon with canisters of small musket balls, called *grapeshot*. Firing cannon in this way had the effect of turning them into rather large shotguns. The attacking royalists knew the guns were there, and they came anyway. After they made it past some barricades, Napoleon had no choice but to shoot. The command was given to fire, and every gun blazed away.

At first, the insurgents faltered, but then they kept coming. Each side was determined to win, but after 15 minutes or so it became clear that there were simply not enough insurgents to overcome the power of the artillery. Through the smoke and noise, they began to withdraw. Sensing victory, Napoleon ordered his infantry to pursue them all the way to the church of St. Roch. There, the insurgents made a desperate last stand, but when artillery was moved into place to fire at close range, their fate was sealed. Today, you can still see potmarks (small holes) in the walls of the church from this confrontation.

Ending an era

The entire affair was over by 6:00 in the evening. Amazingly, only about 400 insurgents were killed. Even so, their resolve was broken, to say nothing of their ability to mount a serious military threat ever again.

Napoleon had been everywhere on the field and had been completely in charge. No one doubted that he was the man of the hour — that the victory had been his alone. Not content with a simple victory, he quickly moved to disarm the sections. Collection points were established, and citizens were ordered to turn in their weapons. Early the next morning, when Napoleon could finally relax a bit, he wrote to his brother Joseph about the events of the day, assuring him that he had suffered no wounds.

During the Revolution, the Parisian working class had formed the most radical basis for Revolutionary action. Often the greatest proponents of violence, the so-called *Paris mob* exerted great influence on the government and was one of the reasons for the radical actions of the Committee on Public Safety. No one was willing, or able, to challenge the Paris mob once it was mobilized.

The Convention may have succumbed to the demands of the Paris mob as well, if not for Napoleon. After his famous "whiff of grapeshot," as the action in defense of the Tuileries would be forever known, the Paris mob would never again exert such influence, whether radical left or royalist right. In that sense, Napoleon's actions brought to an end the French Revolution and ushered in a new era.

Napoleon's success also ended, for a time at least, any talk of a return of the monarchy. The Comte d'Artois had planned to lead a triumphant march into Paris, sweeping aside all who would oppose him. Well, that idea sure was going nowhere, so d'Artois opted for a bit longer stay in exile. When Napoleon heard of this decision, he was rather disgusted. Later, when that same pretender to the throne sought his help, Bonaparte, remembering the character of the man, would have none of it.

Jump-Starting His Career

Even more than he had at Toulon, Napoleon proved with his action in Paris to be an extraordinary leader in extraordinary times. Moreover, he showed that he could use his specialty — artillery — to its fullest advantage. Both Toulon and Paris were situations where an expert artillery officer with imagination, leadership, and daring could turn things around. Napoleon (see Figure 4-1) did just that, and his efforts were rewarded.

Figure 4-1:
This snuffbox shows a confident young Napoleon as he embarks on an amazing career.

The Convention met on October 11, 1795. Barras and Fréron gave speeches that reminded the Convention just how much it owed this young General Bonaparte. Napoleon was clearly the hero of the day, though he was careful not to be seen seeking the limelight and did not give a speech of his own. The Convention had appointed Barras as commander of the Army of the Interior, and now it appointed Napoleon as second in command. The promotion was a great step forward for Napoleon, but the jump-starting of his career was just beginning.

The new constitution called for dissolving the Convention, and on October 26 that body met for the last time. Paul Barras had been chosen as one of the first members of the new Directory, and as such he could not maintain his military position. A grateful Convention, as one of its last acts, appointed Napoleon as commander of the Army of the Interior, with the rank of *général de division*. At 26, he had already accomplished great things. Perhaps to celebrate, and certainly to symbolize his final commitment to France, he gave up the Italian spelling of his name, *Buonaparte,* dropping the *u* to become simply *Bonaparte*.

As he had after Toulon, Napoleon used his new position, with its large salary, to improve his lifestyle and that of his family. He was given a nice home as part of his position as commanding officer, and he was able to send his mother a significant amount of money. He found positions for some of his family as well, arranging for Joseph to be consul in Italy and Lucien an army commissioner. His youngest brother, Louis, soon became Napoleon's *aide-de-camp*.

Napoleon was no longer obscure. Everywhere he went, he was cheered. People sought to shake his hand. He received ovations at the theater and invitations to all manner of social events. He attended many salons and was the topic of conversation in other salons and elsewhere. Everyone, it seemed, wanted to hear of, and better yet, meet, this dashing young general Bonaparte.

Life was good. And it would soon get much better.

Chapter 5

Josephine!

The love story of Napoleon and Josephine is perhaps the aspect of Napoleon's life best known to the general public. It is a modern-day rival to Shakespeare's *Romeo and Juliet* and has been the subject of many books, movies, and television shows. Many people think that the years with Josephine were the best years of Napoleon's life, and when they parted ways Josephine took with her the magic that had sustained Napoleon for those years — magic that was never to return.

As is so often the case, image does not necessarily reflect reality. Their relationship was certainly magical, but beneath the glitter lay a less enchanting reality. In this chapter, I show you the glitter but also some of their problems. I tell you about Napoleon's earlier loves, how he met Josephine, and their marriage.

In later chapters, I check in on the two lovers to see how they are doing. In Chapter 20, I present the sad ending to their story.

Learning about Love

Napoleon did not have a great deal of romantic experience before he met Josephine, but he wasn't a complete novice, either. As a student, Napoleon was dedicated to his learning and didn't have much time for romance. Of course, he was only 9 when he first went to military school in France (see Chapter 2), and most 9-year-old boys have limited romantic experience (except, possibly, with snakes and frogs!). Napoleon was in school through his teenage years, but his poverty and the rigors of his education seem to have kept him plenty busy.

When Napoleon graduated from the Military School of Paris and was assigned to the La Fère Regiment in Valence, things changed. He was no longer strictly confined to a barracks, no longer involved in a 24/7 educational experience, and no longer completely broke (though still quite poor). And, you may add, he was no longer too young for romantic thoughts.

As a dashing young man in a spiffy uniform, he attracted the attention of more than one young lady. While in school, Napoleon had been something of a loner, shy and not very likely to socialize. Free of the constraints of school (and of the indignities he suffered at the hands of some snobbish cadets), he began to socialize more.

Wooing Caroline du Colombier

While in Valence, Napoleon befriended a woman named Madame Grégoire du Colombier, who had a daughter named Caroline. Napoleon escorted Caroline to dances and apparently was quite taken with her.

Alas, as is so often the case with young love, Napoleon's feelings were not reciprocated. Caroline was being wooed by more than one dashing young officer, and she eventually married Captain Garembel de Bressieux. Napoleon was not a sore loser, though. When he became emperor, he gave Caroline and Garembel nice positions, eventually making Garembel a baron.

Learning about feminine charms in Paris

When Napoleon was 18, he was still quite inexperienced in the ways of love — and of sex. On a trip to Paris, he evidently decided to take a step forward in his education. After an evening at the theater, Napoleon took a stroll near the Palais-Royal. The area was home to many cafés and other cheerful places of entertainment — and to ladies of, ahem, easy virtue.

Napoleon was somewhat prudish all his life, but for some reason he seems to have been taken by the opportunities presented to him in abundance that evening. He struck up a conversation with one young lady, whom he fancied to be a cut above the others of her trade. She was soft-spoken and slight of build. They talked, and she told him her tale of woe. Napoleon was touched, and later he continued his education in his room and her arms.

After this educational interlude, Napoleon seems to have withdrawn a bit from his pursuit of love. He certainly met women when he attended various social functions, but there is precious little information available on his love life for the next several years. But things would change dramatically after the siege of Toulon (see Chapter 4), when Napoleon became a brigadier general.

Courting Désirée Clary

Other than his two wives, the woman with whom Napoleon is most associated is Bernardine Eugénie Désirée Clary. Napoleon met her and her sister Julie when he was stationed in Marseille after his success at Toulon.

In 1793, the French Revolutionary government had imprisoned a number of people suspected of being traitors. One of them was Étienne Clary, brother to the two women. Napoleon's brother, Joseph, was instrumental in getting Clary released, which led to Joseph's being a regular visitor to the Clary residence. The head of the household, François Clary, was ill and died in 1794, but he had been a wealthy merchant so both ladies would come with a sizable dowry.

Joseph was initially interested in Désirée, but he switched his affections to the older sister, Julie, when he learned that Napoleon was interested in Désirée. (We know her as Désirée, though Napoleon insisted on calling her Eugénie.) Joseph was a hero to the family, so there were no objections on either side when Joseph proposed marriage. Joseph and Julie were married in August 1794.

Napoleon continued to court Désirée, and he talked of marriage. Désirée, though only 16, seems to have been determined to marry him as well. She was convinced that she was in love and that Napoleon was the one for her. Her wealth would certainly have been a big boost to the Bonaparte family, but before things could progress further, Napoleon was transferred to the Italian front to fight the Austrians. Distracted by his duties, he seems to have cooled a bit in his ardors for Désirée. (This may have been quite fine with Désirée's mother, who is said to have remarked that one Bonaparte in the family was quite enough.)

Transferred again, this time to Paris, it seems that Napoleon's interest in marrying Désirée was rekindled, but her letters to him began to taper off. Napoleon, meanwhile, discovered that Paris offered an abundance of romantic opportunities. As the hero of Toulon, he was very much in demand at social functions. The women there were closer to his age and more sophisticated than Désirée. Napoleon even asked for the hand of an older woman who had been a long-time friend, a widow named Panorier Permon. She was in her 40s and used her age as an excuse to decline the unexpected offer.

When Désirée moved to Genoa with her family shortly thereafter, Napoleon began to shut down the relationship. Désirée swore she would always love him, but her allegiance didn't last long, and she was soon dealing with other suitors. As he was known to do with his own family members, Napoleon tried to arrange a suitable marriage for his former girlfriend. She rejected his nominees and in 1798 married General Jean-Baptiste Bernadotte. (Bernadotte would accompany Napoleon on many of his campaigns but would eventually betray him. In 1818, Bernadotte and Désirée became the king and queen of Sweden, taking the names of King Carl XIV Johan and Queen Katerine.)

A Rose by Any Other Name

Napoleon's next, and greatest, love would come from the Caribbean island of Martinique. Napoleon never went there, but this woman's father, Joseph Gaspard Tascher de la Pagerie, owned a sugar plantation, complete with slaves, on the island. The family had significant wealth and power, and the children led a very comfortable life in an idyllic location.

Marie Josèphe Rose Tascher de la Pagerie was born on June 23, 1763. If you noticed that there is no "Josephine" in her name, you may wonder how that name came about. Her friends and family had always called her Rose, but Napoleon, never content to just go with the flow, called her Josephine (from Josèphe), and that is how she will be forever known.

Growing up and getting wise

Josephine was given an education in a local convent. As was the custom, her family arranged a marriage for her. It was a promising union, as her husband, 19-year-old Alexander de Beauharnais, was a well-educated and quite wealthy viscount. Well-connected at court, he was also considered one of the best dancers in Paris. Alexander seems to have been a little disappointed in his Rose, but she was elated with the match. The two were married in Paris on December 13, 1779. She was 16.

Josephine's future foretold?

Many stories surround the romance of Napoleon and Josephine. Some of them may be true; others are more questionable. This one may very well have happened.

Throughout history, many people have believed in the power of prophesy, of one's future being foretold by fortunetellers. In 1777, when she was 14, Josephine and some friends went to the local fortuneteller to see what lay in store for them. What she was supposedly told may make believers of us all!

Josephine was told that she would have two marriages, the first unhappy and the second to a man who would claim great glory and make Josephine "greater than a queen." But, the fortuneteller went on to say, she would die unhappy, regretting the loss of her easy life on Martinique.

Various historians have questioned if this story is fact or fable, but Josephine mentioned it before she was ever empress, and I'd bet money that it happened.

They had two children, Eugène in 1781 and Hortense in 1783, but the marriage was less than happy. Josephine was a bit plump and was not the elegant lady preferred by high society, while Alexander was every bit the dashing dancer that had so attracted Josephine. Soon, his eyes began to wander, and in 1783 he deserted his wife and returned to Martinique, where he was less than faithful. He was hoping to become involved in the American War of Independence, and he took his mistress along with him to the United States. Over the years, he would father several illegitimate children.

Josephine soon understood the situation. Now, it wasn't all that unusual for a nobleman to have a mistress, but Josephine was not amused; she applied for and received a legal separation, complete with a nice income. She spent some time in a convent, which is not as severe as it may sound. The convent was home to many ladies of the highest social class, and Josephine learned a great deal from them. Later, she stayed with relatives at the chateau of Fontainebleau. She became active on the social scene, which is to say that she had a long string of affairs, some with rather important men.

In 1788, Josephine returned to Martinique, where she spent two years. Among other things, she witnessed a relatively minor slave uprising: All was not well in what she remembered as her idyllic homeland. She returned to Paris, where she had something of a reconciliation with Alexander, though the two never really reunited. Her social life continued, as did her habit of spending far beyond her means. As a result, she was always in financial difficulty.

Josephine's home on Martinique today

Josephine's family lived in a rather nice home on Martinique. Unfortunately, the home was destroyed by a hurricane in 1766. All that is left is the relatively small building that used to be the kitchen, as well as the foundations of the main building. You can also see some of the family's sugar factory down the road; the factory and the kitchen are set in a beautiful park.

The kitchen from the original homestead has been made into a museum, which is full of artifacts from Josephine and her family. The first exhibits remind you that the family's wealth was built on the backs of its slaves. You can then see the bed in which the young Josephine slept, numerous other items of hers, and some of her letters from Napoleon. There is a nice gift shop in what used to be part of the sugar mill.

Nearby, you can visit the church where Josephine was baptized, the church of the Trois-ilets, which also contains the tomb of her mother.

The Savane Square in the center of the nearby town of Fort-de-France has a large statue of Josephine. She is holding a plaque that shows the coronation of she and Napoleon as empress and emperor. A quick inspection of the statue reveals that it is missing its head! Most of the island's inhabitants are black descendents of slaves, some of whom were owned by Josephine's parents. It seems that they have taken out their unhappiness with their familial history on the statue.

Facing the guillotine

Alexander had become a true supporter of the Revolution and had risen to be the president of the National Assembly (see Chapter 3). Later, he was given some important assignments, including command of the Army of the Rhine. But in 1794, to be a nobleman was to be in trouble. As I explain in Chapter 4, the Terror was well underway, and the guillotine was busy separating heads from shoulders.

In March 1794, Alexander was arrested and thrown into prison. To her credit, Josephine did all she could to secure his release. Warned that she was also in danger, she continued her efforts and was put into jail in April. In those days, jail was essentially a way station on a trip to the guillotine. The husband and wife were reunited in prison, though we don't know if they actually reconciled. (Some people believe that while in prison Josephine had an affair with General Louis Lazare Hoche, and it is entirely possible that she did.)

Alexander was executed on July 23, 1794. Josephine had every reason to believe that she would meet the same fate, and sooner rather than later. Her luck turned good, though, because in July, Maximilien Robespierre and his supporters were arrested and executed (see Chapter 4). The Terror was over. Josephine was released on August 6, 1794, after almost four months in prison.

Starting over

Reunited with her children, Josephine set to starting her life over. To do so, she turned to her many friends. One of them was Thérèse Tallien, who had been her friend during Josephine's years of separation from her husband. Another was Paul Barras. One of the best ways to describe Barras would be "survivor," as he had managed to ride out the storm of the Revolution, the Terror, and the fall of Robespierre to emerge as one of the most powerful men in France.

Without question, Josephine's friendship with Barras was the best thing she had going for her. Of course, it seems likely that she was far more than his friend; most historians believe that she was his mistress. The two of them were in a position to help each other out in their various business dealings as well. Josephine had had some really good connections, and some of them were even still alive!

Josephine had beauty and charm, and she knew how to survive — in style. But as all who knew her would eventually discover, one thing that she was really good at was spending money, whether or not she had it to spend.

Meeting and Marrying

There are varying accounts of how Napoleon and Josephine met. Napoleon was a national hero with an up-and-coming career, so he was in great demand for parties all over Paris. He knew Paul Barras and other social luminaries, and it is quite likely that he met Josephine in 1795 at one of the many social functions he attended. Napoleon himself said as much.

I would be remiss, however, if I didn't tell you the more popular, if less likely, story. Better yet, I'll let Josephine's daughter, Hortense, tell you the story as she did in her memoirs, *Memoirs of Queen Hortense (2v),* published in 1927 (Cosmopolita Book Corporation):

> *Following the riots on the 13th Vendémiaire a law was passed forbidding any private citizen to have weapons in his house. My brother, unable to bear the thought of surrendering the sword that had belonged to his father, hurried off to see General Bonaparte, who at that time was in command of the troops stationed in Paris. He told the General he would kill himself rather than give up the sword. The General, touched by his emotion, granted his request and at the same time asked the name of his mother, saying he would be glad to meet a woman who could inspire her son with such ideals.*

As the legend continues, Josephine decided to visit Napoleon to thank him for his kindness toward her son. Napoleon, who was busy with his maps (as usual), saw Josephine and fell head over heels in love with her.

This story is unlikely, but the fact remains that Napoleon was interested in taking a wife and soon decided that Josephine was the woman for him. Now, I must note that Josephine was not completely honest with him. She allowed him to think that she was a bit younger than she was, and of more substantial means. On the plus side, she was a woman of some significant experience, particularly sexual experience. Napoleon, who had very little experience along that line, was probably quite impressed with her charms.

Falling in love

Napoleon fell madly in love with Josephine. His passion is reflected in the many love letters that have survived. One classic example, written in Paris in December 1795, appears to follow an amusing evening, perhaps their first sexual encounter, and can be found in a 1931 edition of their letters:

> *I awake full of you. Your image and last evening's intoxication have left my senses no repose whatever.*

Sweet and incomparable Josephine, what a strange effect do you produce upon my heart! Are you vexed? Do I see you sad? Are you troubled? . . . My soul is crushed with grief, and there is no repose for your lover; but is there any the more when, abandoning myself to the profound emotion which masters me, I draw from your lips, from your heart, a flame which consumes me? Ah! It was last night I really understood that your portrait was not you!

You are leaving at noon; I shall see you in three hours. Meanwhile, mio dolce amor, a thousand kisses; but do not give me any, for they burn my blood.

Napoleon was deeply in love, but Josephine wasn't so sure. She had a pretty good deal going — she was involved in a number of business and other affairs and was maintaining a, ahem, close relationship with Paul Barras. Barras, on the other hand, may well have been anxious to move his rather expensive plaything on to someone else. Indeed, it seems that he arranged for Napoleon to be appointed commander of the French army in Italy in exchange for Napoleon's marrying Josephine.

It's a bit hard to understand why Josephine was interested in Napoleon at all. Sure, he was a young hero, but he was also penniless and fairly lacking in social graces. Josephine, on the other hand, had pretty much made it by the time she met him. She had climbed to the very top of the social ladder and was involved in all sorts of interesting things.

And then there was the little matter of Napoleon's family. Josephine was 32 years old, 6 years older than Napoleon. She was previously married, had two half-grown children, and had little in the way of money, plus her connections were dubious in their nature. Napoleon's siblings and mother were convinced that he could do far better and that Josephine would be a disaster for him. They did everything they could to discourage the marriage. Had Napoleon's mother, Leticia, been on hand in Paris, she likely would have exerted her influence, and the marriage would not have taken place.

Questioning her future

Josephine was also not convinced that marrying this young general was the best decision she could make. Marrying a general may sound like a good deal to you and me, but generals have a tendency to be sent to far-away places where they can end up being killed. In addition, generals were still very political, and if they fell out of favor they could find themselves at the very least out of a job. Napoleon had already discovered how easy it was to suddenly be on half pay (see Chapter 4). Josephine, who was involved in military supply dealings, was well aware of the downside to military careers.

Josephine's friends counseled against the marriage. Of greater importance was the opposition of her daughter, Hortense. But Josephine may well have figured that any daughter would fear losing her mother to a man who would not be her real father. As it happened, Napoleon was an excellent stepfather to both of Josephine's children.

And then there was the little matter of General Hoche, whom Josephine had met, so to speak, while in prison (see the earlier section "Facing the guillotine"). Not only was Josephine not in love with Napoleon; she had hoped that General Hoche would leave his wife and marry her. (She finally realized that he would never do so, which may be why she eventually agreed to marry Napoleon.)

It seems that Napoleon was not the greatest lover in the world, either. Though Josephine was adept in such matters and taught Napoleon a great deal, his approach was similar to his military strategy: He offered little in the way of preliminaries, preferring a quick attack with the fastest possible victory.

Not in love and faced with the opposition of friends and his family, Josephine stalled when Napoleon asked her to marry him. His passion worried her, as she was unable to match it. Besides, any fire can cool quickly, so Josephine made Napoleon wait through the winter of 1795–1796. Finally, faced with her increasing age, diminishing prospects, and Napoleon's persistence, Josephine relented and agreed to marry him.

Marrying their future

Napoleon and Josephine agreed to a civil ceremony at 8:00 p.m. on March 9, 1796. Josephine was there early, wearing Napoleon's famous gift to her, an enameled medallion engraved "To Destiny." (They could not have possibly imagined how significant those words would be.) Barras, serving as a witness, was on time, as were other members of the wedding party. Only one person was missing: the groom!

Anyone can be a little late, even to his own wedding, but as the minutes dragged on into first one hour and then two, emotions must have been on edge. The official who was to marry them left, and an underling was on hand for the ceremony, even if the groom was not. You can only imagine what thoughts were going through the various minds there assembled.

If any of them had known Napoleon well, none of this would have been all that big a surprise. As general in chief of the Army of France in Italy, Napoleon had been planning a campaign and had become so engrossed in his maps that he had completely lost track of time. Clearly, his priorities were not those expected of a typical groom. Then again, Napoleon was not a typical groom.

Nothing about the wedding was normal. Josephine lied about her age on the marriage certificate, claiming to be 4 years younger, and Napoleon added 18 months to his age. The end result was that they appeared to be roughly the same age.

If the wedding was unusual, the wedding night was downright bizarre. Okay, lots of folks are really tired on their wedding night, and it may not really be the best possible time for an evening of wild sexual abandon. Still, Napoleon's passion and Josephine's inclinations would suggest that some kind of activity was likely. But upon coming to bed, Napoleon discovered that he was expected to share his wedding bed with another male!

That would be Fortuné, Josephine's little pug dog. Now, Napoleon wasn't a big fan of dogs (or cats, for that matter). Even if you're an animal lover (as I am), you can forgive him for being upset on this occasion. Josephine, who may have still been a bit upset from the long delay in the wedding ceremony, informed Napoleon that the dog was used to sleeping in her bed and that there was no reason for that to change. An unamused Napoleon nevertheless attempted to claim his husbandly rights (or perform his husbandly duties, take your pick), but the miserable dog, evidently unhappy with the competition, bit him in the shin. (Were it me, that dog would have quickly gone to doggy heaven — or, more likely, hell — but Napoleon, perhaps feeling guilty, let it pass.)

Josephine's children had been apprehensive about their mother's marriage to this young general. True, Napoleon had treated her son with kindness in the matter of his father's sword (if that story is really true), but like any children, they worried about how their stepfather would relate to them.

The day after the wedding, the newlyweds went to visit her children. Napoleon was at his most charming and generous. He arranged to send his own younger brother Jérôme to go to school with Eugène, visited their school, and generally did whatever he could to make them feel comfortable with him. By the end of the visit, Josephine's children knew that they had a new father they could trust — and love.

Napoleon and Josephine were married. One of the greatest love stories in history had begun. But it didn't start out very promising. Within a couple days, Napoleon was off to Italy and glory, while Josephine was to stay home where she would . . . well, more on that subject in Chapter 6.

Part II
Building an Empire

The 5th Wave   By Rich Tennant

Napoleon in Italy

Il Menu

"The troops are in place, we have the area surrounded, but the maitre'd says we still need a reservation before he can seat us all at the same table."

In this part . . .

Napoleon regularly appears in books and documentaries on "conquerors" or "empire builders," and there is no question that he deserves to be considered one of the greatest military leaders ever. He didn't start out at the top; he had to work his way up by leading armies in Italy and Egypt. But when his opportunity to seize power came, well, *carpe diem,* he seized the day — and the government. He went on to defeat enemies all across Europe and for a time controlled one of history's greatest empires. Want to find out how he did all that in just a few short years? Read on!

Chapter 6

Improvising an Army in Italy

● ●

In This Chapter

▶ Preparing to battle Austria

▶ Taking legendary measures

▶ Gaining victories in Italy

▶ Becoming a hero (again)

● ●

*T*he French Revolution hit Europe like a thunderbolt. Its fundamental idea —
that the people could change their government, overthrow and even exe-
cute their king, and establish a new political and social order — was horrify-
ing to the rulers of the rest of Europe. Worse yet (in the eyes of those rulers,
anyway), leaders of Revolutionary France seemed to feel that their Revolution
should be exported, that all of Europe should join in their new Enlightenment.

Naturally, the leaders of other European nations were not going to take this
situation sitting down, on their thrones or elsewhere. They quickly began to
take steps to protect their own interests. Not content to simply contain the
Revolution in France, they were determined to force France to restore the
Bourbon monarchy to the throne. Exiled French royalists began to conspire
for the monarchy's return and to lobby the other nations of Europe to help in
their endeavor. Unfortunately for France, some nations agreed to help.

Many of the royalist exiles had fled to England, and England seemed most
interested in supporting their cause. The British government provided much
of the money and helped organize various coalitions against Revolutionary
France. There was some irony in this situation, as France and England were
probably the two most progressive nations in Europe and should have been
natural allies.

When other European nations aligned themselves against Revolutionary
France, Napoleon went into action. In this chapter, I show you how Napoleon
inspired and led his men to an amazing string of victories in what was his
first full military campaign. You'll see how his legend was already beginning
to develop, as well as how he had to deal with troubles on the domestic front.

Assessing the Austrian Threat

No nation saw itself as having more to lose by the gains of Revolutionary France than the ancient empire of Austria. Austria was governed by Emperor Francis II of Germany, which was to say the old Holy Roman Empire. (He later changed his title to Emperor Francis I of Austria when, in 1806, Napoleon eliminated the Holy Roman Empire.) Francis was an unimaginative man steeped in tradition and determined to maintain what he considered the "natural order" even if doing so meant war. Francis and his government were exactly the kind of government that the French Revolution meant to topple, and he knew it.

Austria had other reasons to distrust and even hate the Revolutionary government. One of the daughters of the Austrian monarchy, Marie Antoinette, had married King Louis XVI of France and had been executed by the guillotine. As a result, the grudge between the two nations was at least somewhat personal, as well as ideological.

To say that there was no love lost between the two nations would be an understatement. And a quick look at a map (see Appendix B) will show that the place where the two nations could most likely clash would be northern Italy.

Fulfilling a Geographical Destiny

Some people say that geography is destiny. Geography was certainly an important factor in what would become known as Napoleon's first Italian campaign.

The Italy of the late 18th century was not the Italy we know today. Well, okay, the people spoke Italian and probably had great food and wine, and Rome had the Coliseum, but Italy wasn't a unified country the way it is today. Instead, the "boot" of Europe (called that because of geography, not because of Italy's well-deserved reputation for excellence in fine fashion, including leather footwear!) was divided into a number of separate and independent kingdoms:

- In the south was the Kingdom of the Two Sicilies.

- The Papal States, controlled by the Pope in Rome, took up much of central Italy.

- In the north were a number of smaller kingdoms, including the Venetian Republic, the Duchy of Parma, the Republic of Genoa, and the Kingdom of Sardinia.

The Kingdom of Sardinia included a critical area known as the Piedmont in northwestern Italy. Ruled by King Victor Amadeus III, Sardinia had taken the side of the royalists and the Austrians, a decision that would prove its undoing.

The Piedmont lies just east of France and includes some critical coastal areas. Austria hoped to use its alliance with Sardinia to put pressure on France through the Piedmont and along the coast. France was not about to just let this happen, and in 1793 it sent an army into northern Italy to put an end to this nonsense. The French thought they would drive the Austrians out of the area and defeat the Piedmontese, assuring their coastal security in the bargain. Then they could negotiate a treaty that would assure France of peace in that area.

Unfortunately, by 1796, the French army had accomplished very little. Its leadership had been less than aggressive, and the campaign had become bogged down. Indeed, disaster was looming. The army was in difficult shape and needed new leadership. And new leadership was exactly what it would get.

Getting Napoleon on Board

Back in France, Napoleon had become a national hero by saving the French government from a royalist effort to overthrow it and reinstall a monarchy (see Chapter 4). Indeed, everything seemed to be going Napoleon's way, as he had also met Josephine and fallen in love (see Chapter 5). Their marriage plans had political implications, as Josephine had been the mistress of one of the most powerful men in France — Paul Barras — who was grateful to Napoleon for taking her off his hands.

Barras had been instrumental in giving Napoleon the chance to save the government, and he would make one more effort on Napoleon's behalf. Partly as a reward for saving the government, partly in thanks for taking Josephine (at least that's what many people suspected), and partly because Napoleon was seen as a potentially great general, Barras appointed Napoleon Commander-in-Chief of the Army of France in Italy (as it was officially known).

Napoleon was given his command on March 2, 1796. One week later, he married Josephine, and two days later he left to take his command. He was clearly a man in a hurry! (See Figure 6-1 to get an idea how he looked at the time.) His first stop was Nice, where he met with his staff for the first time. Josephine remained in Paris, a decision that seemed logical but which Napoleon would have reason to regret.

Figure 6-1:
This pen and ink on vellum drawing was made in 1796 and shows a very different image of Napoleon, but one that was likely fairly accurate.

NAPOLEONE BONAPARTE

Building a Winning Army

Napoleon was confident and ambitious. He was determined to act fast and defeat the enemy before it knew what was happening. He envisioned something of a lightening war (much like Julius Caesar fought against the Helvetii in Gaul some 1,800 years before).

Napoleon may have been anxious to get going, but he first needed to form his staff. Many historians believe that the staff Napoleon put together for this campaign was one of the finest ever assembled, and it certainly gave quite a few officers their start with Napoleon, which for many would translate into long careers in his service.

Assembling a leadership team

Perhaps the most critical support position for any commander is his chief of staff. This person is responsible for interpreting and disseminating the commander's orders to the rest of the generals in the field. If your commander has poor handwriting and often writes confusing orders, your job as chief of staff is all the more difficult. Napoleon fit both categories but was smart enough to select Louis Alexandre Berthier as his chief of staff. Berthier was a master at his job and would stay with Napoleon until defeat in 1814 drove Napoleon from his throne (see Chapter 14). (Berthier's absence in the Waterloo campaign due to his mysterious death likely was a major factor in Napoleon's defeat at Waterloo, which I discuss in Chapter 15.)

If Berthier was the most solid member of Napoleon's staff, his *aide-de-camp,* Colonel Joachim Murat, was surely the most flamboyant, known for his flashy uniforms and dashing nature. Murat was the young captain who had secured the artillery that Napoleon used for his famous "whiff of grapeshot" that saved the French government the year before (see Chapter 4), and he had attached his star to this bright young general, even suggesting his own appointment as *aide-de-camp.* (Murat would eventually marry Napoleon's sister Caroline and become a Marshal of the Empire and King of Naples. Perhaps the greatest cavalry commander of his day, his absence at Waterloo, too, would prove disastrous, but his treachery would be equally so — see Chapter 25.)

Napoleon had with him in Italy other officers who would stay with him throughout his career, usually for the better, sometimes for the worse. These included Andoche Junot, Auguste Marmont, and Napoleon's brother Louis.

Hats off: Winning over the skeptics

When this team arrived in Nice, they met with two senior generals, André Masséna and Charles Augereau. Both would become important in Napoleon's future campaigns, and some historians believe that Masséna, who would become a Marshal of the Empire, was Napoleon's best overall marshal. But for now, these gentlemen, especially Masséna, were not very happy about the situation.

Masséna (and some of the other generals and officers) had two problems with Napoleon:

- ✔ First, they considered his appointment to be a political one, and as career officers, they had seen what kind of leadership they often got from political generals.

- ✔ Second, Napoleon was young and quite inexperienced to boot. Why would he possibly be given command of such an important army? Well, they knew why: as a reward for wooing Josephine, which was outrageous as far as they were concerned.

Masséna (see Figure 6-2) was a proven leader and a senior general. He wanted and felt he should have been given command of the army.

Figure 6-2:
André Masséna was one of Napoleon's greatest commanders. This is a very rare porcelain statue from 1850.

There is a story that Masséna and the senior staff were going to put Napoleon in his proper place by declining to remove their hats when he came into the command tent. This act would have been a great insult that even the young and, they suspected, naive Napoleon could hardly have missed. The story goes that when Napoleon entered the tent, they immediately understood that they had underestimated this young general, who had a commanding personality that *they* couldn't miss. Off came the hats!

Hats or no hats, there is little doubt that Napoleon's staff, like all who met him, were taken with his personality. People who met him would later write of how impressive Napoleon was in person. It was said that when he entered a crowded ballroom, all eyes would become quickly fixed on him.

Lacking hats (and supplies and motivation)

His leadership team assembled and on board, Napoleon turned his attention to his soldiers. He cannot have liked what he saw. First, the position of the army was about as bad as it could get; it was huddled along a crest of the Maritime Alps. Now, this is beautiful country if you're a tourist, but it's not much good for providing food or anything else that an army may need to survive. Moreover, the army's links to home were problematic. The British fleet controlled the coastline, and it was often difficult to get supplies or communications from France. The army was more or less sandwiched between the enemy in front and the enemy in the rear. It was also out of about everything, including uniforms, many of which had simply worn out.

Napoleon's army is often described as ragtag and demoralized, and that is a pretty good description. There were about 41,000 soldiers in the Army of France in Italy, and they faced a Piedmontese/Austrian force of around 47,000 well-equipped soldiers, as well as the British fleet at their rear. Their situation was precarious all the way around, so it is little wonder that they had not been anxious to start an offensive. Worse yet, mutiny and insubordination were in the air, and royalist sentiments could be heard. Napoleon would soon change their attitude!

Inspiring the troops

Napoleon could be inspirational with words, both in writing and in speaking. He knew he had to inspire his troops in Italy. He is reported to have given a speech to his soldiers along the following lines. Now, I don't care how loud his voice was, only a few could possibly have heard it. And there is some reason to doubt that this particular speech was ever actually given. But by all accounts, he probably said this kind of thing to quite a few soldiers and officers, and this speech is quoted in countless sources. (This version came from Albert Sidney Britt's *The Wars of Napoleon* [Avery Publishing Group]). Whatever he said, it worked, as morale soon improved.

> *Soldiers: you are hungry and naked. The government owes you much but can give you nothing. Your patience and courage, displayed among these rocks, are admirable, but that brings you no glory. I will lead you into the most fertile plains on earth. Rich provinces, wealthy cities, all will be at your disposal. There you will find honor, glory and riches!*

Perhaps it was speeches like this that caused image makers to really take notice. Figure 6-3 is an excellent example of the kind of thing that was beginning to appear in Paris and elsewhere.

Leading the Campaign

Great speeches are nice, but talk is cheap! The best way to inspire his troops was to lead them to those rich provinces, and Napoleon resolved to do just that. His job was to gain control of the Piedmont, but it would soon become clear that he had a much wider agenda.

Figure 6-3:
This very rare gold and tortoise shell snuffbox from about 1796 shows Napoleon as a young general. The image is painted in gold underneath the glass.

Winning at Montenotte

As he would do so often throughout his career, Napoleon would defeat a larger force by dividing it and then defeating each isolated part in turn. He managed to come between the Austrian forces of General Johann Peter Beaulieu and General Mercy d'Argenteau, which were near the town of Montenotte. An early morning fog helped conceal Napoleon's movements.

On the morning of April 12, 1796, Napoleon attacked a little over 6,000 Austrians with 9,000 French at Montenotte. The result was a route, with Masséna wiping out Argenteau's right flank while Napoleon's main body decimated its center. By the end of the day, the Austrians had sustained some 2,500 casualties. It was Napoleon's first victory as a commanding general against an army.

The Battle of Montenotte was important militarily but perhaps even more important from the standpoint of the morale of the French troops. No longer could they see themselves as losers, and no longer could they question Napoleon's ability as a leader. Napoleon was on a roll, and he wasn't about to stop anytime soon!

Avoiding disaster at Dego

Napoleon left Masséna to hold off General Beaulieu's army by taking a position at the village of Dego, while Napoleon went after the Piedmontese. At first, Masséna did quite well. After discovering that the town was controlled by as many as 5,000 enemy soldiers, he attacked on April 14 and gained a great victory, including the capture or killing of around 4,000 soldiers! Unfortunately, the next day, while Masséna's soldiers were foraging in the area, another Austrian force unexpectedly attacked, and the French faced almost certain defeat. Fortunately, Napoleon had gotten word of the situation and returned in time to chase away the Austrians and restore order.

Dego was important because it taught Napoleon the importance of being in constant contact with all parts of an operation. It was a lesson that would serve him well, and when he forgot it, bad things would happen.

After Dego, Napoleon won a series of battles against the Piedmontese. While Masséna was dealing with things in Dego on the 14th, General Augereau was defeating a detachment of the enemy near the village of Millesimo. A couple days later, Napoleon had Augereau and General Jean-Mathieu Sérurier attack a major Piedmontese/Austrian force at Ceva, which they successfully drove back toward the town of Mondovi.

Claiming victory in the Piedmont

Once again, Napoleon had Masséna hold off the main Austrian force while proceeding to do what he was under orders to do, namely defeat the Piedmontese and remove that area as a threat to France. Napoleon took his main force of 25,000 troops and attacked the last remaining major Piedmontese force of 13,000 soldiers led by General Michel Colli at Mondovi. There, on April 21, 1796, Napoleon won a major victory, which turned into a route. The Piedmontese were soundly defeated at the Battle of Mondovi.

Napoleon was prepared to march on the major city of Turin, determined to administer a final, crushing blow to the Piedmontese army. This proved unnecessary, however, as within a few days King Amadeus of Sardinia sued for peace. On April 28, the two sides signed the Armistice of Cherasco, which effectively ceded control of the Piedmont to France and took the Piedmontese army out of the conflict. Napoleon promptly sent the treaty to Paris for the approval of the Directory (the governing body in France), which was quickly and gratefully given.

The "fertile plains" promised by Napoleon were now in the hands of his army. Napoleon's first engagement of the campaign had been on April 12, 1796, and by the end of the month he had successfully routed the army of the Piedmont and gained control of its important territory. How's *that* for inspiring the troops?!

Napoleon won because he was willing to be aggressive and flexible in his movements. He moved his forces quickly and was excellent at responding to changing situations. He attacked the center and then moved decisively on the now-separate wings of his enemy. The Austrian and Piedmont armies, on the other hand, were very rigid in their formations and slow in their movements. It really was no contest. Napoleon was using a modern army to defeat an enemy that was using yesterday's tactics.

That said, victory was not certain until the very end. Throughout much of the campaign, Napoleon's army had still been undernourished and very short on provisions, including weapons. Only after the Battle of Mondovi did they obtain enough weapons to be a truly effective fighting force. That battle really turned the tide for Napoleon's army; before it, he was not certain he could maintain his troops in good fighting order.

Napoleon had been hampered by a lack of funds from Paris. The French government had promised adequate money on which to run the campaign, but it was quite clear that it would prefer that wealth travel from Italy to Paris, not the other way around.

Being gracious in victory

Napoleon's terms with the Piedmontese were fair, and looting was kept to a minimum. This was no small order, as Napoleon's soldiers were determined to take their fill of whatever the local countryside had to offer, including bedding the women, drinking the wine, and eating the food. Napoleon was strict in his admonitions against such behavior and administered severe punishments.

The Directory in Paris would actually have preferred harsher terms with the Piedmontese and wanted more loot. But in the end, the Directory could hardly argue with success, and it left Napoleon alone. (To be clear, Napoleon was sending a pretty fair amount of loot back to Paris. To the victor belongs the spoils.)

Napoleon tried, with some success and justification, to portray his campaign as a war of liberation designed to give the northern Italians freedom from domination by Austria. In the end, this was probably a pretty fair assessment of what he did, and today the people of Italy see Napoleon as one of the founders of Italian unification. (See the sidebar "Napoleon and Italian unity.")

LEGEND

Napoleon and Italian unity

As I discuss in Chapter 22, some nations of Europe have mixed emotions about Napoleon. Not so Italy. Napoleon's Italian campaigns drove out the Austrians and began the process of creating unity out of a collection of small, weak kingdoms. Napoleon's role in this unification is celebrated in the Museo de la Risorgimento in Milan. *Risorgimento* literally means "resurgence"; in this case, it really means the drive for unity. Thanks in part to Napoleon, Italy underwent a resurgence that brought to mind her unified days as the center of the Roman Empire.

The museum has a wonderful collection of artifacts from Napoleon's two Italian campaigns, as well as from his coronation as King of Italy after he was made Emperor of the French in 1804. It contains the first flag of the Cisalpine Republic (which I discuss later in this chapter) and the crown and robe used in his coronation.

Other artifacts include French Eagles (gold decorations used at the top of flagpoles that represented the French Empire), items used by Napoleon in exile, and an 1802 flag that lists Napoleon as President of Italy. Add to that a magnificent collection of miniatures, snuff boxes, engravings, and documents, and you have another excellent excuse to lobby for that Italian vacation you've always wanted!

Dealing with the Austrians

With the Piedmont firmly in control, Napoleon turned his attention to the Austrian troops commanded by General Beaulieu. Napoleon moved quickly to try to catch Beaulieu in northern Italy; he crossed the Po River in only two days, thanks in part to decisive action by yet another general who would make his name under Napoleon, Jean Lannes. Lannes managed to cross the river and establish a safe bridgehead on the other side. Napoleon then had a boat bridge built, and his army crossed far faster than anyone, especially the Austrians, could have imagined. By doing this, Napoleon outflanked Beaulieu and the Austrian army, who soon discovered that they were in serious trouble.

Beaulieu had some indecisive actions with the French and then withdrew to the western side of the Adda River. He moved to the small village of Lodi, where he left a rear guard of 10,000 men to hold the bridge while he took his main force to safety. Beaulieu had virtually surrendered Milan and all of Lombardy to the French. But to consolidate his gains, Napoleon would have to cross the Adda River at Lodi and deal with the remaining Austrians.

Creating a legend at Lodi

Napoleon's advance guard quickly pushed the Austrians across the bridge, which was about 200 yards long and 12 feet wide. No one could have known it just yet, but these soldiers were about to participate in one of the most important actions of Napoleon's career, an action that would establish his reputation, create his legend, and set the stage for his future.

Napoleon understood that the bridge at Lodi had to be protected at all costs. He quickly climbed into a church steeple and directed the placement of his artillery. (I have climbed into that very steeple, though more recent construction around it has hampered considerably the view that it offered Napoleon.) Napoleon then personally sighted the guns, earning one of his nicknames, "the little corporal," as it was normally a corporal's job to sight the guns. His artillery training was showing itself.

Like it or not, Napoleon had little choice but to send his troops across the bridge against what would be withering fire from the Austrians on the other side. He gave his troops yet another inspirational speech. You can still see the narrow, winding streets where his soldiers gathered. (In Chapter 24, I discuss what you find in Lodi today.)

Napoleon understood that success would depend on a flanking action that could silence the Austrian artillery. He sent his cavalry up the Adda River where it was to find a good place to cross and then come sweeping down on the unsuspecting Austrians. Then, led by Masséna, Berthier, and Lannes, the French infantry stormed the bridge. The going was tough (no surprise!), and the advance was slow. As expected, the fire was murderous, and the attack began to falter.

Then, just in time, as if on cue, the cavalry came swooping down on the Austrian positions. The fighting was fierce for a while longer, but soon the Austrian guns were silent, and the French poured across the bridge. After losing 2,000 men to death or capture, the Austrians beat a hasty retreat to rejoin their main force. For all the fighting, Napoleon lost only around 200 men and gained 16 Austrian guns.

Napoleon had been an absolute whirlwind of action, seemingly everywhere at once. He had inspired his officers and his men to undertake what some considered an action whose danger outweighed its benefits. He showed his men that he could be a good general not only from a tactical standpoint but also from the emotional standpoint.

Gaining self-confidence and acclaim

The action at the bridge of Lodi has taken its place as one of the most important actions that contributed to the legend of Napoleon. It was also one of the first actions that convinced Napoleon that he was something special — that he may really accomplish something important in life. Lodi taught Napoleon that he was a good, perhaps a great, leader. While in exile on St. Helena (see

Chapter 16), Napoleon wrote that it was only at Lodi he came to see himself as a "superior man," capable of accomplishing things about which he had previously only dreamed.

A few days after Lodi, Napoleon marched triumphantly into Milan. There, he was received as a conquering hero, a liberator. He lived in the local palace where he received tribute from the city fathers. The city coffers allowed him to pay his troops better than he had ever been able to before, a fact that certainly improved *their* morale. Napoleon was treated as royalty, and his generals received similar accolades. Streets were renamed in his honor. The citizens were no doubt impressed by the fact that this French general could speak to them in *Italian.* Many of his officers received the, uh, attentions of the local ladies, but Napoleon eschewed that, preferring to wait for Josephine's arrival.

Napoleon did enjoy the company of Milan's elite, including scholars, writers, artists, and, of course, political leaders from all over the region known as Lombardy. The Austrians had controlled this area for the better part of 100 years, and the Italians really did see Napoleon as their liberator. Napoleon had no problem at all with that image, which continues to this day (see the sidebar "Napoleon and Italian unity.")

In the time-honored tradition of conquering armies, the French began to collect tribute — read *loot* — to send home to Paris. Napoleon had always enjoyed the company of scholars and was delighted when the great mathematician and scholar Gaspard Monge came to Milan, joined by the distinguished chemist Claude-Louis Berthollet. The three of them spent many hours together in intellectual discussions, but they were also there to help select items of great interest to send to France.

Precious works of art, ancient documents, and other historical and scientific artifacts went streaming to Paris, where many of them would ultimately end up in the Louvre, one of the world's great museums. Other items helped enrich various politicians, as well as the commanding general. Napoleon would never again be poor.

Napoleon was truly at the top of his game. But two things were about to happen that would create professional and personal turmoil.

Dividing a command

Napoleon had not been the only general fighting the Austrians. Further to the north, the French Army of the Rhine had been fighting the Austrians across the Rhine River. The army had been successful, and the Directory wanted to put the squeeze on the Austrians in that area. The Directory sent Napoleon notice that his command would be divided. General François Kellerman would take half the army and fight the Austrians in the northern campaign, while Napoleon would take command of half the army and campaign against the Papal States and perhaps Naples.

Kellerman was Napoleon's senior and had been a hero at the Battle of Valmy, which had been the first victory over the Austrians by the army of Revolutionary France, back in 1792. Napoleon could well imagine that a hero like that fighting the Austrians would soon overshadow a young general leading a small army against the Pope. He was not happy, and no one could blame him.

In typical Napoleonic fashion, he immediately took steps to prevent the division from happening. He wrote to the Directory, complaining that the division would make no sense. If it wished, Napoleon wrote, the Directory should give Kellerman overall command but not divide the army. Famously, Napoleon went on to say that "one bad general is better than two good ones."

Underlying Napoleon's comments was an implied threat to resign his command. This action would have been devastating. After all, Napoleon had given the Directory great military success, as well as fabulous riches; it could hardly afford to let him go. The Directory eventually gave up on the idea of a divided command.

Consolidating a victory

Napoleon then moved against what remained of General Beaulieu's army. He chased the Austrians out of northern Italy, but they managed to maintain a presence in the fortress of Mantua. Napoleon immediately ordered a siege, which began in June. If he could drive the Austrians out of this last stronghold, he could, if necessary, continue moving north, even to the gates of Vienna, to force them to make peace.

The forces inside the fortress were greatly outnumbered, and disease was a major problem. Austria sent two forces to try to lift the siege, but they would not arrive for some time. There was time for Napoleon to do other things.

The Directory had another assignment for Napoleon. He was told to swoop down into the Papal States and Tuscany, which had been supportive of the Austrians. He promptly did so (leaving behind a force of 9,000 soldiers to keep up the siege), liberating cities such as Bologna and Florence from papal control. This was a popular move with the people, and Napoleon again was seen as a liberator. Within six weeks, he was back in Milan, arriving there on July 13, 1796.

Not long afterward, Napoleon faced the Austrian forces led by General Dagobert Würmser, whose goal was to relieve the siege of Mantua and then to drive Napoleon out of Italy. Under unexpected attack, Napoleon called off the siege of Mantua, and Würmser was able to send in reinforcements to that strategic stronghold. But on August 5, 1796, Napoleon defeated the Austrians at the Battle of Castiglione. The victory wasn't overwhelming, but it sent the Austrians packing, at least for the moment. Napoleon returned to Milan, where his personal life had taken a rather abrupt change.

Longing for Josephine

Throughout the Italian campaign, Napoleon kept up his torrid advances to Josephine (see Chapter 5). He wrote her on a daily basis, and his letters were hot, to say the least. He spoke of his passion, of his yearning for her company. This should not surprise anyone; after all, he was a newlywed husband, whose passion for his bride could hardly have had time to cool. He wrote phrases like, "I have not passed a day without loving you; I have not passed a night without clasping you in my arms; I have not taken a cup of tea without cursing that glory and that ambition which keep me separated from the soul of my life." You get the picture.

So did Josephine, and she was not all that amused by it. She had never been all that passionate toward Napoleon and was embarrassed by his expressions of love, both before and after they were married. Her letters to him were rather chilly, even formal. For example, she used the formal French word for you, *vous,* rather than the familiar (and far more appropriate for a wife writing to a husband) *tu.* This angered and confused Napoleon, who once wrote, "You treat me to a vous? Vous yourself! Ah, wicked one, how could you have written those letters? How cold they are."

The average young husband who is sent away from a wife he passionately loves naturally wants to see her as soon as possible. And if that same wife started writing rather formal and cool letters, that would be all the more reason for that husband to want to see her — and, perhaps, to be just a little bit suspicious. Napoleon was certainly lonesome for his Josephine, but he was unable to return to Paris on leave.

As the campaign wore on, he became more and more upset and determined to have Josephine join him in Italy. When he defeated the Piedmontese, he sent General Joachim Murat to Paris to retrieve her. Murat arrived several days prior to the Battle of Lodi and reported that she was in ill health and could not travel. There was the possibility that she was pregnant. This news certainly brightened Napoleon's mood, and he gave up thoughts of her joining him soon.

But as time went by, Napoleon was less and less happy with his wife's absence. She no longer claimed ill health, and no more was heard of a possible pregnancy. Napoleon became a bit suspicious and said so. As it happened, he had good reason for his concerns.

Josephine was a young woman with lots of time on her hands and no husband present to keep her company and keep her satisfied. She fell for young Lieutenant Hippolyte Charles, a staff officer to General Victor Leclerc. His job gave him a lot of time to spare as well, and he and Josephine were able to spend many hours together, no doubt discussing Napoleon's Italian victories long into the night. Or not. Charles was the very image of a dashing *hussar* (a member of the light elite cavalry), and he was charming and humorous in the bargain. He swept her off her feet in a way that Napoleon had never been able to do.

By July, Josephine could no longer avoid joining her husband, who was holding court in Milan. This burden would be lightened considerably by the fact that she had arranged for Lieutenant Charles to provide her escort to Italy, riding in her coach.

Josephine arrived in Milan with Lieutenant Charles as her *aide-de-camp*. Napoleon was elated to see his wife and apparently didn't notice the not entirely hidden relationship that she brought with her. Napoleon was a hero and now had his lovely young wife with him. Life was good.

Continuing the Fight Against Austria

Life was good, but Napoleon was still running a military campaign. The Austrians were in Mantua, and two armies had been sent to relieve them. The humiliated General Beaulieu had been replaced by General Würmser, who ordered a three-pronged attack on northern Italy. The Austrians' primary goal was to relieve the siege of Mantua and then to drive this upstart French general back to France. The ultimate effect would be to add to Napoleon's growing reputation.

Battling across the bridge at Arcola

Napoleon, not surprisingly, took the offensive. He won a great victory at Bassano on September 8, 1796. General Würmser, having resupplied the fortress of Mantua, was now obliged to seek shelter in it. The French promptly placed it under siege again.

The Austrians continued to try to lift the siege of Mantua and sent more armies against Napoleon. They next faced off near the town of Arcola, near Verona. The bridge over the Alpone River was critical. On the opposite side from the French waited the Austrians, led by General Josef Alvintzi. The battle for the bridge went on all day on November 15th, and the French were getting nowhere.

Determined to force a victory, Napoleon personally led an attack across the bridge, waving a French flag. At one point, he actually was pushed into the river, where he had to be retrieved by his brother Louis and his friend General Marmont. The French victory didn't actually come for two more days, but the image of the young General Bonaparte leading the attack across the bridge has become one of the most enduring symbols of his legend (see Figure 6-4).

Figure 6-4: This pressed-horn snuffbox in the shape of Napoleon's famous hat, from about 1830, shows Napoleon on the bridge.

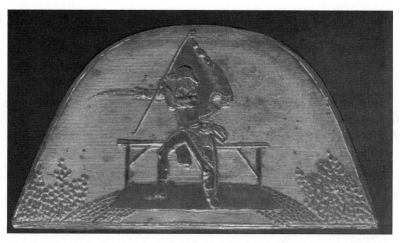

The Austrians regrouped and moved their forces toward Verona. The Austrians surprised Napoleon near the town of Rivoli. He was outnumbered but was more than up to the challenge. On January 14, 1797, Napoleon defeated the forces of General Alvintzi at Rivoli and then turned to defeat General Johann Provera at La Favorita.

This action effectively ended any Austrian chances in northern Italy, though they may not have realized it just yet. The Austrians in Mantua, seeing no possibility of any relief, surrendered on February 2, 1797. General Würmser and his soldiers were treated with all honor and allowed to return to Austria in exchange for promising not to fight against France for at least a year. The general himself was impressed and grateful, and the gesture no doubt improved Napoleon's image in the Viennese court.

Dealing with the Pope (again)

Napoleon turned once again to the Papal States, which had continued in their support of the Austrians, notwithstanding Napoleon's earlier success against them. Napoleon crushed all their forces, and on February 19, 1797, Pope Pius VI agreed to the Treaty of Tolentino. The terms of the treaty called for him to sever all ties to the Austrian cause and to pay 30 million francs to the Directory. The Directory would also gain a great many additional works of art, many personally selected by Napoleon's friend, Gaspard Monge.

Napoleon could have been harsher on the Pope, but with this treaty he demonstrated his understanding of the political realities of Italy and beyond. By being relatively generous to the Pope, he was able to keep other, even less friendly, forces at bay, all the while keeping the Directory happy. Napoleon was only 28 years old, and it would not be the last time that he showed such political acumen.

The Austrians made one last effort to gain some advantage in northern Italy. Their best general, 25-year-old Archduke Charles, brother of the Emperor of Austria, led an army to try to defeat Napoleon in northern Italy. His efforts came to little good, however, and Napoleon pushed him back into Austria. Soon the French army was literally in sight of Vienna. That was too much for Emperor Francis, who had very little in the way of a defense available for his capital.

Securing peace

The Austrians accepted a preliminary agreement at Leoben on April 18, 1797, and then, on October 17th, agreed to the Treaty of Campo Formio. Austria agreed to give up the Duchy of Milan and make peace with France. It also lost Belgium and recognized France's "natural borders" on the left bank (the western side) of the Rhine River. France's gain of Belgium came with its own set of issues. Great Britain was not likely to sit by while her archenemy, France, gained ports in Belgium and Holland that were the closest part of the Continent, just across the English Channel. So in the long run, this gain may have contributed to problems that would haunt Napoleon and Europe for many years.

In an often-overlooked aspect of the treaty, Napoleon was able to secure the release of a man who was both a French and American hero: General Lafayette. After his invaluable help to General Washington in the American Revolution, Lafayette had returned to France and been involved in the French Revolution. He soon soured on its excesses and sought refuge with the Austrians, who promptly tossed him in jail.

Hosting a Troubled Family Reunion

After the preliminary agreement at Leoben, many of Napoleon's family members came to visit him at his palace. What a difference from those dangerous days in Corsica (see Chapter 3)! His mother, Leticia, was there, along with several brothers and sisters and Josephine's children. Napoleon was the gracious host, but all was not well.

The family had never warmed to Josephine, and this visit did very little to change that situation. Worse, they were not shy about letting her know where she stood. They saw her as a spendthrift and a superficial social gadfly. They may have even suspected that she was unfaithful to Napoleon.

For her part, Josephine was not happy in Italy. As elegant as their accommodations were, they were not in Paris. She found the surroundings and the social life absolutely provincial and longed to be back in the exciting environs of Paris.

Settling Scores, Creating Countries

Napoleon now moved to consolidate his gains in Italy. He wanted to organize the area into countries that reflected the progressive ideals of the French Revolution — and that would be loyal allies to France. In so doing, he laid the groundwork for Italy's ultimate unification (see Chapter 22).

The Venetian Republic

After dealing with the Austrians, Napoleon settled some old French scores with Venice. In early 1797, Venetian citizens had massacred a number of French soldiers, so Napoleon took action at once. In May he intimidated the Venetian *Doge* (ruler) into paying France a sizeable indemnity which included, among many other things, paintings and historical artifacts. As part of the Treaty of Campo Formio, Austria was given some of what had been Venetian territory.

The Cisalpine Republic

Napoleon was never one to shy away from doing something unusual. But in the Treaty of Campo Formio, he even outdid himself. It was unusual enough that a mere general would negotiate a peace treaty. Far more unusual would be that same general actually forming a new country. But that is exactly what Napoleon did. Out of the former Austrian territories Milan, Bologna, and Modena, Napoleon formed a new nation, the Cisalpine Republic.

This action was, of course, far beyond his authority. The Directory may have been quite upset with him, but we don't have evidence of that. After all, Napoleon had brought his government unheard-of success, to say nothing of riches, so it could hardly complain. Moreover, Napoleon's popularity in Italy and in France was greater than that of anyone else, including the Directory, so it remained silent.

Napoleon was quite serious about his new republic. He organized its government, wrote its new constitution, and appointed its first leaders. The republic grew as time went on and, in 1805, became the Kingdom of Italy.

The Ligurian Republic

The Republic of Genoa had been weak, and after Napoleon's reorganization of Italy, it collapsed. Napoleon took charge, happy to see the demise of the very nation that had for so long oppressed his native Corsica. As he had done with the Cisalpine Republic, Napoleon created a new republic out of the territory controlled by Genoa. This he called the Ligurian Republic. In both republics, Napoleon promoted the ideals of the French Revolution but also preached moderation in all things political. As a result, all social classes and political parties found something to like about his new governments.

Small wonder, then, that the Italians today see Napoleon as a liberator and founder of Italian unity.

His Italian campaign over, Napoleon prepared to return to Paris. In a very short period of time, he had snatched victory from defeat and led France to a major triumph over her archenemy, Austria. In the process, he had made a name for himself that even he could not have possibly imagined.

And the people of Paris were about to let him know what they thought of him.

Chapter 7

Mixing Art, Science, and Guns in Egypt

• •

In This Chapter

▶ Gathering accolades

▶ Embarking on a new campaign

▶ Following in the footsteps of greatness

▶ Winning and losing

▶ Securing immortality

• •

As I explain in Chapter 6, Napoleon had great success in defeating the Austrian army that was threatening France in northern Italy. He was also successful in negotiating the Treaty of Campo Formio, which brought peace between France and Austria in that region. Napoleon's success had not entirely pleased the Directory, France's ruling body in Paris, which was beginning to fear this ambitious young general who seemed to constantly overstep his authority. However, it could do little to rein him in. Napoleon was at the top of his game, idolized in Italy and France and respected in Austria and Germany. In November 1797, the Directory sent him to Rastadt, Germany, where final negotiations for a comprehensive peace with Austria were underway.

On his way north to Germany, Napoleon toured much of northern Italy, where he was greeted everywhere as a hero for having freed the region from Austrian dominance. He stayed in Rastadt just long enough to bask in some glory and exchange very nice gifts with the principals, including accepting some magnificent Lipizzaner horses from the Emperor of Austria. His duties and pleasures completed, Napoleon soon left for Paris, where the people anxiously awaited their chance to shower him with glory.

In this chapter, I tell you about the next phase of Napoleon's storied career, a phase that is in many ways the most romantic of them all. His campaign in Egypt and the Holy Land led to a greater understanding of that mysterious region and to an inevitable comparison of Napoleon to Alexander the Great. I also check in on Josephine and show how Napoleon reacted to her less than stellar behavior.

Basking in the Glow of Glory

When the 28-year-old General Napoleon Bonaparte returned to Paris in early December 1797, it must have seemed like he had the entire world at his feet. In a very short period of time, he had saved his government from overthrow at home and defended her against attack from abroad. The Italian campaign had been an overwhelming success, and everyone knew it. The Directory's financial picture was good only to the extent that Napoleon had managed to send incredible riches home, and Paris was now the home to some of the world's greatest artistic and historic treasures.

Everyone loves a hero, and Parisians were certainly no exception. Napoleon was wined and dined at every opportunity. Generals, diplomats, and politicians paid homage at his home, which was often quite crowded. Napoleon was in great demand at every imaginable social function, and he also held court at numerous *salons* — afternoon meetings of intellectuals and others.

In some ways, the salons may have been Napoleon's favorite activity. He quite rightfully saw himself as an intellectual and scholar, and the salons, run by fashionable ladies whose husbands were of means (which means they had money!), gave him the opportunity to rub shoulders with the best intellectual minds of Paris.

Achieving high honors

The greatest tribute that can be paid to an intellectual in France is election to the National Institute of Sciences and Arts of France, which had been created on August 22, 1795. That august body, known today as the French Institute, is made up of the *crème de la crème* of France's intellectual elite, and membership is closely controlled. Napoleon's election to the Institute was a telling measure of the esteem in which he was held. It was a well-deserved tribute and one that Napoleon always held with great pride. And he would soon justify the honor many times over.

Image makers of the day quickly picked up on "Napoleon the warrior and scholar." Figure 7-1 is a fine example of a graphic that combines the images of intellect and war.

With Napoleon's credentials even more firmly established, he was in even greater demand on the social circuit. He met intellectuals of all stripes. The most notorious of these was Madame Anne Louise Germaine de Staël. Her salon was perhaps the most important, and she met Napoleon at numerous social functions. At first enamored with Napoleon, in time she turned against him and was his nemesis for many years, writing scathing criticisms of his rule. Even so, Madame de Staël (as she is generally known) was one of the most important and influential women of her time.

Figure 7-1:
This extremely rare period engraving shows Napoleon as a scholar general.

Other tributes ranged from the humorous to the touching. The Directory paid Napoleon several honors, including throwing banquets for him, despite its growing concern over his popularity and his disdain for the governing body's lack of competence. Composers and poets wrote in his honor, and he was given the best seats at any performance he wished to attend. Finally, the street his home was on was renamed *Rue de la Victoire* ("Street of Victory") in his honor. Glory can be fleeting, and Napoleon understood this well, but for the moment, things were great.

However, not everything was as it seemed.

Looking for a new campaign

Napoleon had had great success and had achieved a position of enormous popularity. Now, who could possibly have a problem with that? For one, the Directory — a collection of incompetent, greedy politicians that was running France. It was one thing to have a popular General Bonaparte running around in Italy; it was quite another to have him running around in Paris. Napoleon was obviously ambitious, and the Directory feared he might turn that ambition in its general direction.

Napoleon, to his credit, kept out of politics and played the game more or less to the satisfaction of all. Still, the Directory wanted him out of town, soon. A new campaign was needed, and one was quickly found. Only England remained in opposition to France, and England had to be defeated, one way or another.

The most obvious way to defeat England would be by direct invasion. This idea had been around a long time, of course, but now France seemed ready. Victorious on land, her armies led by a great general (who, as it happened, the Directory wanted out of Paris — now!), the time seemed incredibly ripe. But the idea just wouldn't float.

The idea of invading England literally wouldn't float, as it happens. Any invasion would have to deal with the little matter of the English Channel, that body of water between the British Isles and Continental Europe that had always been England's first line of defense. To invade England, France would have to go by ship, and therein lay a problem: England had the greatest navy in the world, and France had not much of a navy at all.

That little detail didn't stop the French from having a go at it. The French were allied with Spain at the time, and Spain did have a pretty decent fleet. Napoleon put together a plan of battle but kept coming up against the fact that he simply would not have sufficient sea power to prevail. By February 1798, he was finally forced to face reality. He wrote the Directory, suggesting that at best the invasion was at least a year away, and at worst the time had already come and gone. France would have to look elsewhere for a victory over her archenemy, England.

Napoleon was anxious for a new campaign to keep his glory alive. The Directory was anxious to see him off on just such a campaign, the farther away from Paris the better. Soon, the two would agree on a win-win plan: Napoleon would invade Egypt.

Setting Sights on Egypt

There is some question as to the origin of the idea for the Egyptian campaign. The basic idea went back as far as the 17th century, and Napoleon had certainly suggested invading Egypt more than once. But some historians believe that the person who proposed it at just the right moment was Charles Maurice de Talleyrand-Périgord, who was serving as France's foreign minister at the time. Almost from the start, Talleyrand's scheming would be both good news and bad news for Napoleon, and few people would be so involved in, and influential on, Napoleon's career. (Talleyrand shows up later in this chapter, as well as in subsequent chapters.)

At first blush, the idea of invading Egypt may seem madness. First, the Mediterranean is still *water* last I checked, and the British fleet was quite active in the area. Second, a quick look at a map would *seem* to indicate that Egypt is quite the opposite direction from England! While all that is true, it rather misses the point:

- ✔ The Mediterranean is much larger than the English Channel, so French ships might easily avoid British ships. (Think of a needle in a haystack, and you have the basic idea.)
- ✔ Egypt was a key element in the British trade system, especially for its trade with the Far East, particularly India.
- ✔ Invading Egypt would be a significant psychological blow to the British ego, while adding to French presence in the Mediterranean.

The Directory immediately latched onto the idea. Not only would it offer all of the above advantages, but it would also get Napoleon out of Paris. Paris? Heck, it would get him out of France. With any luck, he would bring greater glory to France. With any better luck, he might get killed in the process.

Napoleon must have been equally delighted with the idea. He understood that glory can be fleeting and that his success in Italy would quickly fade away if he didn't add to its luster. An invasion of England may have been preferable, but it simply wasn't in the cards. Egypt, on the other hand, was very doable and had the potential to capture the imagination of all of France. Yes, Napoleon was pleased indeed, and he immediately began to plan the expedition.

Planning to conquer a world of mystery

At the time, Egypt was seen as a very romantic and mysterious place. Little was known about it, though certainly people remembered the history of the ancient Pharaohs. Anyone who could conquer that distant and ancient land would surely gain immortality. Of course, all parties assumed that there would be great riches to be had as well. If Italian works of art could be plundered, er, that is, appropriated, why not equally valuable Egyptian treasures?

Napoleon was in a pretty strong position, so when the Directory asked him to put together a plan of action, he could more or less write his own ticket. He selected his staff and began to put together an invasion force. His staff maintained secrecy and kept up the front that they were preparing an invasion of England. Napoleon put Generals Louis Alexandre Berthier, Jean Lannes, and Joachim Murat on his staff. They would first seize the island of Malta, whose government had been unfriendly to the Revolution and friendly to French royalists.

After taking Malta, they would then seize Egypt itself, on the pretext of restoring full control to the Turks, who at least in theory controlled the country. Since the Crusades, Egypt had really been run by the *Mamelukes,* warrior slaves from Georgia, Armenia, and other locations. By restoring Turkish control,

France would strengthen its ties to Turkey, which would shut the British out of the area and give France an advantage in the trade routes to the Far East. If France could establish a trading colony just across the Mediterranean and do a bit of plundering at the same time, well, that would just be icing on the cake!

Sabotaging the effort

France had perfectly justifiable reasons for its expedition, as long as the Turks understood and agreed. Technically, the French forces would be helping Turkey regain control over its lands in Egypt. Talleyrand, who would increasingly become Napoleon's nemesis, was supposed to go to Turkey and explain the situation to the Turkish sultan, Selim III, who wasn't expected to object.

Unfortunately, Talleyrand never quite got around to making that trip. No one really knows why, though I suspect that he was not greatly interested in promoting this young and ambitious general. Or perhaps the Directory ordered him not to go. Regardless, he didn't go, so as far as the Turks were concerned, the French were invading their territory. They would not stand idly by, and eventually Napoleon would have to deal with them.

Napoleon, of course, knew nothing of this situation as he prepared to leave. In what can only be seen as an amazing organizational feat, he put together an invasion force of over 35,000 men. There were infantry, cavalry, artillerymen, and other soldiers of war. The flagship, *l'Orient,* was the finest ship of its kind. He had 13 ships of the line (roughly equivalent to battleships today), 4 frigates, and hundreds of troop transports. It was a major war machine.

And then there were the scholars.

Emulating Alexander

Napoleon had always been fascinated with Alexander the Great and his campaigns. When it was clear that Napoleon was about to follow in his footsteps, the future emperor read everything he could find on the subject. He may or may not have seen himself as the new Alexander, but he certainly put together a campaign that contained many similarities to Alexander's.

Bringing scholars along

Alexander the Great had been tutored by no less than Aristotle, one of the greatest minds in human history, and when Alexander went on campaign, he took with him many scholars, determined to learn what he could about the new lands he was about to conquer. He was careful to send samples of plants and animals back to Aristotle to help preserve the knowledge gained from the campaign.

Napoleon wanted to do something very similar. He brought with him 167 top scholars from several different fields. They were led by no less than Napoleon's favorite scholars, Gaspard Monge and Claude-Louis Berthollet (see Chapter 6). Egypt was about to become a lot less mysterious. Napoleon's entourage included cartographers to produce maps, artists to record everything that they saw (remember, there were no cameras in those days), surveyors, naturalists, linguists, and numerous other scientists, all of whom were determined to learn all they could and share it with the world. Vivant Denon, the finest engraver of his day, was along to supervise the production of graphic representations of all they saw.

In addition to the top scholars, there were hundreds of additional savants, as well as an enormous amount of equipment, including printing presses, scientific equipment, hot air balloons, and several personal libraries of significant size. Napoleon's library alone numbered some 300 volumes. Remember, these folks were going off to war, so it says a great deal that they were taking all these scientists and their equipment along for the ride.

While he was in Egypt, Napoleon would create the Egyptian Institute — a scholarly association dedicated to the study of all things Egyptian.

Learning was not the only thing on the agenda for the academics on board. The French hoped to gain the trust and support of the Egyptian people and were prepared to make every possible effort in that direction. This included sharing the knowledge of the western world with them. Advances in agriculture, medicine, and other areas were to be widely disseminated.

Finding the Rosetta stone

The scientific effort would not go unrewarded. Probably the most famous discovery during the Egyptian campaign was the Rosetta stone. The scholars didn't find it; a couple of soldiers found it in a wall in the town of Rosetta, but even they understood immediately how important the stone was.

The stone is about 3.7 feet tall and 2.3 feet wide and dates to 196 BCE. It contains an inscription in Greek (the language of the rulers and educated classes), in *demotic* (the common language of Egyptians), and in *hieroglyphics* (the picture-writing used by the ancient Egyptians in the days of the Pharaohs, mainly in religious texts). Humanity had long forgotten how to read hieroglyphics, so all of the inscriptions on tombs, temples, and papyrus scrolls were virtually meaningless.

The members of the Egyptian Institute immediately went to work making rubbings of the stone for scholars to study. It's a good thing, too, as a couple years later the British would end up with the stone. Today, it sits in the British Museum in London. The rubbings were taken to France, and in 1822, anthropologist Jean-François Champollion was able to translate the stone: The secrets of the Pharaohs were unleashed forever.

Documenting the journey

Another huge accomplishment of the Egyptian campaign was the output of the artists and engravers working under Vivant Denon's direction. Denon, named art director of the Egyptian Institute, produced over 200 drawings and supervised countless more created by other artists. They made drawings of everything from ancient temples and tombs to modern-day Cairo. At times, they had mere minutes to record their observations as battles drew closer. At one point in the campaign, Denon and a number of his fellow artists and scholars accompanied General Louis Desaix on a campaign into upper Egypt, where they made it all the way past the first cataracts (waterfalls) to Aswan and beyond, recording the existence of countless temples and other treasures.

When this artistic team returned to France, its members set to work making copper engravings of what they had drawn. Soon it was possible to purchase inexpensive prints in shops all over France, and then the rest of Europe. The expedition set off a virtual frenzy of interest in all things Egyptian. Clothing and furniture styles, decorative arts — all adopted Egyptian motifs, and their popularity continues to this day.

Denon was not content to produce mere penny-prints for the local shops. Over a period of 20 years, some 400 engravers produced an incredible work known as the *Description de l'Egypt* ("Description of Egypt"). This was a ten-volume extra large folio edition of all the engravings that were produced as a result of the expedition. Produced by order of Napoleon himself, it is the crowning achievement of the scholarly aspect of the expedition, containing 837 copper engravings (which are on paper, of course, but made with a copper plate in the printing process) and over 2,000 other drawings.

Sailing (and Marching) into History

On May 19, 1798, Napoleon stepped on board his flagship, *l'Orient,* and set sail, leaving from the port city that had helped start his career, Toulon (see Chapter 4). The voyage was uneventful, with Napoleon spending much of his time reading and engaging in what must have been fascinating discussions with some of the scholars on board.

Gaining Malta

Three weeks after setting sail, Napoleon's fleet arrived at the island of Malta. That island had long been controlled by the Knights of St. John, a religious order dating to the Middle Ages, but they had become weak and corrupt. When Napoleon's army set foot on the island, the knights quickly surrendered (not that they had any real choice). Napoleon was generous to them, sending them to France with a nice pension.

In the first Punic War between Rome and Carthage (264–221 BCE), Malta was one of the spoils of victory gained by the Romans. Though small, it is key to controlling the Mediterranean, and the French were pleased to now control its rather impressive citadel. They were also happy to gain several ships, quite a few military arms and supplies, and a large treasure. It was a pretty good haul for not having to fire a shot!

The citizens of Malta gained as well. As he had done in Italy when he created the Cisalpine Republic (see Chapter 6), Napoleon immediately reorganized the island's government and instituted reforms that would be echoed throughout his career. He granted religious freedom to the Jews and tossed out the old feudal system, along with slavery. He wrote a modern constitution, reorganized the educational and legal systems, and set up military defenses, including a garrison of several thousand French soldiers.

And all that in a week! Napoleon was a whirlwind of action. Malta was a reflection of Italy and a look into the future, all at the same time.

With Malta properly settled, Napoleon left for Egypt. The trip would take just under two weeks. All the while, Napoleon had to be on the lookout for the British fleet, led in this region by Rear Admiral Horatio Nelson. The British had finally gotten word of the expedition and had sent Nelson to destroy the French fleet. The two fleets came close to each other several times but never made contact. That was certainly good news for the French, who would have been at a decided disadvantage in spite of their good ships; the French navy was generally no match for the Brits.

Reassuring the Egyptian people

Napoleon understood that the people of Egypt might be just a bit suspicious of a French military expedition. He did everything he could to reassure them of his honorable intentions. He prepared an Arabic-language proclamation telling the people of his intention to liberate them from the dreaded Beys (the leaders of the Mamelukes). He also assured them that he would respect their religion, which was Islam. He criticized the Beys, who he said had grabbed all the goodies for themselves, including female slaves, horses, land, and palaces.

Since the French were coming to help them, the proclamation went on to say, the Egyptian people should receive them as liberators and offer their full cooperation. Anyone who cooperated, or at least stayed in their homes and out of the way, would be treated with generosity and respect. Anyone who fought against the French would be destroyed.

In a proclamation to his soldiers, Napoleon told them that they would be striking a fatal blow against the hated British, all the while helping an enslaved people. He compared his army to that of the Roman legions and reminded soldiers that the Romans protected the religious beliefs of people they conquered. His men were ordered to respect Islam, even though it was quite different from their own beliefs (for example, in its treatment of women).

While on that subject, he gave the strictest orders that rape and pillage would not be tolerated, and anyone guilty of rape would be shot. An army of liberation does not take such liberties with the very people it is trying to free.

As a great fan of Alexander, Napoleon must have been excited to turn to securing the most famous of the many cities that carried his name, Alexandria. It was here that Alexander the Great had briefly ruled as Pharaoh of Egypt, and it was here that Ptolemy I brought Alexander's body (which has subsequently disappeared).

The French forces marched from their beachhead and soon were storming the gates of Alexandria. Despite a spirited defense, helped by a deadly heat for which the French were ill-prepared, the city fell. Napoleon put General Jean-Baptiste Kléber in command of the city.

Marching to Cairo

With Alexandria secure, Napoleon sent his army toward Cairo. He had already sent an advance guard, commanded by General Louis Charles Desaix. It moved both on land and with a small flotilla of ships on the Nile. On July 6, Napoleon left Alexandria with his main army. The march was awful. The heat was unbearable, there was precious little water to be had along the way, the uniforms were heavy and inappropriate for the climate, and morale was understandably dismal. But all that changed when the soldiers reached the village of El Rahmanyeh, where Desaix's troops were waiting for them. The reunion was no doubt gratifying, but even greater was the discovery of the cool waters of the Nile; long cool baths were the order of the day.

Refreshed, the army turned to the business at hand. Napoleon had an excellent army, but it was quite short on cavalry. Local leaders had promised horses, but those horses had not materialized. The Mameluke commander, Mourad-Bey, had a fearsome collection of 3,000 Mameluke cavalry as part of a total force of perhaps 15,000. The battle was fierce, but the Mameluke cavalry could not break the French squares, so they broke off combat and melted away. Round one to the French.

On July 21, 1798, the French faced off against a combined Egyptian force of approximately 24,000, including at least 10,000 cavalry. The Mamelukes were impressive to see and were probably convinced that they were about to have these upstart infidels for breakfast. The battle took place virtually in the shadow of the great pyramids of Giza. Napoleon exclaimed to his soldiers, "Forty centuries of history look down on you," and artists ranging from those of the day to modern-day poster artists have used the image of Napoleon and his army with the pyramids in the background. (See Figure 7-2 for an example.) It is one of the mainstays of Napoleon's legend.

Figure 7-2:
General Bonaparte points to the Pyramids and exclaims, "Forty centuries of history look down on you!" This is a rare gold snuffbox.

The Battle of the Pyramids was also one of Napoleon's greatest victories. The Mamelukes were fearsome and brave, but they had never had to deal with heavy guns and couldn't figure out how to break infantry squares. They tried and tried again, but to no avail. The large crowds of civilians who had turned out to witness the slaughter of the French were no doubt disappointed, but Napoleon was elated. In only a couple hours, he defeated the entire enemy army. Much of it lay dead on the field of battle or at the bottom of the Nile, drowned in an effort to escape.

Napoleon was in command of Cairo and most of lower Egypt. As he had in Italy, Napoleon was more than willing to share the glory. He wrote of the bravery of many of his soldiers and officers and put many of them in for promotions. Napoleon reorganized Cairo, both militarily and politically. He was disappointed at the lack of wealth and supplies but began to make arrangements for more material to be sent from Malta and France. These were heady days, and Napoleon could have been forgiven if he saw himself as a new Alexander.

Heady days they were indeed, but fate was about to strike twin blows against Napoleon.

Learning of disaster

The first disaster was brought to Napoleon's attention by a letter from General Kléber (who was in command of Alexandria). On August 2, 1798, Admiral Nelson caught up to the French fleet, which was anchored at Aboukir Bay, and destroyed it. (For much more on this situation, see Chapter 11.) Any hope of a regular stream of communication and supplies by sea to Malta and France was now over. The British ruled the Mediterranean, and future French resupply would be sporadic at best.

If this wasn't enough, Napoleon soon learned of Talleyrand's treachery (or incompetence, take your pick!). Talleyrand had never told the Turkish sultan, Selim III, of France's intentions, so the sultan was, naturally enough, incensed to discover that his lands had been invaded. In September, the sultan declared war on France. It would only be a matter of time before his army would march to Egypt to drive out the invading French. The Turkish soldiers had a well-deserved reputation as fierce fighters who would give no quarter. Sultan Selim sent two armies against Napoleon. One was sent by sea, but poor sailing conditions meant that it would not arrive for some time. The other was coming on ground through the Holy Land, and Napoleon would have to face this army first.

Before that, however, Napoleon had to deal with an uprising in Cairo. It seems that not all Egyptians fully appreciated the opportunities for improvement afforded by the French presence. The uprising was a bloody affair that lasted two days, October 21 and 22, but it was finally brought under control. This happened largely through the efforts of General Thomas-Alexander Dumas (who was the father of Alexander Dumas, the author of *The Count of Monte Cristo* and *The Three Musketeers*). The insurrection was put down, but Napoleon now fully realized he was in a hostile land.

Struggling with Josephine

The campaign in Egypt was not Napoleon's only source of bad news. As I explain in Chapter 6, when Napoleon was in Italy, he discovered that his new wife, Josephine, felt less than passionate toward her husband. She was, in fact, having a torrid affair with a young officer named Hippolyte Charles. When she finally visited Napoleon in Italy, she even brought her lover along as an aide, but Napoleon chose to ignore the signs and concentrate on his own love for her — and his victories in the field.

Facing reality

Napoleon was kept rather busy in Egypt, but his thoughts were seldom far from Josephine. Whatever suspicions he had, he kept them to himself and, unlike many of his officers, he did not take a local mistress. When his friend General Andoche Junot showed Napoleon a letter concerning Josephine's relationship with Captain Charles, he could no longer ignore reality. Josephine and Charles had traveled together and were seen together all over Paris. When Napoleon asked other friends about this, they grimly confirmed what they had been fearful of telling him before: Josephine was having an affair.

If that were not enough, Josephine was known for her war profiteering, as she was involved in the procurement of military supplies. No doubt she felt she needed the money, as her spending had become prolific. All of Paris was aware of the situation, which could not do an ambitious general like Napoleon any good at all.

Napoleon was outraged and depressed over the news. He wrote his brother, Joseph, "I have great private unhappiness; the veil has at last quite fallen from my eyes." Napoleon's unhappiness was no doubt increased when this letter was intercepted by the British and published in the papers! Napoleon soon became a laughingstock in Paris.

Finding a new Cleopatra

Napoleon was a man of action, and he quickly resolved to take two steps. One would have to wait: He planned to divorce Josephine when he returned to Paris. But as long as he was in Egypt, he may as well do what so many of his officers had been doing: namely, take a mistress. He had little use for local women, but fortunately for him, especially given his rank as commanding general, another option was available.

Pauline Fourès was a very attractive 29-year-old leggy blond who had been smuggled into Egypt as a soldier by her husband, Lieutenant Jean-Noël Fourès. They were living openly but were not completely happy with each other. Napoleon soon fell for her, and she was more than happy to become his mistress. Napoleon sent her husband on assignment to France, and he and Pauline took up "open and notorious" companionship. All seemed well, but when the British captured her husband and, rather mischievously, returned him to Egypt, things got a bit dicey.

After some no doubt lengthy discussions, the young couple obtained a divorce. Napoleon and Pauline, whom both he and his soldiers called his "Cleopatra," were then seen together everywhere. Napoleon undoubtedly hoped word would get back to Paris, and it did. The news may not have made Josephine happy, but it no doubt increased his standing with the public.

When Napoleon left Egypt, Pauline became the mistress to General Kléber, whom Napoleon left in command. Pauline later returned to Paris where she remarried and lived quietly.

Campaigning in the Holy Land

After taking Cairo, Napoleon turned his full attention to the Turkish threat to the north. Napoleon was determined to deal with the Turkish army before it reached Egypt. The Turks were known for their violence toward all in their path, including civilians, women, and children. To protect the people he claimed to be there to protect, Napoleon had to move into Syria, the name for the Holy Land at the time. Napoleon marched into the Sinai Desert with an army of about 14,000 men. The march through the desert was awful, but when the soldiers arrived in Gaza, they found ample food and water. Some images, such as the medallion in Figure 7-3, suggest that Napoleon rode a camel or a camel-drawn chariot, but he actually went on horseback.

Figure 7-3:
This medallion from 1799 shows an unlikely image of Napoleon riding a chariot drawn by two camels.

When the army arrived at the fortress of El Arish in Gaza, it suffered an unexpected delay. Though it easily captured the town and then, with a night attack, the armed camp outside the fortress, the fortress itself continued to hold out. When the fortress eventually capitulated, Napoleon was faced with another problem. He had taken as prisoner some 2,000 Turks, but he could not spare the forces to either send them to Cairo or imprison them at El Arish. Nor could he take them with him, as his food supplies were dangerously low.

What Napoleon decided to do was quite common in those days in European wars: He got the prisoners to promise that they would not fight him for at least one year, and then he released them "on parole." Like so many westerners before and after his campaign, Napoleon would soon discover that when fighting invading infidels, Muslim warriors in this region paid little regard to western codes of honor.

Confronting a terrible dilemma

Napoleon and his army continued to march up the coast to Jaffa, a city that today is a suburb of Tel Aviv in Israel. This city had an important port and a large number of supplies, so its capture was essential. On March 7, 1799, Napoleon's forces successfully took the city. In so doing, he captured 4,000 prisoners. Much to his surprise, Napoleon discovered that many of them were the very prisoners he had released on parole in Gaza.

This discovery put Napoleon in a real quandary. If he released the prisoners, they would eventually fight again and kill more of his soldiers. If he kept them prisoner, they would either starve or cause his soldiers to starve, as there was already a serious shortage of food. There was no good choice. But according to the rules of war followed by Europe at the time, if an army continues to fight after the walls are breached, the soldiers can be executed. (This is not unlike the rule that allows a retreating army to be fair game, while soldiers who surrender must be spared.) Moreover, the commandant had beheaded Napoleon's emissary and put his head on a pike. This action enraged Napoleon and his soldiers.

Napoleon held war councils, consulted his generals, and no doubt looked into his conscience. In the end, his concern for the welfare of his men won out, and he ordered the prisoners executed. It was an awful decision to have to make, and some historians have seized on it to question his character, but it is hard to imagine that Napoleon could have done anything else. (I would not have wanted to be the father of a son killed by one of those combatants had they been released and allowed to fight again.)

The French soldiers remembered well the fate of their emissary and the fact that many of their comrades had died at the hands of paroled soldiers, and they took out their fury on the population of Jaffa. Throughout the night, they raped and pillaged their way through the city, and only in the morning could Napoleon and his officers restore order.

The locals got some measure of revenge when many of the soldiers got the plague as a result of their evening activities. Napoleon had those soldiers put up in a monastery-turned-hospital, and they were given the best treatment. And, in a move that both endeared him to his men and added another chapter to his legend, Napoleon personally visited the stricken soldiers, speaking to them, touching them, and helping move a corpse. Little was known about the plague in those days, but everyone did know that the disease was contagious, so Napoleon's bravery in touching diseased soldiers was astonishing. This scene was made famous in a painting by Antoine Jean Gros. (I visited the room where this scene happened and can tell you that even today it is an emotional experience.)

Reaching the end of the line

Jaffa secured, Napoleon marched up the coast to the town of Acre, also known as Acco or Akko. There he met Turkish forces led by Djezzar Pasha, whose nickname "the butcher" probably tells us all we need to know. He had been joined, thanks to Napoleon's delay at El Arish, by Sir Sydney Smith, who commanded some 800 British sailors.

Smith had been at Toulon when Napoleon had driven the British out (see Chapter 4) and had later been imprisoned in Paris. He was spirited out of prison by a royalist named Picard de Phélippeaux, who had been a classmate of Napoleon's and was now his bitter enemy. Smith managed to capture Napoleon's siege cannon that had been sent by ship up the coast, and he worked hard to strengthen Acre's defenses.

Napoleon tried to take the city by bombardment, by frontal assault, and by a combination of the two. His attacks met only limited success and in every case were beat back. The siege lasted six weeks. During that time, Napoleon sent Generals Junot, Kléber, and Murat to defeat elements of the Turkish and Mameluke armies. They had great initial success, but Kléber got into a tricky situation near Mount Tabor, not far from Nazareth. Kléber played defense for the better part of a day, but when Napoleon suddenly arrived with a division of men, the rout was on.

The Battle of Mount Tabor and the skirmishes that led to it made the trip into the Holy Land worthwhile, as they finished the Mamelukes as a fighting force and kept the Turks from thinking of moving toward Cairo.

The success at Mount Tabor notwithstanding, it soon became clear that Napoleon's siege of Acre was going nowhere. Napoleon had observation balloons with him but failed to use them (see Chapter 25). Had he done so, he would have learned of the exact nature of the defenses, including a double-wall construction that proved quite effective. But the delays earlier in the campaign that allowed the British to reinforce Acre caused his ultimate failure in the siege.

Some historians describe this campaign in the Holy Land as a total failure, but it did accomplish its most fundamental goal, which was to protect Cairo from the oncoming Turks. Still, the march back was no fun, despite Napoleon's efforts to put the best possible face on it. Napoleon had arranged for the worst sick to be taken care of along the way — there is no truth to a rumor that he had some of them poisoned — and for Cairo to give a great welcome to the returning army. Cairo went all out, holding an orgy of celebration that lasted for several days.

Defending against the Turks

Napoleon had little time to rest. The second Turkish army, the one sent by sea, landed near Alexandria at Aboukir on July 11, 1799. Napoleon was ready for them. The Turks were caught between Napoleon's forces and the sea. Nine thousand Turks had been landed by 60 transports supported by Sir Sydney Smith, and they faced only 8,000 French. Even so, the contest wasn't even close. The Turks established a beachhead and gained control of a small fortress called Fort Aboukir. The fort was of little use, and most of their forces were stretched out over at least half a mile in relatively open ground.

Napoleon sent General Murat's cavalry crashing into them, supported by a massive artillery barrage and General Lanne's infantry. As Napoleon planned, the beachhead collapsed, and the Turks were literally pushed into the sea. Of the 9,000 Turks that began the engagement, 7,000 were either shot or drowned, and the rest were captured. It was a decisive victory that cost the French only around 100 killed and several hundred wounded, including the dashing Murat, who received a slight pistol wound in the cheek.

Many people characterize Napoleon's Egyptian campaign as a failure. On one level, there is some truth to the charge. His successes didn't last long, and in a couple years the British were back in force. But this turn of events is hardly to be laid at Napoleon's feet. Military incompetence on the part of his admiral (see Chapter 9) deprived him of his fleet, and political treachery by Talleyrand meant that he had to fight two Turkish armies in addition to the Mamelukes. To his military credit, he defeated both Turkish armies and the Mamelukes. Only at Acre did he fail in his primary objective, and had his fleet been available, he likely would have met success there as well.

In short, Napoleon achieved at the very least success in his short-term military goals. And when added to the incredible accomplishment of his savants, who are generally credited with the development of modern Egyptology, the campaign can hardly be seen as a disaster.

Suffering European Setbacks

Whatever success Napoleon did or did not have in Egypt, while he was there it soon became clear that France was in trouble at home. England, Austria, and Russia had joined in the Second Coalition against France, and France had taken the field against Austria in Germany. Unfortunately, the Archduke Charles, brother to Emperor Francis of Austria, defeated General Jean Baptiste Jourdan, who was forced to retreat back across the Rhine River.

The situation in Italy was even worse, at least from Napoleon's point of view. The Austrians and the Russians had invaded northern Italy and pushed the French back to Genoa. The Cisalpine Republic, Napoleon's pride and joy, was retaken and its government dissolved. The situation seemed grim and in need of strong leadership.

Preparing to leave

Napoleon was determined to be that strong leader. After all, he had defeated the Austrians in Italy and was perhaps the only general capable of doing so again. Just ask him! There was, however, the little matter that he was under orders to command the French forces in Egypt, and those orders had not been changed. For Napoleon to leave for France without proper orders would be to desert his army. It was a risky move, but Napoleon was nothing if not a risk-taker.

Napoleon's main concern was the safety and security of France. But there is little doubt that he was also concerned with his own ambition. Egypt was fast becoming at best a side show, and Napoleon needed to be where the real action was.

After Napoleon's victory against the Turks at Aboukir, he returned to Cairo and outwardly continued his incredible pace of work to study and modernize Egypt. But he also informed a number of his closest associates, including his secretary Bourrienne; Generals Murat, Lannes, Marmont, Antoine-François Andréossy, and Berthier; and his friends and scholars Monge and Berthollet that they would soon be leaving Cairo.

Heading back to France

The biggest concern, of course, was the fact that the British fleet made departure from Egypt rather risky business. But when Napoleon was told that the Brits had sailed away, he acted quickly. He dashed off letters to a number of people, including General Kléber (whom he left in charge); said goodbye to his Cleopatra, Pauline Fourès; and collected his belongings. On August 22, 1799, Napoleon and his entourage boarded two frigates and sailed away.

Three weeks later, they reached Corsica where, due to wind conditions, they remained for six days. This was quite a time for Napoleon, who had become a local hero. Large crowds formed wherever he went, and he often seemed under siege by adoring fans in his own home. (If you visit his home, you can see the trap door that he sometimes used to sneak out of the house.)

Napoleon could not have known it at the time, but when he left Corsica he did so for the last time, never again to return. On October 9, 1799, he and his followers arrived at Fréjus, where they were again welcomed as heroes. Napoleon had already added the conquest of Egypt to his growing legend, and the hero had returned to save France. A week later, he was in Paris. He was about to take the world by storm.

Chapter 8

Gaining Control of France

. . . .

In This Chapter

▶ Coming to terms with Josephine

▶ Choosing the winning conspiracy

. . . .

*W*hen Napoleon returned to France from Egypt in October 1799, he found his nation in serious trouble. England, Austria, and Russia, joined by the lesser powers of Naples, Portugal, and Turkey, had formed the Second Coalition against France and had become emboldened by military success against the French in Germany and Italy. The desire of these nations to replace the Revolutionary government with a Bourbon king had not gone away.

At home, the governing body — the Directory — had continued to demonstrate that it was competent only at staying in power. France's economy, the poor performance of which was a root cause of the French Revolution, had not improved under the corrupt leadership of the Directory. Among other things,

✔ Inflation had destroyed the value of French currency.

✔ Roads, bridges, and other infrastructure were in sharp decline due to general neglect.

✔ Businesses were in serious trouble.

If a government's primary duty is to provide economic and military security for its people, then the Directory was a failure of the first magnitude.

In this chapter, I explain how Napoleon became involved in a move to replace the Directory and ended up as the undisputed leader of France. First, however, I describe Napoleon's return to Paris and his fateful meeting with Josephine.

Returning Home a Hero

Napoleon arrived in Paris on October 16, 1799. Though he had been received as a hero on Corsica and along the way to the capital city (see Chapter 7), he was not at all certain what kind of reception to expect from the Directory. On one hand, the populace considered him a conquering hero, and the mania with all things Egyptian that resulted from his expedition had already begun. On the other hand, he had technically deserted his soldiers. The Directory had actually sent him a letter suggesting he return to France, but he had never received it; he made the decision to leave Egypt on his own.

Napoleon could have been in serious trouble, but that simply wasn't going to happen. The Directory was very unpopular and incompetent. Napoleon was very popular and then some, and he had a reputation as the most competent person in France. Politicians (the Directory) need to attach themselves to popular causes and people (Napoleon). You do the math.

Dealing with Josephine

Napoleon returned to Paris still angry and heartbroken over Josephine's infidelity while he was in Egypt (see Chapter 7). He was determined to divorce her and said so to his friends and family. When he went to his home, he found that she had spent a fortune redecorating it — a fortune "paid" for by going ever deeper into debt — but Josephine was nowhere in sight. He naturally supposed she was with her lover, but that was not the case.

When she heard that Napoleon was coming home, Josephine had mixed emotions. She hardly missed him as a lover or even a husband, and his return would certainly create difficulties for some of her romantic and business adventures. Indeed, she was working on a possible new romance with Louis Gohier, who was none other than the new head of the Directory. On the other hand, Napoleon might be able to bail her out of her financial problems. And she was, after all, quite fond of him, so she determined that she should try to save her marriage.

But saving her marriage might prove quite difficult, especially if Napoleon were able to talk with his brothers first. They would certainly fill his ears with lurid stories. Napoleon's family had never really warmed to Josephine, and her escapades had only reinforced their coolness toward her. Josephine understood the situation very well, so she left Paris to intercept Napoleon en route before his brothers could get to him.

Unfortunately for Josephine, her driver took one route south while Napoleon was taking another route north! Josephine wasn't able to return to Paris until two days after Napoleon's arrival, and she found her belongings packed and Napoleon locked in his room, refusing to see her. Responding to the situation in the only way she could, given the circumstances, Josephine spent the night crying outside Napoleon's door, pleading her case, promising eternal fidelity and devotion. None of it worked; Napoleon wasn't interested.

Desperate, Josephine called in the big guns. She got her children, Hortense and Eugène, to plead her case. Eugène was one of Napoleon's aides, and he was very fond of the boy. Napoleon was also fond of the younger Hortense and, in the end, relented.

Josephine (see Figure 8-1) had used all her resources to keep Napoleon and would henceforth be a rather devoted wife, content to follow Napoleon's lead. Her political and social connections proved of great value to his career, and she enriched his personal life as well. Napoleon later lost much of his initial passion for Josephine, but he settled into a very comfortable marriage. All's well that ends well!

This whole episode may well have changed Napoleon's outlook on life. Always a hard worker, after Egypt he developed a well-deserved reputation for his constant devotion to work. And, given what lay just ahead, hard work was needed.

Figure 8-1:
Josephine was beautiful and cunning, and she needed both attributes to keep Napoleon as her husband. This is an early engraving after a painting by Isabey.

Being a Hero in a Troubled Nation

Napoleon was treated as a returning hero of mythic proportions. To the French people, he was Caesar and Alexander rolled into one. The streets were full of his admirers. The Council of Ancients (one of France's legislative bodies) gave him a standing ovation when he appeared before them.

Behind all the public show was a floundering government. Various political factions, ranging from radical Revolutionaries on one side to royalists on the other, were vying for power. Military success in the field, most especially by General André Masséna, had at least temporarily stymied the efforts of the Second Coalition (the alliance of Austria, Russia, and England to overthrow the French government), but domestic problems loomed. Some of the problems included the following:

✔ Some areas, such as the Vendée, were again considering secession from France. (In Chapter 4, I discuss earlier opposition to the Revolutionary government.)

✔ Chouan rebels, conservative Catholic royalists supported by the clergy and whose leaders were paid by the British, were threatening civil war.

✔ The highways were as unsafe as they had been in the years leading up to the Revolution. (Even Napoleon's baggage had been broken into on the trip to Paris.)

✔ Armed groups of hoodlums, some quite large, terrorized the populace.

Napoleon wondered out loud what had happened to his country, and it was a good question. The government and citizens understood that something needed to be done, but few could agree on what that something *was*.

Napoleon knew he was very popular, but he also understood the fleeting nature of popularity. The question *What have you done for me lately?* has sunk many a political career, and Napoleon was determined not to let it happen to him. Everywhere he looked, he saw incompetence and threats to his beloved French Republic, and he was determined to play a major role in protecting the gains of the Revolution.

At first, he considered becoming a member of the Directory. This step would have been simple enough but for the fact that he was only 30 and the constitution required Directory members to be at least 40. There was little support for changing a constitution to put a general on the Directory, so Napoleon had to dig deeper.

Analyzing the political situation

The French political situation was chaotic at best. The legislative branch had come under the strong influence of a strong royalist faction, and there was a possibility that royalists would soon control that branch of the government.

The executive wing, the Directory, was a major defender of the Revolution. Yes, it was corrupt and mainly interested in staying in power long enough to get rich (which didn't actually take that long, as it happens), but it was also more in tune with the wishes and needs of the people than was the legislative branch.

Another, perhaps surprising, supporter of the Revolution (and hence part of the "liberal" wing of government) was the army. In the old days, the army had been run by the nobility, but now there was scarcely a noble to be found in or out of the army. Made up largely of the very common people the Revolution was designed to protect, the army was, by and large, interested in protecting the Revolution. It had become a strong political force, and anyone who sought to change the government would need the support of the army.

Unveiling conspiracies

Against this backdrop, a major plot was underway to replace the government. Well, actually, there were at least two major plots. Our old friend Paul Barras (see Figure 8-2), a member of the Directory who had helped bring Napoleon to the forefront (see Chapter 3), was involved in a major effort to bring back a Bourbon monarchy. A corrupt womanizer to his very core, Barras was less a royalist than a man seeking additional power and wealth, in this case perhaps as many as 12 million francs.

Figure 8-2:
Paul Barras, seen in this 19th-century engraving, was a scoundrel, but few people had more influence on Napoleon's career.

In addition to Barras on the right, the minister of war, General Jean-Baptiste Bernadotte, a strong supporter of Jacobin causes, was considering leading a coup of his own. Bernadotte had married Napoleon's first girlfriend, Désirée Clary (see Chapter 5), and though he would serve in Napoleon's army, he would always be his rival and ultimately turn on him.

Barras and Bernadotte were not the only people involved in conspiracies. One of the major players in the third significant plot was none other than Napoleon's youngest brother, Lucien Bonaparte. Long active in Revolutionary politics, he had been elected to the Council of Five Hundred (the other legislative branch) and, just months earlier, had become its president.

Lucien was supporting a plot by Emmanuel Joseph Sieyès and Roger Ducos, both of whom he had helped become members of the Directory. Sieyès had been a major player in the very earliest days of the Revolution and now believed it was his job to give France a more stable and effective government, as well as to protect it from any royalist plots. To do that, Sieyès and his supporters believed they needed to replace the Directory with a three-man Consulate that would run France more or less as a dictatorship.

Sieyès and Lucien Bonaparte had enlisted the support of several other powerful politicians in Paris, including Joseph Fouché, Jean-Jacques Régis de Cambacérès, and Charles Maurice de Talleyrand-Périgord, better known simply as Talleyrand. As I explain in Chapter 7, Talleyrand had previously failed to alert the Turks of the French expedition to Egypt and had thus caused Napoleon a great deal of difficulty.

This group had the support of a number of other politicians, but all recognized that they needed the support of the army. To get that, they needed their "sword," a general who would support them and who could bring support of the army with him. Hmmmm. Who do you suppose will end up with *that* job?

Actually, Sieyès originally had someone else in mind. General Barthelemy Joubert was born in the same year as Napoleon and had established a good name for himself, largely in Italy. Sieyès thought he could control Joubert, which made him an ideal candidate. Unfortunately for these plans, to say nothing of the young Joubert, he was killed at the Battle of Novi in Italy on Napoleon's 30th birthday, August 15, 1799.

Providing a sword

Sieyès then turned to plan B. That would be B as in Bonaparte. Napoleon had far more to offer than any other general. For starters, he was a national hero. Any enterprise that involved him would have instant credibility and popularity, at least at the beginning. Napoleon was also one of the most competent people around. Not only was he an excellent and successful general, but he had already shown his administrative abilities in Italy, Malta, and Egypt. Moreover — and this was very important to Sieyès — Napoleon had well-established republican beliefs; he would be an excellent shield against any royalist efforts. Of course, Sieyès wasn't too happy with Napoleon's obvious ambition, but he figured he could keep that under control.

Besides, time was of the essence. Barras and Bernadotte were not going to dawdle forever; there was no time like the present to get things underway. Napoleon was offered the chance to play his role, and after some consideration, he accepted. He knew that something had to be done to improve France's government, and he wanted to be the one to do it.

The plot thickens

The conspirators began to take action, and at first all went well. On November 9, 1799, the Council of Ancients put Napoleon in charge of the troops in Paris and its outlying areas, and then it decreed that the legislative bodies would move to the suburbs, to a town called St. Cloud, for their own security. This move was really intended just to get them out of Paris proper and away from the prying eyes of Parisian citizens. Meanwhile, Talleyrand was sent to bribe Barras to resign from the Directory. The bribe was eagerly accepted.

The stage was set, but one of the actors did not behave as well as he could have. That would be none other than Napoleon. On November 10th, Napoleon first went to the Council of Ancients to convince them of the need for change. According to at least some eyewitnesses, Napoleon lost his cool and may even have become somewhat incoherent. He seemed, to some, to be threatening force. He was roundly booed and left the hall in disgrace.

Napoleon then went to the Council of Five Hundred, where Lucien was presiding, to seek their support for change. This encounter should have been a cakewalk, but again Napoleon found himself facing increasingly angry politicians. Curses were shouted, and Napoleon was actually physically attacked. Several soldiers came in and escorted him to safety. The members of the Council then turned on Lucien, demanding that he declare his brother an outlaw (see Figure 8-3). He refused but was able to calm the crowd down somewhat. He sent a note to Napoleon indicating that he had but a few minutes to act.

Napoleon's first thought was his brother's safety, so he sent a group of soldiers in to rescue Lucien. Ever the loyal brother, Lucien then addressed the soldiers who were assembled outside the Council's meeting hall — soldiers who were thoroughly confused as to what was going on — and told them that armed royalists were attempting to seize control and it was up to them to take action to protect the republic. Holding his sword up, Lucien promised to run it through Napoleon himself if necessary in the republic's defense.

Napoleon then spoke to his soldiers. He had really hoped not to have to use force in this coup, but force was clearly needed now, else he be declared an outlaw and shot. His composure now back in full order, he told his soldiers that he had attempted to speak to the Council and had been instead attacked with daggers. The soldiers were outraged; the drums sounded, and the grenadiers, bayonets fixed, marched into the hall. Many of the members of the Council took the opportunity to discover the joys of a quick exit through the windows.

Remaining members of the two branches of the legislature immediately met and appointed Napoleon, Sieyès, and Ducos as Consuls in a new provisional government. It was a bloodless coup; that, at least, had gone according to plan.

The days of November 9th and 10th fall into the Revolutionary calendar month of *Brumaire,* so Napoleon's rise to power is usually referred to as the *Coup d'état de Brumaire.*

Consolidating power

Napoleon was only one of three provisional Consuls and, in theory, not necessarily any more powerful than the other two. This fiction must have lasted all of a few minutes. Napoleon very quickly took charge, leading discussions about everything imaginable. Sieyès is said to have remarked that Napoleon was a man who knew how to do everything, was able to do everything, and wanted to do everything. He was exactly right. Napoleon and his new allies quickly appointed their supporters to important positions and began to write a constitution.

Napoleon was determined that the new constitution would be progressive and give new rights to the people. So the constitution included universal male suffrage at age 21 and a system of *plebiscites* (public votes) to confirm the new constitution and its new government. A legislative branch was established, but it was clear to one and all that the real power rested in the executive branch, embodied by the three Consuls.

Sieyès tried to marginalize Napoleon's power, but in the end the First Consul had the real power in the government, and Napoleon was to be First Consul. Sieyès was convinced to resign and accept the presidency of the Senate. Ducos also resigned and accepted a series of relatively minor political positions.

Napoleon then appointed Jean-Jacques Régis de Cambacérès, a respected lawyer, as Second Consul and Charles François Lebrun, a moderate known for his expertise in finances, as Third Consul (see Figure 8-4).

Figure 8-4:
This period engraving shows Napoleon and the other two Consuls, along with symbols showing peace, prosperity, and victory.

The French people adopted the new constitution on December 14, 1799. At the ripe old age of 30, Napoleon was the leader of France. A lot of things had contributed to his rise to power, including

- ✔ Personal characteristics such as his intelligence, determination, and force of will
- ✔ Family support
- ✔ Powerful and influential friends
- ✔ His willingness to take risks
- ✔ The opportunities afforded by the French Revolution and its aftermath
- ✔ His luck
- ✔ Most importantly, his sheer ability

Europe was about to find out just how important the events of late 1799 had been.

Securing domestic peace

Napoleon's first order of business as First Consul was to eliminate some of the internal threats to the public order. The previous government had been reluctant to send the army after the rebel bands, but Napoleon, aware that domestic peace was crucial to the success of his new government, had no such qualms. He sent soldiers in with a vengeance, along with proclamations that warned citizens that they would be shot on sight if caught collaborating with rebel groups.

Adding the carrot to the stick, Napoleon offered generous terms to those rebels who would renounce their efforts. He offered to allow nobles who had left during the Revolution, called *émigrés,* to return peacefully, though without having their lands restored. Priests, who had also suffered under the Revolution, were also given fair terms without actually restoring their powers.

By February 1800, most of France's internal disorder had been eliminated, and Napoleon could turn to other matters.

Chapter 9

Winning His Greatest Victories

● ●

In This Chapter

▶ Conquering Italy again

▶ Achieving imperial glory

● ●

After Napoleon took control of France in November 1799 (see Chapter 8), he began to institute a series of domestic reforms to improve living conditions in the country. Unfortunately, the enemies of the French Revolution were now the enemies of Napoleon, and for the next several years, Napoleon was forced to defend France against a series of coalitions, often led and bankrolled by England.

In this chapter, I discuss how Napoleon conquered the European continent by dealing with threats in Italy and Germany in the early 1800s.

Seeking Peace in Europe

After taking power, Napoleon was determined to consolidate gains that he (and France) had made in earlier years. His first efforts were in Egypt, where he ordered additional troops and supplies to be sent in relief of General Jean-Baptiste Kléber, whom he had left in charge just a few months earlier. He also began to organize his fleet to gain control of the Mediterranean and attack British trading vessels in the Atlantic. Finally, he prepared an expedition to the island of San Domingo to support a revolution there, which was being led by General Pierre Dominique Toussaint l'Ouverture.

Napoleon, naturally enough, wanted peace on the European continent. Peace would allow him to focus on securing France's gains in other territories, as well as to implement his domestic reforms (which I discuss in Chapter 19). To this end, Napoleon wrote a conciliatory letter to King George III of England, asking for peace. But England replied by saying that peace would come when the Bourbon monarchy was restored to the throne and France returned to its borders of 1789. (See Chapter 3 for details on how the Bourbons were removed from power during the French Revolution.) Meanwhile, England would continue its "just and defensive" war.

In other words, if France gave up all the territories she had gained and pretended that the French Revolution had never occurred, *then* England would make peace. This harsh response served only to strengthen the resolve of the French people to defend their Revolution against those outsiders who would destroy it in the name of the very Bourbons the French had tossed out of power.

Napoleon also wrote to Emperor Francis of Austria, with much the same result. Austria would pretend to consider peace, but the war would continue. In June 1799, England, Austria, and Russia had formed what was called the Second Coalition against France, and they were convinced that they had the upper hand. It would be up to Napoleon to call their bluff. The situation was not entirely bad from Napoleon's standpoint. For one thing, it allowed him to seize the moral high ground: He was seeking peace, but his enemies wanted nothing but the forceful overthrow of the French government.

There was another benefit as well. Military leaders need great victories to maintain their popularity. Julius Caesar certainly understood the political benefits of military success, and Napoleon was a student of Caesar. Domestic reforms take time, but Napoleon was determined to bring France new military glory quickly. And to do that, he turned once again to northern Italy.

Fighting the Austrians in Italy — Again!

While Napoleon had been in Egypt (see Chapter 7), the Austrian army had moved back into the very same areas that the French had pushed them out of in the 1796–1797 Italian campaign (see Chapter 6). As a result, in 1800, France was once again facing the Austrians (who were receiving British financial support), and once again they would clash in Germany and northern Italy. In southwestern Germany, a French army under the command of General Jean Victor Moreau faced Austrian forces led by General Paul Kray. The Austrians were east of the Rhine River in the Black Forest, and the situation was more or less a stalemate.

Russian troops led by Field Marshal Alexander Vasilivich Suvorov had been a part of this mix; in 1799 they had actually driven the French out of the northern Italian areas that Napoleon had acquired for France with the Treaty of Campo Formio (see Chapter 6). But some of Suvorov's army had been badly defeated by General André Masséna in September 1799, and Suvorov and the rest of his army were chased out of the area. This defeat led Russian Tsar Paul to pull Russia out of the Second Coalition.

As he did in 1796, Napoleon led the French army into Italy in 1800. But this time he was not just a general; he was the leader of France. In fact, he was not technically in command of his new army, called the Army of the Reserve. To assure a separation between the executive leadership of the nation and the military, the new constitution prevented a Consul from commanding an army. So Napoleon put his friend Louis Alexandre Berthier in command. But who do you think was really calling the shots?

In 1796, had Napoleon moved along the southern coast of France to join an army that was already there. This time, he was leading an army into Italy, and he attempted to surprise the Austrians by doing what they least expected. He led his army through the snowy passes of the Alps and descended upon them from the north. He planned to go through the Great Saint Bernard Pass (on the Italian-French border), sweep into Milan, and move south to face the main Austrian force led by General Michael Melas.

Meanwhile, General André Masséna, fresh from his victory over the Russians, had taken command of a French army in Genoa, which Napoleon anticipated would keep a significant number of Austrians away from his attack. But Masséna's army was in terrible shape (about as bad as Napoleon's army had been in 1796), and before long he was trapped behind the walls of Genoa, hoping for rescue by Napoleon. He had rations for 30 days, barely enough to hold out until the end of May, so Napoleon needed to hurry.

Trekking through the Alps

Napoleon and his Army of the Reserve began their trek through the Alps, and on May 15, 1800 they entered the Great Saint Bernard Pass (elevation 8,100 feet). This portion of the trip was made famous by a well-known painting by Jacques-Louis David, probably the most important French painter of the Napoleonic period. You may well have seen it: Napoleon on a rearing white horse; his cape flowing in the wind; the names of Hannibal, Charlemagne, and Bonaparte inscribed on rocks at his feet. (Hannibal had passed that way to torment the Romans in the Punic Wars, while Charlemagne had crossed the Alps to defend the Pope in the eighth century.)

The reality of the passage was likely less romantic and more dangerous. You may think of May flowers, but the Great Saint Bernard Pass is often quite snowed in at that time of year, and Napoleon was on a mule for much of the trip (an image shown in another painting, this one by Paul Delaroche). The French had to slip past Fort Bard, which the Austrians had refused to surrender, but they did have the pleasure of receiving cheese and wine at the Hospice of Saint Bernard. The few Austrians encountered along the way were stunned by the French presence. Napoleon said it best, "We have struck like a thunderbolt . . . the enemy can scarcely believe it."

Napoleon's plan worked like a charm. He sent units against all known Austrian forces in the area and gained victories over each of them. On June 2, 1800, he entered Milan much as he had in 1796, a victor over the occupying Austrians. Once again, he was received as a hero by the people of Milan. He ordered the restoration of the Cisalpine Republic (see Chapter 6), a move that solidified his role in the historic unification of Italy.

Napoleon was a blur of action, planning the campaign, dealing with issues in France, receiving the adulations of the Milanese, and establishing a *very* close relationship with the noted Italian opera singer Madame Giuseppina Grassini. Grassini performed at the famed opera house La Scala and was frequently seen with her lover, Napoleon. (Many historians believe that in 1814, she was also the lover of Napoleon's famous nemesis, Arthur Wellesley, the Duke of Wellington, the victor at the Battle of Waterloo. More on him in Chapter 15.)

Facing the Austrian response

Austrian General Melas had not fully understood the importance of French movements in northern Italy. But as the end of May approached, he began to understand the danger. French control of northern Italy would cut him off from his home base in Austria, a disaster for any army.

Melas began to organize for a move north to meet Napoleon, and he was prepared to lift his siege of Genoa. About that time, Masséna surrendered — he was out of rations and had no real choice — but requested quite favorable terms. Melas was so concerned with Napoleon that he met those terms, which allowed Masséna to march out with his army to rejoin other French forces. Meanwhile, Napoleon's French army tightened the noose and completely severed Melas's communications with Austria.

Faulty intelligence

Napoleon quickly moved south to engage the Austrians, and the two armies began to converge near the town of Alessandria and a small nearby village named Marengo. Napoleon began to fear that the Austrians were fleeing, and so on June 13th he sent two units to cut off their possible escape routes. One of these units was commanded by General Louis Charles Desaix, who had served with Napoleon in Egypt and was one of Napoleon's best friends.

Napoleon was unclear both as to the location and size of the Austrian forces. He received a report that the Austrian forces around the town of Alessandria were light. He sent only one scout to confirm this report, and this scout failed to fully report obvious signs of an Austrian effort to build up its forces in the area, such as the construction of a new bridge. Moreover, a double agent gave Napoleon misinformation. Thus, Napoleon thought he was facing only the Austrian rear guard that was covering the army's retreat, rather than the main Austrian force.

The Battle of Marengo

On June 14th, the Austrians made a surprise move on Napoleon's forces at Marengo. Napoleon had supposed that the Austrians were fleeing; instead, they had consolidated their forces and now outnumbered Napoleon's army 30,000 to 22,000. It didn't take Napoleon long to realize his mistake, and he quickly sent urgent messages to the two French units out looking for retreating Austrians. His note to Desaix was quite to the point: "I had thought to attack Mélas. He has attacked me first. For God's sake come up if you still can." But Desaix and all other French forces were likely too far away to be of any help.

The battle began, and it was soon clear that the French were in serious trouble. Outnumbered, outgunned, and low on ammunition, things were looking rather grim. The fighting was deadly, much of it at point-blank range. By mid-afternoon, the Austrians were certain of victory and began to regroup for a final push. Mélas, tired, had actually retired from the field, leaving the final push to subordinates.

Then, a miracle occurred. General Desaix had been delayed by poor roads and had not gotten all that far from Marengo. When he heard guns firing, he followed the old admonition to "march to the sound of the guns" and headed back to Marengo. Thus, before the Austrians could make their final push, Desaix arrived on the scene, exclaiming that this battle was lost, "but there is still time to win another."

The French quickly regrouped, with the fresh troops inspiring the others to renew their fight. A massive artillery barrage prevented the Austrians from moving forward, and when the French counterattacked, the Austrians collapsed (see Figure 9-1). The victory became a rout. Thoroughly beaten, the Austrians sued for peace, requesting only that they be allowed to retire to Austrian territory.

The Austrian casualties were much heavier than the French, but Napoleon suffered a deep personal blow. General Desaix, whose timely action had saved the day, was killed in the battle. Upon hearing of his friend's death, Napoleon said, "Why am I not allowed to weep?" He ordered monuments erected and eulogies spoken to the memory of his friend, and Desaix's statue is near Napoleon's at the battlefield to this day.

Napoleon's sadness was later compounded by the news that on the very same day, General Jean-Baptiste Kléber, whom Napoleon had left in charge in Egypt, had been assassinated by a religious fanatic. French forces there were now in the hands of far less capable leaders, and within a year they would be forced by the British to withdraw.

Figure 9-1: This 1824 engraving by George Crunkshank after Carl Vernet shows the action at the Battle of Marengo.

NAPOLEON'S DECISIVE VICTORY OVER THE AUSTRIANS, AT THE BATTLE OF MARENGO.

The victory at Marengo had almost been a disaster, in more ways than one. Had Napoleon lost, the legitimacy of his government may have been questioned. He ruled at least in part due to his image as a leader who simply never failed, an image that a defeat at Marengo would have dashed forever. Napoleon always understood that he was as little as one defeat away from oblivion. To keep his position, he needed to keep winning victories, at least for now. Napoleon learned one lesson: In the future, he would send out more than one scout.

Napoleon returned in triumph to Milan, where he was warmly welcomed by an adoring public. He sent letters to Austria's Emperor Francis and opened peace negotiations. He returned to Paris in July 1800 to deal with domestic issues. There, as in Milan, he was welcomed by crowds that were convinced he was invincible.

Securing the peace

Napoleon was in great spirits, but he soon discovered that the peace talks with Austria were bogged down. Disgusted with the situation and fearful that the Austrians were simply stalling while they regrouped, Napoleon ordered General Moreau's Army of the Rhine to find and destroy the Austrian army under General Kray. Moreau caught up to Kray at Hohenlinden, near Munich, and on December 3, 1800 won a great victory. A series of other victories followed, which left the Austrian court despondent. On Christmas Day, Kray and Moreau signed an armistice.

On the February 8, 1801, Austria and France signed the Peace of Luneville. Napoleon was generous to the Austrians. He wanted a lasting peace and realized that a nation that is treated badly in a treaty may feel compelled to regain its honor in the near future. Under the Peace of Luneville, Austria

- ✔ Agreed to the terms of the earlier Treaty of Campo Formio (see Chapter 6).
- ✔ Gave France the left (west) bank of the Rhine River.

Later treaties with Naples and Tuscany brought peace to the European continent. Only England remained in opposition to France; the war of the Second Coalition was over.

Fighting the Austrians and Russians — Yet Again!

For the next several years, Napoleon ruled as First Consul and instituted a number of important reforms in France. (I discuss these reforms in Part IV.) Peace with England came and went, as I discuss in Chapter 21. But since this chapter is all about conquering a continent, I now tell you about Napoleon's most famous victorious campaign, that of 1805.

Setting the stage

In 1804, Napoleon was proclaimed Napoleon I, Emperor of the French, and, shortly thereafter, King of Italy. (I explain how these titles came to him in Chapter 20.) He sought peace with all the nations of Europe. England, however, was uninterested in allowing Napoleon to rule.

Stubborn England

England was organizing a Third Coalition, which included Russia and Austria, to threaten France's security. Napoleon realized that as long as England was able to finance coalitions against France, the French people would not be secure, and an overall peace would not be possible. This situation was unacceptable to France. Napoleon felt he would have to invade England to finally bring peace to Europe. To be fair, England felt that French control of so much territory, especially right across the English Channel, was a threat to her own security.

Napoleon massed his troops along the English Channel, with his headquarters at the French port city of Boulogne, just a stone's throw from the British coast. Ah, but therein lay the rub. To get from here to there required ships, of which England had many and France had few. This was long before the construction of the *Chunnel,* the tunnel that now allows for high-speed train travel between England and France beneath the Channel. Don't think Napoleon didn't think of building one, but the technology just wasn't there.

The Third Coalition

Why would other European nations want to engage Napoleon yet again? After all, wasn't there peace on most of the Continent? Unfortunately, the usual suspects still weren't happy:

- The Pope didn't appreciate Napoleon's being crowned King of Italy.

- Austria had several grievances:

    - She still resented being ousted from Italy.

    - Napoleon's increasing influence in Germany positively galled her.

    - Napoleon had created new allies in Germany — Bavaria, Baden, and Württemberg — greatly reducing Austria's influence.

- Russia feared French expansion into Central Europe and an imbalance of power that might threaten her interests in the east.

And behind everything was England and her money. Determined to roll back the clock, England made it clear to one and all that she was quite prepared to bankroll any additional wars against Napoleonic France.

Trouble brewing

Now, you may think that the Austrians, the Russians, and the Pope had learned their lesson. But you would be wrong. While Napoleon was reorganizing his army along the coast, including giving it the name that stuck for the rest of his reign, *La Grande Armée* (the Great Army), moves were afoot in the east to challenge Napoleon. Austria and Russia were moving across central Europe, and Austria, Russia, and some of the smaller countries in Italy were threatening France's interests in that country. Notice a trend here?

Napoleon didn't want a Continental war, but he was quite prepared to do what was necessary to protect the gains he had made, both at home and abroad. If the Russians and Austrians were determined to do battle, so be it. But he would not attack them in force in Italy, as he had done in two previous campaigns. Instead, he would move his *Grande Armée* straight across Europe to confront what became known as the Third Coalition head-on. The campaign that followed, known as the War of the Third Coalition, was Napoleon's greatest and assured him a place in the pantheon of great commanders.

Dividing and conquering

In terms of raw numbers, the Austrian and Russian forces moving westward were quite impressive. Each side could, at least on paper, promise some 200,000 troops. But the numbers of the Third Coalition alone did not tell the complete story:

- The Austrians had sent a vanguard fairly far west, commanded by General Karl Mack.

- The Russians, under General Mikhail Kutusov, were moving to join Mack but were still quite far to the rear.

- The main Austrian force was still near Vienna.

- Another Austrian force, commanded by Archduke Charles, the Austrian emperor's brother, was in Italy, being held at bay by Masséna.

Napoleon had an army of some 210,000 men. If he could bring that army to bear against the divided Austrian and Russian forces, victory should be easy. There was just one little problem: Napoleon and his army were on the English Channel, several hundred miles from Ülm, the German city where Mack was headed.

As he had done in Italy in 1800, where he surprised the Austrians by marching through the Alps to "descend like a thunderbolt," Napoleon pulled off one of the most amazing military maneuvers in history. He marched his entire *Grande Armée* from the coast clear across Europe into Germany — in secret! No Bulletins were issued save those designed to give the impression that the army was still in Boulogne. An army of almost a quarter million men marched across Europe, and its enemies had not a clue what was about to happen to them.

Austrian General Mack had occupied Ülm and was busying himself improving the fortifications and waiting for the Russian reinforcements to arrive. He had approximately 50,000 men under his command. But he was a man without any idea of his real situation. Napoleon not only moved his army to Ülm, he moved it *around* that city, completely encircling the Austrians. Mack made several efforts to extricate himself from the situation, but it was no use. He had been completely bamboozled by Napoleon, and on October 20, 1805, he surrendered to the French. As he presented himself to Napoleon, he said, "Here you have the unfortunate General Mack." Unfortunate indeed. Mack was allowed to return to Vienna, where he was promptly court-martialed.

A few days after taking Ülm, Napoleon went to Munich, where he was received much as he had been in Milan twice before. He enjoyed his rest there but could stay only a few days. He had defeated a substantial Austrian army, but the main conflict lay ahead. Archduke Charles and his brother, Archduke John, had over 100,000 men in northern Italy and were beginning to move toward Austria, having heard of the disaster at Ülm.

Capturing Vienna

Napoleon moved quickly down the Danube River toward the Austrian capital city of Vienna. Several times, he wrote to Austrian Emperor Francis suggesting peace. Francis probably should have agreed, but he was convinced that his brothers would move up from Italy to join the Austrian and Russian armies north of Vienna and that together they could crush Napoleon.

Meanwhile, French forces were defeating the Austrians in every skirmish they fought, and Vienna was in clear danger. After defeating a substantial Russian force, the French moved into Vienna, and Napoleon occupied the palace of Schönbrunn, one of the world's most beautiful. With the capture of Vienna, Napoleon gained enormous stores of food, ammunition, and other materials necessary for the campaign.

Napoleon's mood was decidedly dampened, however, when he heard news of a naval disaster at the Battle of Trafalgar, which I explain in Chapter 11. Clearly, it was time to crush his opponents.

Preparing for combat

Napoleon moved north to Brünn. The Austrians and Russians had recently evacuated that town and move some 50 miles to the east, taking positions at the fortress of Olmütz, where they hoped to be joined in time by the Archduke Charles and his men. There was also the possibility that Prussia would renounce her neutrality and join the Coalition, a move that would be a disaster for the French. Clearly, Napoleon needed to take quick action before any of these possibilities came to pass. As things stood now, Napoleon had the advantage, but that could quickly change for the worse. So he moved his army east and took up positions at Austerlitz, a short distance from Brünn.

Russian Tsar Alexander I, a 28 year old who had recently advanced to the throne with the murder of his father, Tsar Paul I, arrived to join the Austrian Emperor Francis. Their combined army numbered around 85,000 men. Napoleon had an army of some 73,000 men in the immediate vicinity, with other units in the region. These were not terrible odds, as long as the Prussians or the Archduke didn't enter into the equation.

By the way, Tsar Paul I was a bit insane and also was quite pro-French in his foreign policy. There is a real possibility that his son, Alexander, participated in his murder. Ah, the joys of family politics! In any event, Russia's foreign policy toward France abruptly changed as a result of Alexander's accession to the throne.

Conveying weakness

Napoleon sent General Jean Savary as an envoy to the tsar. He spent several days at Olmütz, mainly trying to convince the tsar that Napoleon was weak and most anxious for peace. The brash young tsar was taken in by this ruse and began to demand that the Coalition forces attack Napoleon and end his reign once and for all.

This, of course, is exactly what Napoleon wanted. He was certain that the key to victory would be to convince the Austrians and Russians that he, Napoleon, was in a weakened state and thus entice them to attack before their reinforcements arrived. To further give this impression, Napoleon moved his troops off the high ground, known as the Pratzen Heights, a clear sign that he was considering retreating. (No army ever voluntarily gives up the high ground.) The allies, sensing blood, quickly moved onto the heights and prepared their next move.

When General Savary returned, he brought with him an emissary from Tsar Alexander, one Prince Peter Dolgoruki. Dolgoruki was arrogant and lectured Napoleon on the political realities, as he saw them, informing Napoleon that the key to peace was for Napoleon to give up pretty much all that he had gained. Napoleon held his temper in check, giving the impression that he could not completely disagree with Dolgoruki, who reported Napoleon's "weakness" to his superiors. The trap was set and would soon be sprung!

On December 1, 1805, the night before the battle, Napoleon went on a tour of his positions. His soldiers, inspired by the sight of him and remembering that the next day was the anniversary of his coronation as emperor (see Chapter 20), lit huge bonfires and torches of straw, crying out "Vive l' Empereur!" ("Long live the Emperor!") as he passed by. Napoleon later said that that evening had been the finest of his life. Napoleon wrote that he expected all would go well the next day, but that if the outcome were in any doubt, he would personally lead his soldiers into battle.

The Battle of Austerlitz is also sometimes called the Battle of the Three Emperors, because Tsar (Emperor) Alexander of Russia, Emperor Francis of Austria, and Emperor Napoleon of France were all present at the scene. When the battle was over, only one of the three would be pleased with the outcome.

Fighting at Austerlitz

The Coalition allies were convinced that they had Napoleon on the ropes. They were also convinced that he was far weaker than he really was, as

Napoleon had managed to conceal much of his strength, including the late arrival of reinforcements to his right flank.

And then there was the famous fog of Austerlitz. An early morning heavy mist or fog completely obscured Napoleon's center from view of those atop the Pratzen Heights. Not expecting an attack on the Pratzen itself, Allied forces, most of whom were commanded by Russian General Friedrich Buxhöwden, streamed off the heights to attack Napoleon's presumably weak right flank. They soon found resistance stronger than anticipated, which only encouraged their commanders to order more reinforcements from their center. The Allied position on the Pratzen Heights was now far weaker than it should have been, but the fog and a small hill had successfully hidden Napoleon's true intentions.

Around 9:00 in the morning, Napoleon judged the Allied center to be sufficiently weakened for him to strike. He ordered Marshal Nicolas Soult to attack the center. As the sun began to burn off the morning fog, the Allied commanders were astonished to discover that a massive French force, spearheaded by General Dominique Vandamme's forces, was sweeping up the hill right toward them! They undertook emergency measures to try to stop the French, but it was to no avail. In a short time, they were forced off the Heights. An Allied counterattack threatened the French position there, but when Napoleon sent in his elite fighting force, the cavalry of the Imperial Guard, the French controlled the Pratzen Heights once and for all (see Figure 9-2).

Figure 9-2: This engraving from about 1830 shows Napoleon on the Pratzen Heights with his marshals behind him and prisoners on the ground. The battle rages in the valley below.

After the Pratzen Heights were secured, Soult, joined now by the infantry of the Imperial Guard, was able to send his forces down the Heights in pursuit of Buxhöwden's Russians. Buxhöwden found himself between a hammer and anvil, and he suffered tremendous losses. Many Russian soldiers tried to escape across some frozen lakes, but French artillery broke the ice, and thousands drowned in the freezing water. By now, the Allied sovereigns, Tsar Alexander and Emperor Francis, were leaving the field. The battle was over shortly after 4:00 in the afternoon.

The Russian right flank, commanded by General Peter Bagration, retreated in good order. He had been having some success against the French left wing, but when he saw that all was lost, he was able to extricate his men. His actions made him the only true Allied hero of the day; all other glory was claimed by the French.

Gaining a glorious victory

And glory there was to claim. At the end of the day, the Russians alone had lost 18,000 men. The devastating Allied losses also included 180 artillery pieces and 30,000 prisoners of war, including 20 generals. In contrast, about 1,400 French were killed.

When the Austrian losses at Ülm are included, it is clear that the forces of the Third Coalition had been not only defeated but humiliated by the French campaign. Prussia quickly gave up any thought of joining the now-discredited Coalition, and the Russians limped back home. Pursuing French forces may have done more damage to the retreating Russians and even captured the tsar, but Alexander fooled the French into thinking an armistice had been signed, delaying pursuit until the Russians were safely gone. This blunder didn't bother Napoleon a great deal, as he generally had very little respect for the Russian army and anticipated that they would go home and cease meddling in the affairs of Western Europe.

The Russians could retreat home, but Austria really had nowhere to go and nothing to do. Further fighting would simply have added to its casualty lists. Austrian Emperor Francis requested a personal meeting with Napoleon, which Napoleon granted. An armistice soon followed, with Napoleon warning his commanders to be prepared in case of renewed hostilities, a definite possibility if Archduke Charles arrived on the scene. This was unlikely, however, and negotiations for a peace treaty soon commenced.

Napoleon was usually generous in victory, but he was bitter at continued Austrian opposition to his rule and determined to punish her once and for all. The subsequent Treaty of Pressburg, signed on December 26, 1805, stripped Austria of substantial territory in Italy and Germany and required her to pay a large indemnity. As he twice had done in his Italian campaigns, Napoleon ordered a large number of art and historic treasures sent to Paris. The French also gained a couple thousand cannon and numerous additional military supplies, including much-needed horses.

Francis also gave Napoleon his personal word to never again fight against Napoleonic France. It was a promise he would break all too soon. Francis also was told to fire his foreign minister, Count Johann Cobenzl, whom Napoleon blamed for having been heavily influenced (and paid) by the British to get Austria into the Third Coalition.

Rewarding his soldiers

Napoleon understood that his victories belonged as much to his officers and men as they did to him. He was careful to point out brave or brilliant actions taken by individuals and units, and to give medals to all who were deserving of them. After Austerlitz, Napoleon was especially generous because he recognized the very special importance of the victory. In his proclamation of December 3rd, the day after the battle, he proclaimed, *"Soldats! Je suis content de vous!"* (Soldiers! I am pleased with you!) I provide an excerpt of the proclamation in the sidebar "Napoleon's proclamation after the Battle of Austerlitz."

In his Bulletins (written accounts of his actions published on a regular basis), Napoleon also listed numerous men and units for special recognition. This gave them recognition within the army as well as back in France, as the Bulletins were published and widely distributed (see Chapter 18).

Words are nice, but Napoleon gave his soldiers far more than simple recognition:

- ✔ By Imperial Decree, he gave widows of those killed in the battle lifetime pensions, ranging from 6,000 francs per year to widows of generals to 200 francs per year to widows of privates.

- ✔ He personally adopted the children of those killed, finding husbands for daughters and jobs for sons.

- ✔ He also provided for these children's education and allowed each to add the name *Napoleon* to his or her own.

Soldiers who had been wounded received bonus pay, and countless promotions and awards were given out, including France's top honor that had been organized by Napoleon himself, the Legion of Honor. Napoleon also honored the brave officers and men on the Allied side, mentioning some in his Bulletins and often seeing to it that their commanders were made aware of their bravery. This was good politics, as Napoleon hoped to be at peace with these countries, and establishing good relations with other armies is never a bad thing.

Napoleon's proclamation after the Battle of Austerlitz

Napoleon won what was generally considered his greatest victory at the Battle of Austerlitz on December 2, 1805. The next day, he issued a proclamation (which I reproduce here only in part) to his soldiers to express his great satisfaction with them. The proclamation comes from my book *Imperial Glory: The Bulletins of Napoleon's Grande Armée, 1805–1814* (Greenhill).

Soldiers! I am pleased with you. On the day of Austerlitz, you have justified what I expected from your intrepidity. You have decorated your eagles with an immortal glory. In less than four hours an army of 100,000 men, commanded by the Emperors of Russia and Austria, has been cut down or dispersed. . . . Thus, in two months the third coalition is conquered and dissolved. Peace can no longer be at a great distance; but, as I promised to my people before crossing the Rhine, I will only make a peace that gives you some guarantees and assures some recompenses to our allies . . . Soldiers! When everything necessary to the happiness and prosperity of our country will have been achieved, I will lead you back to France. There you will be the objects of my most tender solicitudes. My people will see you again with joy, and it will be enough for you to say: "I was at the battle of Austerlitz," for them to reply, "There is a brave man!"

The Battle of Austerlitz is generally considered Napoleon's greatest military victory. It showed the world the depth of his ability to engage in virtually every aspect of warfare and to combine them all into a devastating defeat for his enemies. It ranks with some of the greatest victories in history and would alone mark Napoleon as one of history's great commanders.

Austerlitz destroyed the Third Coalition and further isolated England. It should have ushered in an era of peace and prosperity for all of Europe. Unfortunately, not everyone saw it that way, and war would continue.

Chapter 10

Conquering a Continent

- -

In This Chapter

▶ Fighting the Prussians and the Russians

▶ Teaching the Austrians a lesson (again!)

- -

After winning the Battle of Austerlitz in Austria in December 1805 (see Chapter 9), Napoleon returned to Paris in late January 1806, once again a national hero. He had just defeated all but one of France's enemies — that would be England, of course — and peace and prosperity seemed possible. In this chapter, I discuss what happened to foil hopes for peace and how Napoleon gained control of much of Europe.

Reorganizing Europe

Napoleon took quick action to try to secure peace in Europe. For example,

✔ He granted some new territory to Prussia in exchange for her continued neutrality.

✔ He took steps to eliminate the ancient Holy Roman Empire, headed by Emperor Francis of Austria. In July 1806, Napoleon got 16 German states to leave the Holy Roman Empire and join a new organization, the Confederation of the Rhine. These states would be allied to, and under the protection of, France. In time, many of them would institute reforms similar to those Napoleon promoted in France (see Chapter 19). This action effectively spelled the end of the Holy Roman Empire, though that name would persist until World War I.

✔ Napoleon sought to secure his position through the establishment of blood ties:

• He arranged the marriage of his stepson, Eugène de Beauharnais, to Princess Amelia Augusta, the daughter of the King of Bavaria, a key kingdom in the area. Bavaria had refused to join the Third Coalition against France and had been invaded by Austria. Bavaria had provided some 25,000 soldiers in support of the French in 1805, and she was now reaping her rewards.

- He installed his brother, Joseph, as the King of Naples, ousting the pro-British King Ferdinand IV and Queen Caroline. Joseph became known as a progressive, reform-oriented monarch (see Figure 10-1). As he did with all his conquests in Italy, as well as the rest of Europe, Napoleon gave people new rights and reforms, and he eliminated repressive regimes and feudalistic social and political systems.

- He installed his brother, Louis, as King of Holland.

Even England seemed a possible partner in peace. The strongly anti-French prime minister, William Pitt, had died in 1806. (Many people believe that news of Napoleon's victory at the Battle of Austerlitz led directly to Pitt's demise.) In his place was Lord William Grenville, who, along with Foreign Minister Sir Charles James Fox, wanted peace with France. France and England opened negotiations, but they eventually failed, especially after Fox died later in the year. A new British government soon took over, dashing those short-lived hopes for peace.

Figure 10-1:
This German engraving from the period shows Napoleon's brother, Joseph, as the King of Naples and Sicily.

Tussling with Prussia and Russia

Prussian King William III was not one of Europe's brightest lights. Napoleon had given Prussia some territory, but even so, Prussia was suspicious and concerned regarding French intentions in Germany. The Confederation of the Rhine was seen as a threat, as was the stationing of large French armies near the Prussian border. Napoleon did what he could to establish good relations — he much preferred diplomacy to war — but he was dealing with a king easily swayed by members of his court, who were anxious to go to war with Napoleon.

Chief among the proponents of war was the king's wife, Queen Louise. She headed what could be called the war party in the Prussian court, and she never missed a chance to promote her cause. Her husband, weak and vacillating man that he was, was no match for her determination. Aware that England and Russia were forming a Fourth Coalition, King William tried to use that fact to his advantage. With Russian support, he demanded that French troops evacuate all of Germany. The evacuation had been likely prior to King William's demand, but after it, the French troops were there to stay.

The 36-year-old king needed a reality check:

- ✔ The Prussian army was large, but it was unbelievably old-fashioned and incapable of fighting a modern Napoleonic war; it was poorly organized, slow, and lacking leadership.
- ✔ The Prussians would be fighting a French army that had just swept the field, led by a man who was remaking the face of warfare.

Ah, but the Prussians had Russian support and English money and promises. Mind you, this was support from the same Russian army that had just been humiliated by the French, and the same English money and promises that had been less than effective at Austerlitz. And at Austerlitz, the Third Coalition allies had Austria, which was now allied to France. It was a fool's errand for the Prussian army to take on France, but the kingdom's leaders were determined to play it out. Had they joined the allies at Austerlitz, perhaps they could have made a real difference. Now, they were just committing suicide.

Routing Prussian forces

Apparently determined to hand their collective heads to Napoleon on a platter, the Prussians ignored the obvious need to wait for their Russian allies to join them before engaging the French. In August 1806, the Prussian army advanced toward the French armies that were mobilizing to meet it. Much like Austrian General Mack at Ülm (see Chapter 9), the Prussians advanced too far, too fast, and found themselves isolated. Worse yet, they were also divided, with one part of their army facing Napoleon at Jena, Germany and another facing Marshal Louis Davout at Auerstädt.

On October 14, 1806, Napoleon thought he was facing the entire Prussian army, but he was really facing only a small force of 38,000 men led by General Friedrich Hohenlohe. Napoleon had in excess of 90,000 men, but Hohenlohe thought he was facing a much smaller French force.

As had happened at Austerlitz, when a morning fog lifted at Jena, Hohenlohe discovered the true situation, but it was too late. He quickly called for reinforcements, which never came, and he did what he could to withstand the French advance. By 3 p.m., his men were retreating, and Marshal Joachim Murat's spirited cavalry pursuit turned the Prussian defeat into a rout. Total French losses were around 5,000 at Jena, compared with Prussian losses of over 25,000.

Napoleon was understandably elated, but he soon learned that he had not faced the main Prussian army after all. That army, commanded by King William, was facing Marshal Davout at Auerstädt. Prussian forces numbered 63,000 while Davout had only 27,000, but the result was the same: a complete French victory. Davout's triumph over such overwhelming odds entered him into the ranks of Napoleon's finest marshals. (In contrast, Marshal Jean Bernadotte ignored Napoleon's orders to move in support of Davout, which was an outrage and a sign of problems to come.)

In a week, Napoleon had completely defeated the Prussians, killed or captured tens of thousands of their men, captured all their artillery and baggage, and made it clear to one and all that the French victories in 1805 had not been flukes.

Napoleon followed France's twin victories at Jena and Auerstädt by marching on the capital city of Berlin, stopping along the way to visit the tomb of Frederick the Great at Potsdam. Napoleon entered Berlin on October 27th and took possession of an immense arsenal. Meanwhile, an unchastened (and foolish) King William fled to Königsberg (modern-day Kaliningrad in Russia) to await Russian reinforcements.

While in Berlin in 1806, Napoleon issued orders that France, its territories, and its allies were prohibited from trading with Great Britain. The British had tried to starve France economically by sinking her merchant ships; now France would play the economic warfare game with new rules. These sanctions would become known as the Continental System and would have decidedly mixed results for Napoleon. (See Chapter 21 for more on the Continental System.)

Fighting a winter battle against Russia

Notwithstanding the French success against Prussia, to say nothing of French success against the Russians at Austerlitz a year earlier, Russian forces led by General Levin Bennigsen continued to move west to confront the French. Napoleon's forces were tired and definitely deserved a break, but the Russians were determined to force what Bennigsen thought was his advantage.

Napoleon, never one to sit back and wait for his enemy to force a fight on its terms, moved into Poland, taking Warsaw and moving north. After some inconclusive skirmishes, including the Battle of Pultusk on December 26, 1806, the two forces met at the town of Eylau, sometimes called Prussian-Eylau. (Eylau is now the town of Bagrationovsk in Russia, named for the Russian general Peter Bagration.)

It would be hard to imagine worse fighting conditions than those faced by the French and Russians during the two-day Battle of Eylau on February 7–8, 1807. It was bitter cold and snowing heavily much of the time. Bennigsen had some 67,000 men to Napoleon's 45,000, but Napoleon could count on at least some reinforcements in short order.

On the first day of the battle, the two sides fought for control of the city. The fighting was desperate, and it was often difficult to see what was going on. By evening, however, the French had captured the city. That was important to Napoleon but perhaps even more so to his soldiers, who now had decent shelter from the bitter night to follow.

The next day saw more of the same bitter fighting for control of the city. While a blizzard howled about them, soldiers fought, often hand-to-hand, for control of small pieces of land. Napoleon's headquarters were in a church, and at one point his personal guard was surprised by a substantial Russian force that was nearly able to capture Napoleon himself! The Russians, not fully realizing their opportunity, didn't push their advantage and were eventually driven away. Even so, it was a close call.

As the day wore on, the Russians appeared to be gaining the upper hand. Their reinforcements were arriving before the French reinforcements, and the French situation looked alarming. A massive cavalry attack led by Marshal Murat at least temporarily devastated the Russian center, and Marshal Davout pushed back the Russian left. But evening fell before either side could gain advantage, and overnight Bennigsen withdrew to the east. Napoleon held the field and could thus claim the victory, but it was an indecisive bloodbath, with both sides losing perhaps as many as 25,000. Neither side was in any condition to keep fighting, and each retired to winter quarters.

Finding a Polish love

When Napoleon had first entered Warsaw, the Poles had sought to take advantage of his presence. Poland had historically been claimed by one major power or another, most notably Russia, Austria, and Prussia — three countries hated by Polish patriots and generally at war with Napoleon. Poland had long hoped to become an independent state. Napoleon had the power to make that happen, and the Poles pressed their case to him, figuring he wouldn't mind doing something that would stick it to his enemies.

As part of their approach, they used a secret weapon named Marie Walewska. This 20-year-old ravishing beauty was married to wealthy 71-year-old Count Anastase Walewski. Polish patriots, including her husband, persuaded her that she should do whatever was necessary to convince Napoleon to support their cause. Napoleon, who was lonely and not necessarily ill-disposed toward warm female companionship on cold Polish winter nights, was quite taken by young Marie — and her Polish cause.

They were soon sharing a bed, and the relationship blossomed. Napoleon fell quite in love with Marie, and the feeling was mutual. When Napoleon was apart from her, he wrote her letters that were every bit as passionate as those he wrote to Josephine. (Speaking of Josephine, she eventually became aware of Marie's existence, but there was little she could do about the relationship.)

After the Battle of Eylau, Napoleon moved his headquarters in Poland to the castle at Osteröde and then to the mansion called Finkenstein, where he spent more than two months. Marie joined him there, and together they spent what for Napoleon were some of the happiest times of his life.

Though the lovers would part company when Napoleon left to continue his campaign against the Russians, they would meet again several times over the coming years. Marie joined him in Paris and, in 1809, for several weeks in Vienna. That visit provided the lovers more than just the great pleasure of their mutual company, as Marie became pregnant with Napoleon's child. In May 1810, she gave birth to Alexandre Florian Joseph Walewski. He was an illegitimate son, but when Napoleon's nephew became the Emperor of France many years later, Alexander was given the post of foreign minister. Alexander's descendents are today the only living direct descendents of Napoleon.

The birth of Napoleon's son proved that the lack of children with Josephine was not Napoleon's fault. As I discuss in Chapter 20, the lack of an heir to the throne eventually led Napoleon to divorce Josephine. The romantic in Napoleon may have led him to marry Marie, but the politician led him to other choices. Even so, Marie remained loyal to Napoleon, even visiting him in exile on Elba (see Chapter 14).

Napoleon's Polish love nest at Finkenstein

Napoleon and Marie Walewska spent a little over two months in the mansion of Finkenstein, also sometimes known as *Kamieniec-Finkenstein* for the region of Poland in which it is found. This magnificent structure was built in 1706 by one of the richest men in the area, who made his living providing agricultural products to the army and the government. The mansion became a social center for 200 years, with Napoleon and Marie being its most famous visitors.

Its most infamous visitor was Adolf Hitler, who stayed there briefly during World War II, using the same room occupied by Napoleon. That room was known as the Yellow Room and was, not surprisingly, the best in the building. Hitler's dog is buried on the grounds, and visitors still come today to see the grave.

Because Hitler had stayed there, the Germans didn't destroy the mansion when they retreated from Poland. The Russians, however, were determined to destroy all traces of German heritage in the area. One story says that Russian soldiers got drunk and set fire to the place, but there was a great deal of looting and some locals still have certain artifacts, such as knives, from its glory days.

The mansion is now in ruins, but a new foundation has been established to raise funds for its restoration. This foundation is known as the *Kamieniec–Finkenstein–Napoleon I in Poland and Central Europe* and was formed by the Pultusk School of the Humanities, the Napoleon Foundation in Paris, and the company GERO, which owns the facility. My wife, Barbara, and I were pleased to give the first financial contribution to this foundation, and we hope that one day the mansion will be restored to its former grandeur. (The figure shows how it looks today. Napoleon's room is on the second story in the right hand corner.)

As to Poland, Napoleon never did grant its wish of becoming an independent state encompassing all Polish territory. But as I explain in the upcoming section "Signing a peace, gaining a friend," he did create a smaller independent state called the *Grand Duchy of Warsaw* from some of the Polish territory. The Grand Duchy of Warsaw undertook numerous reforms, such as freeing the serfs and abolishing slavery. As a result, the Poles were ever grateful to him and remained loyal to his cause to the very end. Even today, Napoleon is seen as a very positive force in their history.

Continuing the campaign

In May 1807, the Russian commander Bennigsen reopened the campaign to drive Napoleon out of Germany. No one knows why he was so sure of success, but away he went. He was seriously outnumbered: Around 220,000 French soldiers would face just under 120,000 Russians. The Prussian city of Danzig (modern-day Gdansk in Poland) had been put under siege by Napoleon, and the Russians sought to send reinforcements to drive the French away. Instead, Danzig capitulated, giving the French a virtual treasure trove of supplies.

The Russians were stymied in their effort to relieve Danzig and began to withdraw to the east, taking up positions at the fortified city of Heilsberg in eastern Prussia. There, on June 10, 1807, the two forces fought to more or less a draw that ended with the withdrawal of the Russians and the taking of the city by the French. Like Eylau, this was a victory in name only, but it set the stage for one of Napoleon's most decisive victories. Bennigsen withdrew to his base camp near the east Prussian town of Friedland (now in Russia, only a short drive from Eylau) on the left bank of the Alle River.

Crushin' the Russian army

When Napoleon approached the town of Friedland, he did not have all his forces with him. Still, the French slightly outnumbered the Russians, and Napoleon was determined to crush them if at all possible. This determination increased when he decided that the Russian position was weak and dangerous, as the Russians had their backs to the river and were not otherwise well-positioned.

The Russians struck first, attacking Marshal Jean Lannes's force with their own much larger force. But Lannes held out on the evening of June 13th and again early in the morning of the 14th.

When Napoleon arrived on the scene at noon, he could have played it conservatively and waited for all his reinforcements to arrive, but he feared that he might lose his opportunity. He began his attack on June 14th at 5:30 p.m.

Artists of the day depicted the conflict at Friedland as consisting of glorious cavalry charges, which is at least a partially fair image (see Figure 10-2 for an example). Marshal Michel Ney led some of those glorious charges, sweeping many of the Russians into the river. Another image, less glorious, is a more accurate description of the essence of the battle. Thousands of Russians were tightly wedged between the French guns and the river. The French used them for target practice, and the devastation was awful.

Figure 10-2: This engraving, based on the famous painting by Messionier, shows one of the great cavalry charges at Friedland.

Most of this action was on the Russian left and center. The devastation would have been complete, but hesitation on the French left flank (the Russian right), hallmarked by General Emanuel Grouchy's failure to press his advantage with what could have been a wildly successful cavalry charge, allowed Bennigsen and much of his army to escape across the river. Napoleon did sent cavalry in pursuit, and by 11 p.m. the battle was over. The scene throughout the town was as ghastly as anyone could imagine. The battle cost the French 10,000 men, but the Russians lost at least twice that many and were on the run. They may not have completely realized it at the time, but Bennigsen's army was spent.

News of the Friedland victory spread quickly. The Russians evacuated Königsberg, giving the French access to a huge collection of supplies. The main Russian army fled to Tilsit in eastern Prussia, near the Niemen River, where Tsar Alexander was staying. When Murat's cavalry arrived on the scene, the tsar had had enough and sent word to Napoleon that he would like a personal meeting to arrange peace. Napoleon was delighted and quickly agreed. If he could win a peace, maybe even get Alexander as an ally, he would be sitting pretty. Perhaps even the British would have to settle.

Prussia, meanwhile, was quite apprehensive of its future, to say the least. Queen Louisa had visited Napoleon the day before he met the tsar, pleading her case. (She was the one who had practically pushed her husband into war with Napoleon.) Napoleon remembered well what she had done, and she met with no success. A young woman of great beauty, perhaps she thought she could replicate Marie Walewska's use of her charm. She certainly tried, flirting outrageously, but it gained her nothing.

Signing a peace, gaining a friend

Napoleon had never thought highly of the brash young Russian Tsar Alexander, and Alexander had returned the favor. Still, reality dictated that they meet, which they did on a raft in the middle of the Nieman River on June 25, 1807. They were accompanied by aides but quickly went into private conversation while their respective armies waited on opposite shores, all hoping that the fighting was over.

Perhaps unexpectedly, the two men hit it off quite well. Napoleon could charm anyone, and Alexander was no exception. He quickly came under Napoleon's spell. Napoleon was also more impressed with Alexander than he had ever expected to be. In short, the two men began what would become a very friendly relationship.

On June 26th, they were joined by King William of Prussia. Not surprisingly, King William did not fare all that well. Some images of that meeting have Napoleon and Alexander hugging while the king stands off to one side (see Figure 10-3). Napoleon treated King William disdainfully, a treatment that would continue in the coming days when the negotiations moved to the city of Tilsit itself.

On July 7th, Russia and France signed an alliance called the Treaty of Tilsit. The big loser was — surprise! — Prussia, which lost an enormous amount of territory. A new kingdom called *Westphalia* was to be carved out of several Prussian provinces. The new King of Westphalia would be Napoleon's brother, Jérôme.

The Poles were probably the biggest winners (other than France), for they were granted the Grand Duchy of Warsaw. They were to be under the rule of the King of Saxony and a part of the French Empire, but Napoleon gave them a constitution, and they had more than they would ever have had were it not for Napoleon.

The Grand Duchy of Warsaw was a great gift to the Poles, but it was a thorn in the side of Russia, which didn't want the Poles to be independent and didn't like French soldiers so close to its own border. For the moment, all was well, but soon the Polish question would become a great difficulty.

Other than the Grand Duchy of Warsaw, Russia came out quite well. She lost no territory and received the alliance of France and the friendship of Napoleon. Russia agreed to help Napoleon negotiate a peace with England and, if that failed, to join in the Continental System (see Chapter 21) and use the tsar's influence to get others in as well.

Figure 10-3:
This gold snuffbox shows Napoleon embracing Tsar Alexander of Russia while King William of Prussia looks on.

Napoleon was at the top of his game. Sure, his army was tired and he had not swept to glorious victory every single time (remember Eylau), but he had not been defeated. Going back to Austerlitz in 1805,

- ✔ He had defeated the Austrians, the Prussians, and the Russians (in two campaigns) and was master of western and central Europe.

- ✔ He had consolidated his position in Italy and put brothers on various thrones.

- ✔ He would soon put his brother Joseph on the throne of Spain and his brother-in-law Joachim Murat on the throne of Naples.

The downside to all this, of course, was the fact that Great Britain refused to make peace. Moreover, some of Napoleon's allies were not all that excited about their roles in his new empire. Chief among them was Austria, whose emperor had sworn to never again make war on Napoleon. The next great challenge to Napoleon would come from that supposed ally.

Facing Another Austrian Threat

By 1808, Austria had become quite restless. Influenced by English money and promises, still unhappy over the loss of territory and of influence in Italy and elsewhere, Emperor Francis began to imagine that he could defeat Napoleon and set himself up as the great savior of Europe.

Declaring war on France

At the time, Napoleon had much of the cream of his army tied down in Spain (see Chapter 12), and some of Napoleon's European holdings, especially in Germany, were showing signs of wanting out of his imperial system. Having convinced himself of his glorious role in the liberation of Europe, Emperor Francis joined England in a Fifth Coalition, turned on his French ally, and declared war on France in April 1809.

Austrian forces moved on French forces in Bavaria and achieved initial success, largely due to the element of surprise. Napoleon quickly rushed to the front. On April 20th, the French army defeated the Austrians at the Battle of Abensberg. The French prevailed again the next day at the Battle of Landshut. And the next day, the French were again victorious, this time at the Battle of Eckmühl. The Austrians had thus far lost some 30,000 troops but had been able to retreat in good order. After resting his exhausted troops, Napoleon moved on Vienna, occupying the city on May 13th.

Napoleon moved his army to the large island of Lobau, in the Danube River, and then, on May 20th, sent Marshal André Masséna to occupy the towns of Aspern and Essling on the river's left bank. The French were shocked to discover that the left bank held a substantial force of 95,000 Austrian troops led by Archduke Charles. Napoleon had only about 24,000 soldiers on the left bank and rushed to get more over as quickly as possible. The river had a very fast current, however, and the Austrians cleverly floated debris down the river, which damaged the bridge and prevented French troops from crossing. (Normally, engineers would have built protective devices to prevent such tactics, but in their haste they had failed to do so this time.)

Napoleon did get the bridge repaired and brought over more soldiers on May 21st, but his momentum was stalled and he was still outnumbered. That afternoon, Charles attacked. The French held their ground, but their advance was stopped. That night, even more French made it over the bridge, and early in the morning the French army regained control of Aspern, lost the day before to the Austrians. Throughout the morning, the French and Austrians clashed with little advantage to either side, but Napoleon's position was by far the more precarious, with his back to the river and only one bridge for either reinforcements or retreat.

By mid-afternoon, Napoleon could see that there was little to be gained, and much to be lost, from continued conflict. He ordered a withdrawal to Lobau Island. The withdrawal was made in good order and the bridge destroyed. Archduke Charles had succeeded in holding the left bank of the Danube, but Napoleon was in a secure position on an island that he quickly turned into a fortress.

Both sides had suffered heavy casualties, most notable of which was the death of Marshal Lannes. Napoleon had always been especially fond of Lannes, who was not only one of his best military leaders but also a friend. Lannes was also quite popular throughout the army, and his death was mourned by everyone.

Napoleon was in an unhappy position. He had been forced to cede the battlefield to his opponent for the first time in his career. This didn't go over well in France but gave hope to those who sought his demise. This situation was not unlike his position after Eylau, though there he had actually held the battlefield. Clearly, Napoleon needed to follow the Battle of Aspern-Essling with the equivalent of the Battle of Friedland.

And that is exactly what he would do.

Winning Wagram

Napoleon spent the winter preparing for the great conflict that would come with warm weather. He fortified the island, built well-protected bridges to the right bank of the Danube, and called in reinforcements. By July, he had almost 200,000 soldiers at his disposal. Archduke Charles, meanwhile, had never tried to follow up on his success, being content to simply hold his ground for the winter. Charles had about 155,000 men a few miles from the shores of the Danube, near the town of Wagram, located further north (away from the river) of Aspern and Essling. He was convinced that he had Napoleon boxed in. Not likely.

On the evening of July 4, 1809, the French put ten well-built pontoon bridges across the river, and troops began to stream across. Charles had been convinced that any French effort would be at a different location and was, therefore, quite taken by surprise at this action. The fighting became furious, but French efforts to break the Austrian center failed, as did Austrian efforts to do the same against the French.

The next day brought more of the same. Charles made the first move, soundly defeating the forces led by Marshal Bernadotte, whom Napoleon ordered off the field in disgrace. The French left was soon in serious trouble, but Marshal Masséna saved the day by halting the Austrian advance. Marshal Davout was containing things on the right, and Napoleon launched a massive attack on the Austrian center. (Figure 10-4 shows Napoleon giving orders on the field of battle.) Soon, the Austrian army was split in half, and Charles was forced to order a retreat. French pursuit caught up to him a few days later near the town of Znaim. There, General Auguste Frédéric Louis Marmont, joined by Marshal Masséna, forced Charles to seek an armistice, which the French were happy to grant. It was signed on July 12th. Napoleon was delighted with the performance of his two military commanders and gave Marmont his marshal's baton the same day the armistice was signed.

Completing the victory

Wagram was a great victory, but the war was not necessarily over yet. Austria's ally, England, landed 40,000 soldiers on the island of Walcheren in The Netherlands on July 29th. They achieved some success but were slow to exploit their situation. Marshal Bernadotte soon arrived to take charge of a French counteroffensive. Little French effort was necessary, however, as disease had depleted the British ranks, and they soon withdrew. The whole affair had been a wasted effort, and the effect on British and Austrian morale was predictable.

Emperor Francis finally realized that the Fifth Coalition had failed, and he agreed to the Treaty of Schönbrunn on October 14, 1809. Napoleon was not unduly harsh toward the man who had personally betrayed him. Austria lost some territories, including some given to the Grand Duchy of Warsaw in return for Polish support in the campaign. Austria also had to promise to rejoin the Continental System, reduce the size of her army, and pay a sizable indemnity.

Looking toward the future

Napoleon was reasonably easy on Austria for some very good reasons. More than anything else, he wanted peace. His 1809 campaign had been victorious, but there were some bad signs that came out of his victories. For one thing, the victories had not been as overwhelming as he may have wanted; he had not crushed his enemies. This was probably due to several factors, not the least of which was that his enemies were fighting better these days. Perhaps they had learned from Napoleon, but they were better organized and fought harder.

Another bad sign had been the approach taken by his friend and ally, Tsar Alexander of Russia. Alexander had talked a good game, but when it came to action, the promised Russian troops in support of the French were nowhere to be seen. Napoleon fought the Austrians with precious little help outside of the Poles. He and Alexander were still friends and allies, but it was clear to Napoleon that the alliance was not all it could be. For now, though, he treated Russia as a dear friend, even giving her some of Austria's eastern territories.

In this chapter and Chapter 9, I show you the campaigns that were most responsible for Napoleon's image as a great warrior, as well as for his dominance of Europe. I also show you that the so-called *Napoleonic Wars* are better described as wars of various coalitions organized by England and others to remove Napoleon from his throne. Indeed, many historians refer to them as the *War of the First Coalition,* the *War of the Second Coalition,* and so on.

These two chapters could give you the impression that Napoleon was invincible. Indeed, many people saw him as exactly that, and Figure 10-5 is typical of the imagery that supports that feeling. But as I show you in the next few chapters, Napoleon was anything but.

Figure 10-5:
The Battles of Marengo, Wagram, and Austerlitz are among Napoleon's finest and are commemorated on this bronze and marble inkwell.

Part III
Losing an Empire

The 5th Wave   By Rich Tennant

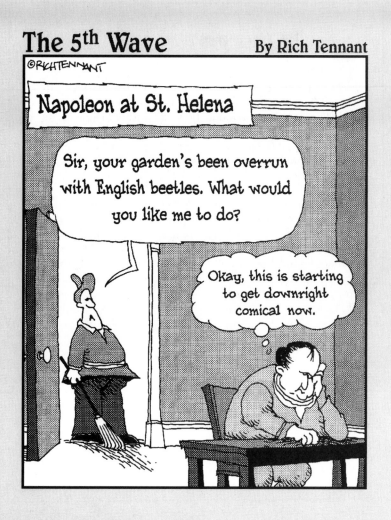

In this part . . .

*E*ver hear the old rule of physics that "What goes up must come down"? That seems to be true with empires as well (just ask the Romans!), and it was certainly true with Napoleon's. As good as he was on the battlefield, he ultimately had just too many enemies arrayed against him. Great Britain kept dashing his hopes on the sea, and his Continental opponents (often paid by the British) just kept coming.

And then there were the mistakes. Some things seem like good ideas at the time but just don't work out. That was the case with Napoleon's campaigns in Spain and Russia, which I cover in this part. To "meet your Waterloo" means to meet your ultimate defeat, and in this part I tell you how Napoleon met his. Finally, I relate the rather sad story of Napoleon's exile and death on the remote island of St. Helena.

Chapter 11

Sailing into Disaster with the British

In preceding chapters, I discuss several of Napoleon's most famous battles and show you why Napoleon is considered one of the greatest military commanders in history. These battles, and others that I didn't have the space to discuss, all had at least one thing in common: They were fought on land. When it came to land battles, Napoleon had no peer.

Unfortunately for Napoleon, his greatest adversary was the island nation of Great Britain. Not surprisingly for an island nation, the British had a long tradition of having a great navy. You've probably heard the chorus to Britain's unofficial national anthem:

> Rule Britannia, Britannia rule the waves.

> Britons never will be slaves.

Well, the Brits took that anthem seriously; they really *did* rule the waves. That was why Napoleon was never able to invade them; that darned English Channel kept getting in the way.

Not that Napoleon didn't try. He built ships and made alliances with nations that had ships. But he was sailing into the wind in trying to match the British at sea. As a result, he was never able to completely dominate Europe. The lesson here is that land supremacy alone is not sufficient to conquer a continent.

In this chapter, I describe three important French naval disasters that affected Napoleon. The first happened while Napoleon was just a general, but it had far-reaching consequences. The second two came as Napoleon was busy winning battles on land. Not surprisingly, all three disasters came at the hands of the British.

Facing Denial in Egypt

Okay, so that's one of the oldest and worst puns around. But there is no question that the French naval defeat that I am about to discuss denied Napoleon the chance for a much more successful Egyptian campaign in 1798. (For the complete story on that fascinating campaign, see Chapter 7.)

Dodging the British

To get to Egypt, Napoleon sailed from France across the Mediterranean Sea to the island of Malta. He then went on to Aboukir Bay in Egypt. The whole time, his biggest fear was that the British fleet would find the French ships. Napoleon knew that even though he had some of France's finest ships, he was unlikely to win a confrontation at sea, and so he naturally hoped to avoid one.

The British, on the other hand, would have loved to nip that little expedition in the bud. The French tried to keep their plans a secret, but the Brits eventually found out and dispatched a fleet to find them. The fleet was commanded by then 40-year-old Rear Admiral Horatio Nelson. To say that finding the French fleet was a long shot would be a major understatement. Talk about a needle in a haystack!

The two fleets actually came fairly close to each other, probably more by luck than by design, but Napoleon managed to get in and out of Malta and to Aboukir Bay on the Egyptian coast without difficulty. As it happened, Nelson had been at Aboukir just a few days earlier. Motivated by the knowledge that Nelson might return at any moment, Napoleon quickly put ashore on July 1, 1798. He left a rear guard, including shore artillery, and moved inland.

Nelson had been searching all over the Mediterranean and was actually in Greece when he learned that the French fleet was anchored at Aboukir Bay, 15 miles east of the city of Alexandria. Nelson quickly set off for Egypt, anxious for battle.

It was a battle that probably never should have occurred. It certainly shouldn't have turned out the way it did.

Improperly anchoring the French fleet

The fleet Napoleon used to get to Egypt was commanded by Admiral François-Paul Brueys. But Napoleon was commander of the French army and in overall command of the expedition, so he could tell Brueys what to do with his fleet after the soldiers were disembarked. He told Brueys to either put the fleet in the port of Alexandria, where it would be safe from any British attack, or take it to a port on the island of Corfu, then under French control, where it would also be safe.

For reasons that are not at all clear, Brueys chose to do neither of these. He believed that he could position his 13 ships where they were, near the coast, in a line formation that would present formidable fire power against any attacking navy. Further, one side of this line would be protected by the shore batteries that would force any attackers to run the gauntlet between the French ships and the French shore gun emplacements.

Now, all this sounds well and good, but there were huge problems with the way Admiral Brueys carried out his plan. His first mistake was in positioning his ships too far from shore, around a mile and a half to be exact. This created several problems:

✔ His ships would no longer be protected by the shallow water near the shore that would make it impossible for British ships to maneuver.

✔ British ships would now be out of range of the shore batteries.

✔ Small ships bringing supplies and men back and forth between the shore and the ships would now take much longer than necessary, a fact that could be disastrous in an emergency situation.

As a result of this mistake, the British would be able to encircle the French fleet. In ideal circumstances, this may not have spelled disaster, but Brueys was shorthanded, and having to man guns on both sides of every ship was a real stretch of his capabilities.

Brueys's second mistake was in the actual formation of his ships. He placed them in a long line that stretched for at least a mile and connected each ship with a cable. So far, so good, as the line formation was the traditional way of presenting to an attacking navy (allowing all the guns on one side to blast away), and the cable was designed to keep the British from weaving in and out between ships. The problem was that the ships were too far apart from each other, making assistance and communication more difficult. Moreover, Brueys had not allowed for any need to maneuver or, if necessary, try to beat a hasty retreat. Brueys had served honorably and with distinction throughout his career; there was no excuse for these mistakes, for which the French would pay dearly.

Getting surrounded

Nelson and his fleet arrived shortly after noon on August 1, 1798. A lesser commander may have decided to wait until the next day to attack, but Nelson ordered an immediate attack, not wanting the French to have the chance to redeploy or escape. The French first saw the British masts around 2 p.m. and quickly sounded the alarm. Because of the distance involved, many of the sailors on shore were unable to return to their ships, further reducing the available number of gunners and other important positions.

Given the problems with the French fleet's position, the outcome was never really in doubt. Several British ships sailed between the shore and the French ships, dropped anchor, and opened fire at very close range. Other British ships got equally close on the opposite side of the French, who now found themselves surrounded and under awful fire. Admiral Brueys was killed shortly after the action commenced, and many others would follow him to a watery grave.

The French ships at the front of the line were hit hardest and earliest. Several of them were knocked out of action very early in the conflict. And the British did not escape major damage, either, as several ships were severely damaged and Nelson himself was wounded and briefly convinced he was dying.

The battle raged, and the French got the worst of it by far. At a little past 10 p.m., the French flagship *l'Orient*, which had been on fire for some time, blew to smithereens in an explosion that could be seen and heard for many miles (see Figure 11-1). It was an awesome sight that stunned the rest of the combatants. All fighting stopped for at least ten minutes, possibly longer, before both sides returned to the grim task at hand. The battle raged throughout the night.

Figure 11-1:
This snuffbox from the period shows the French flagship *l'Orient* exploding. Note the British lifeboats rescuing survivors, both British and French.

The French may have fared better but for the action, or rather the inaction, of French Rear Admiral Pierre-Charles de Villeneuve. He commanded several ships at the rear of the French line and never suffered a direct attack. On land, generals are bound by the adage to "march to the sound of the guns," but apparently Admiral de Villeneuve felt no such need. Instead of sailing forward in support of the other French vessels, and possibly putting some of the British in the same two-front battle being experienced by the French, he chose to sail away with four ships, claiming that he was simply preserving what he could of the now decimated French fleet.

The battle continued until late on August 2nd. When it was finally over, Nelson and the British had achieved an overwhelming victory, the likes of which had scarcely been seen before.

Dealing with long-term effects

The implications to Napoleon's campaign in Egypt and beyond were enormous. After the Battle of the Nile, as this engagement is called, the French would no longer be able to dream of dominating the Mediterranean. The French fleet suffered damages that would take years to repair. Napoleon was effectively cut off from France, so precious few supplies and reinforcements would make it to Egypt. (Only small, fast ships would be able to run the British blockade, and not all of them would be successful.)

As a result, Napoleon's campaign in Egypt would be far different than he had hoped and imagined. He would lose the Battle of Acre largely because the British ships were there and his were not (see Chapter 7). And any hopes of continuing to the east, *a la* Alexander the Great, were quashed by Nelson's victory. It is interesting to speculate on the effect such a campaign would have had, both on Napoleon's career and on the French-British rivalry. But it was not to be.

It was a complete disaster for the French.

Rediscovering the Battle of the Nile

The Battle of the Nile made an unexpected reappearance 200 years after the fact. Land archaeology is well-known to most people, but underwater archaeology is far less known. In 1983, divers discovered the wreckage of *l'Orient,* and 13 years later serious exploration of the area began.

In the years since, countless priceless artifacts have been brought to the surface and displayed in museums. The story of the underwater exploration, and the artifacts, were presented in a Discovery Channel program and in

an accompanying book by Laura Foreman and Ellen Phillips, *Napoleon's Lost Fleet* (Discovery Books). The book also does a nice job of telling the details of the battle, though the authors clearly have a low opinion of Napoleon.

The archaeological "dig" also allows historians to see the actual position of the ships, especially those like *l'Orient* that sank quickly and pretty much straight down. Several ships have been discovered, and their position confirms the arguments of those who criticize Admiral Brueys's battle plan.

Destroying the Danish Fleet (Twice)

British action against the French fleet in 1798 was understandable and within the accepted rules of war. But the British actions I describe in this section, taken against Danish fleets in their own harbor of Copenhagen, were not quite so appropriate.

Engaging in trade wars

By 1800, England and France were engaged in a rather serious trade war. Each side sought to keep its allies from trading with its archenemy. Great Britain, however, seemed willing to go beyond that. She felt justified in attacking ships of neutral countries to prevent their trading with France. This was a questionable policy at best and prompted reaction from some of those neutral countries. Tsar Paul I of Russia formed the Armed Neutrality of the North Agreement (also called the *Armed Neutrality League*) between Russia, Sweden, Denmark, and Prussia in December 1800. These countries agreed not to trade with England and to protect each other against English actions against their shipping.

England was outraged and felt quite threatened. She was dependent on trade for her very survival, and it didn't take long before she began to feel the consequences of this embargo. Rather than negotiate a treaty or change her policy of stopping neutral ships on the open sea, England decided to make a preemptive strike against the best navy of the group, namely Denmark.

Forcing Denmark out of the League

The British tried to coerce the Danes into deserting the Armed Neutrality League. To assist in the "negotiations," they sent a fleet of 56 ships to lay siege to Copenhagen's harbor. Inside the harbor were 18 Danish warships, as well as substantial numbers of commercial vessels. The harbor was guarded by a major battery on an island near its entrance. The British fleet was commanded by Admiral Sir Hyde Parker, and his second in command was none other than Vice Admiral Nelson, of Battle of the Nile fame. Parker was not known for his aggressiveness, but Nelson was. The British fleet arrived on March 21, 1801 and awaited further developments.

British efforts to intimidate the Danes failed, so on March 30th the British navy moved into position outside the entrance to the harbor. On April 1st, Nelson was sent into the harbor with a squadron of about a dozen ships with orders to destroy the Danish fleet. The wind was right on April 2nd, and the battle began early in the morning. Successful at first, the British soon began to encounter problems. Several ships ran aground, and British casualties were mounting.

Nelson's superior, Admiral Parker, tried to render assistance but was unable to enter the harbor due to improper winds. Convinced that Nelson was headed for disaster, he signaled him to withdraw. When Nelson was informed of this by subordinates, he rather famously put his telescope to his blind eye and claimed he couldn't confirm the signal!

As a result, the fighting continued with heavy losses on each side. The Danes finally agreed to an armistice and to leave the Armed Neutrality League soon. The Danes lost a little over 1,000 men and the British a little under that number. But the British gained possession of a number of ships and achieved their diplomatic goal as well.

The British were prepared to next turn against the Russians, but the death of Paul I and the ascension of Alexander I, who cared little for the League, made that unnecessary. However, the League had taught England that she was clearly vulnerable to economic warfare, and her problems with the League were part of her motivation for eventually agreeing to peace with France later that year (see Chapter 21).

Bombarding the Danes

Denmark, it seems, cannot catch a break. She remained neutral in the conflict between France and England, but the Brits continued to harass her shipping, in violation of international shipping law and British/Danish agreements. In 1807, after Napoleon signed the Treaty of Tilsit with the Russians (see Chapter 10), he began to pressure Denmark into joining economic warfare against England in the form of the Continental System, which I explain in Chapter 21. The Danes were not excited about the idea, but neither were they pleased with England, which was pressuring Denmark to join her in opposition to France.

What's a crown prince to do? For a time, Denmark's Crown Prince Frederick seemed to do nothing. His inaction didn't please the Brits, who sent a massive fleet of 25 *ships of the line* (the major warships of the day) and almost 30,000 marines to invade Copenhagen. The Danes were furious (and who can blame them?). They refused to simply roll over and play dead. The Brits responded on September 2, 1807 by bombarding and invading the city and the port, burning much of the city and killing at least 2,000 civilians.

The Danes were no match for the Brits and soon surrendered. The British action gained them the entire Danish fleet and many supplies. Happy with their victory, they sailed away.

The Brits may have won the battle, but they suffered greatly in the war of public opinion. People throughout Europe, and even some in England, were outraged at the idea that a nation could, without a declaration of war or any reasonably just cause, take military action against a nation that had taken no action against her. The question of the justification of a preemptive strike continues to be a factor in international relations even today.

Great Britain had always attempted to seize the moral high ground, claiming that France was a threat to peace and freedom. That argument was now much harder to make. Napoleon would have dearly loved to have those Danish ships on his side, but he was probably equally glad with the end result: Denmark agreed to join the Continental System against Great Britain. Another door into continental Europe was closed to France's greatest enemy.

Sinking the Spanish and French at Trafalgar

The most famous naval battle of the Napoleonic period took place on October 21, 1805. It was the final result of a convoluted effort to use a combined French and Spanish armada to draw the British navy all the way to the West Indies. The initial plan was that the French and Spanish were to dash back to the English Channel to support an invasion of England. Napoleon was a master of war on land. His understanding of the capabilities and condition of his navy was less complete.

Lacking leadership

The French lacked strong naval leadership. The main French fleet, harbored at Toulon in the Mediterranean, was commanded by our old friend Admiral Villeneuve. Remember him? At the Battle of the Nile, he hemmed and hawed for awhile and then decided to sail away rather than taking the fight to the British. Mr. Indecision himself.

At first, things went more or less according to the French plan. Admiral Villeneuve managed to slip out of Toulon harbor, meet up with some other French and Spanish ships, and sail away to the Caribbean. Somewhat belatedly, the English navy followed, led by another of our old friends from earlier in this chapter, Admiral Horatio Nelson. The French and Spanish reached the island of Martinique, then turned around and sailed all the way back to Europe, keeping several days ahead of the British.

On the way back, the French and Spanish fought a short engagement with British ships on July 22nd, and then they sought shelter in several harbors. They eventually ended up in the Spanish harbor of Cadiz, where Villeneuve was well-protected by shore batteries. This situation suited him just fine, but Napoleon was furious with Villeneuve's lack of decisiveness and ordered him replaced. Napoleon was a man of action and expected his subordinates to take the battle to the enemy rather than seeking safety. Of course, Napoleon never really understood naval warfare all that well, but it is reasonable to say that Villeneuve should have been more aggressive.

By this time, Napoleon had abandoned his plans to invade England and was preparing to move his *Grande Armée* into central Europe. To assist in the coming campaign, Napoleon planned to move his navy (under new leadership) from Cadiz to Italy, where it would land soldiers and await further orders.

Battling Nelson again

Meanwhile, Nelson had reappeared and instituted a blockade on Cadiz harbor. Clever lad that he was, he put many of his ships out of sight so that the French and Spanish would have reason to believe they could escape and fulfill their mission. If you read about the Battle of Austerlitz in Chapter 9, you may realize that Napoleon did much the same thing with his ground forces there. Great minds think alike.

Admiral Villeneuve would probably have preferred to stay where he was, but he was quite concerned about his career and had heard that he was about to be replaced. In a desperate bid to save his reputation, he sailed out of Cadiz harbor on October 19th, and in so doing, he played right into the hands of Admiral Nelson, who caught up to them two days later off nearby Cape Trafalgar.

The British held off engagement until the French and Spanish ships were well out of the harbor and beyond the range of the harbor guns. Then, the Brits sent in the *ships of the line,* the main warships of navies in those days. (They were called that because naval battles were usually fought by the two sides lining up against each other and then just blasting away until someone cried "Uncle.") Nelson had his flagship hoist the famous flag signal, "England expects that every man will do his duty." And his men most certainly did theirs.

When the French and Spanish saw the British ships approaching, they attempted to turn and return to the safety of Cadiz. This action only served to break their line of battle, and the engagement soon turned into something of a one-on-one. The battle continued for much of the day, with a number of the French and Spanish ships sailing off to safety rather than turning and fighting. (Hmmm. Does that sound familiar?)

The ships that stayed paid a heavy price. By the end of the day, the British had captured 18 ships and lost not a one. It was an overwhelming victory, though most of the captured ships would be destroyed in a big storm shortly thereafter. Admiral Villeneuve was taken prisoner. A broken man who was now associated with both of France's overwhelming naval defeats at the hand of Admiral Nelson, he committed suicide in 1806, just as he was about to be sent to France on parole.

Villeneuve was not the only admiral to lose his life as a result of Trafalgar. Admiral Nelson's flagship, *Victory,* was heavily engaged in the action. Shortly after 1 p.m. on October 21, 1805, a sharpshooter on the French ship *Redoubtable* shot Nelson, who died a few hours later. One of England's greatest heroes, Nelson is remembered and respected by all. England erected a huge monument to Trafalgar — and Nelson — in London, called Trafalgar Square.

Facing reality

In some ways, the Battle of Trafalgar changed nothing. France was never likely to challenge Great Britain for dominance of the seas. True, if Napoleon's scheme had been instituted while his *Grande Armée* was still on the French coast opposite England, *and* if sufficient troop carriers had been available, then perhaps Napoleon could have carried out the long-planned invasion. But by the time of Trafalgar, those plans had been scrapped, and Napoleon had pretty much given up ever being able to invade his greatest foe. In fact, he said as much as early as 1798, before he turned his attention to Egypt.

But Napoleon still had a fleet and still had allies who had fleets, most notably the Spanish and the Danes. Those fleets would, from time to time, keep the British occupied and even at bay, and they did prevent the various coalitions against France from having much success in invading anywhere but Portugal (see Chapter 12).

On the other hand, the Battle of Trafalgar set both physical and psychological limits on French expansion. No longer could Napoleon convince anyone, including himself, that an invasion of England was possible. This set the British people's minds to rest and allowed them the luxury of opposing Napoleon at every opportunity, secure in the knowledge that the French would never be able to take the battle to them.

If Trafalgar was a boost to the spirits of the British, it was quite the opposite to the French, Napoleon in particular. It meant that Napoleonic France would be restricted to being a great land power, with an empire restricted to continental Europe. Foreign colonies were unlikely, as were any expeditions to the far east, other than by following in Alexander the Great's footsteps and marching there.

As a result, Napoleon would turn to other ways to defeat England. Earlier in this chapter, I mention the economic blockade known as the *Continental System,* which I discuss further in Chapter 21. That effort at economic warfare was one of the outcomes of the Battle of Trafalgar. Unfortunately for Napoleon, it would be no more successful.

Chapter 12

Bleeding in Spain

· ·

In This Chapter

▶ Closing off the Brits

▶ Making Spain a family affair

▶ Fighting a new kind of war

▶ Draining needed resources

· ·

As I show in previous chapters, for most of his career, Napoleon had great success against land armies. He fought against traditional armies using his new, improved *Grande Armée,* and his opponents just couldn't keep up. In this chapter, I show you what happened when Napoleon's armies had to face a very different situation. In Spain, the French faced not only a tradi- tional army but also a new way of fighting. We used to call this kind of fighting *guerrilla warfare,* but now we often hear it described as a *war against insur- gents.* As Napoleon found out, it's tough to win against insurgents.

Napoleon was in Spain and Portugal to try to close off the entire European continent to British trade. This economic embargo was called the *Continental System,* and I tell you all about it in Chapter 21.

In this chapter, I give you an introduction to Spanish politics and how Napoleon became involved in matters concerning the Spanish crown. I show you that being progressive is not always popular with the common people, and I explain why the French campaign in Spain soon became known as Napoleon's *Spanish Ulcer.*

And oh, yes. In this chapter, we have our first introduction to a fellow named Arthur Wellesley, the future Duke of Wellington.

Gaining Control of Portugal

Spain and France had an on again, off again relationship. Spain had been unhappy with the French Revolution and had not been all that thrilled with Napoleon. In 1807, Spain and France were again allies, but Napoleon was not very pleased with Spain's lack of enthusiasm about that alliance. Still, Spain had been fairly cooperative. She had at least loosely tried to enforce the Continental System.

Portugal, on the other hand, had been unwilling to cooperate with France. So in 1807, Napoleon sent General Andoche Junot (see Figure 12-1) to occupy that small country on the western edge of the Iberian Peninsula. (Spain and Portugal share the Iberian Peninsula, and the conflict I describe in this chapter is usually called the *Peninsular War* or the *Peninsular Campaign*.)

Figure 12-1: This period painting on ivory in a gilt frame shows General Andoche Junot in his uniform.

Junot had little difficulty moving his troops through Spain. (Because Spain was an ally, she did not object.) They marched into Lisbon, the capital of Portugal. There they discovered that the Portuguese fleet and royal family had left for Brazil two days earlier. Junot was appointed governor, and Portugal was, for a time at least, under the control of France. This action closed the largest gap in the Continental System and was a major accomplishment for Napoleon's strategic goals.

Taking Advantage of Spain's Political Turmoil

Even with Portugal on board, Spain continued to be lax in its enforcement of the Continental System. Napoleon became determined to fix that situation once and for all. Turmoil in the Spanish court would give him his opportunity.

Sorting out Spanish court politics

Spain was run by a king named Charles (*Carlos* in Spanish) IV, a member of the Bourbon family that had once ruled France as well. (All those Louies were Bourbons.) Charles IV was nobody's idea of an ideal monarch:

- ✔ He was not very bright.
- ✔ He may have been quite mentally unbalanced.
- ✔ For good measure, he was a complete despot, ruling with an iron hand.

Being married to such a man was probably not much fun for Queen Maria Luisa, but she did what she could to cope. She coped by befriending a man who would become her notorious lover, Manuel de Godoy, whom she soon had installed as prime minister. Their behavior was flagrant, and the common people were outraged. The Spanish people were generally very conservative Catholics. They hated the French Revolution for its anticlerical actions, and they were none too fond of the impious actions of their queen and her lover.

The royal couple's son, Ferdinand, was unhappy as well. Queen Maria Luisa and Godoy, who was actually given the title "prince of peace," were running the country, and Ferdinand's father was as ineffective as he was despotic. There were plots and counterplots, with Godoy siding with the king against his son. King Charles actually had Ferdinand arrested for treason, though little came of that.

Convincing the royals to abdicate

The situation became out of control, and both King Charles and Prince Ferdinand appealed to Napoleon for mediation. This gave Napoleon the opening he needed. He had been looking for an excuse to occupy Spain and gain control of not only the country but also all of her (presumably) wealthy overseas colonies. Napoleon quietly put his military in charge of Spanish forts along the border between Spain and France, in the Pyrenees Mountains. He also increased French military strength in Spain itself. He then sent Marshal Joachim Murat to occupy the Spanish capital of Madrid, which he did on March 24, 1808.

Napoleon convinced the royal family to become his "guests" in the French city of Bayonne, and they arrived there on April 30th. The idea was to mediate their differences, but it was soon clear that the real point was to remove all of them from power in Spain. Both Charles and Ferdinand abdicated their rights to the throne, and Godoy was removed from all further influence in Spain. (See Figure 12-2 for period images of Charles and Godoy.) Since none of them were really capable of leadership, at least some of the Spanish people were not particularly sad to see them gone.

Figure 12-2:
Manuel de
Godoy (A)
and King
Charles IV
(B), from
Godoy's
memoirs
of 1823.

A   B

The Peasants Are Revolting (and So Are the Clergy)

At first, the Spanish peasants and especially the citizens of Madrid took
kindly to Napoleon's actions. They had been quite unhappy with the bickering between the king and his son, and they were disgusted with the relationship between the queen and her prime minister. But they quickly tired of
French military occupation. Marshal Murat was determined to keep order,
and most people don't like soldiers on every street corner and seemingly
quartered in every bed. Especially foreign soldiers. Nobody likes foreign
troops stationed in their city for very long at all.

All may have been well if Murat had simply recognized Prince Ferdinand as
the new ruler, with the French there to help in the transition. But Murat
couldn't do that, of course, as Napoleon had other plans. This didn't sit well
with the good citizens of Madrid, no matter how much they liked their French
allies. French General Emmanuel Grouchy was installed as Madrid's military
governor, and while he was able to keep things reasonably quiet for a time,
he soon ran into difficulty. A riot broke out on April 1st, but Grouchy was able
to restore order quickly.

When word of the complete removal of the Spanish royal family from power,
(and the pending arrest of royal family members still in Spain) reached
Madrid, the people had had enough. Allies or not, the French had to go.
Resentment of the French Revolution's perceived destruction of the Catholic

Church bubbled to the surface, and the clergy joined the general citizenry in their goal of sending the French packing.

On May 2, 1808, the citizens of Madrid rioted. Any French soldier caught alone or in a small group was likely to be hung from the nearest street lamp. French cavalry and artillery restored order after several hours, but the streets ran red with blood.

Marshal Murat (see Figure 12-3) then managed to make things worse. Rather than seeking a way to pacify at least some of the anti-French factions, he instead declared martial law and cracked down hard on the citizens of Madrid. He rounded up as many insurgents as he could and had many of them shot. This action is reflected in some of Francisco José de Goya's paintings, notably his *Dos de Mayo* and *Tres de Mayo* (Second of May and Third of May). Goya would continue to paint scenes of the Spanish conflict with France, showing alleged scenes of French atrocities. His viewpoint was understandably partisan, not showing equally horrific scenes of Spanish atrocities against the French, but his paintings stand out as some of the most powerful of the period.

Figure 12-3: Marshal Joachim Murat, shown here in a period engraving, was one of the flashiest of all Napoleon's marshals.

Keeping Control All in the Family

Having deposed the Spanish royal family, and with order somewhat restored in Madrid, Napoleon moved to place someone from his own family on the Spanish throne. This action was not as odd or inappropriate as you may think; kings did not always come from the country they ruled. King George III of England, for example, was from Hanover, and in a few years Sweden would choose French Marshal Jean-Baptiste Bernadotte as its king.

Going from brother to brother

Napoleon first offered the Spanish throne to his brother Louis. When Louis declined the honor, he offered it to another brother, Jérôme. Both of these brothers were smart enough to turn it down. And who could blame them? Let's see. Their brother had deposed the rightful rulers, Murat had caused anti-French rioting with substantial bloodshed in the capital, and the peasants and clergy really didn't like France's secular government anyway.

Napoleon was not to be denied, however, and turned next to his eldest brother, Joseph. Now, brother Joseph was quite content where he was, sitting on the relatively peaceful throne of Naples. He had a nice palace, beautiful beaches, and plenty of Roman ruins to visit. But Napoleon insisted, and when Napoleon insisted, one had little choice. On June 6th, Joseph was declared King Joseph (*José* in Spanish) of Spain. Napoleon then removed Murat from Madrid and made him the King of Naples. Murat had wanted to stay in Spain, but given his lack of local popularity, it was probably just as well that he left, which he did in July.

Meeting popular resistance

The people of Spain did not appreciate their new French monarch. Rioting became widespread, and organized resistance to the French occupation grew. Napoleon could not have completely understood it yet, but his efforts in Spain were doomed. Without the support of the people, it would be impossible for Joseph to be an effective ruler.

There is much irony in all of this. Joseph was a moderate and quite likeable person who wanted to be a good king. He brought with him the liberal reforms that had been so popular in France and elsewhere. The Spanish Catholic Church had been anything but progressive: This was, after all, the home of the Spanish Inquisition, where even the suspicion that you weren't a good Catholic could get you tortured to death. The Church was extremely wealthy and corrupt, and it was very unpopular with the intelligentsia of the country. Those educated people supported Joseph and his reforms, and they hoped that the Church would lose its stranglehold on the populace.

Napoleon made the mistake of assuming that the intelligentsia, along with the merchant class that wanted increased trade with France, represented the population as a whole. Even in the area of religion, Napoleon thought the fact that he had established good relations with the Pope would stand him in good stead. (See Chapters 20 and 23 for more on Napoleon's relations with the Pope.)

The enlightened reforms offered to the Spanish people by Napoleon through Joseph would have been a big improvement in their lives — Napoleon ended the Inquisition, for example — but the peasants were not interested. French clerical reforms, such as religious tolerance, divorce rights, and secular control of public policy, were of no interest to the conservative Catholics of Spain. Napoleon thought he'd be seen as a liberator. Instead, he was seen as a usurper of power and a threat to religion. Kind of hard to rule with that kind of image!

Battling the British

Joseph well understood what he was facing. He arrived in Madrid on July 20, 1808, and by the 24th he already had written to Napoleon that he, Joseph, had no support and that Napoleon's "glory will be shipwrecked in Spain." Joseph was all too correct. Things very quickly began to unravel. Pro-French provincial and city governors were assassinated, and some Spanish governors appealed to the British for help.

The British are coming

By mid-summer of 1808, the British government responded to Spain's requests for help by sending an army into Portugal. This army was led by a general named Arthur Wellesley. If Spain were to kick the French out of their country, they would need all the British help they could get, as the regular Spanish army was not very effective. The British consolidated their position and then began to move toward French forces.

Before the Brits could do much, the Spanish insurgents claimed a big victory in southern Spain with the July 22nd defeat of the French at the Battle of Bailen. General Pierre Dupont's corps of over 20,000 men surrendered. It was a stunning defeat, though the fact that Dupont's men were raw recruits was a significant factor. When Joseph got wind of this development, he beat a hasty retreat, abandoning Madrid for the safety of secure French positions in the north.

On August 21st, General Junot's army attacked the slightly larger force commanded by Wellesley in Portugal. The resulting action led to a decisive French defeat, and Junot was forced to surrender his entire command. Wellesley's superiors insisted on cutting a quick deal, though, and the resulting Convention of Cintra allowed Junot's army to evacuate Portugal for France, keeping all its baggage and the plunder it had accumulated. The soldiers even sailed home on British ships! This kind of deal was unheard of, and the British government recalled the top three commanders, including Wellesley, leaving General Sir John Moore in command. Wellesley, cleared of any wrongdoing, returned in April 1809.

Napoleon is coming

Napoleon was quite displeased with the situation in Spain and its consequences to his overall position. While he was at peace on his eastern front with Austria and Russia (see Chapters 9 and 10), past experience had shown that he could not count on that peace to last. If it didn't, and if Spain were still tying down a substantial part of his army, he would be fighting a two-front war, which is never a good idea. Napoleon had expected Spain to fall into place with no difficulty and had sent second-rate soldiers to do the job. They and their leaders (including Joseph) had failed him, so Napoleon would just have to do it himself.

After substantial preparation, Napoleon led his offensive into Spain in early November 1808. His forces numbered 100,000, including units commanded by some of his best marshals, such as Nicolas Soult, Michel Ney, and Jean Lannes. They met with considerable success (see Figure 12-4), and by early December, Napoleon was in Madrid. There, he managed to humiliate his brother, King Joseph, by pretty much ignoring him while taking complete charge of everything.

Figure 12-4:
This period snuffbox celebrates Napoleon's initial victories in the Pyrenees.

Napoleon meant well in Spain, but he still just didn't get it. He undertook reforms that were much needed and were popular with the educated classes. He abolished the Inquisition and completely restructured the relationship between the Church and the government. As he had in France and elsewhere, he instated financial, social, and political reforms, attempting to modernize a nation that in many ways was still stuck in the Middle Ages. Actually, many common people approved of at least quite a few of these reforms, but they didn't appreciate the way they were instituted. (Perhaps if their new King Joseph had been the one to announce them, they may have gone over better.)

The British are leaving

British forces under Sir John Moore's command began to move from Portugal into Spain and threaten the French position there. Napoleon soon rushed forces to stop them and to drive them back into the sea from whence they came. Moore began to retreat, but the process kept French forces busy when they should have been dealing with more serious threats elsewhere.

Finally, on January 11, 1809, Moore's forces were pinned against the ocean at Corunna, in northwestern Spain. A few days later, British transport ships arrived to remove the soldiers, and by the time Marshal Soult attacked, most of the Brits were gone. Though some people criticized Moore for not standing and fighting, his actions may have saved a significant part of the British forces, and they certainly distracted the French. Moore was not around to hear the criticism or receive any accolades, however, as he was killed by a French cannonball.

Napoleon is leaving

Madrid secure, his reforms in place, and the countryside now being pacified by some of his best marshals, Napoleon decided he could leave Spain and attend to matters back home. A couple things needed his immediate attention:

✔ Austria was trying to take advantage of Napoleon's absence, and that of so many of his soldiers and marshals, by threatening war. That war would come, as I discuss in Chapter 10, and Austria would regret her actions.

✔ There were problems on the homefront as well. Joseph Fouché, Napoleon's minister of police, and Charles Maurice de Talleyrand-Périgord, Napoleon's foreign minister, were invaluable to maintaining control over France and dealing with other European countries. However, these two men had not been exactly trustworthy over the years, and there was some evidence that they were hatching up a plot to relieve Napoleon of the burdens of empire by organizing a *coup d'état* (overthrow of the government). No specific plot was uncovered, so Napoleon just gave them what amounted to a slap on the wrist.

The Spanish Ulcer

Napoleon couldn't be everywhere at once, and he was probably needed more elsewhere than in Spain. He planned to return but never did. Had he done so, the history of the Peninsular War may have been quite different. Napoleon left behind forces sufficient to pacify Spain and throw the British out of Iberia. But his forces failed to do either of those two things.

There were several problems:

- ✔ Joseph was a weak leader who commanded very little respect from either his military leaders or the Spanish people.

- ✔ Joseph was not a military commander and could not really take charge of the campaign.

- ✔ The marshals Napoleon left behind had enormous egos and resented any restrictions on their commands, save from Napoleon himself. Their feuds with each other and disdain for Joseph did little to help them unify against the growing Spanish and British military threats.

- ✔ Napoleon took with him many of his best soldiers.

- ✔ The Spanish people had never been happy with what had happened to the Church in France and the mistreatment they felt Napoleon gave the Pope. The clergy regularly gave fiery sermons calling for the Spanish people to rise up against the French. Opposition to the French took on the nature of a religious crusade, a losing proposition for any occupying army.

- ✔ The Spanish campaign was beginning to cost the French treasury a great deal. As a result, Napoleon began to demand that Spanish taxes be raised, which did nothing to improve the attitude of the Spanish people toward the French.

Making one last effort

Over the next several years, things went from bad to worse. When Napoleon was successful against Austria in 1809 (see Chapter 10), he could have returned to Spain to take personal charge of the campaign. Instead, he sent Marshal André Masséna to assume overall command, and he sent Marshal Louis Alexandre Berthier as his chief of staff. Along with them, Napoleon sent 80,000 good soldiers. Their goal was to drive the British out of Portugal and then deal with the Spanish.

At first, the French had some success, both against the British and against the regular Spanish army. General Wellesley (Wellington) retreated to strong positions in Portugal, with Masséna in pursuit and Marshal Michel Ney as second in command. In September 1810, the French reached the British defensive position known as the *Lines of Torres Vedras*. These were three defensive lines of walls and other fortified positions.

Both Masséna and Ney, who often agreed on very little, agreed that these positions were pretty much impregnable, and they wrote that analysis to Napoleon. The French lay siege for a month, but lack of supplies (his army was essentially starving) led Masséna to eventually withdraw in November to the town of Santarem to wait out the winter. The Lines of Torres Vedras stopped the French advance on the British position in Portugal and shifted the momentum to Wellesley and the British. Knowing that they could always retreat to this fortified position, the British were soon on the offensive.

Stopping the French momentum

It was all downhill for the French after Torres Vedras. The French army soon found itself fighting on three fronts:

- The British, who provided the most disciplined and traditional army in opposition
- The Spanish regular army
- The Spanish guerrillas, or insurgents. These fighters captured the imagination of people on both sides of the conflict. Operating in bands ranging from a few dozen to several thousand, Spanish insurgents would harass French units and sometimes inflict great damage.

It's easy to idealize the heroic nature of these insurgents, but the reality was often quite different. Many of these groups were in it for the loot as much as for any patriotic fervor, and they often did not trust each other. But what was especially bad about the conflict between the French army and the insurgents was the total lack of anything resembling the "rules of war." Earlier in the chapter, I mention the French atrocities depicted in Goya's paintings, and there is no doubt that the French were often guilty as charged. But many French atrocities were in reaction to similar actions on the part of the insurgents.

A more modern example of the idealizing of the insurgency campaign was the television series regarding one Richard Sharpe (played by Sean Bean), a soldier in Wellesley's army. It's wonderful entertainment (my wife, Barbara, can watch Sean Bean for hours), but it seems that the insurgents are always good and the French are always bad (as well as incompetent soldiers, which was hardly the case).

The fact is that neither side wanted to take prisoners, and neither side would be content, or safe, until the other was completely annihilated. It is impossible to say how many on either side were killed. I've seen estimates of as many as 50,000 French casualties from both guerrilla attacks and pitched battles, and there can be no disputing the fact that the French got the worst of it.

French armies would deal with insurgent actions on a large scale once again during their campaign in Russia in 1812, especially during their withdrawal (see Chapter 13). History really does repeat itself. In the late 20th and early 21st centuries, we've seen major insurgency movements in Afghanistan against the Russians and in Vietnam and Iraq against the Americans, to name but three.

Pushing the French out of Spain

The French armies did have some successes in Spain. For example, their victory at Ocana in November 1809 halted a Spanish effort to move on Madrid. But their overall position became steadily weaker. With Masséna withdrawing from Portugal, Wellesley was able to turn his attention to other French positions in that country. He was in the process of forcing them out when, in late 1811, Napoleon ordered a new push to reestablish control of at least part of Spain. The push eventually stalled, however, especially when Napoleon withdrew some of the best troops for his 1812 campaign in Russia.

Fighting a two-front war was not going to be easy. Or successful, as it turned out.

Wellesley won a stunning victory at the Battle of Salamanca on July 22, 1812 against French forces led by Marshal Soult. That loss forced the French to retreat to the north, abandoning Madrid. Allied forces took that city without a fight on August 12, 1812.

As French forces moved northward, they were able to consolidate. Though frequently outflanked by Wellesley, King Joseph, who had assumed overall command, made a major stand at Vitoria on June 21, 1813. Joseph had 66,000 soldiers defending his positions, and they faced almost 80,000 allied forces. Wellesley's forces attacked from several directions at once. Overwhelmed, Joseph and his army were forced to retreat, leaving behind artillery and other important supplies. French losses were about 8,000, compared with 5,000 for the allied forces. The large amount of loot that the French left behind sidetracked Wellesley's soldiers such that pursuit was not possible, and the French managed to escape.

Vitoria was a major victory for Wellesley, who by now was a field marshal and had the title Arthur, Duke of Wellington. See Figure 12-5 for an engraving from the period showing Wellington. From now on, I call him *Wellington,* as he is generally known.

Defending France

The French were never again a major threat in Spain. Joseph returned to Paris, leaving the army in the command of Marshal Soult. In July 1813, Soult ordered a counterattack and won engagements in some of the mountain passes. But Wellington defeated him at Sorauren on July 30th, and Soult withdrew to the north. Defeated again at Vera and San Marcial on August 31st, Soult withdrew again, this time to prepare his defense of France against a British invasion.

Figure 12-5:
This somewhat stylized engraving of Wellington was produced in 1815.

That invasion came in late 1813, and Soult would be pushed back, slowly but surely, until Napoleon's abdication in 1814 (see Chapter 14) brought an end to action. The final action took place at the Battle of Toulouse (a city in southern France). There, Wellington defeated French forces led by Marshal Soult on April 10, 1814. The next night Soult withdrew his forces to the medieval city of Carcassonne. The two sides agreed to an armistice when word of Napoleon's abdication arrived, thus ending the Peninsular Campaign.

The Peninsular Campaign had seemed to offer Napoleon an excellent opportunity to consolidate his position on the Continent. But Napoleon had not understood the nature of the Spanish people and had not anticipated the determination of the British to contribute to his defeat. As a result, the Peninsular Campaign was, in many ways, Napoleon's worst defeat. It bled him dry for years, tied up his soldiers and marshals, ate away at his image (and pocketbook), and ultimately led to a British invasion of France herself. It is no wonder, then, that it is often considered Napoleon's biggest mistake.

Chapter 13

Reeling from Russia

• •

In This Chapter

▶ Feeling the tension between Russia and France

▶ Marching forward to victory

▶ Winning the only real battle

▶ Capturing Moscow and watching it burn

▶ Waiting for nothing

▶ Leaving a disaster

• •

*A*fter the Treaty of Tilsit between France and Russia in 1807 (see Chapter 10), those two nations became allies. Equally important was the fact that the two emperors, Napoleon of France and Tsar Alexander I of Russia, became friends. Napoleon saw this friendship as a very important move toward peace on the European continent. After all, what country would possibly want to take on both France *and* Russia at the same time?

But it soon became evident that the friendship, both personal and political, had its limits. Alexander didn't provide France much help against Austria in 1809 (see Chapter 10), and in the years that followed there were other signs of growing disillusionment on both sides.

In this chapter, I tell you about some of the issues that divided the two countries and what they tried — and didn't try — to do about them. Then I describe France's 1812 campaign in Russia and discuss that campaign's long-term implications for Napoleon.

Watching Storm Clouds Gather

The Treaty of Tilsit in 1807 was much better to France than to Russia. That's fair, because France had just defeated Russia for the second time in two years. But a one-sided treaty can sometimes lead to problems, and that is exactly what happened. Two things in particular created problems for Russia, and thus for the alliance between the two nations. I discuss these two things in the following sections.

Polish pain

The Treaty of Tilsit created the Grand Duchy of Warsaw out of what today is part of Poland. This step elated the Poles and made them steadfast allies of Napoleon, but it deeply concerned the Russians. Here's why:

- ✔ The Russian nobility, and some people in Alexander's family, had hoped to expand Russian borders to the west. In fact, they wanted to swallow up most of Poland and were not at all happy when Napoleon created an independent state, under his protection, right on their border.

- ✔ Worse yet, creation of the Grand Duchy gave Napoleon an excuse to station French troops alarmingly close to Russia. This fact did not sit at all well with the Russian nobility, and they let Alexander know it at every opportunity.

Another reason the Russian nobility didn't like the creation of the Grand Duchy of Warsaw was that Napoleon instituted many of the same reforms he had brought to France. He abolished the old feudal system, freed the serfs, and brought other legal and social reforms to the Poles. He promoted religious freedom and tolerance, and he opened the Jewish ghettos.

Not surprisingly, the feudalistic nobility of Russia was not at all pleased with this development so close to home. If the serfs on one side of the border could be freed, why not on the other side? And religious freedom was not exactly at the top of their priority list either, as the relationship between the state and the Orthodox Church was, shall we say, quite close. In short, the Russian nobility looked across the border and didn't like what they saw one little bit. They pressured Alexander to get Napoleon to desert the Poles, but Napoleon refused to cooperate. He never gave the Poles the completely independent state they really wanted, but neither did he desert them to the whims of their Russian neighbor, and for this they were exceedingly grateful.

Napoleon felt compelled to keep his word to the Poles, but he had other concerns as well. If he deserted the Poles, Russia would move in, sooner rather than later. Then she would likely try to expand further west, causing tension with Napoleon's other allies. That circumstance would likely lead to war, but on Russia's terms rather than on France's. This would not be good news for France, and Napoleon knew it. Thus, Poland was in several ways at the heart of the eventual war between Russia and France.

Continental divide

The other major problem was the provision of the Treaty of Tilsit that brought Russia into the Continental System. That system was an economic blockade of Great Britain, which meant that Russia was not allowed to trade with the British. Again, the Russian nobles were upset, along with the merchant class.

Russia depended a great deal on trade and had historically had substantial trade with Great Britain. To have this source of income removed just so Napoleon could bring the British to terms was more than many people in Russia could swallow.

It's important to understand that while Tsar Alexander I was, well, a tsar, he couldn't completely ignore the wishes and needs of his nobility or his merchants. Tsars who fell out of favor were susceptible to sudden illness and death, among other things. (After all, Alexander's father, Paul I, met an untimely death.) Indeed, some nobles were less than subtle in their pressures on Alexander to abandon his friendship with Napoleon. Absolute rulers are never as absolute as they may like to be, or as their image may suggest. (The term *tsar* is based on the name Caesar, as in Julius Caesar, and we all know what happened to him!) It didn't help Napoleon's cause that Alexander's mother was completely opposed to Napoleon and to any good relations between the two countries. Even a tsar must listen to his mother!

The Continental System was almost as harmful to its participants as it was to England, and Russia suffered as much as (or more than) anyone. As a result,

- ✔ By 1810, Russia was opening its ports to neutral ships carrying British goods. This was a sham, as many of the ships were simply flying bogus flags, including American.

- ✔ At about the same time, the Russians also began to put prohibitive tariffs on French goods. These taxes made it very difficult for French merchants to sell items to the Russians, and it was tantamount to an act of economic warfare by Russia.

- ✔ Alexander also made threatening moves toward Warsaw, but the presence in that city of Marshal Davout and his army prevented further Russian adventures.

Each side continued posturing as 1812 approached. In April of that year, Tsar Alexander offered to reinvigorate his efforts (such as they were) to enforce the Continental System, but his offer came with conditions that were unacceptable to Napoleon. He wanted Napoleon to give him part of the Grand Duchy of Warsaw and allow Russia to continue to trade with so-called neutral ships. Napoleon wasn't about to do either of these. Both sides wanted peace, but both sides realized that war was inevitable and began to make preparations.

Getting Russia Ready for War

When Tsar Alexander realized that war with France was just over the horizon, he began to get his ducks lined up:

✔ To secure his northern flank, he cut a deal with Swedish Crown Prince Jean-Baptiste Bernadotte (see Figure 13-1). This is the same Bernadotte who married Napoleon's first love, Désirée Clary (see Chapter 5). Bernadotte had previously asked Napoleon to help him regain control of Norway, but Napoleon had declined. When Alexander showed signs of cooperation in that area, Bernadotte offered to support him in any war with France. The Convention of St. Petersburg, signed in April 1812, tied Sweden and Russia together and secured Alexander's northern border.

Figure 13-1:
Marshal Bernadotte, seen here in a 19th-century engraving, married Napoleon's first girl-friend and was a thorn in his side ever after.

✔ Russia had been involved in a war with Turkey since 1806, but Alexander managed to bring it to an end by May 1812.

✔ Alexander negotiated a trade treaty with England, which was finalized in July.

Also, since 1810, Alexander had been working hard to reform the Russian army — not one of the finest armies in Europe. Alexander followed Napoleon's lead in organizing his army in an efficient corps system (see Chapter 17). He also improved its weaponry, as well as its level of artillery support. While it was not as good an army as that fielded by Napoleon, it was an improvement over the Russian armies that fought at Austerlitz and Friedland (see Chapter 10).

Preparing France for War

Napoleon had long anticipated the possibility of war with Alexander and had planned accordingly. For two years leading up to 1812, he reinforced his military outposts in the Grand Duchy of Warsaw and in Germany. In 1811, he even tried to negotiate a peace with Great Britain, anticipating that her difficulties with the United States might make her, finally, willing to come to terms with France. Great Britain's troubles with the United States did worsen, leading to the War of 1812, but that wasn't enough to get her to agree to peace with France. Instead, she threw in her lot with Russia. Very few people were surprised by this development.

Growing the army

One advantage of Napoleon's system of empire and alliances was that countries other than France got to provide soldiers for the *Grande Armée.* This was just as well. France's war with Spain, which I discuss in Chapter 12, was tying down a quarter million troops, and conscriptions were both unpopular and increasingly unproductive. Napoleon had to fight a two-front war, and he needed soldiers.

To augment his army, Napoleon signed treaties with Austria and Prussia that gained him a total of at least 50,000 men and assured him that neither country would take advantage of the situation to move against Napoleon. Naples, various states in the Confederation of the Rhine, the Grand Duchy of Warsaw, and other allies would further increase Napoleon's effective fighting strength.

Napoleon's efforts to bolster the size of his army were hugely successful. He amassed an army of almost 600,000 men for this campaign. It was the most massive army in history up to that point, and it seemed capable of simply rolling over any opponent, especially because it was commanded by the greatest military commander of his (and perhaps of any) time. However, it was not without its problems:

✔ This was an allied army, no more than half of which was French. This meant that

- Twenty different nations were represented.

- Each nation had its own uniform and its own flag.

- Each army also had its own *language,* making communication difficult and slow. (Luckily, French was the language of the educated classes, which included the officer corps of virtually all armies.)

- Non-French soldiers were not as motivated and dedicated, to say nothing of loyal, as their French counterparts.

✔ Some of Napoleon's leaders were not all they could be:

- Field Marshal Prince Karl Schwarzenberg of Austria and other foreign commanders were only fair generals, and their loyalty to Napoleon was more than likely limited.

- While some of Napoleon's marshals and generals, such as Louis Davout and Joachim Murat, were among his very best, others were mediocre.

Stocking supplies

While Napoleon may have preferred that Alexander attack the Grand Duchy of Warsaw, thus giving Napoleon the moral high ground, he knew that he would likely have to invade Russia. It made some sense to take the war to Russia rather than allow it to be fought on allied territory. Accordingly, Napoleon began to increase his stores of supplies at all of his most forward positions. Everything from medical supplies to food, from ammunition to wine was sent as far east as possible. Napoleon was determined that his soldiers should not want for anything.

One thing that they did want for, unfortunately, was horses. For at least two years, the French army and its allied forces were short of horses. Napoleon did all he could to purchase horses from any possible source, but his effort was just barely successful. There would be no spare horses for the Russian campaign, which would eventually impact his soldiers greatly.

Hoping for a quick battle

A final problem faced by Napoleon and his army was the very nature of the war they were about to fight. Napoleon understood history, and he knew that no recent invading force had been successful in Russia. Still, he anticipated that the Russians would defend their country by giving battle right away. Napoleon expected to win that battle, and any others that followed, and quickly achieve victory. Had Russia done that, his expectations would have likely been fulfilled.

But Napoleon should have paid attention to what Alexander was saying (and to what made perfect sense). If he had, he may have realized that the Russians wouldn't engage the French allied troops in an immediate battle. Instead, Alexander would withdraw his forces deeper and deeper into Mother Russia, stretching the French lines of communication and running them low on supplies.

In looking at all the problems facing Napoleon, it is easy to fall into the trap of believing that the Russian campaign was a foolish mistake. But at the time, to the casual observer and careful analyst alike, it seemed that Napoleon would most likely succeed. His allies thought so, and many people in Russia thought so as well. Indeed, some thought Napoleon would not stop with Russia. These people believed that after Napoleon defeated Russia and once again secured Alexander's friendship, he would follow in the footsteps of Alexander the Great and march all the way to India. Things just didn't turn out that way.

Invading Mother Russia

For all the causes of concern, it was clearly an impressive and optimistic sight when Napoleon's *Grande Armée* marched across the Niemen River on June 24, 1812. Any Russian on the other side would have certainly wondered if anyone could stand up to this mass of military might. What's more, the Russians seemed to be playing right into Napoleon's hands. Their force was divided into three armies:

- ✔ The First Western Army, commanded by General Barclay de Tolly, fielded about 127,000 men.

- ✔ The Second Western Army, commanded by General Peter Bagration, had a little under 50,000 soldiers.

- ✔ The Third Western Army, commanded by General Alexander Tormazov, was just being organized and would eventually have perhaps 43,000 men.

Seeking a battle

Napoleon's basic plan was simple: He would try to position his main force between the two Russian armies and defeat each of them in turn. It was the old divide-and-conquer approach that had worked so well in the past, and it was a perfectly reasonable approach here as well. Unfortunately for Napoleon, it didn't work out as well as he had expected.

We may never know if the Russian strategy was predetermined, but there is no question as to its success. Rather than standing and fighting, the Russians simply continued to withdraw in the face of overwhelming odds. The French managed to force some skirmishes and won them all, but Napoleon initially was frustrated in his desire to seek a major battle.

Napoleon and his commanders were partly to blame for the turn of events. Exasperating delays were the order of the day. Because of the sheer size of the *Grande Armée,* it moved very slowly, and the roads became so clogged that supplies could hardly get to the front. In some cases, soldiers were near starvation because of the supply problems. Communication, usually a strong point in Napoleon's campaigns, was slow at best. Add to that some indecisive leadership by certain subordinates, as well as uncooperative weather, and already things were not going well.

That uncooperative weather deserves a mention. Later in this chapter, I discuss how awful the weather was during Napoleon's withdrawal from Russia. But the weather on the way in was just about as bad. It was so hot that many soldiers died from exhaustion or thirst.

Horses were especially hard-hit by the weather — thousands of them died along the way — and Napoleon had no extra horses to spare. Horses pull baggage carts and cannon, as well as carry cavalry, so in some ways men were more expendable than horses. In the entire Russian campaign, Napoleon would lose as many as 200,000 horses, and in the campaigns of 1813 and 1814 (see Chapter 14), he would dearly miss them.

All the delays cost the French several chances for an important victory. For example, General de Tolly had been surprised by the French advance and may have been caught in an open and isolated position. But Prince Eugène de Beauharnais (Napoleon's stepson, who was Prince of Bavaria) was unable to get his force into position in time, and de Tolly escaped. General Bagration was similarly able to evade the forces of Prince Jérôme (Napoleon's brother), and he later avoided major contact with Marshal Davout's forces when Eugène and Jérôme each failed to arrive with timely support.

Waiting for Alexander

Napoleon continued to push forward into Russia, and on June 28th he entered the town of Vilna. So far, he had won several skirmishes and pushed the Russians back. By most standards, he was doing fine. So fine that he figured Alexander, knowing what he was up against, would seek peace terms. Or, if not peace, Alexander would offer a battle to decide the issue once and for all.

Napoleon sat in Vilna for 18 days, but nothing came from Alexander or any of his commanders. By mid-July, it was clear that Alexander wasn't sending any envoys seeking peace and the Russian armies were not coming to give battle. Napoleon had to make a decision. He considered staying in Vilna until the next spring (almost a full year). He could use that time to

✔ Consolidate his position.

✔ Reorganize his army.

✔ Bring supplies forward.

✔ Fortify the town to serve as a safe base for future operations.

✔ Prepare for a spring push, either to St. Petersburg (where the tsar was) or to Moscow.

But Napoleon scrapped the plan to stay in Vilna, fearing that an idle army would be of little use by the next spring. Instead, he began to move forward, still seeking that one, decisive battle with the Russians.

As he moved toward the Russian town of Vitebsk, on his northern, or left, flank, Napoleon found out that General de Tolly had been isolated there, with Marshal Davout keeping General Bagration from coming to his support. This situation was just what Napoleon wanted, and he pushed forward quickly.

Then, just when he had his chance for victory, Napoleon delayed his action against General de Tolly by a day, waiting for reinforcements. General de Tolly took full advantage of this delay and beat a hasty retreat. Napoleon took the city after some minor engagements, but the main Russian force had once again eluded him. Both Russian forces moved toward the city of Smolensk, where they could finally unite.

His army exhausted and the summer fading fast, Napoleon again gave thought to calling a halt to operations until the following spring. He had defeated the Russians in their major encounters and now controlled much of their western territory. If he made it clear he was in Russia to stay, perhaps Alexander would come to his senses and seek peace. But staying there and doing nothing might look weak, and declaring victory and going home might look weaker yet. So, after a two-week stay to rest the soldiers and bring up supplies and reinforcements, onward the allied army went.

Taking a city by storm

Napoleon moved on Smolensk and discovered to his pleasure that the two Russian armies were there. Though they had combined forces, Napoleon was happy because he was finally going to get the battle he wanted. Had he moved immediately, he could have fought them in front of Smolensk. Instead, he declared a cessation of hostilities for one day. That was August 15th, his birthday. But the birthday present was to the Russians, who withdrew into Smolensk and prepared its defenses.

For the next two days, fighting raged in the suburbs of Smolensk. On August 18th, there was a lull in the action. During the lull, and rather amazingly, from the French point of view, Bagration's army withdrew, leaving General de Tolly to fight an overwhelmingly superior French force! Napoleon, perhaps unable to believe his good fortune, failed to quickly pursue the retreating Bagration or to attack General de Tolly's remaining forces. As a result, both Russian forces faded from the scene, leaving Napoleon with a sacked and partially burned Smolensk.

While the engagement in Smolensk was going on, French forces under Marshal Nicolas Oudinot and General Gouvion St-Cyr pushed back Russians led by General Ludwig Wittgenstein in what is known as the *First Battle of Polotsk* on August 17–18, 1812. This battle, depicted in Figure 13-2, led Napoleon to believe that all was going well and that it was safe to move further into Russia. (The Russians and French would fight there again in November, with the French winning again.)

Figure 13-2:
The First Battle of Polotsk. This 19th-century engraving shows the second day of the battle with General Gouvion St-Cyr leading a charge.

Decisions, decisions

Now Napoleon had some really tough decisions to make. It was moving on toward late August; summer was fading fast. He had had limited success against the Russians, but they had had no success against him, save their success at continually retreating. Napoleon could stay in Smolensk and crank out publicity saying that he had conquered much of western Russia and had two Russian armies on the run. He was not too overextended and would be fairly secure in Smolensk.

While he was there, he could really stick it to Alexander by declaring Poland a fully independent nation. This would make him an even greater Polish hero, and Russia would really have a hornet's nest on its border. Napoleon could do that, declare victory, keep his captured territory, and dare Alexander to do anything about it. And if Smolensk was not a good place to winter, having been burned and sacked by the retreating Russians, it would have been easy to move his army to Vitebsk, where he would have had plenty of everything and his supply lines would have been shorter. (Since his soldiers did not have winter uniforms, supplies were an important consideration.)

The allure of these options notwithstanding, Napoleon became convinced that the only real option was to take the fight to the Russians. He still wanted to win a peace and get back to Paris in 1812. So he had to decide whether to move on St. Petersburg, where the tsar was headquartered, or on Moscow, in which direction the Russian army had withdrawn. Seeking a fight, Napoleon moved toward Moscow. That city was the emotional center of Russia; surely the army would not surrender it without a fight.

Giving a beating at Borodino

For once in this campaign, Napoleon was right. The Russian people would not tolerate a tsar who simply yielded the holy city of Moscow to the infidel French. Alexander sent Field Marshal Prince Mikhail Kutusov to assume command of the two Russian armies, with orders to finally confront the French. That confrontation came near the town of Borodino, only about 70 miles from Moscow.

By this time, Napoleon was down to 130,000 men and 600 cannon. A fair number of soldiers had died or deserted along the way, and Napoleon had to leave a number of units to guard his flanks and his supply lines in the rear. Several of these units were involved in significant action against smaller Russian forces. Garrisons also were stationed at several cities, including Smolensk and Vitebsk. Opposing him was Kutusov with 154,000 men and 624 cannon. Moreover, the Russians had the advantage of having selected their positions and fortified them.

On September 5th, heavy fighting gained the French control of the Schevardino Redoubt, a key element to their forward progress. (A *redoubt* is usually a fortified hill with a trench around it, a very good defensive position.) On September 6th, both sides rested and reorganized for the battle that both knew would come the next day.

Fighting began on the morning of the 7th, and at first it went well for the French. Prince Eugène captured the village of Borodino, and Marshal Michel Ney grabbed portions of an important defensive site known as the *Three Arrows.* Ney asked Napoleon to send in the Imperial Guard cavalry to deliver a crushing blow, but Napoleon declined. (Criticism of Napoleon for this decision is misguided second-guessing. Had he thrown in the Imperial Guard and had it been defeated, the *Grand Armée* would have been finished, and Napoleon with it. It would have been the ultimate gamble: Thousands of miles from home, toss the dice for either a complete victory or a complete disaster.)

The major battle was fought over what was called the *Great Redoubt* (see Figure 13-3). The Russians were dug in, and they poured grapeshot and musket fire on the attacking French. The French soldiers were tenacious, and by late in the day the Great Redoubt was in French hands. As the Russians withdrew from the redoubt, they were fired on by their own cannon but not pursued by Murat's cavalry. During the night, the Russians left the field of battle with little interference by the French. Napoleon chose to consolidate his victory rather than try to destroy the Russian army. (If you want to criticize any of Napoleon's decisions, this one may deserve it.)

Figure 13-3:
This 19th-century engraving shows French soldiers charging a Russian redoubt at the Battle of Borodino, also known as the Battle of the Moskova.

On paper, the Battle of Borodino was a French victory. Russian losses were over 44,000, compared to 33,000 French. But the battle was a bloodbath for both sides, with the French much less able to replace their losses.

One major loss for the Russians was Prince Peter Bagration. One of Russia's finest commanders, he had been responsible for saving much of the Russian army at the Battle of Austerlitz in 1805 (see Chapter 9). He fought bravely at Borodino but was fatally wounded, dying a few days after the battle.

Entering Moscow

The Russians retreated to Moscow but quickly decided not to attempt its defense. The Russian rear guard was leaving as Murat's cavalry was entering, but neither side sought a confrontation. By all normal standards of war, the French had won. They had defeated the Russians at every encounter, captured several important cities, and were now moving into the Kremlin itself. (The Kremlin is a huge walled city within a city, a major fortress that is still the most dominant feature of Moscow.) Both the French and the Russians anticipated that Alexander and Napoleon would agree to peace terms and that the war would shortly be over. No one wants to be the *last* soldier killed in a war!

Count Fyodor Vasilievich Rostopchin, the governor of Moscow, had also deserted the city, but he had left orders to destroy everything that could possibly be of any use to the French. He took with him all available firefighting equipment. Shortly after Napoleon entered the city on September 15, 1812, the Russians set fire to their own city. Napoleon was forced to abandon the Kremlin (which ultimately was not harmed by the fire) and watch 80 percent of the city go up in flames from a vantage point on a nearby hill. For much of the 200 years since the campaign, people have blamed the French for the fires. But the French were ill-served by the destruction of the very city upon which they then depended for food and shelter, and we now know that the Russians themselves burned Moscow.

Burning the city was probably a brilliant move, as it effectively removed Moscow as a likely winter home for the French army. Napoleon stayed there for 35 days, sending peace overtures to Alexander, as well as to Kutusov. Neither man gave Napoleon the courtesy of a reply. Napoleon considered wintering in Moscow, but that option was finally rejected; they were just too far from home. The supply lines would be a nightmare to maintain, and there was too great a risk of political intrigue in Paris if Napoleon were gone that long. When Murat's cavalry, which had been living in extremely poor conditions outside of Moscow, was surprised by a Russian attack and handed a defeat on October 18th, Napoleon quickly decided to leave. The next day, the first elements of the no longer so *Grande Armée* began to leave Moscow.

Making the Long Return Home

Napoleon wisely decided to return by way of a more southerly route, rather than go back through Borodino. This decision would avoid returning through land that had already been stripped bare. There was only one problem: Kutusov stood in his way. The two faced each other at Maloyaroslavets, 68 miles southwest of Moscow. Napoleon won that engagement but was concerned that Kutusov would be able to regroup his forces and attack again. Had Napoleon reconnoitered over the ridge in front of him, he would have discovered that the Russians had melted away and the way was relatively clear. But Napoleon didn't do that. Instead, he turned north, where eventually he would retrace his steps through Borodino and on to Smolensk.

Borodino was a ghastly sight, with tens of thousands of bloated bodies still strewn about the field and on the roads. On November 6th, winter struck hard, and the withdrawal became more and more a desperate fleeing to safety. On the 9th, Napoleon reached Smolensk, but supplies there were almost immediately devoured by the first soldiers to arrive. There would be no winter quartering in that city, and Napoleon pushed on.

Fighting "General Frost"

The winter soon became the greatest enemy. Men froze to death while walking or while asleep. Warm clothing and food were at a premium; horse meat was a delicacy. What few horses they still had left were unlikely to survive, and the consequent loss of cavalry made their military situation precarious. Only reuniting with several rear-guard forces gave the men any hope at all.

The horrors of the winter withdrawal from Russia provide one of the most lasting images of that campaign and, indeed, of all of Napoleon's campaigns. The British caricature shown in Figure 13-4 (which, ironically, I bought in Moscow) pretty much tells the story of Napoleon's real enemy, "General Frost." As I explain in Chapter 21, this kind of caricature was quite common during Napoleon's time.

Figure 13-4:
This British caricature from 1812 shows "General Frost" wearing a hat labeled "Mountains of Ice" and threatening to bury "Little Boney" for having invaded his country.

GENERAL FROST *Shaving* LITTLE BONEY

The last major obstacle to Napoleon's withdrawal from Russia was the Beresina River. As bitter as the winter was, it was not bitter enough to freeze the river sufficiently to allow crossing on the ice. Existing bridges had been destroyed by the Russians, and Napoleon has jettisoned his pontoon bridge building equipment just days earlier, as he had expected the river to be frozen solid. Under these circumstances, Napoleon and his engineers really proved their mettle. With Napoleon directing and providing inspiration, his engineers built two bridges, one for men and one for horses and carts. In spite of Russian efforts and a last-minute panic by some soldiers and many camp followers (women, pro-French Russians, and other hangers on), most of the army got across the river (see Figure 13-5), and the bridges were then destroyed to keep the Russians from following. Thousands died or were wounded in the crossing, but the army was saved.

With the army now reasonably safe from the Russians, though not from the bitter cold, Napoleon determined that he was needed in Paris to counter fears that he had been killed. Napoleon had already been told of an unsuccessful plot to overthrow his government that had used as its excuse Napoleon's alleged death. The plot, led by General Claude-François Malet, had failed, but it was enough to convince Napoleon and his staff that he needed to get to Paris as quickly as possible. The next several Bulletins would end with the phrase, "The Emperor's health was never better."

Figure 13-5:
This period engraving by Raffet shows both the tenderness and horror of the French situation at the crossing of the Beresina River.

Very few heroes were created during the Russian campaign. One of the few was Marshal Michel Ney, a tall, red-headed cavalryman with unequaled bravery and a fondness for profanity. Already one of Napoleon's best marshals (though he was less than bright and not much good at thinking for himself in certain situations), Ney had been given the title *Prince of the Moskova* for his bravery at Borodino. During the march back to France, Ney commanded the rear guard and tenaciously defended against Russian attacks, allowing what little was left of the *Grande Armée* to get safely out of Russia. Ney, it is generally believed, was the last French commander to leave Russia. For all this, he received another well-deserved title: The Bravest of the Brave (see Figure 13-6).

Understanding the consequences

The Russian campaign of 1812 was a disaster. Napoleon probably had little choice in undertaking it, as he could hardly let Russia do as she pleased regarding Poland and the Continental System. But Napoleon had several choices along the way, and he often made the wrong one. His delays and indecisions, and those of his subordinates, kept him from wrapping up the campaign in the summer or fall, when there would still have been time for his army to establish suitable winter quarters. He allowed himself to be drawn far deeper into Russia than he had ever planned; even Smolensk was beyond what he had anticipated. His delay in Moscow was inexcusable and was the single greatest error of the campaign. Had he left after only two weeks, his trip home would have been far, far different.

Figure 13-6:
Marshal
Michel Ney,
Prince
of the
Moskova,
Bravest of
the Brave, is
shown in
this period
engraving
returning
from Russia.

Napoleon never really recovered from the debacle of 1812. He lost half a million men, French and allied, and as many as 200,000 horses. In the campaigns to come, he would miss them all, especially the horses. The loss in cannon and supplies was immeasurable and would take a long time to replace.

But the worst consequence for Napoleon was the loss of his reputation. Spain had tarnished it, but much of the problem in Spain was that Napoleon was not there in person. He *was* there in Russia and had shown the world that he was not invincible after all. Still tough, still determined, still brilliant, but not invincible. That knowledge was all that some of his old enemies needed, and as the year 1812 drew to a close, some of them were about to start settling old scores.

Chapter 14

Defeat and Resurrection

· ·

In This Chapter

▶ Defending an empire and a nation

▶ Winning and losing, but mostly losing

▶ Coming so close but yet so far

▶ Gaining a new "empire"

▶ Returning as Caesar

▶ Preparing for Armageddon

· ·

After the disastrous 1812 campaign in Russia (see Chapter 13), Napoleon returned to Paris and organized a new army to prepare to defend the core of his empire: France and Germany. Tsar Alexander I of Russia seemed intent on pursuing the French army far beyond the Russian borders. The tsar began to see himself as the leader of a holy crusade, and we all know how determined people can be when they feel they are fighting for God.

But Napoleon still had a decent army and quite a few allies, so the result of Russia's crusade was not a foregone conclusion. And besides, Napoleon was, well, Napoleon. Anyone who thought defeating this master of war was going to be a cakewalk might find himself being served up on a platter!

In this chapter, I explain how Napoleon spent 1813 defending Germany and much of 1814 defending France. I show you that military opposition isn't the only thing he had to face at the time — there was also plenty of politics to go around — and I take you with Napoleon into exile on the island of Elba. After a short visit (sorry, no time to lie on the beach), we join Napoleon as he returns to France for one last throw of the dice.

Trying to Keep the Wolves at Bay

In Chapter 13, I mention that while Napoleon was busy in Russia, there was an attempted coup in France led by a somewhat crazy general named Claude-François Malet. That coup was based on the rumor that Napoleon was dead. Although the coup failed, it raised the question of why no one tried to rally behind Napoleon's new wife, the Empress Marie Louise, or the son they had together in 1811, who held the title of King of Rome. (Yes, I know, last you checked Napoleon was married to Josephine. See Chapter 20 for how all of that changed, and why.)

Napoleon's appearance in Paris put an end to the rumors and to any further coup attempts. Still, Napoleon had discovered just how fragile his empire was and how much it depended on his success on the battlefield.

Facing a Sixth Coalition

Napoleon's invasion of Russia failed, as I explain in Chapter 13. But most of Europe was still, at least on paper, allied with Napoleon or part of his empire. Thus, it was entirely possible that Russia would advance to her borders, look across at the French, cry out "Take that, sucker," and go back home.

There were two problems with that scenario:

✔ Tsar Alexander I did not like the Grand Duchy of Warsaw — the independent Polish state created by Napoleon. At the very least, he was determined to incorporate all or most of it into Russian territory.

✔ Napoleon's reputation had been tarnished so badly by the problems in Russia that at least two of his so-called allies — Prussia and Austria — were thinking seriously of jumping ship.

Losing Prussia as an ally

The first of these erstwhile friends to jump ship was Prussia. She had been bitter toward Napoleon ever since her defeat in 1806 (see Chapter 10), and her loyalty to the French Empire was tenuous at best. Indeed, as the Russian army advanced, more than a few Prussian soldiers simply switched sides.

The government of Prussia declared war on France on March 13, 1813, and by spring a Sixth Coalition was forming, consisting at first of Russia, Sweden, Great Britain, and Prussia. (As I explain in previous chapters, the first five coalitions had each been formed with the goal of defeating France as well. None had succeeded.)

Anticipating the coming conflict, Napoleon worked hard to reform his army. He had factories working overtime to make more cannon, and he recruited everyone he could lay his hands on. He tried to get as many horses as possible, but they were especially difficult to obtain. Trained horses were just about nonexistent, at least in the numbers he needed.

Some of the major players in the Sixth Coalition, including Prussia and, later, Austria, were not as intent on destroying Napoleon as they were on driving the French out of Germany. For that reason, Napoleon suspected that his allies in Germany, particularly Saxony and Bavaria, might be willing to jump into the Coalition. Russia, on the other hand, was on a holy war that would end only in Paris itself.

These differing views of Coalition goals left an opening for Napoleon. If he could achieve some quick victories, his alliance might hold, and the Coalition might falter. If not, anything was possible.

Taking on the Prussian troops

By May 1813, Napoleon's army was in pretty good fighting condition. He took personal command as it moved east to fight the Coalition at the Battle of Lützen on May 2 in the northern German region of Saxony. Marshal Michel Ney was taking on a sizable, allied, Prussian-Russian force, led by Russian General Prince Ludwig Wittgenstein. Ney fought bravely, and when Napoleon brought up troops to reinforce him, the rout was on. Unfortunately, Napoleon's lack of horses meant that he had precious little cavalry. His pursuit of the fleeing enemy was mediocre at best, and the combined forces withdrew.

Each side lost around 20,000 men at the battle, but the French held the field and claimed the victory. Even with such high losses, the victory did wonders for French morale and made the Coalition allies wonder at least a bit if they had made a mistake taking on Napoleon again.

Napoleon well understood that he had to maintain what advantage he had, so he had his army press on after the allied Prussian and Russian forces. He caught up to them at Bautzen. Napoleon had 150,000 men, while the Coalition forces, led by Field Marshal Gebhardt Lebrecht von Blücher, had just under 100,000 in a defensive position. Even with that advantage, Napoleon's lack of adequate cavalry, plus some mistakes made by Ney in getting his forces lined up, caused the French to take their time in preparing for battle.

The battle commenced at noon on May 20, and by nightfall the French had made significant advances. The fighting continued the next day, with the French pushing the Coalition back. Ney took forever to get into position and, as a result, was never able to outflank the Coalition forces, which allowed them to again escape with their army pretty much intact.

As at Lützen, each side lost around 20,000 men. Napoleon had won two decisive victories but would end up with little to show for it. Napoleon may well have cried out, "My kingdom for a horse," as in both battles the lack of horses kept his victories from being complete routs of the enemy.

The Coalition allies, on the other hand, had just suffered two defeats and were pretty fed up. They decided it would be a good idea to have at least an *armistice* (a temporary lull in fighting while each side explores the possibility of peace). Austria, in theory still an ally of France, agreed to mediate between the two sides.

Things seemed to look reasonably good for Napoleon. He had won two victories, the leadership of the Coalition forces against him was unable to agree on strategy, and his reputation as a great commander was on the mend.

Being undermined by Austria

Napoleon was also confident that he had the support of his ally Austria. His wife, Marie Louise, was the daughter of the Austrian emperor, Francis. The purpose of the marriage was in large part to tie Napoleon's new French Empire to one of the oldest empires in Europe, the Hapsburg Empire. The marriage in 1810 seemed a good idea for both Austria and France, and Francis was quite pleased with the arrangement. (See Chapter 20 for more on Napoleon's second marriage.)

Austria hadn't been the greatest of allies, but she had provided soldiers for the disastrous campaign in Russia. Most of her troops had not been involved in the heart of the campaign, instead playing flanking and rear-guard roles. When the Russians chased Napoleon out of Russia and then kept on coming, they didn't pay much attention to either the Prussians or the Austrians, hoping in both cases to gain them as allies against Napoleon.

Napoleon was quite aware of Austrians' general lack of enthusiasm for their alliance with France, and he did everything he could to cement the relationship. He had named his son his heir and also named Marie Louise as *regent* (someone who runs a country until the legitimate ruler is old enough to take charge for himself). In short, Napoleon played the family ties thing for all it was worth. As it turned out, it wasn't worth very much at all.

Francis had promised to provide soldiers to help Napoleon take the fight to the oncoming Prussians and Russians. Had he done so, Napoleon's victories may well have been overwhelming, and the Prussians, at least, may have decided to duck out of the action. But Francis's soldiers were phantoms: They never materialized.

Holding talks that lead to nowhere

When Napoleon defeated the Coalition forces for the second time in 1813, both sides were interested in an armistice. Emperor Francis, anxious to get involved, offered his foreign minister, Count Clemens Metternich, to mediate between the two sides. Both sides were pleased with the chance to rest their armies and train raw recruits. (Many of Napoleon's new recruits were just in their teens, but they proved loyal to the end. They were frequently referred to as *Marie-Louises,* after the young empress.)

It soon became clear that Metternich was less interested in mediation than he was in forcing an unacceptable peace down Napoleon's throat. He joined

Prussia and Russia in insisting that Napoleon give up virtually everything he had gained since 1800. While Napoleon may have received at least a temporary peace in return, his acceptance to these terms would have been a disaster at home. All the fighting, all the wars, all the deaths would have been for almost nothing. The people of France would not stand for it, and Napoleon — and Metternich — knew it. It was a fool's bargain, and Napoleon was no fool.

The offer had one big advantage for the Coalition partners: They could claim that the subsequent war with France was the result of Napoleon's ego and refusal to make peace. The truth was that the Coalition was determined to destroy him. Nonetheless, the image of an egotistical and war-mongering Napoleon has lingered for 200 years. It is one reason that so many people, incorrectly, refer to the *Napoleonic Wars* rather than the *Wars of the Coalitions Against Napoleonic France.*

The armistice and talks led to the final break between France and Austria. Despite Marie Louise, despite the alliance, despite all that Napoleon had done to maintain good relations with Francis, Metternich and Francis determined that Napoleon's star was no longer rising and that they would be better off joining the Coalition. So, on August 12, 1813, Austria declared war on France. The armistice was over, and war would commence.

Trying a new Coalition tactic

Napoleon's reputation had been somewhat restored by his victories against the Prussians and Russians, so the Coalition partners agreed on at least one thing: They would try to avoid facing Napoleon directly, instead concentrating on defeating his marshals and generals who were detached from Napoleon's main force. This could be a risky approach, as Napoleon might win some great victory that would negate Coalition victories elsewhere. But the strategy ended up being just about perfect.

Napoleon was able to relieve besieged French forces at Dresden and win a decisive victory on August 27, 1813. This was very important, as Dresden was a major supply depot for Napoleon and was located in Saxony, one of his key allies. It was a major victory, with at least 38,000 Coalition casualties compared to about 10,000 French losses. But French General Dominique Vandamme was unable to trap and destroy the retreating Coalition army, and Coalition victories over other French marshals took the shine off Napoleon's victory.

Napoleon wanted to capture Berlin and perhaps drive the Prussians out of the Coalition. But every time he made moves in that direction, Coalition forces elsewhere required his attention. For much of the time, Napoleon was kept off balance and unable to isolate and decisively defeat any of his opponents. On October 6, Bavaria switched sides, joining the Coalition in return for guarantees of her independence. Napoleon's Confederation of the Rhine — the collection of small German states that were allied to France — was starting to come apart.

Napoleon marshaled his forces at Leipzig, having perhaps a quarter of a million men at his disposal, though less than that in the immediate vicinity. He managed to catch Marshal Blücher at Düben on October 9, but the Prussian commander had already begun to withdraw, and Napoleon was only able to claim victory over a rear guard. By that time, Coalition forces were converging on Leipzig, setting up the major battle of the campaign.

Facing disaster at Leipzig

Napoleon had almost 200,000 soldiers in Leipzig and the surrounding area, but the Coalition forces numbered over 200,000 with more on the way. It was a difficult situation, but Napoleon was determined to make the best of it. He ordered his army to strike at forming Coalition forces before they could completely unite against the French. French attacks, and counterattacks against moves by the Coalition, worked for a time, but Napoleon's outmanned forces were constantly kept off balance. The lack of cavalry continued to haunt French efforts.

The first day of conflict, October 16, 1813, was indecisive. The French lost fewer soldiers, but little territory changed hands. Worse, the Coalition was awaiting the arrival of about 150,000 soldiers, while Napoleon could only hope for 10 percent of that total to arrive in his support. It was a bad situation and about to get worse.

October 17 saw little action, as both sides rested and consolidated their positions. This was much better news for the Coalition than for Napoleon, as major reinforcements arrived throughout the day. Napoleon was aware of the situation and belatedly decided to withdraw in the early hours of October 18. Heavy rain hampered the withdrawal efforts, but as the day progressed much of the army managed to get across some bridges near the Leipzig suburb of Lindenau.

French forces were stunned by the sudden defection of two divisions of the Saxon army, who literally turned around and started firing on their allies of moments ago. The defectors were repulsed by the French, but the significance of their actions was not lost on anyone.

Napoleon attempted to buy some time by offering an armistice to Austria and the Coalition. The Coalition forces, smelling blood, refused to show much interest, though the effort did delay major military moves on their part until mid-morning of October 19.

Napoleon had decided that his supplies were too low to continue fighting and had ordered a general retreat across the one remaining bridge, with Marshal Nicolas Oudinot and Prince Marshal Joseph Poniatowski (who had achieved that rank just the previous day) directing the rear guard. All was going reasonably well, and the rear guard was about to be evacuated. The retreat would have signaled a French defeat, but Leipzig would not have been considered a disaster.

Unfortunately, some underling who had been put in charge of blowing up the bridge *after* the French had all escaped instead blew it up *before* the French were across. Indeed, the bridge was full of French soldiers when the explosion hit. Some of the French managed to swim across the river to join their comrades, but at least 15,000 were captured as a result of this tragic mistake. Many others died in the resulting action.

The saddest of these losses was Prince Poniatowski, who attempted to get across the river on his horse but drowned in the effort. A symbol of the loyalty of the Poles to Napoleon's cause, Poniatowski was one of the true heroes of this period and is still a revered figure in Poland. You can see him in Figure 14-1.

Figure 14-1:
Polish
Prince
Poniatowski
was one of
Napoleon's
most loyal
supporters.

Leipzig was a disaster of monumental proportions for the French, in some ways worse than any others they suffered during the Napoleonic period:

- ✔ France lost almost 40,000 killed or wounded and another 30,000 captured.

- ✔ Napoleon's supplies were mostly destroyed or captured, and he lost several hundred vital cannon.

- ✔ Bavaria and Saxony were gone, and most of the rest of the Confederation of the Rhine would soon follow.

Napoleon had spent most of his career fighting enemies of France on foreign soil. Now, he would be forced to defend France on her own soil.

Defending the Homeland

As 1814 opened, Napoleon was in tough shape, to say the least!

- ✔ He had lost tens of thousands of troops and countless horses, supplies, and cannon during the campaign for Germany in 1813.

- ✔ His reputation was greatly tarnished and erstwhile allies were, or soon would be, leaving him like rats leaving a sinking ship.

- ✔ His son-in-law, Prince Eugène, was being defeated by the Austrians in Italy.

- ✔ Arthur Wellesley, the Duke of Wellington (known just as *Wellington*), was no longer fighting the French in Spain; he was fighting the French in France. His forces had driven quite far into the southwestern region of the country, with no end in sight.

- ✔ France was being weakened by a British economic blockade, and there was considerable political unrest in Paris, largely fomented by the treacherous Charles Maurice de Talleyrand-Périgord (otherwise known as Talleyrand), Napoleon's one-time Minister of Foreign Affairs.

- ✔ Napoleon was outnumbered and had precious few additional resources on which to draw.

But Napoleon was not without a few cards of his own to play:

- ✔ For starters, his enemies were not entirely sure just what they wanted to do. Austria had not paid a *whole* lot of attention to the fact that her emperor's daughter was on the French throne as empress, but that inconvenient fact did carry some weight. Emperor Francis wasn't sure how far he wanted to carry the campaign against Napoleon.

- ✔ Napoleon's one-time marshal Jean Bernadotte, now the Crown Prince of Sweden, likewise had some misgivings about attempting to crush Napoleon, or at least France, completely. For one thing, he was French, so a little loyalty to the homeland might be in order. He also had the (delusional) hope that France might depose Napoleon and put him, Bernadotte, on the throne. (Not bloody likely.)

- ✔ Even Great Britain was not as intent on destroying France as may be expected. Her greatest fear had always been that a Continental power would become so powerful that it could challenge England for supremacy, even on the high seas. For years, France had been the embodiment of this fear, but a resurgent Austria or, worse yet, Russia, could be just as dangerous. Better for England to find a way to obtain a peace that left France in decent shape, though preferably without Napoleon in charge.

Preparing Paris

Napoleon returned to Paris and immediately set about preparing to defend the motherland. His brother, Joseph, had been ousted as King of Spain by the combination of Spanish insurgents and Wellington's soldiers (see Chapter 12). He had done such a good job there (choke!) that Napoleon placed him in charge of governing France from Paris while Napoleon was away on campaign with his army. Joseph was no match for Talleyrand when it came to politics, so Napoleon's support in his capital city was less than he may have expected.

Nevertheless, Napoleon did what he could while he was there. He organized the defense of Paris against an anticipated attack, and he publicly reaffirmed Marie Louise as regent for his son, who held the title of King of Rome. Napoleon clearly hoped that even his defeat would not destroy his hereditary rule and that his son would be allowed to replace him with the daughter of Austria as regent. It was a pipe dream, but Napoleon could be excused for the hope, which was in keeping with how these sorts of things *usually* worked.

With Paris prepared as well as could be, Napoleon left on January 25, 1814 to rejoin his army and seek a major victory that might still turn the tide in his favor.

Seeking an elusive peace

The Coalition forces were still divided as to their ultimate goal — so much so that they decided to offer Napoleon an out. On November 16, 1813, they had offered Napoleon peace if France would withdraw to her borders of 1799. These were her so-called *natural frontiers,* which included the western bank of the Rhine River. Napoleon at first stalled and then provisionally agreed to the terms, calling for an international conference to work out the details.

If the forces allied against Napoleon had been serious, they may well have seen to it that this offer became the basis for peace. At that point, there was little likelihood of Napoleon becoming an aggressor again. The *natural frontiers* would keep France as one of the major, but not dominant, powers on the European continent. Napoleon may have been content to solidify his domestic reforms (which I discuss in Chapter 19), and the people of France may have been willing to accept the loss of their empire for a lasting peace.

Perhaps it was fear that their proposal might be accepted, perhaps it was simple distrust of Napoleon, or perhaps it was bloodlust toward the man who had defeated them so many times. Whatever the reason, the Coalition allies withdrew their offer on February 6, 1814 and made the absurd offer of peace if France would withdraw to her 1792 borders. They wanted to pretend that over 20 years of history simply didn't exist. The French people would never tolerate that, and Napoleon couldn't agree to it. The Coalition allies knew that quite well. The entire process was a sham, and hostilities soon commenced.

More bad news for Napoleon soon followed. Brussels fell in the north, which was not unexpected. What may have been unexpected was the desertion of King Joachim Murat of Naples. Murat was married to Napoleon's sister Caroline and was one of Napoleon's major marshals. Murat was expected to keep pressure on the Austrians in northern Italy. Instead, he cut a deal with the Austrians and withdrew as a French ally.

By this time, the people of Paris were beyond nervous, and many were deserting the city, fearing the worst. Talleyrand was in his treacherous element and was negotiating on a regular basis with the future Louis XVIII.

Reliving the good old days: The six-day war

For all the bad news surrounding him, Napoleon never gave up hope and never stopped trying. The Coalition forces were moving toward Paris, but they were split into forces led by Prince Karl Schwarzenberg and forces led by Marshal Blücher. The Austrian Schwarzenberg (not to be confused, as my spellchecker sometimes is, with the Austrian Arnold Schwarzenegger) was further away, so Napoleon moved to pounce on Blücher's forces, which were spread out rather thin. The campaign that followed, generally called the *Six Day Campaign,* is often considered one of Napoleon's finest, though some of the credit goes to ineffective Coalition action.

Napoleon had only about 30,000 men, but one Russian attachment to Blücher's forces had only 5,000 near the town of Champaubert. Marshals Auguste Frédéric Louis Marmont and Michel Ney defeated the Russians on February 10, 1814, killing or capturing 4,000 of the Russians. Napoleon arrived shortly thereafter to discover that his forces had lost only around 200 casualties and were now in Napoleon's classic position between the two wings of Blücher's forces.

Napoleon knew he had no time to lose; any victory would depend on speed. He led his soldiers on an overnight forced march in rain and mud to catch another Russian corps. Napoleon routed that corps the next day, February 11, enjoying a one-to-two advantage in casualties. The victory wasn't as decisive as Champaubert, but it did put Blücher on the defensive.

Determined to keep the momentum going, Napoleon turned to pursue the retreating Russians. He caught up to them near the village of Château-Thierry, and on February 12, he managed to rout them. Unfortunately for Napoleon, his lack of cavalry and the failure of a corps led by Marshal Jacques Macdonald to follow instructions allowed most of the Russians to escape. Still, it was yet another victory for Napoleon, and people were beginning to take notice.

Napoleon left with part of his force to face Prince Schwarzenberg's troops (see Figure 14-2). Blücher attempted to take advantage of the situation by attacking French forces under Marshal Marmont on February 13. The attack stalled, and Napoleon quickly brought over the Imperial Guard (Napoleon's elite fighting force) to reinforce Marmont. On February 14, the combined French forces routed Blücher's forces, though the poor (muddy) conditions of the field prevented proper use of French artillery. Even so, Blücher lost at least 7,000 men while Napoleon lost no more than 600.

Figure 14-2:
Prince Schwarzenberg commanded the Austrian forces and was temporarily defeated by Napoleon.

The good news just kept on coming, at least for a little while longer. Prince Schwarzenberg had taken advantage of Napoleon's departure to fight Blücher to make his own move on Paris. He was blocked by French forces at Valjouan (whose numbers he couldn't immediately determine), so he stopped to review the situation. Big mistake. Napoleon and his Imperial Guard moved quickly to join those French forces, and on February 17 they chased away the corps led by General Carl Wrede and gained yet another French victory. Suddenly, Schwarzenberg was no longer attacking; he was on the run. Napoleon had seemed to stymie both wings of the attacking Coalition army.

Napoleon pursued Schwarzenberg's army and caught up to it near the town of Montereau, on the Seine River. Napoleon tried to cross the river first and cut the army off. Unfortunately for the French, Marshal Claude Victor failed to follow orders, and the French army failed in its goal. Napoleon was justifiably furious and replaced Victor with General Maurice Etienne Gérard. On February 18, the French stormed Montereau, which was held by forces led by General Württemberg. The French captured all the bridges and then the town itself, and they sent Württemberg's forces retreating in extreme disarray. Württemberg lost 6,000 troops, and Napoleon less than half that number.

Failing peace

Throughout all this action, the peace talks had been off again and on again. First, the Coalition allies seemed willing to talk peace; then they suspended the talks. Napoleon initially demanded that France maintain its 1799 borders, but when he realized that his position wasn't as strong as his string of victories made it seem, he decided to settle for the borders of 1792 (an offer he had refused just a few months earlier). But by then, it was too late. The Coalition forces had finally reached an agreement to continue the war until Napoleon had been deposed.

The two sides parried at each other, but Napoleon was more and more on the defensive. His marshals and generals were unable to achieve victory without Napoleon's presence, and Napoleon simply could not be everywhere at once. Those marshals were beginning to lose heart, and Napoleon knew it. Still, he and his army fought on, hoping against hope to somehow inflict a decisive blow against an enemy that was becoming increasingly bolder.

Some marshals lost more than heart. Marshal Pierre-François-Charles Augereau had been placed in command of forces near Lyon. Defeated on March 18, 1814 and again on March 23, he abandoned Napoleon and called for the restoration of the Bourbon monarchy. Napoleon was sickened by the news, but it was a portent of things to come.

By late March, the two Coalition armies were moving toward Paris. Napoleon had to make a choice. He had a decent army, and by consolidating with forces led by Marshals Marmont and Eduoard Mortier (as well as forces in assorted fortresses), he could rampage on the enemy's lines of communication and supply and overwhelm the occasional isolated unit. He could even consider marching to join his stepson (Josephine's son) Prince Eugène in Italy, where he would have the support of the local population and maybe even the turncoat Murat.

Tsar Alexander had abandoned Moscow in 1812. Could Napoleon do the same to Paris in 1814? The answer was a resounding *non!* The French would never stand for it, nor would Napoleon's military commanders. Napoleon must beat the Coalition forces to Paris. If everything worked well, he might possibly trap many of them between Marmont's forces and his own. The race was on!

Racing to Paris

It was a race he'd lose. Word of the approach of the enemy reached Paris, and its citizens panicked. Marie Louise and her son with Napoleon, the King of Rome, left the city on March 29, and with them left any possible imperial symbol to rally the citizens of Paris. Had she stayed, perhaps Paris would have rallied to the cause; it is impossible to say. She may also have been a counter to the move to restore the Bourbon monarchy to the throne; after all, there she was, with the King of Rome, ready to take charge if Napoleon fell. (The Coalition allies didn't have a great desire to put another Louis on the throne; they were united by the desire to bring Napoleon down.)

Lest you assume Marie Louise was not loyal to her husband, she actually objected to leaving Paris but was told to do so by Napoleon's brother, Joseph, who had been left in charge. She wrote to her father, Emperor Francis of Austria, and tried to convince him not to support the deposing of Napoleon. Unfortunately, he was not swayed.

One of Napoleon's biggest problems was that Talleyrand had stayed behind and was working hard to pave the way for a Bourbon restoration. For whatever reason (including, most likely, what he saw as good for his own future), Talleyrand was determined to prevent Marie Louise and the King of Rome from replacing Napoleon on the throne of France. He had encouraged Marie Louise and Joseph to leave town, leaving the way open for his treachery.

On March 30, Joseph and what few loyal government officials remained joined in the exodus. The Coalition forces moved into the capital. Napoleon had left orders that no one was to negotiate with or even greet them. Never one to pass up an opportunity to promote his own importance (along with his current vision of what was best for France), Talleyrand had stayed behind. Claiming to speak for France, he soon declared the French Empire at an end.

When Tsar Alexander of Russia entered Paris (see Figure 14-3), he stayed at Talleyrand's home. The tsar was actually quite willing to consider putting the King of Rome on the throne with Marie Louise as regent. But Talleyrand was determined to bring back a Bourbon monarchy in the person of Louis XVIII, and Talleyrand had the tsar's ear.

Figure 14-3:
This engraving, done in 1814, shows Tsar Alexander I of Russia as he looked when he entered Paris.

Napoleon arrived in Paris a few hours after the Coalition had moved in. He was four hours too late to defend Paris, four hours too late to rally its citizens to the cause, four hours too late to negotiate in favor of his son from a position of at least some strength. Instead, he moved into Fontainebleau Palace to await developments. He hoped to rally his army and his marshals and find a way to carry the fight to the Coalition. It was a fight that would not happen.

Losing his marshals

On April 3, a group of Napoleon's marshals, including Ney, Macdonald, Oudinot, Louis Alexandre Berthier, and Francois Lefebvre, met with Napoleon and demanded that he abdicate his throne in favor of his son. This meeting is usually called "the revolt of the marshals," though Napoleon may have called it "the revolting marshals." Whatever you call it, the marshals made it clear that they would not fight for him any longer and that any further efforts on his part would be seen as fighting for the cause of *Napoleon* rather than for the cause of *France*. Reluctantly, Napoleon agreed, and the marshals took his agreement to Tsar Alexander, who had assumed overall leadership of Coalition forces.

Tsar Alexander was quite prepared to accept a solution that secured a quick peace and had the potential for unifying France under someone other than Napoleon or Louis XVIII. But Talleyrand was determined to have a Bourbon king, and Talleyrand was resourceful.

Under Talleyrand's arrangements, Marshal Marmont took his 11,000 soldiers straight into the Austrian camp, where the Austrian soldiers were waiting for them. The French soldiers were livid when they realized what had happened, but they had no choice but to lay down their arms. Marmont's treachery ranks with the worst in history.

Napoleon was now pretty much without an army, which meant he was pretty much without any negotiating strength, which meant any hope for the King of Rome was gone. On April 5, the provisional government (which meant Talleyrand for all practical purposes) asked Louis-Stanislas-Xavier, brother to King Louis XVI, to assume the Bourbon throne of France.

Losing his position

No longer fearful of Napoleon's ability to continue to wage war, the tsar demanded Napoleon's unconditional abdication. Napoleon was finished; even some of his closest friends and companions, such as his chief of staff, Berthier, and his first valet, Wairy Constant, left him, never to return. Despondent, Napoleon knew he had no choice. On April 11, Napoleon abdicated unconditionally. The next day, he received a copy of the Treaty of Fontainebleau. He was to be exiled as Emperor of Elba, a small island off the coast of Italy.

One extremely important issue for Napoleon was his desire to be reunited with his wife and son. It seemed a reasonable request, but many of the Coalition leaders did not want the former Emperor of the French reunited with such a close tie to the current Emperor of Austria. Napoleon also understood that Elba was small, so he asked the Coalition to grant Marie Louise dominion over Tuscany, a part of Italy just across from Elba. Instead, the treaty gave her the Duchy of Parma, a landlocked territory north of Tuscany and substantially further away. It seemed clear that they had no intention of ever allowing the two (and their son) to reunite. On its surface, the treaty seemed honorable, but its treatment of Napoleon and his wife gave reason to wonder what its ultimate result would be.

To her credit, Marie Louise tried to rejoin Napoleon right away. But politics intervened, and Count Clemens Metternich, Austria's foreign minister, convinced her to go visit her father first. She would never see Napoleon again, nor would their son. The letters she exchanged with her husband during this period are some of the most poignant I've ever read.

On April 13, Napoleon tried to kill himself by taking some poison that he always carried with him. He was fearful of what the Coalition really had in store for him, and he preferred death to the indignity and worse that lay ahead. But the poison was old and weak, and Napoleon's doctor was able to save him. The next day, feeling more optimistic, he received a hopeful letter from Marie Louise and wrote a letter to Josephine, who was still living at their former home at Malmaison.

Becoming the Emperor of Elba

For a man who had been defeated at every turn, Napoleon got what, on the surface at least, seemed a pretty good deal:

- ✔ He kept the title of emperor, albeit of a small island rather than of a vast empire.
- ✔ His family members kept their titles and estates.
- ✔ He was given a military guard and a pension of 2 million francs from France.
- ✔ Contrary to what most history books will tell you, he was not forbidden to leave the island; he was not a prisoner.

What he didn't get, of course, was his wife and child.

Prior to leaving for Elba, Napoleon visited with friends, made arrangements, and read books on his new dominion. On April 20, 1814, he assembled his *Old Guard* (the longest-serving members of the Imperial Guard), the elite of his army who had been with him for most of his campaigns, in the courtyard of

Fontainebleau Palace a few miles from Paris. The scene is one of the most famous, and emotional, in all of the Napoleonic legend. Napoleon addressed his soldiers, who were standing at attention, reminding them of their years together and of their steadfastness and glory throughout it all. "Goodbye my children," he said. "I should like to press you all to my heart; at least I shall kiss your flag . . ." When he symbolically kissed the flag, there wasn't a dry eye in the courtyard, including among the foreign commissioners who were to escort Napoleon to Elba (see Figure 14-4). The ceremony over, Napoleon left in his carriage for the long ride to the south coast of France.

Figure 14-4:
This engraving, made shortly after the event, shows Napoleon kissing the flag as a symbolic farewell to soldiers at Fontainebleau Palace.

The trip to the coast was an unhappy one for Napoleon. He passed through areas where his support had waned, and there were moments when he feared for his safety. But he made it to the coast and set sail for Elba on a British ship on April 28, and he arrived at his new home on April 30. The British assigned Colonel Sir Neil Campbell to be their commissioner on the island. His job was to keep an eye on Napoleon's activities, as well as to be of some protection to Napoleon by providing a British presence that would remind all that Napoleon was there with the support of the British and their allies.

Losing Josephine

Shortly after arriving on Elba, Napoleon received sad news. His beloved Josephine had died of pneumonia. She had led an active social life and had become chilled while hosting a party for the tsar in Paris. Alexander had even provided his personal doctor, but it was all for naught. Napoleon and Josephine had remained friends after their divorce and perhaps still loved each other. On top of all his other problems, this news was a real blow for Napoleon. He was in mourning for two days.

Creating a new life

Napoleon did everything he could to keep busy on Elba and to be a good emperor. He made numerous improvements to the island's infrastructure, such as roads and defenses, and he actually made it a defensible island. As he had done in France and across Europe, he reviewed and revised the legal codes and tax system, making both a reflection of the progressive systems he established in the French Empire (see Chapter 19).

Although Napoleon could not see his wife and son, he did not lack for company. His sister Pauline came to live on the island, and she soon became the center of social attention, playing hostess to many social events. Napoleon's mother came to live there also; Corsican family ties are strong, and at least some of Napoleon's family rallied around him.

Also rallying around him was his Polish mistress, Marie Walewska, with their son. Napoleon and Marie had kept touch over the years, and she offered to stay. It probably would have been good for Napoleon to have her there, but he feared a scandal. Besides, he still entertained hopes that his wife would be allowed to return to him.

Such was not to be. Marie Louise's father had ordered the dashing General Count Adam Adalbert von Neipperg to seduce her, which he did. She soon turned her attentions completely to him and stopped writing Napoleon. (After Napoleon died, Marie Louise and Neipperg would marry and rule as the Duke and Duchess of Parma in Italy. Napoleon's son lived as the Duke of Reichstadt in Vienna until he died of tuberculosis in 1832 at the age of 21.)

Being the center of attention

Napoleon had once been at the center of the European stage, and much of his old audience still held a deep fascination with the man. As a result, Napoleon found that many people, important and not so important, beat a path to his door. He maintained a court, a small-scale version of the one he had had at Paris, and received political leaders, scientists, and other important people. He especially enjoyed meeting with British visitors, and the descriptions that some of them wrote of their interviews make for quite interesting reading. Colonel Campbell frequented Napoleon's court, and the two got along well.

Tempting fate

But there was a problem. Actually, there were several problems. For starters, Napoleon was soon quite bored. This is a man who had ruled Europe and traveled across most of it several times. Elba was a small island with only a few thousand people. Hey, even *I'd* be bored after awhile!

Confining Napoleon in this way was a fatal miscalculation by the Coalition. If they had put Marie Louise on the Italian coast, or even let her reunite with her husband, he may have been content to write his memoirs and live out his live in luxury, visiting Italy from time to time. (He had planned to write his memoirs on Elba, and said so many times, but he never even started on them.)

Worse than boredom was fear. Napoleon soon came to believe, with some justification, that the Coalition leaders would not be content having him living comfortably so close to them. He — and they — knew that he still was popular in France and elsewhere (most notably in Poland and Italy). Napoleon knew that Louis XVIII had spies on the island and that Talleyrand was probably up to his old tricks. Also, the British press was still attacking Napoleon at every opportunity, and there were rumors of assassination or prison. Napoleon had fortified the island and had about 1,000 men to guard him, but that could hardly keep all of Europe at bay.

All these rumors were floating around a meeting of the Coalition leaders in Vienna, called the Congress of Vienna. Talleyrand represented France, and that couldn't be good for Napoleon. Napoleon's spies there told him that exile to the remote island of St. Helena was a much-discussed possibility. The rest of Europe, he feared, was not prepared to let him alone.

Then disaster struck. Louis XVIII (see Figure 14-5) was obligated by treaty to pay Napoleon 2 million francs a year and to pay very large sums to Napoleon's mother and his sister Pauline, along with the rest of the Bonaparte family. These sums, along with the wealth that the Bonapartes could tap into, would have been enough to keep Napoleon — and his small army — in good condition.

Figure 14-5:
Louis XVIII, shown here in a period engraving, probably never looked better!

But in a move that defies all logic, Louis refused to pay Napoleon so much as a thin dime. I have never been able to figure out why he did this. Maybe he just figured he'd save the money and that Napoleon didn't need it. A more sinister possibility was that he was trying to drive Napoleon into poverty so he couldn't afford his army, making him a sitting duck. Whatever the case, it was really dumb, and Louis's allies knew it. They told him to pay it, but he refused. (I suppose they could have paid it themselves, but that didn't happen either.)

Napoleon, naturally enough, was not pleased, and he could easily see the possible results down the line. It's likely that he would have enough money to live comfortably *if* he didn't have to fear for his safety, but, of course, he did. So the lack of funds wasn't just inconvenient; it was dangerous. His exact financial picture is unknown, as we don't know precisely how much money he brought with him to Elba. But he was facing a bleak financial future, which was likely the reason he took the drastic measure he did.

Considering options

Napoleon was Emperor of Elba with a small army (if you can even call 1,000 men an army!) and a few ships. Given the right circumstances, he may have been content to stay on the island. But he had other options as well:

- ✔ **Napoleon may have considered making a run for the United States.** He could have lived as a wealthy gentleman in the very French city of New Orleans or even in Washington, D.C. He would certainly have been the center of attention there, and the leaders of Europe may have been content to leave him alone. Then again, they may have sent assassins after him, just as he feared they'd do on Elba.

- ✔ **He could have considered taking his army and moving into Italy.** He had always been very popular there and could probably count on the support of the locals as well as of the military forces. Despite the previous betrayal of his brother-in-law, Prince Joachim Murat, King of Naples, the two had gotten on better terms, and Napoleon's wife controlled the Duchy of Parma. With a base of strength and popular support, backed by Napoleon's pledge to stay put, a war-weary Europe may have been willing to give that situation a try.

- ✔ **Napoleon could consider trying to regain power in France.** It had not taken long for the people of France to become disillusioned with Louis XVIII. That king was well-meaning — he had even granted the French a Charter of Rights, a document meant to assure French citizens that they would not lose all the rights they gained as a result of the French Revolution and Napoleon — but his advisors and the hordes of returning exiled nobles were not. They wanted their lands returned to them, never mind that other people had lived on them for 20 years. They also wanted Church lands returned. Worst of all, they wanted all their old privileges back. In other words, they wanted to pretend that the French Revolution and 25 years of history had never happened.

The veterans of Napoleon's army had not been treated well either, with many of them discharged or put on half-pay. Many had begun to really miss the glory days of the French Empire and longed for Napoleon's return. He had always been their hero, and nothing had happened to change their deep feelings of affection for their emperor.

Returning to France

It was this last option that most excited Napoleon's imagination and which he eventually chose to follow. Fearful of assassination, prison, or a more remote exile, Napoleon decided to roll the dice one more time and make another bid for power in France. Encouraged by his mother and some of his advisors, Napoleon organized his army, prepared his ships, and waited for the right moment. When he heard that the English commissioner, Sir Neil Campbell, was leaving for a long trip to Italy, he took advantage of the resulting lack of English observation.

On February 25, 1815, Napoleon and his small army set sail for France in his "armada" of three ships. He had 1,100 men, 40 horses, and a grand total of 4 cannon. He prepared Bulletins for distribution to the people of France, including his old army. "Soldiers! In my exile I heard your voice!" he wrote. "I have arrived, despite all obstacles and perils! Your general, called to the throne by the peoples' choice and raised upon your shields, has been returned to you; come and join him!"

Napoleon understood that he needed to retake power without firing a shot. As soon as there was any outward sign that the people, and especially his old army, opposed his return, he was finished. His Bulletins reminded people that he had been defeated by the treachery of some of his generals (Augereau and Marmont, in particular) and of politicians in Paris (especially Talleyrand). He assured the leaders of Europe of his intention to rule only France, and he reminded his soldiers that they needed to forget that they had once ruled most of Europe.

On March 1, Napoleon landed at Golf Juan on the French Mediterranean coast. There was no opposition to his landing. One of the great adventures and legends of his career (or anyone else's career, for that matter) had begun. Think about it. Napoleon with 1,100 men was going to march all the way to Paris and depose a king who commanded a major army and who was supported by the other countries of Europe? Madness! Well, madness it may have been, but it worked (see Figure 14-6).

Figure 14-6:
This engraving from the One Hundred Days shows Napoleon returning as Caesar, with winged victory above and a list of his accomplishments below.

The One Hundred Days

When Napoleon set foot on French soil on March 1, 1815, he began a period known as the One Hundred Days. That period included his march to Paris, his becoming emperor again, and, as I discuss in the next chapter, his final defeat at Waterloo. (Okay, so now you know that it doesn't end all that well, but things did start out promising enough.)

Marching on the Route Napoléon

Napoleon understood that he was not universally loved in all areas of France, so he planned his march to Paris so as to avoid some of the most royalist areas. This meant that instead of marching straight north through the province of Provence, he took a much more difficult mountain route toward Grenoble. (I have driven that route and can tell you that even now it is much slower than the direct route.)

It would be a great story if I could tell you that Napoleon was immediately acclaimed as France's savior by all the people he met along the way. But that isn't what happened. Some folks were bemused by his presence, some delighted, and some rather alarmed. This latter group feared renewed hostilities and possible retribution by the Coalition forces. No one opposed him directly, but there was no groundswell of support, either.

Slowly but surely, Napoleon did pick up supporters. The odd soldier would fall into formation, the odd citizen would offer support. As the slowly expanding force marched up and down mountain trails, their cannon and wagons long since abandoned due to the nature of the roads, the idea of Napoleon's return began to capture the imaginations of people along the way. Napoleon sent messages to his supporters in Grenoble and elsewhere, trying to lay a groundwork for his plan to return without a fight.

By March 5, King Louis XVIII was told of Napoleon's adventure. Louis was in Paris and controlled a massive military machine. Napoleon was nearing Grenoble with only a few thousand troops at most. At this stage, Napoleon hardly seemed a major threat, but Louis nevertheless began to organize forces to capture the *Corsican Usurper,* as some of the British cartoonists had labeled him. Marshal Ney promised to bring Napoleon back in an iron cage, and other marshals were sent to block Napoleon.

It was at the town of Laffrey, near Grenoble, that Napoleon met his first real challenge. By then, each village was producing crowds of cheering people and new recruits for his army. At Laffrey, however, Napoleon would face a battalion of the 5th Regiment that had been given orders to capture or kill him. Napoleon had gotten wind of this, and his spies suggested that the soldiers were not likely to fire on their old commander, but the situation was still quite tense — and dangerous. Napoleon walked in front of his troops, whom he had ordered to carry their weapons at rest. The order was given to fire at Napoleon, but no soldier complied. There was an uneasy silence. Then Napoleon cried out, "Soldiers! I am your Emperor. Do you recognize me? If there is one among you who would kill his general, HERE I AM!"

Today, this site is a small park with a monument to the occasion, and a commemorative plaque contains that statement. Of course, no one fired. Instead, there were cries of "Vive l'Empereur!" ("Long live the Emperor!"), followed by cheers and a rushing of the two sides to embrace each other in their mutual joy of being reunited under their old leader. It was a scene like none other in history. Later that same day, another major unit defected to Napoleon's cause. Napoleon now had momentum and would prove unstoppable.

Receiving the gates of Grenoble

Napoleon's next obstacle was Grenoble, whose military commanders refused to open the gates. No problem. The citizens tore down the gates and carried Napoleon to the Hotel of the Three Dauphins. Later, they presented him with the remains of the gates. He addressed the citizens from a balcony on the city hall in a park across from the hotel.

Napoleon was on a roll. He had turned back all opposition without firing a shot, and his army was expanding by leaps and bounds. Now, all over France there was excitement at his return, though that excitement was not universal, to be sure. Napoleon sent out countless declarations, all of which made the basic point that he did not want any war and had no intentions of any further conquest. He portrayed himself as the embodiment of the French Revolution and protector of all that France had accomplished in the years since the Revolution's beginning in 1789. It was a popular approach to take, as France no longer wanted war, and many people did resent the rolling back of the gains of the Revolution by the newly reinstated nobility.

Years later, Napoleon wrote that before Grenoble he had been an adventurer, but afterwards, a reigning prince.

Napoleon continued his march, and the result was always the same. When units sent by the king met units sent by Napoleon, they were likely to drink together, and they never fought each other. Marshal Macdonald tried to defend Lyon, but his troops refused to fight, instead switching to Napoleon's side.

Marshal Michel Ney also tried to inspire his troops to defend the king but got nowhere with that effort. Suffering an acute case of torn loyalties, Ney switched sides himself, issuing a proclamation to his soldiers to join him in the "immortal phalanx, which the Emperor Napoleon is conducting to Paris." On March 18, Napoleon and Ney met at Auxerre and joined forces. At this point, there was no hope for the king, who left the country on March 19.

Paris was alive with excitement at Napoleon's return. Broadsheets and other items celebrating his arrival in France were issued every day. Marshal Macdonald's memoirs (I use the first English edition from 1892) and other sources relate the following set of broadsheet headlines, which wonderfully portray what was happening:

LEGEND

The Tiger has broken out of his den!

The Ogre was three days at sea.

The Wretch has landed at Frejus.

The Brigand has arrived at Antibes.

The Invader has reached Grenoble.

The General has entered Lyons.

Napoleon slept last night at Fontainebleau.

The Emperor proceeds to the Tuileries today.

His Imperial Majesty will address his loyal subjects tomorrow!

Entering Paris

Napoleon entered Paris on March 20, 1815. His journey had been nothing less than a spectacular event in history. Only Caesar's march across the Rubicon River to take power in Rome seems to match Napoleon's march along the *Route Napoléon* for dramatic effect. And Caesar's march happened 2,000 years ago!

When Napoleon entered Paris, he was met by thousands of people who were shouting his name and slogans of the Revolution. Unfortunately, Marie Louise and their son, the King of Rome, had not been allowed by Austrian Emperor Francis I to return to Paris (see Figure 14-7). That fact no doubt took some of the edge off Napoleon's celebration — and provided a clue of what would soon follow. Other than that, however, it seemed as though Napoleon had returned from a great victory or had secured a lasting peace. It seemed that the good old days had returned.

Figure 14-7:
This gold snuffbox shows Napoleon, Marie Louise, and their son reunited on March 20, 1815, their son's birthday. Too bad it didn't happen that way.

Except they hadn't. Napoleon had some very difficult work to do, and he knew it:

✔ Not everyone in government, or in the nation as a whole, was all that pleased with his return. Napoleon had to win over the old Revolutionaries who probably would not support a return to the more or less absolute power that he had enjoyed for much of his reign.

He handled this situation brilliantly by convincing one of his fiercest critics, Benjamin Constant, to join in writing a new constitution.

Constant was a great intellectual who had led much of the liberal opposition to Napoleon's becoming emperor. When Constant agreed to Napoleon's request, liberal support was assured. On April 22, the people ratified a new constitution. For the moment, Napoleon was secure on his throne.

✔ Napoleon needed to guarantee peace. He could not afford to have any nation attack him: The people of France would not support another war, and his army was hardly in top fighting condition. He wrote the leaders of all the major nations that had once been allied against him, pledging to keep France within the 1792 boundaries and giving up all claims to Belgium and Holland, which had been England's biggest concern. Unfortunately, none of the leaders he wrote to gave him a positive response.

Suffering a fatal, if unavoidable, flaw

For all the good things that happened as Napoleon returned to power, there was one thing that was decidedly unfavorable to his continued success. The leaders of Europe had been meeting in the Congress of Vienna, making an effort to secure a lasting peace and maintain a balance of power on the Continent. Napoleon knew this and was not happy that all the Coalition leaders, including his now archenemy Talleyrand, would be in one place. Napoleon had had no choice, however. The Congress, which was essentially one great party after another, seemed to be never-ending, while Napoleon was convinced that his days on Elba were limited and that he needed to act with expediency. If he waited for the Congress of Vienna to end, he may have waited too long.

Napoleon's concerns were well placed. When the leaders of Europe heard of Napoleon's return, they were furious. Had they been each in their respective capital cities, it would have taken a long time for them to communicate and to agree on a plan of action. And perhaps Napoleon's pleas to his father-in-law, Emperor Francis of Austria, or to his old friend Tsar Alexander of Russia may have had some positive effect.

But the European leaders were not in their capitals; they were in Vienna. And Talleyrand was there, waving the Bourbon flag, calling for Napoleon to be declared an outlaw.

Possibly working in Napoleon's favor was the fact that Austria and England were now allied to France by treaty. Treaties do not specify the names of rulers, only of governments. Thus, to declare war on France, they would have to break the very treaty they had signed just months earlier. Add to that the family connection and the fact that Belgium and Holland were off the table, and those two powers should have remained neutral or even taken France's side.

Yeah, right, like that was going to happen! Austria and England sidestepped the issue by declaring war not on France but on Napoleon! I know of no other time that people declared war on a person rather than a country, but such was their hatred or fear of Napoleon. The assembled leaders quickly formed a Seventh Coalition against Napoleon.

With friends like this . . .

If all this weren't bad enough, King Murat of Naples decided that he would "help" Napoleon by trying to drive the Austrians out of Italy. Austria couldn't know for sure if Napoleon was behind this action or not (he most definitely wasn't), but it sure gave them a reason to feel that Napoleon couldn't be trusted. I don't know if Austria would have behaved differently without Murat's interference, but she not only beat back his rather pathetic effort but also joined the Seventh Coalition against Napoleon.

The Coalition decided to move in a coordinated attack on Napoleon. The British and Prussians were in nearby Belgium, but the Austrians were not yet mobilized and the Russians were easily the farthest away. They agreed not to attack Napoleon until all their forces were ready. The Coalition forces were on the move, but Napoleon would have the chance to strike first.

Chapter 15

Waterloo

· ·

· ·

Waterloo is a small town a few miles south of Brussels, Belgium. It's an unassuming place, with a church, a few inns, and some homes surrounded by old stone farmhouses and lots of open fields. Those farms and fields are its claim to fame, because one of the most famous battles in history was fought on them.

The Battle of Waterloo, as it has come to be known, is always included on lists of battles that changed the course of history. Napoleon was considered one of the greatest generals ever, yet he is often defined by this one terrific loss at the end of his career. The word has entered our language: You probably know what it means when we say someone has *met their Waterloo,* even if you don't know anything about the actual battle. In this chapter, I tell you about the battle itself and why it spelled the final end of Napoleon's political and military aspirations.

Feeling the Weight of Waterloo

For Napoleon, Waterloo was the final struggle against the forces that battled him since the very beginning of his career. For almost 20 years, he had fought various coalitions of British, Austrian, Russian, and Prussian armies, and the usual suspects were at it again. Only this time, it was to be for all the marbles — not just to determine whether Napoleon would stay in power. The outcome of the battle would go a long way in determining whether the move toward political liberalization started by the French Revolution (see Chapter 3) and continued by Napoleon would continue or be greatly slowed.

If Napoleon (see Figure 15-1) had won, perhaps the European Union would have happened a great deal sooner. Or perhaps not. That's the frustrating but fun aspect of history: You can never be sure what would have happened if one thing (like a battle) had turned out differently.

In preparing for the battle, Napoleon appeared to make all the right moves, both on the diplomatic and military fronts. He started strong. But in the end he had too little, too late.

Figure 15-1: This period painting on a snuffbox shows Napoleon as he may have looked as he prepared to meet his Waterloo.

Organizing an Army and Seeking Peace

After Napoleon entered Paris and reclaimed power without firing a shot (see Chapter 14), events unfolded quickly. The Coalition that was allied against him was going to act fast to get rid of him once and for all. The Russian and Austrian armies were mobilizing in the east while the British and Prussian armies were very near the French border, in Belgium. To allow all four armies to act in concert against the French would be a disaster. But if he could pick them off one by one, perhaps he could succeed.

The Austrians and Russians were fairly far away, so for the moment, Napoleon could ignore them. The British and Prussians were another matter. The British, under the Duke of Wellington, were hanging out in Brussels, with the officers attending parties and the men sitting around grumbling. The Prussians were some miles away, also biding their time but (being Prussians) without the parties.

Napoleon really didn't want war. He was old and fat and would have been content to just rule France (okay, and maybe Belgium), bringing reforms and enjoying life with his young wife, Marie Louise, and their son, both of whom he adored. But even his father-in-law, Emperor Francis I of Austria, was against him, preventing his wife and son from joining him in Paris. So war it would be.

Napoleon took several critical steps to try to prepare for (or in some cases, avoid) fighting the Coalition forces:

- ✔ He sent an envoy to the Austrians asking for peace, which was ignored.

- ✔ He wrote a personal letter to the Prince Regent of England asking for peace. It was returned, unopened.

- ✔ He increased the army from 200,000 to 300,000 just by inspiring many of his old veterans to reenlist.

- ✔ He called up the National Guard to defend the homeland.

- ✔ He fortified Paris with troops and artillery.

- ✔ He asked his father-in-law, the Emperor of Austria, to send his wife and son back to him, with the possibility that they would rule France if he had to abdicate again. In this request, he was also ignored.

- ✔ He secured the support of the legislative body by agreeing to a new, more liberal constitution written by some of his old liberal foes.

All this was not enough. Armies and countries need leaders, so he had to recruit the best and brightest and do so quickly. Naturally, he first turned to those who had been with him before his abdication.

Picking a New Team

The most important post Napoleon had to fill was that of chief of staff. Louis Alexandre Berthier was top-notch at the job and had been for many years. He had stayed in France and been loyal to the Bourbons after Napoleon's first abdication, but that was then and this was now.

Losing Berthier

Many people believed that Berthier would rally to Napoleon's cause, which was no small matter. You think your doctor's prescriptions are hard to read? You should try Napoleon's orders! *Sacré bleu!* Berthier, however, was a master at understanding Napoleon and passing (greatly clarified) orders along to subordinate officers. So imagine the shock to Napoleon when news came that on June 1, 1815, Berthier had a fatal fall from a window in his estate. (Did he fall, or did he receive a not-so-friendly shove? I've been in that room, and frankly it is hard to imagine how someone would fall without some assistance.)

Napoleon lost more than an old friend. Some historians believe that Berthier's death effectively ended any real chance of success for Napoleon. Berthier's fall from his window may have led to Napoleon's fall from power.

Settling on a B team

With Berthier gone, Napoleon made a series of personnel decisions that put pretty good people in pretty inappropriate positions:

- He picked Marshal Nicolas Soult, one of his top commanders, as his chief of staff. Soult was out of his league in this job, and it showed.

- Napoleon compounded the problem by leaving his best warrior in Paris: He appointed Marshal Louis Davout as Minister of War. Sure, he needed someone good at that job, but his best warrior? Davout should have been with him on the front lines, not minding the home front. (That would be like Agamemnon telling Achilles to stay home and mind the store rather than go to Troy.)

- Napoleon made Marshal Michel Ney commander of his left wing. Ney was fearless and had earned the title *the Bravest of the Brave* in the Russian campaign (see Chapter 13). He was a great cavalry commander and a good political appointment. But he had little experience commanding at this level and insufficient imagination for the job.

- Equally inappropriate was the appointment of Marshal Emanuel Grouchy to command the right wing. An excellent cavalry commander of smaller units, Grouchy was sorely lacking in the kind of initiative that he would ultimately need as commander of an entire wing.

Finally, there was the dog that didn't bark, or at least the cavalry leader who didn't lead. That would be perhaps the greatest cavalry commander of his day, Marshal Joachim Murat, who was also Napoleon's brother-in-law. Okay, so he had turned on Napoleon in an earlier campaign, and he had made a fool of himself in Naples by trying to support Napoleon by attacking the Austrians, which only convinced them not to trust Napoleon. Sometimes you just have to overlook those kinds of little details. Napoleon needed the best he could get, but he turned down Murat's pleas to serve in the 1815 campaign. Remember that fact when you read of the futile cavalry charges led by Ney at Waterloo.

There is a lot of irony in all this. Throughout his career, Napoleon was renowned for picking the best person for the best job. (Well, perhaps not every time — he did initially trust the traitor Talleyrand.) But he generally had the best staff on the field, and that fact served him well. Now, when he needed that advantage more than ever before, it wasn't there. Napoleon may have been sick or perhaps just over-stressed. Whatever the case, the battle may have been over before it began.

Yet, in spite of the obstacles, Napoleon nearly won it all.

Marching to War

Diplomatic efforts concluded, his staff selected, and the army mobilized, Napoleon moved north into Belgium. There, he would meet his fate in a battle that has captured the imagination of historians and the general public ever since. The outcome was close. In the words of the British commander, the Duke of Wellington, the battle was "a near run thing."

Hoping to divide and conquer again

As I note in earlier chapters, Napoleon was the master of using a divide and conquer approach. Before he went to battle this time around, he tried using this approach through diplomacy, writing to various people in an effort to get one or more of them on his side: his father-in-law, the Emperor Francis I of Austria; his old friend Tsar Alexander I of Russia; the Prince Regent of Great Britain; and even his wife, Marie Louise (who was kept under pretty tight wraps in Vienna). But when they all failed to respond, he turned to military action.

With the British and Prussian forces just north of the French border, they were the obvious targets. Very quickly, and with a great deal of secrecy, Napoleon moved his army of about 125,000 men north, hoping to divide and conquer the two opposing forces. If this worked, he might send the Prussians hightailing it to Berlin and the British swimming to England. It was Napoleon's only real chance to win, and he almost pulled it off.

Surprising the Prussians

The Prussians were the first to discover Napoleon's plan of action, and they were none the better off for it. He surprised them at the little town of Charleroi and sent them packing in the direction of Ligny. Wellington, the British commander, was at a formal ball in Brussels when he heard the news. (If you watch the movie *Waterloo* with Rod Steiger and Christopher Plummer, you'll get a pretty good idea of what that scene must have been like. Indeed, that movie gives a good overall flavor of the campaign, though you shouldn't depend on it for exact historical accuracy.)

Napoleon, meanwhile, was chasing the Prussians to Ligny while leaving a force under Marshal Ney at Quatre Bras, six miles northwest of Ligny. Napoleon wanted Ney to keep Wellington at bay and, if at all possible, defeat him. For his plan to work, he would need speed, secrecy, and perfect execution. He got the first two but came up short on the all-important matter of execution.

In the past, Napoleon would divide his enemy and concentrate his forces first on one wing of the split enemy and then, having defeated it, on the other wing. By splitting his forces between Quatre Bras and Ligny, he violated his own rule, and he would live to regret it. He would also live to regret his choice of Ney to head the forces at Quatre Bras, as Ney dawdled throughout the day and eventually allowed Wellington to escape unhindered.

Napoleon, joined by the wing of his army under Grouchy's command, moved to take on the Prussians under Marshal Gebhardt Lebrecht von Blücher. After a slow start, the battle began to go well for the French, with Blücher forced to give ground. Napoleon sought to call up reinforcements to attack the Prussian right flank from the rear and crush their army. This action led to one of the biggest disasters of the campaign.

Marching to and fro

General Jean-Baptiste d'Erlon commanded a French corps that was positioned close to Napoleon's left flank. Napoleon sent orders to d'Erlon to move right, directly across toward Ligny, and fall on the Prussian rear. Unfortunately, Napoleon's orders were not completely clear, and d'Erlon ended up at Napoleon's rear instead! If Berthier were still Napoleon's chief of staff, he would never have let that happen.

The mistake was corrected, and things were moving forward. Victory was in sight! Then, one of the most amazing events in this campaign took place. Ney, finally thinking of doing something useful at Quatre Bras, sent an order to d'Erlon to come to *his* support. Apparently nobody bothered to tell Ney of the emperor's orders.

Imagine d'Erlon's surprise and confusion. He was caught in the middle: His immediate superior ordered him one way and his emperor another. For my money, the emperor would prevail, but d'Erlon was possibly confused by Napoleon's order, possibly intimidated by Ney, and possibly just not very bright. Whatever the reason, he decided to move back toward Quatre Bras. As a result, he and his men spent the day marching back and forth and were never able to play a significant role in either action.

The lesson to be learned here is profound: No matter how great a leader may be, lousy staff work can lead to disaster.

Missing key opportunities

Another real "if only" occurred when the Prussian leader Blücher was actually thrown from his horse. French cavalry rode right by him without realizing it, and he got away. Many historians are convinced that if he had been captured, the Prussians would have most likely retreated toward Berlin rather than rally to Wellington's cause at Waterloo.

In another error of major proportion, Napoleon was slow to send pursuit after the Prussians. When he finally did, he sent Marshal Grouchy, whose approach was, shall we say, less than urgent. He was in command of about a third of Napoleon's army but was slow getting started and slow in his movements. When push came to shove at Waterloo, Napoleon needed those men, but he got the Prussians instead.

Waiting on the weather

Meanwhile, back at Quatre Bras, Ney was still not doing very much, and Wellington had assembled a formidable fighting force. When Wellington heard of Blücher's defeat and withdrawal, he retreated north toward Brussels. Ney could have inflicted great damage on the retreating British. Soldiers who are retreating are very vulnerable to a pursuing army, which can pound them with mobile artillery and "slice and dice" them with cavalry. It was a golden opportunity.

Instead, Ney waited for Napoleon, letting the British escape relatively unmolested. Later, Napoleon and Ney marched north in a heavy rain. On the evening of May 17, 1815, they arrived at the fields near the small town of Waterloo. Wellington had gotten there first, of course, and had already staked out the high ground. In spite of everything, Napoleon would have a chance to inflict a second defeat on his enemies, which just might be enough to keep him in power.

On the morning of June 18, Napoleon was facing Wellington's forces, who had grabbed the best defensive positions at Mont St. Jean. Normally, battles start early in the day, but the heavy rains had made the fields a quagmire. Sure, the British would have been disadvantaged by the rain as well, but they were already in position and playing defense. It was the French who had to move heavy cannon into position and run across muddy fields into withering fire. Maybe they should have done just that, but instead they delayed, waiting for the ground to dry just a bit. Unknown to them, the Prussians had eluded Grouchy and were moving ever closer to Waterloo.

Moving from fight to flight

By mid-morning, the fight was underway. Napoleon sent forces to try to take a nearby walled farm called Hougoumont, but the farm would never fall to the French, who hadn't bothered to take any cannon along with them. It would have been difficult to move cannon through the heavy woods around the farm, but even a couple of light cannon would have made all the difference.

Napoleon sent his freshest troops against Wellington. That would be d'Erlon's troops, who had done a fair amount of marching but precious little fighting. The British beat them back and then sent in the Scots Greys cavalry, one of the best such units around. They overextended, and when Napoleon sent in the *cuirassiers* (heavy cavalry wearing breastplates) and *lancers* (light cavalry carrying lances), the Scots Greys were toast. (If it sounds a bit like the Charge of the Light Brigade, you've got it!)

Missing Grouchy

By the afternoon, it was clear that the Prussians were going to be a factor after all. Napoleon expected to see French troops (Grouchy's) appearing on his right flank; instead he saw Prussians. As the day wore on, it became clear that for all intents and purposes, Grouchy and one-third of Napoleon's army had disappeared into thin air. Somewhere along the line Napoleon must surely have cried out, "Where's Grouchy?"

Misusing the cavalry

The dubious award for Biggest Bonehead of the Battle must, however, fall to Marshal Michel Ney. He led a force of as many as 9,000 cavalry in a series of glorious but futile charges against Wellington's forces.

It was the stuff of movies: Ney, hatless and sword in hand, exhorting his troops onward to glory. Impressive, but doomed to failure because Ney neglected to include infantry in his attack. To defend against massed cavalry, infantry forms into squares, presenting themselves as prickly boxes that are very difficult for a horse to break through. Ah, but if the cavalry fades away to reveal infantry preparing to fire, well, the squares are sitting ducks. But there would be no infantry, no sitting ducks, and no glory for Ney.

Ney could have accomplished something even without the needed infantry. In front of the British infantry was a line of artillery. Each gun was a cannon that was fired by a fuse at its closed end. As the cavalry swept by, the cannoneers retreated into the squares for safety, leaving the guns in the control of the French.

Cavalrymen are not likely to be carrying around long ramrods, but they do carry small bags of lead spikes and a hammer. Had a few of them dismounted and driven those spikes into the fuse holes, the cannon would have been disabled for the duration of the battle. Instead, after each cavalry charge, the

British went right back to the cannon and blasted their attackers. Without the cannon, the battle would have been much shorter and had a much happier ending for the French! (Then at the ensuing party, the cannon spikers could have enjoyed spiked punch in honor of their efforts. Or not, as it turned out.)

Making a last-ditch effort

In spite of all this, Napoleon had one last shot at victory. Night was approaching, and he made one last effort to dislodge the British, whose lines were getting fairly thin. He had taken a walled farm known as La Haye Sainte, and therefore he had a good launching position and artillery support for his soldiers.

Ney finally got it right and began to push back portions of the British line with a combined cavalry, infantry, and artillery assault. In time, finally sensing victory, Napoleon threw five battalions of his feared Imperial Guard against Wellington, and for a time it looked like they would succeed. But the appearance of fresh Prussian troops demoralized the French; they wavered and then began to fall back in increasing disorder.

Napoleon seemed determined to stay and fight, perhaps wanting to meet his fate right there. Instead, he was given protection by a square of the Guard and eventually escaped on horseback to Paris. There, he was soon joined by the relatively rested forces of Marshal Grouchy.

Bad News Travels Fastest

Napoleon had lost the Battle of Waterloo but, back in Paris, still expected to remain in power and carry the fight further. After all, he was emperor, and there were plenty of other military forces at his disposal.

Alas, it was not to be. Napoleon as a winner was all powerful; as a loser, it was best that he get out of town quickly. He tried to abdicate in favor of his son, but that idea went nowhere. Napoleon's enemies were determined to bring back King Louis XVIII, and that is exactly what happened. In the end, Napoleon abdicated his throne with no assurances regarding his future.

Napoleon lingered at his home at Malmaison, receiving a visit from his Polish mistress, Marie Walewska, and their son. It was their last visit. The United States had always been a possible destination for a dethroned Napoleon, but he had to act quickly. He went to the coast and considered his options, but he took too long, allowing the British to establish a blockade. There was still the possibility of making a run for it, perhaps hidden in a barrel on a French ship, but that seemed beneath the dignity of the Emperor of the French. In the end, Napoleon decided to surrender to the British, fully expecting to be allowed to retire as a country gentleman in England. Instead, he was taken to the remote island of St. Helena.

Whatever happened to . . .?

Some of the folks who rallied to Napoleon's cause during the One Hundred Days were killed in battle. Others' lives went back to pretty much normal after Napoleon abdicated the second and final time. Two of his most famous allies, however, met rather different fates:

✔ Marshal Joachim Murat decided he would retake his Kingdom of Naples the way Napoleon reclaimed his own throne, so shortly after Waterloo he landed in Italy. Unfortunately for him, the local folks didn't agree with his plan. Shortly after landing in Italy, Murat was captured, tried and quickly executed.

✔ Marshal Michel Ney was tried for treason and found guilty. Because he was a true French military hero, many people felt he should be spared. Instead, he was executed by firing squad on December 7, 1815. (To this day, some people believe that he escaped and came to the United States to teach school. It is an amusing idea, but not very likely.)

Chapter 16

St. Helena: Napoleon's Final Island

After Napoleon's defeat at the Battle of Waterloo (see Chapter 15), he made his way to the small island of Aix on the Atlantic coast of France. There, he considered his options, which included trying to escape to the United States. In the end, he decided to surrender to the British ships that were trying to blockade the bay.

He wrote to the Prince Regent (the son of the king, who was really running the show in England at that time) asking to be allowed to retire peacefully to England. This was a common thing to do, and Napoleon could have lived out the rest of his life as a country gentleman. But too many people still feared Napoleon, so instead he was sent to the remote island of St. Helena off the coast of southern Africa, a thousand miles from nowhere.

A lot of people felt that the British treated Napoleon miserably and should have allowed him to retire to England like other former heads of governments. The British refusal to grant to Napoleon what was typically granted to other deposed heads of state enraged Napoleon and his entourage, along with many other people of the day, and has for almost 200 years been a black mark against the British government of that time.

In this chapter, I briefly describe the process of sending Napoleon to the island, and then I tell you a bit about his life there. I discuss the controversy surrounding his death and tell you of his ultimate fate.

Putting His Fate in British Hands

In July 1815, Napoleon sent negotiators to Captain Frederick Maitland of the *HMS Bellerophon* to secure an agreement that Napoleon would be treated properly and sent to England. They also negotiated how many of his entourage could join him. Maitland was not authorized to make any promises as to Napoleon's ultimate fate, but his respectful treatment of the French was encouraging, and eventually Napoleon decided that he had little choice but to essentially throw himself on England's mercy. (I'd have advised him to come to the United States instead. Imagine how fascinating his time here may have been. Can you say "Senator Bonaparte"?)

On July 15, Napoleon, with full honors, boarded the *Bellerophon* (see Figure 16-1). Maitland and Napoleon got along quite well; Maitland gave Napoleon a great deal of respect, which was reciprocated. Napoleon, whose charming personality had always been one of his strong points, was soon on excellent terms with everyone on board.

The *Bellerophon* sailed to England and weighed anchor in Plymouth. Almost immediately, the harbor was filled with people anxious to get a glimpse of their hated enemy, the Ogre of Corsica. Napoleon seemed to enjoy this attention and would often walk about on deck where he could be seen by one and all.

Figure 16-1:
This period engraving shows Napoleon boarding the *Bellerophon* and is based on a description given by someone who was there.

What's in a name?

One of the first issues that the British had to decide was what to call their august prisoner. The obvious answer was *Emperor Napoleon,* because he had been Emperor of the French twice and Emperor of Elba once. For reasons I don't understand, the Brits were not willing to call him that. They made some noises about the question of legitimacy, but they had recognized Napoleon as emperor for many years.

Nor were they willing to then fall back on *First Consul Bonaparte,* the title he held before becoming emperor. That would have still acknowledged the fact that he had been head of state, which they were not willing to do. They decided instead to call him *General,* as though 15 years of ruling France meant nothing. While they were at it, they reverted to the Italian spelling of his last name, *Buonaparte.* Another unnecessary insult.

Now that he was a general, he was to be considered a prisoner of war. But wait! Under the rules of those days, officers were released on parole and allowed to live in certain communities until the end of hostilities. Napoleon had asked to do just that, and as an officer POW it should have been a no-brainer. But the Brits were not interested in having him on their islands.

There was another glaring inconsistency in all of this. If Napoleon was a POW, why wasn't he released at the end of hostilities? That's what happens to POWs, officers, and enlisted men alike. Everyone, it seems, but General Buonaparte. It was not England's finest hour.

The decision to send Napoleon to St. Helena was not made without some serious consideration. There was considerable risk that the party in power may be seen as cruel and as having betrayed Napoleon who, after all, had thrown himself on their mercy. (Some mercy!) British politics was such that there was a sizable block of politicians and their supporters that thought Napoleon should have been allowed to immigrate to Great Britain and live the life of a retired country nobleman.

But in the end, the British government decided that the only way it could be certain of keeping Napoleon out of European politics — and providing for his personal safety — was to send him into distant exile on the island of St. Helena. When Napoleon was told of the decision, he was predictably furious and made his feelings quite clear both verbally and in writing. But by then, it was too late: His fate was sealed.

An interesting entourage

On August 5, 1815, Napoleon and his entourage were transferred to *HMS Northumberland,* commanded by Rear Admiral Sir George Cockburn. They quickly set sail for the 67-day journey to St. Helena. Napoleon had with him an interesting assortment of people:

- ✔ **General Henri-Gatien Bertrand, the 42-year-old Grand Marshal of the Palace (the person in charge of, among other things, Napoleon's schedule), along with his wife, Fanny, and their three children:** Bertrand had been with Napoleon on many campaigns and had served him on Elba. His wife was less than thrilled with the thought of going to St. Helena, but Napoleon really liked Bertrand, and his presence was much appreciated.

- ✔ **Count Charles Tristan Montholon, and his wife, Albine, and their youngest son:** The 33-year-old Montholon was a bit of an oddity. He had been a royalist who rallied to Napoleon, but his career had not been distinguished, and he was constantly in debt. Most people were surprised that he went to St. Helena, and he figures prominently in the controversy over Napoleon's death. Albine also figures prominently, but in a far different way. Napoleon, not surprisingly, became lonely for female companionship, and Albine was quite willing to fill that role as long as she was on the island.

- ✔ **General Baron Gaspar Gourgaud:** The 32-year-old Gourgaud had served Napoleon as an orderly officer since 1811 and was promoted to brigadier general at Waterloo. He had been Napoleon's chief negotiator with Maitland and would write important memoirs on St. Helena.

- ✔ **Marquis Emmanuel-August-Dieudonné, de Las Cases:** Las Cases had immigrated to England after the French Revolution and lived there for ten years, becoming fluent in English. When Napoleon declared a general amnesty for exiled nobles, Las Cases returned and became a respected politician. Now 49, his knowledge of English was invaluable to Napoleon. His goal all along seems to have been to get rich by writing memoirs of his time on St. Helena, and he was quite successful in doing just that.

- ✔ **Barry Edward O'Meara:** O'Meara was an Irishman serving as the British naval surgeon on board the *Bellerophon.* Napoleon had enjoyed his company, especially because O'Meara was fluent in Napoleon's native tongue, Italian. When the French doctor originally expected to join Napoleon in exile backed out, Napoleon requested O'Meara, and the British were all too pleased to have one of their own as his physician. Their pleasure was lessened when O'Meara got too close to Napoleon, and within three years O'Meara was drummed out of the service. He had the last laugh, though, as his memoirs raced through several editions in no time at all, generating a great deal of sympathy for Napoleon's plight.

- ✔ **First valet Louis-Joseph Marchand, *maître d'hôtel* (butler) Cipriani Franceschi, and second valet Louis Etienne St. Denis (known as *Ali*):** All three wrote memoirs of their time on St. Helena. They helped run a staff of eight additional members in various positions.

The voyage was generally uneventful, even boring. Napoleon was treated with great respect and got along fine with Cockburn and the other officers.

He played cards, discussed politics, and got a fair amount of exercise. At dinner, he sat at the head of the admiral's table.

If Napoleon tried to make the best of it, the same cannot be said for many members of his entourage. Already, the petty bickering and infighting that would run rampant on St. Helena could be seen. Small wonder that Napoleon often preferred the company of the officers of the crew, as well as of the officers of the British artillery company that accompanied them on the voyage. Among these officers was James Verling, another Irish doctor in the British military who would figure in Napoleon's last years.

Arriving on a Tiny Rock 1,000 Miles from Nowhere

Napoleon arrived at St. Helena on October 15, 1815 and spent his first night in the town of Jamestown, the only town on the small island. Did I say small island? It was all of 10 miles long and never more than 6½ miles wide. Three sides of the island were cliffs, and the harbor was well defended. You could see any ship arriving as far away as 60 miles. England was over 4,000 miles away, the African coast was 1,200 miles distant, and Ascension Island was a mere 700 miles distant. A more perfect island prison could not be imagined. Plus, there was a large military garrison already there (in anticipation of Napoleon's arrival), with more arriving on Napoleon's ship.

St. Helena was actually under the control of the East India Company and was a major stop in its trading routes. Most of the people who lived there were involved in one way or another with that trade.

There was absolutely no way that Napoleon could escape from this island. And yet, the British, with the concurrence of the allies (who sent commissioners to the island to keep an eye on things), placed many restrictions on Napoleon's movement — restrictions that just kept getting worse all the time. He was watched all the time, his mail was censored, and his visitors were screened.

Napoleon wasn't even given great living quarters. His jailors decided that he would live in Longwood House, which was in ill repair and sat on perhaps the worst piece of ground on the island. No trees protected it from the sun and the bitter winds that swept across the plateau. There were other homes that would have been much more suitable for the former emperor, but Longwood it would be.

Now, I know what you are saying: "But he was a *prisoner*, after all, *of course* he didn't get the best house." But remember, he was a former emperor, and other heads of state who had fallen on tough times were given far better treatment. Plus, Napoleon was a prisoner whose only "crime" had been to lose! Even captured French officers were given better treatment than he was: They were allowed to return home to their families.

Enjoying a stay with the Balcombes

Despite the circumstances, Napoleon spent a few weeks actually enjoying his stay on St. Helena. While Longwood was being prepared, Napoleon was expected to stay in Jamestown. But he hated the place and was anxious for other quarters. He visited William Balcombe and his family at their home, known as *the Briars,* and found them to be very nice company. He especially enjoyed Balcombe's 14-year-old daughter, Betsy. Balcombe was superintendent of public sales for the East India Company and partner in a firm that served as purveyor to the ships in the harbor. As such, he was able to live a good life on the island.

As it happened, there was another house on the Balcombe property. It was really more of a pavilion, but it suited Napoleon just fine. All were in agreement, and Napoleon moved right in. The local military engineers provided an additional structure to serve as a dining hall and Napoleon's study.

For the next two months, Napoleon lived a reasonably content life. Betsy loved to play tricks on him, and the two of them became quite the pair, with Napoleon playing the role of the kindly uncle and Betsy the mischievous niece. She could barge in on Napoleon just about anytime she pleased, and Napoleon always seemed to enjoy her company.

The Briars was not perfect, however, and Napoleon soon began to tire of life there. The guards were ever present, and already there were major tensions forming between Napoleon and his jailors. Neither side was willing to budge on what Napoleon should be called. As a result, social opportunities that may have lightened Napoleon's stay were not available, as Napoleon refused to socialize with people who could not or would not refer to him as emperor. (His staff, however, felt perfectly free to socialize with the locals.) People blame both sides for this obviously petty dispute: Napoleon was arrogant and foolish; the Brits were mean-spirited, petty, and hypocritical.

Moving to Longwood

On December 10, Napoleon and his group moved, with great ceremony, to his new quarters at Longwood. It was the beginning of a long and bitter end to Napoleon's life.

Napoleon and Admiral Cockburn had been on good terms on the trip to St. Helena, but now that Cockburn was serving as governor of the island, the relationship began to sour. Napoleon resented the tight restrictions under which he lived, and he resented the condition and location of Longwood. The repairs and additions to the house had been inadequate and poorly done. The house was leaky and drafty, and with the ever-present guards, Napoleon had little in the way of privacy.

Still, for a time Napoleon attempted to make the best of it. He would exercise by taking long walks or by going riding. He held court as best he could, especially at his formal dinners. He received numerous guests, whose later descriptions of their visits often make good reading.

Napoleon would sometimes dictate his memoirs to Las Cases, Gourgaud, or others, and he would engage in long conversations about any number of topics. He continued to study English. Evening entertainment often included playing cards, readings plays, or listening to Albine Montholon sing. (Of course, some evenings she did more than sing for Napoleon.)

Napoleon soon tired of the petty rivalries that were forming in his little band of followers. Each one was jealous of the other, each one convinced that someone else was getting an unfair share of Napoleon's time. Thus, as on the trip over, Napoleon often avoided spending too much time with them. He did enjoy his time with the British officers stationed there, and they were in turn fascinated to be talking with this man, who was England's greatest adversary for so many years.

Slowly but surely, the British improved some of his physical conditions with the arrival of better furnishings. Some restrictions were removed — for a time, at least, Napoleon had the run of the island. But things didn't stay that way for long.

Receiving a Lowe blow

In April 1816, the British sent a new governor to the island. Sir Hudson Lowe was a career officer who had served in numerous campaigns with little distinction but with honor (see Figure 16-2). He made his name as someone who was quite good at following orders right down to the smallest detail, with no wiggle room allowed. This characteristic made him an ideal candidate for some posts and a disastrous candidate for this one.

Not that he didn't make some effort. Lowe's first meetings with Napoleon were cordial, which was helped by the fact that both men spoke Italian. He agreed to build Napoleon a new house elsewhere on the island, to repair Longwood in the meantime, and to allow Napoleon full use of his (Lowe's) extensive library.

Unfortunately, Lowe also made it clear that not only would he not reduce any of the restrictions on Napoleon's movements, but they were likely to get worse (see Figure 16-3). Indeed, Lowe revoked some of the relaxations that

Cockburn had granted, including the right for Napoleon to receive any visitors and to travel wherever he wished on the island. The new house was to be built very near the old one. Even in sending books to Napoleon, Lowe was often petty, being careful to send some that were very critical of Napoleon.

Figure 16-2:
An early engraving of a rather stern looking Sir Hudson Lowe.

Figure 16-3:
This engraving by Currier nicely illustrates Napoleon's isolation on St. Helena.

In short, it soon became clear that Sir Hudson Lowe was determined to make life miserable for Napoleon. While Napoleon could certainly be petty in his own right, he could not hold a candle to Lowe in that department, and it is difficult to imagine what Napoleon could have done to make Lowe act any differently.

Meanwhile, the pettiness of Napoleon's staff had reached a boiling point. Montholon and Gourgaud were very jealous of Las Cases (see Figure 16-4), who had become one of Napoleon's favorites. Las Cases and Napoleon spent hours together, with Napoleon dictating an incredible number of pages of memoirs. Napoleon also greatly enjoyed the company of Las Cases's son, Emmanuel.

Figure 16-4: A period engraving showing Las Cases, one of the people most responsible for the Napoleonic legend.

Las Cases soon got fed up with the pettiness and contrived to get himself deported. The authorities took his notes of Napoleon's dictation, but when he finally reached Europe, he rewrote them all from memory. Entitled *Memorial de Sainte-Hélène,* they soon became a bestseller, and Las Cases became rich. Translated into several languages, they present a very sympathetic view of Napoleon.

Enduring medical follies

Napoleon's medical care on St. Helena was evidence of the petty nature of his exile. His first doctor was the Irishman Barry O'Meara. He and Napoleon got along great — too great for Sir Hudson Lowe, who was suspicious of anyone who showed a favorable attitude toward Napoleon.

O'Meara could see that his patient was beginning to slide into ill health and encouraged him to get more exercise. That is a tough sell to most of us, let alone to a person who is required to be escorted by an armed guard wherever he goes. Not long after Lowe's arrival, Napoleon pretty much stopped taking the nice long walks and rides that had helped keep him in decent physical — and mental — condition.

Napoleon's situation deteriorated in several ways:

✔ In an amazing turn of events, the British decided that Napoleon should help pay for his imprisonment. Napoleon fired back by selling some silver, which humiliated the British into rescinding the policy. The image of the former emperor forced to sell his silver to pay for his own confinement was just too much for the British people to take, and the government feared a political backlash, or, at the very least, an abusive media blitz.

✔ In 1818, Napoleon lost his trusted servant Cipriani Franceschi to a suspicious death.

✔ The Balcombes left in March 1818, having been more or less forced out by Lowe's jealousy of their closeness to Napoleon.

✔ In August 1818, Barry O'Meara was court-martialed and forced to leave the island. Napoleon had liked and trusted his doctor, and his departure was a major blow.

Lowe and the British understood the importance of having a good doctor for Napoleon. It would do the British no good to have the world thinking that the British were trying to kill off Napoleon, or giving him inadequate healthcare. So Lowe turned to the best medical man on the island, an Irish doctor named James Verling (see Figure 16-5).

Figure 16-5:
Dr. James Verling was probably the best doctor on the island but was never able to treat Napoleon.

Napoleon would probably have been willing to see Verling if he had agreed to be his personal doctor and not make his medical condition known to the

British superiors. But Verling refused (no doubt noticing what had happened to O'Meara for doing just that). Napoleon would not see any doctor appointed by and reporting his condition to Sir Hudson Lowe, so he never saw Verling. Napoleon's staff did, and encouraged Napoleon to do so as well, but Napoleon refused.

Verling wrote a daily journal while he was involved with Napoleon, and it makes for some very interesting reading. You can see the pettiness on all sides and have great sympathy for Verling, who was stuck in the middle. (My book *Napoleon and Dr. Verling on St. Helena* [Pen and Sword] includes the entire journal and important related letters between some of the principle players in the soap opera of St. Helena.)

Verling and O'Meara weren't the only doctors to have to deal with this tricky situation. In January 1819, Napoleon fainted. Because Napoleon wouldn't see Verling, Lowe sent Dr. John Stokoe to attend to him. The two men hit it off, and Stokoe agreed to be Napoleon's personal physician. For Stokoe's efforts, Lowe had him court-marshaled and drummed out of the service.

Napoleon's last doctor was sent to the island by Napoleon's family. His name was Francesco Antommarchi, and he arrived in late 1819. Unfortunately, he was grossly incompetent. Napoleon knew it and had little use for him. Still, at least he was somewhat useful: He convinced Napoleon to take up gardening, which got Napoleon outside and in some mode of exercise. Napoleon's health and attitude improved, and for a time it looked like he might recover completely and get into something resembling a normal life (for those circumstances, anyway). Alas, it wasn't to be.

Losing His Last Battle

For the next year and a half, Napoleon's health continued to slide. Every time he seemed to get better, he would suffer yet another decline. Napoleon knew he had little time left. He prepared a will, destroyed it, and prepared another. He suffered extremely sharp pains in his sides and could not keep food down.

As the end drew near, he added more to his will and prepared to die. The end came a little before 6 p.m. on May 5, 1821. Napoleon had been one of the most powerful men in history, but he died on an obscure little island far from his family, surrounded by a small group of friends and servants. He was only 51 years old.

An unmarked grave

Even in death, the pettiness continued. Lowe decreed that Napoleon would be buried in Geranium Valley, where Napoleon used to enjoy some quiet solitude. So far, so good. But what to put on the gravestone? Napoleon's followers wanted *Emperor Napoleon,* but even a dead Napoleon would be called *Napoleon Buonaparte* or nothing at all. Nothing it would be: Napoleon was buried in an unmarked grave.

On May 9, a solemn procession of British soldiers and Napoleon's followers took Napoleon's casket down the long path to his resting place. Lowe had pulled out all the stops; no one would ever accuse him of not giving Napoleon a decent burial. He had been placed in a tin coffin, which was placed inside a mahogany coffin, which was placed inside a lead coffin, which was then placed inside another mahogany coffin.

Bands played funereal music; the local artillery and the ships in the harbor fired salutes. Napoleon was finally lowered into a concrete grave, covered by a large stone cemented into place. A permanent guard was stationed at the grave. Louis-Joseph Marchand wrote that the scene was "overwhelming in its sorrow and grief," but the French writer François René de Châteaubriand commented that Napoleon was buried by the British "as though they feared that he could never be sufficiently imprisoned" (see Figure 16-6). That phrase sums up the whole St. Helena experience.

Figure 16-6: This engraving shows the "Shade [ghost or spirit] of Napoleon" at his tomb on St. Helena. Can you see it between the trees?

Death by . . .?

One of the most intriguing controversies of Napoleon's life is the question of the cause of his death. Antommarchi performed the autopsy under the watchful eyes of seven British doctors and several others. There was general agreement that he likely died of some tumors and ulcers on the stomach. Not everyone agreed on all aspects of the autopsy, however, and its honesty remains in some question yet today.

But the biggest question to be raised regarding Napoleon's death has to do with the possibility that he was poisoned. The biggest proponent of that theory is Ben Weider of Montreal, Canada. Weider is a successful businessman who made his name in bodybuilding and has received numerous honors and awards, including the French Legion of Honor, the Canadian Medal of Honor, and a nomination for the Nobel Peace Prize. (As a matter of full disclosure, I should tell you that he is also the founder and president of the International Napoleonic Society, of which I am Executive Vice-President and Editor-in-Chief. He is also a longtime friend.)

Weider has studied the memoirs of all the people on St. Helena and has had various tests done on strands of Napoleon's hair, including by the U.S. Federal Bureau of Investigation (FBI). These tests show the presence of segments of arsenic that are consistent with the possibility of periodic ingestion. In other words, someone could have been periodically giving Napoleon the poison.

This arsenic would weaken Napoleon, making it look like the climate was slowly doing him in. Then, at the critical moment, the poisoner would administer other substances that would become toxic and kill Napoleon. This method of poisoning was common for the time, and the autopsy results showed conditions that *could* lead to the conclusion that this is what happened.

The obvious question here is just who would want Napoleon dead. When James Bond asked that question of his director, M, the reply was a classic, along the lines of "jealous husbands, outraged chefs, the list is endless." Well, the list isn't quite endless when it comes to Napoleon. The obvious answer would be the British, but they actually stood to gain from having Napoleon alive. He was a good foil to use against the new French monarch Louis XVIII should he prove uncooperative. Besides, the Brits didn't want to be blamed for Napoleon's death; they were much too civilized for that.

Weider believes, and it makes good sense, that if anyone wanted Napoleon dead it would be the French. If anyone stood to lose from Napoleon's possible return, it would be that very same Louis XVIII. Napoleon unleashed could cause a civil war or a coup, neither of which suited Louis.

Weider also believes that the culprit was Count Montholon. He was in charge of the wine, which could easily have been used as the method of poisoning. Montholon had a questionable past, and Napoleon had left him more money than anyone else, despite the fact that others had been much closer to Napoleon before the exile.

There is much more to the story, of course, but this summary gives a good idea of what the controversy is all about. And controversy it is, with most French scholars appalled at the idea of one of their own killing one of France's greatest leaders, while Brits and Americans often seem to find some credibility in the theory. For my part, I think it makes sense, but the only way to be absolutely sure would likely be to exhume Napoleon's body and run tests. Like *that's* going to happen!

Returning to France

Napoleon's body *was* exhumed once. In July 1840, King Louis Philippe of France sent his son to St. Helena to retrieve Napoleon's body. Henri-Gatien Bertrand and Louis-Joseph Marchand were along; Napoleon was finally to come home. When they opened the coffin, his body was as it had been the day he was buried. The body was returned to France (see Figure 16-7) and then made a slow trip up the Seine River to Paris. Along the route, thousands stood in silent tribute. Church bells rang, cannon fired salutes. Marshals and members of the Old Guard (the oldest of Napoleon's elite fighting force) paid their respects.

On December 15, 1840, the casket moved slowly down the Champs-Elysées, under the Arc de Triomphe to Les Invalides, its final resting place. The day was bitter cold, but thousands lined the streets in homage to their former emperor. The king's son, the Prince de Joinville, followed the casket, and behind him were thousands of Napoleon's Old Guard. The ceremony was conducted by the king himself. Afterwards, countless thousands filed past the emperor's casket as he lay in state.

Finally, in 1861, Napoleon was laid to his final rest under the Dome of Les Invalides, as he had requested in his will: He wanted to be "on the banks of the Seine, amongst the French people whom I have loved so well." His tomb is without doubt the grandest I have ever seen.

Figure 16-7:
This wood snuffbox, carved in 1840, shows Napoleon being brought back from St. Helena.

Part IV
A True Revolutionary

The 5th Wave By Rich Tennant

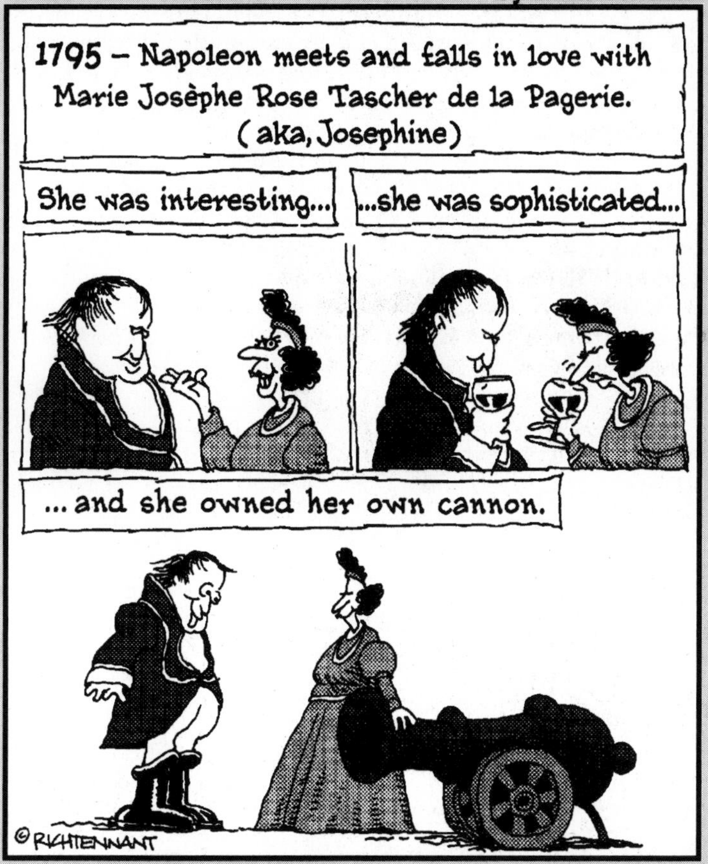

In this part . . .

Napoleon was a conqueror, but that's only part of his story. To understand *how* he earned that title, in this part I tell you a bit about Napoleon's military innovations. And he was innovative off the battlefield as well. He was ahead of his time in areas as divergent as education and the economy, law and logistics. All these topics and more are included here. If you want to understand why Napoleon was so popular in France, read this part.

Like all reformers, Napoleon wanted to ensure that his reforms would last, so I also discuss how he tried to create a family dynasty in France to carry on after he was gone. (As I explain, plenty of folks were trying to see that he was gone sooner rather than later!)

Chapter 17

Marshalling a Great Army

*I*t is fair to say that Napoleon's reputation is largely based on the fact that he was one of the greatest military commanders in history. He went to military school and rose through the ranks in the artillery branch of the French army. He fought in about 60 battles and won most of them. He could inspire his soldiers and convince them to fight well under almost any conditions.

But Napoleon's reputation as a great commander depends on far more than his ability to lead men into battle:

✔ Napoleon was a great military planner whose command of the ebb and flow of a battle was key to his success.

✔ He was also a great military organizer; his organization is still reflected in today's military.

✔ He was a micromanager who knew the details of every aspect of his army; few things escaped his attention.

✔ Napoleon revolutionized the art of war and kept his opponents off balance, until they finally began to copy his approach to war.

In this chapter, I show you what Napoleon did to reorganize the army, and I discuss some of his basic battle tactics.

Revolutionizing the Army Corps System

When you read about massive armies facing each other (perhaps 100,000 on one side, 125,000 on another), you may have an image of one person on a horse leading a massive number of troops behind him. While that image is generally fictional, European armies of the 18th and 19th centuries were loosely based on a system that depended on a centralized command, the head of which was often far to the rear. Moreover, many of the individual units of an army were specialized. That is, there was a heavy cavalry unit, a light cavalry unit, an artillery unit, various types of infantry units, and so forth. All units were under the centralized command of a general, a field marshal, or an emperor.

Recognizing flaws in the old system

There were several problems with this kind of military structure:

- Large armies were often spread out over a wide area, making communication very difficult and slow.

- With a centralized command structure, it was sometimes difficult for one unit to come to the aid of another.

- Worse, if the cavalry units were mostly, say, in the north, and they were suddenly needed in the south, well, lots of luck!

This type of structure led to slow advances with little ability to maneuver to respond to a rapidly changing situation.

Designing a better way

Napoleon looked at the situation and decided there had to be a way to improve the structure of his army to make it a more effective fighting force. Antiquity provided an example for all to see: The Roman legions (which won a battle or two in their day) were largely self-contained units. But few armies since the Romans had attempted to copy that model. Napoleon took that model and perfected it. It was, in many ways, his ace in the hole, the single biggest military advantage he had over his opponents.

The army corps system (called *corps d'armée* in French) was really a very simple concept. Any large army is subdivided into smaller units. But instead of units being specialized (light cavalry, infantry, and so on), Napoleon made each unit completely self-contained — a miniature version of the larger army.

Each corps usually had the following elements:

- A full allotment of artillery, usually including heavy guns and more mobile horse artillery, a Napoleonic specialty

- Heavy or light cavalry, or both

✔ Infantry (usually called *grenadiers*)

✔ Other logistical and support units

✔ A command staff

✔ A marshal in overall command

When you put all these pieces together, you have a miniature army capable of holding off a larger force of a less complete enemy. As to size, flexibility was again the word, with a corps size of anywhere from 9,000 to 25,000 men possible.

Napoleon believed that any corps could hold off virtually any enemy for at least a day. Thus, he tried to have his various corps no more than a day's march from their nearest counterparts. This flexibility allowed his army to take full advantage of varying road conditions, the availability of forage opportunities, and other aspects of a military command. It also allowed for Napoleon's tactics of encirclement, speed, mobility, and a flexible response to changing battlefield conditions.

I should mention one more thing here. Throughout history, leaders have had special military units that were elite fighting forces, often for the protection of, and under the command of, the supreme ruler. As soon as Napoleon became a general, he formed a small elite force for his own protection, called the *Guides.* When he was First Consul, this force was known as the *Consular Guard,* and in 1804 it was reconstituted as the *Imperial Guard.* Membership in the Guard was greatly sought and reserved for the best fighting men. The Guard was Napoleon's top trump, which he could play whenever the battlefield situation required a *coup de grâce.* The Guard was intensely loyal to Napoleon and was the elite of the army. To send in the Guard was usually a sign that the final, decisive blow was about to be administered.

Creating Marshals

On May 19, 1804, Napoleon created a new level of the social and political hierarchy called the *Marshalate.* The men who were chosen as Marshals of the Empire were among the highest in the social pecking order and were usually given additional titles, such as duke or prince, to go along with the lands and wealth that came with the position.

The marshals are most remembered, however, for their military roles, even though technically the position of marshal was not a military position. (These men had the official rank of *general of division* but were — and still are — referred to as *marshals.*) The marshals were usually in command of an army corps, though this was not always the case. So if you read about Marshal Michel Ney's corps or Marshal Nicolas Soult's division, that means that these men were the commanding officers of those units.

This marshal business does get just a little bit confusing. Many of the marshals were given additional titles, often based on their performance at one battle or another. Thus, Marshal Ney also had the title *Prince of the Moskowa, Duke of Elchingen* for his role in those two battles. And Marshal Joachim Murat was a prince, the King of Naples, and the Grand Duke of Berg (a small German principality). When you read Napoleon's military Bulletins and other official pronouncements, rather than saying "Marshal Ney" did such and such, they are more likely to say, "The Prince of the Moskowa" did such and such. With no last name given, it's easy to forget who is who. (You should be pleased that in this book I just call them "Marshal so and so" and let it go at that.)

Oh, and how many of these exalted folk were there, you ask? The initial group contained 18, but by Napoleon's final fall in 1815, the number had risen to 26.

Fighting a Modern War

Napoleon brought far more than military organization to his military campaigns. He also brought a set of tactics that allowed him to defeat his less modern opponents up until the very end of his career. Some of these tactics were based on developing technology. Others were based simply on Napoleon's military genius.

Using artillery effectively

Napoleon's branch of service was the artillery, so it is not surprising that much of his success was due to his expert use of that branch of arms. Both sides of any conflict had cannon, of course, but Napoleon excelled at its use. (By the way, in this book and elsewhere, cannon are also called *field pieces, artillery, guns,* or *heavy guns. Cannon* is one of those words that is both singular and plural.)

As Napoleon entered the military, the technology of cannon was changing, and he was quick to take advantage of it. Before that time, cannon were generally massed into huge batteries, or *artillery parks*. They would blast away from long range at an enemy's position or at attacking cavalry or infantry. Throughout his career, Napoleon was quite willing to use this tactic, often to great advantage.

But smaller, lighter, and more mobile cannon were developed in Napoleon's lifetime. These cannon could be rapidly pulled behind a horse and brought into position to turn the tide of battle. The sudden and unanticipated appearance of such guns could terrorize an attacking army, inspire a defending army, or destroy a retreating army. Retreating armies were especially vulnerable, as they were likely using roads that compressed their numbers, making them sitting ducks for suddenly-arriving horse artillery. Napoleon recognized very early in his career the potential of light artillery and used it effectively throughout his campaigns. For most of this time, his opponents simply did not get it.

Planning an offensive

Napoleon is often called a micromanager, and nowhere was this more true than in planning his military campaigns. Napoleon didn't want to leave anything to chance. He read everything he could find on his opponents: Not just their military tactics, but the nature of their countries, their economies, their individual leaders (both civilian and military) — all were of interest to Napoleon.

Today, military planners use sophisticated computers to design various possible scenarios, including the worst case scenario and several most likely responses to various actions. Napoleon did all of that in his head, using only his knowledge of his opponents and his stacks of maps (see Figure 17-1). A firm believer in intelligence, he had spies wherever possible and sent cavalry reconnaissance to determine the latest enemy troop movements.

Napoleon knew almost to the man the size of his various units and their fighting capabilities. He could move army corps or artillery parks on a battlefield like you or I may move chess pieces on a board.

While it was important to know as much about the enemy as possible, it was also important that they know as little about Napoleon's movements as possible. Napoleon would routinely send out cavalry screens to shield his own movements from enemy eyes. He would also send small units elsewhere to misdirect the enemy's attention. Napoleon would even, as he did in 1805 (see Chapter 9), use the media to disseminate false information on the movements of his troops.

Figure 17-1:
This 19th-century miniature on ivory shows Napoleon studying his maps while his staff awaits his orders.

Taking the fight to the enemy, quickly

I don't know when the old adage "The best defense is a good offense" came to be, but Napoleon certainly believed in it. He had little interest in sitting around and waiting for his enemy to attack him, much preferring to take the fight directly to the enemy instead. At its worst, this philosophy of war could be reckless. But Napoleon waged war at its best, and his planning and security measures seldom let him down. Taking the offensive was almost always the right thing to do militarily, though it did allow people to see him as an aggressor.

If you are going to move forward, you may as well go quickly. Napoleon believed in moving his forces as fast as possible in order to catch his enemy unawares. The army corps system I discuss earlier in the chapter was designed in part to allow for rapid movement.

Napoleon was a master at rapid troop movements, surprising and often overwhelming an enemy that had no idea he was so close. Napoleon's soldiers were fond of saying that Napoleon fought war with their legs rather than with their bayonets, and they had a good point. In campaign after campaign, Napoleon's advantage was often gained by his ability to move far faster than his enemies could even imagine. (See my discussion of the campaign of Ülm and Austerlitz in Chapter 9 for an excellent example of this tactic.)

Dividing and conquering

In battle itself, Napoleon liked to mass his forces against the opponent's center and then defeat each wing in turn. Napoleon's rapidity of movement often allowed him to reach an enemy before it had been able to concentrate its forces. At Austerlitz, for example, Napoleon was able to gain control of the center of the allied position and then turn on the Russian left flank and utterly destroy it (see Chapter 9). At the Battle of Ligny, part of the prelude to Waterloo (see Chapter 15), he did much the same thing against the Prussians, and only the lack of adequate pursuit prevented a similar result.

Austerlitz provides us with an example of a related aspect of Napoleonic strategy. Napoleon would not only attempt to defeat his opponents piecemeal, but he would also try to envelope them, thus cutting off their communications with other units and stopping their line of retreat. Enemy soldiers, often demoralized by Napoleon's sudden arrival on the scene, were then devastated to discover that they were surrounded. (If you don't believe me, just ask "the unfortunate General Mack" at Ülm!)

This approach also was effective if Napoleon could catch part of an enemy army temporarily isolated from its main force. He would use *forced marches* (marching quickly, usually with few if any breaks and often at night) to suddenly appear before — or behind — his enemy, who he would then force to either surrender or be crushed. (Again, talk to General Mack about the effectiveness of this tactic.)

Improving logistics

Part of planning involves, of course, making sure that your army has everything it needs to carry on a campaign. This involves far more than adequate ammunition and weapons. It also involves food, clothing, medical supplies, and other such necessities.

Napoleon was determined that his soldiers would have everything they needed, and he always sought to guard against shortages, either inadvertent or the result of fraud. One story relates how he would stop a wagon and ask to see the *manifest* (the list of what was on board). The wagon master would then be asked to empty the wagon to check the actual contents against what was promised on the manifest, and woe to anyone who came up short!

Preserving food

Carrying food for a long time is problematic: How do you keep the food in good condition? Napoleon recognized the problem and was anxious to find a solution. Before that time, the only way to preserve meat was through packing it in salt or using vinegar to pickle it. Napoleon, who was himself very scientifically inclined, held a competition to seek a more palatable method of preservation. The forerunner to modern canning was the result.

Foraging for supplies

There were no railroads in the early 19th century, just long lines of wagons called *baggage trains*. Baggage trains were necessary, but they could be very slow. To maintain their speed, Napoleonic armies generally depended on their ability to forage from fields and procure necessary supplies from locals. This method often worked quite well, allowing the armies to depend less on baggage trains and to move more quickly.

Providing medical care

One area where Napoleon did not scrimp was in caring for his sick and wounded. Napoleon made sure that his field hospitals were fully stocked and that there were adequate doctors to attend to the often large numbers of wounded. His attention extended beyond his own men: He would order his doctors to attend to enemy wounded as well.

Napoleon's most famous doctor was Dominique-Jean Larrey. Dr. Larrey joined Napoleon during the 1798 campaign in Egypt (see Chapter 7) and was loyal to him all the way to Waterloo (see Chapter 15), where he was wounded while tending to the wounded. His emphasis on sanitation and other practical matters no doubt saved many a life. But he was most known for his invention of the quick and mobile field *flying ambulances* (so-called because they moved very quickly to get the wounded off the battlefield), which allowed wounded to be evacuated to a field hospital rather than being treated on the spot. Larrey became a legend in the army and was among those who paid their respects to Napoleon when his body was returned to France in 1840. Napoleon called Larrey "the most virtuous man I have ever known."

Inspiring soldiers

Logistics, planning, and organization are all important to the success of any army, and they contributed greatly to Napoleon's many victories. But Napoleon had one more ace up his sleeve: He was a true inspiration to his men. While the leaders of the opposing armies were conservative, often stodgy, aristocrats who had no way of connecting to their soldiers, Napoleon was positively inspirational.

For starters, Napoleon had risen on the basis of his own talent and ambition, and he made it clear that other soldiers could do the same. This was a far cry from the armies of Russia and Austria, for example, where soldiers had little hope of any real advancement and where officers were all members of the arrogant nobility.

Napoleon had an incredible memory, and he put it to good use in inspiring his soldiers. He would frequently walk among his men in their evening encampments, chatting with them, recalling that this soldier or that had been with him in Egypt, at Austerlitz, or wherever. A great honor was bestowed if Napoleon would tweak a grenadier's ear or, better yet, offer him some snuff from his personal snuffbox. *That* experience would be talked about around the campfires for years! Napoleon's rapport with his men is itself the stuff of legend, comparable with that of Alexander the Great or Julius Caesar.

Napoleon also understood that men would not fight and die only for a just cause or even for an inspirational leader. Throughout history, armies have rewarded their men with medals and other awards, and Napoleon was careful to do so as well. He instituted a wide range of medals and awards, including swords or muskets of honor. He gave cash awards and, to his top leaders, various titles of nobility. For the common soldier and officer alike, appointment to the Imperial Guard (his elite fighting force) was a great honor.

In 1802, Napoleon instituted a new national award, the Legion of Honor (*Legion d'honneur*). This was — and is — France's highest honor, given to worthy civilians as well as military men (and now women). When opponents of the award derided it as a mere "bauble," Napoleon replied, "It is with such baubles that men are led." That was true then, and it is true now.

Chapter 18

Sustaining Support at Home

In This Chapter

▶ Promoting himself through public relations

▶ Using power to maintain power

▶ Plastering images across France

*L*ike any politician, Napoleon had to maintain his popularity with his "base," in this case a majority of the French people. He approached this task, as he did everything else he undertook, in a methodical manner, and he met with much success. While he may have preferred to make his mark based on his domestic policies (see Chapter 19), he knew that their effects would take time, and he needed shorter term means of maintaining popularity.

Napoleon realized that much of his popularity was based on his military success, his ability to obtain victory and glory on the battlefield. And winning battles certainly was something that Napoleon did quite well. But he also recognized that military glory alone was not enough. He needed additional domestic approaches to maintain his power — approaches that people could instantly see and appreciate. He also needed ways of insuring that alternatives to his rule were not seriously considered and that opponents were not able to obtain a foothold in French politics.

In this chapter, I discuss how Napoleon used some good old fashioned public relations to keep his version of events ever before the people. I also delve into both the positive and negative aspects of his other means of maintaining power at home.

Promoting a Point of View

Any ruler wants the people to see events from his or her point of view. Throughout history, political leaders have sought to control the presentation of their images through control of the media of presentation. Napoleon was no different. He used the media to promote positive images of himself and of France while providing negative images of France's opponents. Sometimes, he also used the media to attempt to win over people in other countries by praising them or by criticizing foreign (usually British) involvement in their affairs.

Determined to control as much as possible the information that people received, Napoleon took both positive and negative (from our point of view) steps toward that end. The following sections consider a few of the approaches that he took.

Issuing Bulletins and proclamations

Julius Caesar was one of the greatest commanders of all time and one of the best at promoting his victorious image. Caesar, like Napoleon 2,000 years later, fully understood the power of the written word and was a master word-smith. He wrote his *Commentaries* while on campaign and had them copied and posted throughout Rome. These descriptions of his campaigns were generally accurate as to what happened but were designed to present Caesar at his very best.

Bulletins

Napoleon took much the same approach with his *Bulletins de la Grande Armée* (Bulletins of the Great Army). Like Caesar's *Commentaries,* these Bulletins were designed to tell what was happening while giving a decidedly pro-Napoleon spin to the telling.

Some cynics suggested then (and still do now) that the Bulletins could not be trusted. There is some truth to this skepticism, as bad news was often (but not always) downplayed, casualty figures tinkered with, and victories sometimes overstated. But, in general, I find them to be as accurate as, say, official reports from Vietnam or Iraq. (And now it's time for a shameless plug: You can read English translations of all of the Bulletins in my book *Imperial Glory: The Bulletins of Napoleon's Grande Armée, 1805–1814,* published by Greenhill.)

The Bulletins were designed for three audiences:

- ✔ **Napoleon's soldiers:** As all soldiers like to hear of their importance, both collectively and individually, the Bulletins would take great care to extol the bravery of various units and individual soldiers. Thus, a unit fought with "the greatest persistence and extreme bravery" or "covered itself in glory," while an individual soldier (in this case, Marshal Michel Ney) "acquitted himself with his usual intelligence and intrepidity." Sometimes the Bulletins would provide lengthy lists of soldiers who excelled, were wounded or killed, or received medals.

- ✔ **The French people:** Citizens of any country are always anxious to hear news from the front, and the Bulletins were reproduced and posted throughout France to give the French people their fill of news. They were also carried in the official newspaper, *Le Moniteur* (*The Monitor*), and elsewhere.

- **Napoleon's opponents (domestic and foreign):** Napoleon understood full well that the Bulletins would be translated and distributed in Great Britain and elsewhere, so he wrote them with this fact in mind. Many of his comments were political in nature, either criticizing or complimenting his opponents. So, England's policy "nauseates us with indignation" and the Russian cavalry known as Cossacks were "hordes of barbarians." On the other hand, members of the Russian regular cavalry at Austerlitz "show intrepidity and resolution."

Proclamations

Proclamations were similar to the Bulletins, though they were less likely to be military in nature. Some announced public policy, some military policy, and some dealt with civil issues of a wide variety. Like the Bulletins, many proclamations were designed for international as well as domestic consumption, and most were designed to promote a positive image of either Napoleon or French policies. Thus, when the French entered Vienna in 1809, Napoleon issued a proclamation telling his soldiers that he placed the Viennese citizens under his protection and that the soldiers should treat them with all respect (see Figure 18-1).

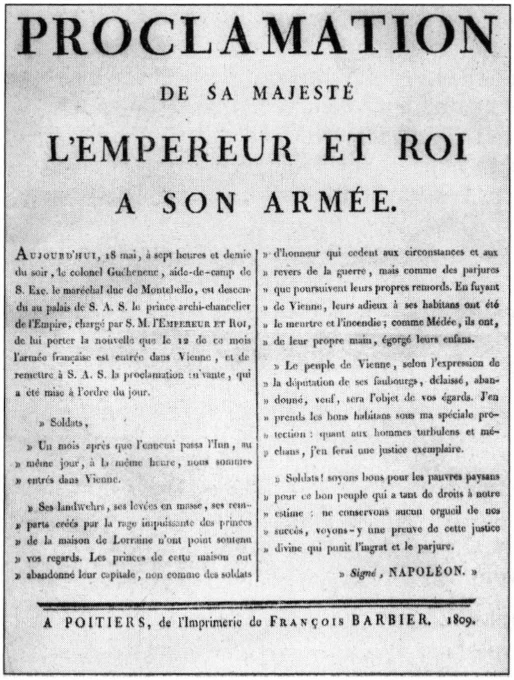

PROCLAMATION

DE SA MAJESTÉ

L'EMPEREUR ET ROI

A SON ARMÉE.

Aujourd'hui, 18 mai, à sept heures et demie du soir, le colonel Guéhenenc, aide-de-camp de S. Exc. le maréchal duc de Montebello, est descendu au palais de S. A. S. le prince archi-chancelier de l'Empire, chargé par S. M. l'Empereur et Roi, de lui porter la nouvelle que le 12 de ce mois l'armée française est entrée dans Vienne, et de remettre à S. A. S. la proclamation suivante, qui a été mise à l'ordre du jour.

» Soldats,

» Un mois après que l'ennemi passa l'Inn, au » même jour, à la même heure, nous sommes » entrés dans Vienne.

» Ses landwehrs, ses levées en masse, ses rem» parts créés par la rage impuissante des princes » de la maison de Lorraine n'ont point soutenu » vos regards. Les princes de cette maison ont » abandonné leur capitale, non comme des soldats » d'honneur qui cedent aux circonstances et aux » revers de la guerre, mais comme des parjures » que poursuivent leurs propres remords. En fuyant » de Vienne, leurs adieux à ses habitans ont été » le meurtre et l'incendie; comme Médée, ils ont, » de leur propre main, égorgé leurs enfans.

» Le peuple de Vienne, selon l'expression de » la députation de ses faubourgs, délaissé, aban» donné, veuf, sera l'objet de vos égards. J'en » prends les bons habitans sous ma spéciale pro» tection : quant aux hommes turbulens et mé» chans, j'en ferai une justice exemplaire.

» Soldats! soyons bons pour les pauvres paysans » pour ce bon peuple qui a tant de droits à notre » estime : ne conservons aucun orgueil de nos » succès, voyons-y une preuve de cette justice » divine qui punit l'ingrat et le parjure.

» *Signé*, NAPOLÉON. »

A POITIERS, de l'Imprimerie de François BARBIER. 1809.

Figure 18-1: This proclamation was distributed not only in Vienna but across the empire to show Napoleon's good treatment of his conquered enemies.

Influencing newspaper coverage

Another way that Napoleon was able to generate support for his regime was through the use of newspapers. This situation had positive and negative sides:

✔ The good news was that Napoleon and his supporters would use papers just like any other politicians would, by providing positively-spun stories for the newspapers' mass audience to consume. Indeed, in an echo of Caesar's approach, when Napoleon was on campaign in Egypt and elsewhere, he took with him portable printing presses that allowed him to produce newspapers both in French and in the local language. This allowed him to promote his cause to the local citizens, as well as to the people back in France.

✔ The bad news was that, especially later in his career, Napoleon would either shut down papers that he felt were not supportive enough or censor the material that was being published. Those of us who live in a 21st-century democracy condemn that action, and Napoleon does stand guilty as charged. Still, France was at war for most of Napoleon's time in power, and many nations engage in censorship during wartime, including modern democracies. I discuss this topic further in the upcoming section "Censoring opposing voices."

A couple newspapers are worthy of special mention here:

✔ **Le Moniteur:** *The Monitor* was the official daily newspaper of the French government and, therefore, of Napoleon. It was allowed a certain amount of editorial freedom, but that freedom diminished over time. *The Monitor* served as the outlet for official pronouncements and documents (much as newspapers do today). Thus, it carried all of the Bulletins and proclamations, as well as any other material that the government wanted disseminated. This material often included letters and proclamations from other countries, either to show support of or to promote anger toward a government (such as Great Britain or Prussia). It also reported on parliamentary debates, foreign politics, and events in Paris and in the provinces.

✔ **Journal de L'Empire:** Like *The Monitor,* the *Journal of the Empire* purported to be a general newspaper with a wide variety of information from home and abroad. But the *Journal of the Empire* was not given as much leeway on what it published and, by 1810 or so, was little more than a mouthpiece for the government.

As Napoleon's military situation began to get worse in 1812 and beyond, the *Journal* (and, to a lesser extent, *The Monitor*) was told not to publish anything that promoted a less than optimistic view of the French situation. (See Figure 18-2 for a sample of this newspaper.)

Figure 18-2: A copy of *Journal de L'Empire* from April 5, 1811. This issue was four pages long and carried stories from several countries, as well as the results of the Imperial Lottery.

Using the Power of Government

All leaders of nations use the power of government to promote their world view, and Napoleon was no different. He was a master at this task and was perfectly comfortable using his control of government in ways that, while effective, may not pass muster in a modern democracy.

Producing information

Napoleon created an enormous publicity machine, much like government leaders do today. For example, the Ministry of the Interior had a number of bureaus that were largely dedicated to the production of information (some would say propaganda). This ministry also included public education and was able to influence the image of Napoleon and of French conquest in the schools. During the later years of his empire, Napoleon created the Imperial University, which assumed the task of overseeing curriculum matters. Napoleon strongly supported education, but at least one of his motives was education's ability to mold student opinions and perceptions in ways favorable to Napoleon's goals. (See Chapter 19 for more on Napoleon's education policies.)

The Ministry of Foreign Affairs generated stories and other information for public consumption. It produced many of the proclamations and other announcements of military success, and it provided the media with information that would put a very positive spin on Napoleon's campaigns and a very negative interpretation of British or other countries' actions.

Even the Ministry of Police got into the act. For example, after Napoleon took power in 1799 (see Chapter 8), his newly appointed Minister of Police, Joseph Fouché, produced a widely-distributed Bulletin that explained and justified the coup that put Napoleon in power (see Figure 18-3).

Figure 18-3:
This original pamphlet was produced by Joseph Fouché to justify Napoleon's having taken power. It came out on November 11, 1799, two days after the coup.

Censoring opposing voices

Napoleon's detractors promulgate an image of a censor gone wild, of a man who was determined to eliminate any voice that was raised in opposition to him or his policies. They are only partly correct. He certainly did want to control the news but not to the extent sometimes claimed. And in any event, he was only partially successful for most of his time in power.

In the early years of his rule, Napoleon divided up governmental responsibility for attempting (and that is the key word here) to control the message put out by the media. The Ministry of the Interior, in addition to having the powers I discuss in the previous section, was expected to oversee such things as the theater. But the government had very limited success in dictating what was produced on stage.

The Ministry of Police, under the control of the notorious Joseph Fouché for most of Napoleon's time in power, was given responsibility for censoring all written material, including the press and literature. The press, especially after 1810, was at least loosely controlled, but literature was more or less ignored.

It's easy to say you're going to control the media; it's quite another thing to actually do so. True, some papers were either suspended from operation for a time or shut down altogether, and a few writers were punished. True also that in Paris after 1810 only four official newspapers were allowed: *Le Moniteur, Le Journal de Paris, La Gazette de France,* and *Le Journal de L'Empire.* (I discuss the first and last of these earlier in the chapter, in the "Influencing newspaper coverage" section.)

Still, there was only a fairly brief period when Napoleon was truly successful in strictly controlling the media. From 1811 to 1813, the crackdown on dissent was fairly harsh. Before then, and especially under the rule of the Consulate (when Napoleon, as First Consul, effectively began his rule of the nation), there was more *talk* of censorship than actual censorship. There were many local papers at the time, and even those who feared the censor were often able to write their stories in such a way as to sneak past the censor while still getting their points across. After 1813, Napoleon was so busy defending France that he hardly had resources to devote to censorship. Moreover, as his grip on power loosened, the press became increasingly bolder and willing to report defeats as well as victories.

Controlling political opposition

In one area, however, the Ministry of Police (that would be Fouché) was very successful. Fouché developed a very good system of domestic spies and was able to eliminate, or at least strictly control, any political opposition to Napoleon.

Some people were arrested, some deported. And a few were even executed. But the people who got such harsh treatment were actually plotting to overthrow the government; treason has its costs. Overall, Napoleon was tolerant of at least mild opposition, and the numbers of people arrested or punished was really quite small. Most people, including many opposed to Napoleon, had little to fear from the secret police. Those who say that Napoleon ran a police state simply have it wrong.

Comparing Napoleon to his peers

Lest the preceding sections leave a bitter taste in your mouth, I want to offer a little perspective on Napoleon's use of government to control the opposition:

- ✔ France had a long history of a centralized government. The kings of France believed themselves to be absolute monarchs and thought nothing of arresting and throwing into the dungeon those who opposed them. During the French Revolution and the rule of the Directory, opposition was not generally tolerated, and many paid for it with their lives. Next to those folks, Napoleon was a model of modern liberalism.

- ✔ Censorship and secret police actions were the order of the day in early 19th-century Europe. Individual liberty was not. The British would round up young men and force them to serve in the navy. Political opponents in Russia were given extended tours of Siberia — if they were lucky. In short, none of the other rulers of the day were there because the people wanted them. They were there because they used the power of government to maintain their position. Only Napoleon could at least somewhat legitimately claim that he held power because of the will of the people.

Controlling Images

Napoleon was a master of spin, and from the very beginning of his career he used a variety of methods to promote his image:

- ✔ **Medallions:** As early as his campaign in Italy in 1796 (see Chapter 6), Napoleon used imagery to assure that the people saw him in the most favorable light possible. The Paris Mint had long produced commemorative medallions, but under Napoleon it produced them in record numbers. Virtually everything he did, from winning battles to visiting hospitals, was celebrated. Limited edition gold and silver medallions were produced for the wealthy and bronze for everyone else. Many people collect these medallions today, and the Paris Mint sometimes issues restrikes (carefully marking them to avoid fraud).

- ✔ **Prints:** Printmakers throughout Europe, and especially in France, would quickly create prints that depicted various Napoleonic victories or events. These would be produced in fairly large numbers and sold in small shops in virtually every town, but especially in Paris.

- ✔ **Decorative arts:** Napoleon understood that any government needs an image that can be recognized everywhere. After he returned from the Egyptian campaign and took power in France (see Chapter 8), he actively promoted the use of certain imagery in the decorative arts. After Napoleon's time in Egypt, for example, Egyptian motifs were very popular, and Napoleon encouraged their use in furniture and homes.

Napoleon hired two designers, Charles Percier and Pierre Fontaine, to design his style, first when he was part of the Consulate and later when he ruled the French Empire. Their designs became the symbols of Napoleon's rule, and collectors today speak of *Consulate* and *Empire* styles of furniture and other items. These styles gave the government a sense of grandeur that helped promote its popularity.

✔ **Foreign loot:** Throughout his military campaigns, Napoleon was careful to send home carefully selected items of plunder. It may be that only the British matched Napoleon in this regard, as many of Europe's finest art treasures made their way to Paris. Napoleon created a new national museum for many of these treasures. Dubbed the *Musée Napoléon* (Napoleon Museum) during his rule, it is now one of the world's greatest museums: the Louvre.

The various types of images I discuss here helped shape France's image of herself and of Napoleon. Designed to promote the idea of a glorious military led by an even more glorious leader, they masked both the costs and the horror of war. A glorious cavalry charge was often shown, while the effect of cannon on that charge was not. As in similar images throughout history, the glory of war overshadowed the reality.

These images continue to shape how we see Napoleon and the time period. Remember, there were no cameras in his day. The only reason we have any idea at all what he looked like is because of the work of the artists of his day.

Our image of Napoleon as a grand military leader surrounded by spectacular furnishings comes from the art and artifacts produced during his day. Today, such items are highly sought after (including by yours truly) and can be found in antique shops around the world. It is through these items that many people "know" Napoleon, so we can safely say that his effort to promote his image was very successful.

Chapter 19

Building a Greater (Middle Class) France

Most of the governments of Europe in the 18th and 19th centuries were by, of, and for the nobility. The French Revolution changed that situation in France. For all its radical imagery, it was really a revolution of the middle class, ultimately rejecting both the elitism of the nobility and clergy and the radical working class upheaval sought by the Parisian workers and others.

When Napoleon took power in late 1799, he sought to secure those middle class values. To do that, he had to provide for stability in government, something that had been absent for some time. After he achieved this stability, he could turn to providing what he considered the most important element of the ideals of the French Revolution: equality. At the heart of middle class values is the idea that all people can rise or fall based on their merits, rather than on the accident of their birth. France alone at the time promoted this concept in Europe. It was joined in this principle only by the United States of America, far across the Atlantic Ocean.

In this chapter, I look at some of Napoleon's primary areas of reform and progress. Without success in these areas, Napoleon would never have been able to stay in power, regardless of his military successes.

Creating a Legal Legacy

Though France had a long history of centralized government, it had almost no legacy of centralized laws. Generally speaking, Germanic law dominated in the north, while Roman law held sway in the south. More specifically, there was an incredible mixture of regional codes, royal decrees (some 15,000 to be exact), and other documents. Many of these so-called laws actually contradicted one another. Small wonder, then, that Napoleon once exclaimed, "We are a nation with 300 books of laws, yet without laws." He made legal reform one of his primary goals.

No country could be truly unified if its legal system was not the same throughout. Napoleon knew that in order for France to be run in an efficient, orderly manner, its legal system needed a complete overhaul.

Writing new civil law: The Code Napoléon

Any legal system has different types of laws, including criminal and civil. Napoleon made civil law his primary priority. As he would do in so many areas, Napoleon called on the best and brightest to help him in this project.

In early 1800, Napoleon formed a committee of legal scholars. In only four months, that committee produced a draft, which was then considered by the Council of State in a long series of meetings. As busy as he was, Napoleon managed to chair about half of the meetings and played a very active role in committee deliberations. You can well imagine that no one dozed off while *he* was chairing the meetings!

The new Civil Code that began to emerge contained several important elements:

- **Secularization of society:** The new code provided for a complete separation of church and state, something France had not known prior to the French Revolution. The privileges of the clergy were removed, and religious freedom was guaranteed. This was especially important for the Jews, as I explain in Chapter 23.

- **Elimination of the feudal order:** Prior to the Revolution, France had been dominated by the hereditary nobility. The new Civil Code removed all vestiges of this throwback to the Middle Ages. Moreover, it provided that feudal (and church) lands that had been confiscated during the French Revolution and distributed or sold to common people would never be returned to their original owners. This action increased stability and made Napoleon all the more popular.

✔ **Individual freedom:** Equality and individual freedom were hallmarks of the Revolution, and the Civil Code sought to assure their continued role in French society. The right of individuals to choose any profession was written into law, along with the ability to engage in free enterprise. People were guaranteed freedom of conscience. However, the ability of workers to organize was limited.

✔ **Marriage and the family:** The most well-known part of the Civil Code was also the source of the most controversy. Women gained some significant property rights within marriage, with husbands no longer in complete charge of community property (itself a new concept in French law, promoted by Napoleon). More importantly, the right to divorce was guaranteed. This part of the code was very difficult to get approved, as the conservative Catholic Church and other traditionalists were bitterly opposed. In the end, however, Napoleon was able to exert his will and have it included.

Women didn't do so well in other areas, however. In matters of family law, the code generally followed the Roman traditions that held that the husband was the head of a household. Thus, husbands were generally in charge of their wives' lives. A classic example of this was the matter of infidelity: Husbands who were caught having an affair were not generally punished for it, while wives caught in the same situation were.

In general, Napoleon was more progressive in what he wanted in the code than were the rest of the people involved in its approval. Thus, his efforts to increase the marriage age were successful, but his efforts to eliminate the dowry system and equalize the inheritance rights of all children (male and female) failed. Many conservatives in society — and in government — resented Napoleon's effort to make French society more progressive and fought him every step of the way. Even so, the code was a major step forward and was finally passed (over conservative objections) in 1804. In 1807, it was renamed the *Code Napoléon* in recognition of his major role in its development.

The *Code Napoléon* was adopted in various forms throughout the empire and remains the basis of French law and the law of numerous other countries still today. Napoleon himself recognized that the glories of his military victories would fade but that his most important legacy, one that would live forever, was the *Code Napoléon*.

Overhauling the rest of the system

Along with any legal system comes a system of courts. Napoleon overhauled the French court system completely. He created a system of *prefects,* which were chief administrators in charge of upholding the law in each *department,* or administrative area. Prefects and judges were to be fair and objective in administering the law, and all French were to be treated equally.

In time, the entire legal system was overhauled with a combination of progressive and conservative elements found in the Civil Code. The Code of Civil Procedure was adopted in 1806, the Commercial Code in 1807, the Criminal Code in 1808, and the Penal Code in 1810. These codes accomplished many improvements, including

- ✔ Promoting better trade by making trade arrangements more efficient and effective, thus helping both workers and merchants
- ✔ Setting up a system of justice that was logical and organized the same throughout France
- ✔ Increasing the use of juries and making soldiers subject to civil law as well as military law

Educating the People

Besides law, education may be the most fundamental institution in a society, and it is certainly the institution most necessary for the formation of a solid middle class. For most of French history, however, education was primarily reserved for the clergy and the nobility, with far fewer educational opportunities for common folk. Moreover, much of the education was provided by the Catholic Church, leading to an emphasis on education on religious dogma rather than on the basic skills necessary to advance in society. And even though educational administration was centralized in Paris, curriculum and educational standards varied widely across France.

The French Revolution led to some changes in France's educational system. These changes included removing religious influence as much as possible, as well as increasing teacher training. A new system of public secondary schools — called *école centrales* (central schools) — was created: One school was established for every 300,000 people.

Becoming a Napoleonic priority

When Napoleon took power (see Figure 19-1), education was high on his list of priorities. Central to his beliefs was the concept of equality and the ability of people to rise or fall based on their merit. For people to have that opportunity, they must be given the chance to receive a good education. Moreover, education was important to the development of a strong middle class. Centralized control of the curriculum would afford an opportunity to include patriotism in the curriculum as well.

Figure 19-1:
This 19th-century snuffbox shows a young Napoleon at the peak of his game.

Napoleon's interest in education was expressed in writing as early as 1797, when he wrote, "The real conquests, the only ones that do not cause regret, are those that are won over ignorance." And this from a man who spent most of his career winning the other kind of battles!

Napoleon wanted to reintegrate the Catholic Church into society, albeit not nearly at the pre-Revolutionary level (see Chapter 23). One way to do this was to give the Church major responsibility for elementary education, especially for girls. When it came to education for girls, Napoleon was both good news and bad news:

✔ The good news was that he believed girls should be educated in a curriculum that included language, history, geography, and science, along with the more traditional domestic arts. In this, Napoleon was quite progressive.

✔ The bad news was that Napoleon didn't think that education for girls was nearly as important as that for boys. Like most people of his day, Napoleon saw education for girls primarily as a step toward finding a husband. Even so, he provided universal education for girls, a more progressive stance than could be found anywhere else in Europe at the time.

Educating the best and brightest

In 1802, when Napoleon essentially ran the French government as the First Consul, France created a new educational system. As before, elementary education was split between a few state schools and many religious schools. But the heart of any middle class educational system is secondary education, which is where Napoleon concentrated his reforms.

The basic secondary schools, covering students from roughly ages 10 to 16, were a mixture of public and private schools, many of the latter being religious. In spite of this mixture, the curriculum was tightly controlled in Paris; even the religious schools had to toe the line. The purpose of these schools was to provide a good basic education and to identify students worthy of moving to the next level. Teachers were given incentives to find and properly prepare the best students. These students would ultimately provide the leadership core in both military and civilian fields, and Napoleon was anxious that the pool of such talent be as large as possible.

Napoleon had benefited from the educational opportunities given him; his career was made possible by his opportunity to go to an elite school and prove his abilities to a skeptical faculty (see Chapter 2). Small wonder, then, that providing all Frenchmen with such an opportunity was high on Napoleon's agenda.

One of the most important changes brought by Napoleon's reforms was the establishment of a new level of post-secondary schools: the *lycées*. Thirty of these schools were established. They received complete funding from the state, which completely controlled their curriculum and other matters. Napoleon established a system of scholarships for these schools. Two-thirds of those scholarships went to the best students coming out of the secondary schools, and the other third was split between sons of the military and of government employees.

Teachers for these schools were carefully selected and well-paid by the standards of the day. They were offered incentives and a pension; a teaching position at one of the *lycées* was highly desired.

Thirty post-secondary schools may seem a bit on the light side for a nation the size of France, but they were augmented by hundreds of regular schools, both public and private. The very best students, the ones with the best futures, worked hard to be admitted to these elite schools.

Centralizing educational authority

When Napoleon became emperor in 1804, education continued to be a major priority. France was becoming more and more centralized under his control, and education was no exception. In 1808, he created the Imperial University, which was given responsibility over every aspect of French education. Nothing was done that didn't first move through the Imperial University. Thus, this institution was both an elite university and a central governing body. I suppose it would be something like having a central university with hundreds of branch campuses, each directly responsible to the central campus.

The basic educational system remained much as it was under the reforms begun in 1802. The major difference was in the addition of several new levels of schools, most notably the *colleges,* or municipal secondary schools, and their private equivalent, *institutes.* Though their names suggest higher education, they were really just a bit below the *lycées,* which were still the heart of the system.

Having a lasting impact

Perhaps the most important thing to remember about Napoleon and French education is that the reforms he instituted are still at the heart of French education today. Like his reform of the legal system, his work to improve French education has been one of his most lasting legacies.

The changes that Napoleon brought to French education were a great improvement over what had existed prior to his reforms. The standardization of the curriculum meant that students throughout France were learning the same basic skills, and a cadre of graduates ready to assume positions in the government and the military was being produced. Literacy rates went up, and the quality and employability of the workforce was improved. The role of the Church in education was reduced, thus contributing to the secularization of society. Most importantly of all, the new system gave an opportunity for young people of merit to climb as far as their merit would take them.

To be sure, his reforms had critics. The Church was not happy to lose its former position of preeminence in educational matters. When Napoleon was emperor, students had to swear an oath of allegiance to him. And Napoleon really couldn't win when it came to women. Those conservatives who didn't want women to have much education complained that Napoleon went too far in that regard. And those people who wanted women treated equally to men complained (and are still complaining today) that he didn't go far enough. But despite these complaints, Napoleon's education reforms are among the best of his legacies.

Reforming the Economy

One word likely expresses the root cause of the French Revolution: the economy. Okay, I know that's two words, but you get the idea. The economy was in the toilet, and the people finally got sick of it and tried to do something about it (see Chapter 3).

Unfortunately for the people, the regimes that replaced Louis XVI were not much better in dealing with France's economic problems. There were still awful shortages, extreme poverty, bread riots, and the like. One of the few economic highlights in the years just before Napoleon took power was the continuing flow of wealth being sent back to Paris from other nations by — you guessed it! — General Bonaparte. (See Chapters 6 and 7 for examples of the bounty that Napoleon sent home from his military campaigns.) Small wonder, then, that the people were quite willing to turn to him to solve their economic problems.

Dealing with massive debt

One of the most difficult economic problems that faced France throughout these years was her massive debt, estimated at as much as three times the value of the national treasury. Payment of civil servants and soldiers alike was sporadic at best. One famous story relates Napoleon's effort to determine how many soldiers were in the army. He quizzed the appropriate functionary in a manner related as follows:

> N: How many men are in the army?
>
> A: We don't know.
>
> N: Then check the payroll records.
>
> A: We do not pay the army.
>
> N: Ration lists?
>
> A: We do not feed the army.
>
> N: Clothing lists?
>
> A: We do not clothe the army.

Napoleon understood that it would be necessary to raise a great deal of money. Some came from bank loans, but the key to success was to raise funds that did not involve increased debt. To do that, as soon as he became First Consul, Napoleon

- ✔ Instituted a national lottery to raise funds (much as lotteries do today)

- ✔ Created a new, full-time cadre of tax collectors

- ✔ Created incentives to insure that all taxes were properly collected

- ✔ Increased taxes on some items

- ✔ Had the government buy bread and other items to distribute to the poor

✔ Organized interest-free loans and other government programs

✔ Provided scholarships for education (as I discuss in the previous section)

✔ Instituted the Bank of France, giving the government better control over the nation's economy

✔ Replaced paper money with coins, which increased people's faith in their currency

Within one year, France's economy had completely turned around. The debt was gone, tax collections were up and being fairly collected, the value of the currency was stable, and poverty was greatly reduced. In short, Napoleon brought about an economic miracle, solving a problem the solution to which had eluded both a king and a Revolution. Napoleon's economic reforms were a major reason for his great popularity. And as to his legacy? The Bank of France is today France's central bank and the pillar of its economic stability.

Rebuilding France (literally)

The list of economic reforms in the previous section is missing one rather important item. Nothing helps an economy like putting people to work. And the easiest and quickest way to put people to work is through a public works program. Two thousand years ago, Julius and Augustus Caesar understood that fact, and ancient Rome is filled with their construction projects. In the 20th century, U.S. President Franklin D. Roosevelt comprehended the idea, and the public works program he instituted started the United States on its road to recovery from the Great Depression. And between these two leaders, Napoleon Bonaparte understood it as well.

One of the most important types of public works is a nation's transportation system. Roads and canals tie a nation together and allow trade to move smoothly throughout a country or a region. Throughout his time in power, Napoleon undertook a number of important transportation projects:

✔ He built key canals linking major river systems, allowing inexpensive and easy transport of goods.

✔ Seaports are important, and he ordered three major ones built at Cherbourg, Brest, and Antwerp.

✔ Major road systems were developed, including several through important passes in the Alps. He ordered trees to line many of them, providing shade for travelers.

✔ He paved the streets of Paris (a first) and instituted the odd-even numbering system for house addresses.

280 Part IV: A True Revolutionary

> ✔ To protect Paris, he started its first fire brigade.
>
> ✔ In Paris and throughout the lands he controlled, Napoleon built triumphal arches, buildings, and other structures to improve the quality of life for the people.

These projects improved France's economy at the time and continued to be important into the 20th century. Many of the road systems developed under Napoleon are the basis of modern roads in France, and his improvements to Paris can still be enjoyed today. (Visitors there will note that they still use the odd-even system for numbering houses, an idea that has spread to much of the world.) Napoleon's seaports are still used today. The canals still have some economic use, and tourists can take romantic boat trips across France in them. Finally, of course, the triumphal arches and buildings are still very much around today, and the *Arc de Triomphe* (Arch of Triumph) he started is second only to the Eiffel Tower as a symbol of Paris.

Chapter 20

Attempting a Dynasty

- -

In This Chapter

▶ Attempts on Napoleon's life

▶ Imperial ambitions

▶ A childless couple

▶ A political marriage

- -

*I*n 1804, Napoleon became Emperor of the French. To some, this was a natural progression in a Europe that was traditionally ruled by emperors and kings. To others, it was proof positive of his insatiable ambition and arrogance.

In fact, Napoleon did not make the decision to become emperor lightly. It was the result of a variety of important factors, including plots against his life after he became the ruler of France in 1799. In the end, the decision would cost him a wife and do him little good in his relations with the other crowned heads of state.

In this chapter, I explain why Napoleon felt he had to become emperor. I also join with you in saying goodbye to Josephine and hello to Marie Louise.

Surviving Assassination Attempts

When Napoleon became First Consul in late 1799, he was the ruler of France in all but name, as the other two consuls had little real power (see Chapter 8). The French Revolution was over, and it was time to consolidate the ideals of that Revolution while attempting to solve the many problems that confronted France. Napoleon had become France's leader largely because of his ambition and the fact that people recognized he was a man of extraordinary talent. A national hero, he immediately turned to the task of problem-solving. (In Chapter 19, I describe many of his reforms.)

Becoming the subject of royalist intrigues

Not everyone was pleased with Napoleon's ascendancy, however. Some of the most radical Revolutionaries, called *Jacobins,* were not pleased with a military leader.

Of greater concern, however, was the desire on the part of many of the royalists to bring a Bourbon king back to the throne of France. Indeed, when Napoleon took over, the Count of Provence, who was Louis XVI's oldest surviving brother (and the future Louis XVIII), wrote to Napoleon to congratulate him on his having ended the Revolution. The Count suggested that Napoleon might now bring him to the throne. Napoleon sent back a polite reply saying, in essence, "Thanks, but no thanks." He pointed out that if the Count tried to return, it would be over the bodies of 100,000 dead French soldiers.

The point was taken, but the royalists were not about to give up. If they couldn't work with Napoleon, they'd eliminate him altogether! This idea suited some of the other powers of Europe just fine, especially the British. Napoleon was wildly popular with the French people, so there was little hope for removing him by election or another coup. With those avenues closed, assassination seemed most logical. Many royalists lived in England, and it was there that they hatched their plots with the full cooperation and financial support of the British government.

One of the major conspirators was a man named Georges Cadoudal. He organized what today we may call a terrorist training camp for would-be assassins. Sheltered as Cadoudal was by England, Napoleon had no opportunity for a preemptive strike.

Ironically, Napoleon had been reaching out to the royalist exiles and allowing them to return to France. Indeed, it was his willingness to accommodate the hated old nobility that most outraged the Jacobins and made *them* inclined to kill Napoleon as well. To Napoleon, the left-wing Revolutionaries, with their history of violence (remember the guillotine!), were most worrisome.

Napoleon's fears notwithstanding, the royalists were actually the greater danger. Several attempts were made on Napoleon's life, and several other plots never came to fruition. But one attempt very nearly succeeded.

The "infernal machine"

On Christmas day of 1800, Napoleon and Josephine were going to see Hayden's *Creation.* Joining them was General Jean Rapp, an *aide-de-camp* to Napoleon;

Josephine's daughter, Hortense; and Napoleon's sister, Caroline. They were taking two carriages. Napoleon left in his, but last-minute changes in attire delayed the ladies, so there was a significant gap between the two carriages.

Along the way, Napoleon's carriage passed a young girl watching over a cart containing a large wine cask. This was no ordinary wine, however. The cask contained gunpowder and broken rocks. It was, in fact, a very large bomb, known to history as the "infernal machine." As Napoleon's carriage neared, the fuse was to be lit and, "boom," no more Napoleon.

Well, we all know it didn't work out that way. Napoleon's carriage raced by before the bomb went off, and Josephine's carriage, which was just approaching, suffered only minor damage. Nine people were killed by the explosion, but what really exploded was the myth that a popular leader like Napoleon was safe, even in his own capital.

Recognizing the source of the problem

Napoleon was convinced that the attack had been orchestrated by the Jacobins and ordered a general crackdown on their activities. In August 1803, however, he came to realize his mistake. Georges Cadoudal, apparently tired of training assassins, decided to become one himself. He left the supportive safety of London and headed off to Paris. He was joined by General Charles Pichegru, an exiled royalist who had dreams of overthrowing Napoleon. The two men were convinced that France was just buzzing with discontented generals who were desperate to restore the Bourbons to the throne. I have no idea where they got that idea, but it was the basis of their plot.

There was one general, Jean Moreau, who they thought might possibly side with them, and the conspirators were determined to win him over. In this, if nothing else, they were successful. The idea was that several generals, including Pichegru and Moreau, would get close to Napoleon, pretending to give him a document, perhaps a petition for clemency, and then, at just the right moment, they would all draw out swords or knives and kill Napoleon.

Then — and this is very important to understanding what would follow — a prince of the House of Bourbon would magically arrive and be declared the new king. Just like that.

Frankly, it sounds to me like they'd had a bit too much cognac and read a bit too much Shakespeare. Such a plot had worked against Julius Caesar, but these guys never got the chance to try it out for themselves. And even with Caesar, it took a long civil war to find a successor. With Napoleon as popular as he was, what *were* those guys thinking!

Napoleon's secret police got wind of the plot and rounded up all the suspects, who were soon executed. Cadoudal should have stayed in London!

Eliminating a Bourbon prince

Cadoudal's plot finally convinced Napoleon that the royalists were the biggest threat to his safety. The particular folks involved in this plot had been executed, but there must have been a Bourbon prince involved too, who was still alive and well. Napoleon had tried hard to win over the old nobility and royalists (without going so far as to hand the country over to them), but it seemed they were not won over at all.

Napoleon was determined to send the royalists a message they couldn't possibly misinterpret. He had no way to know just which Bourbon prince was involved in the plot (assuming that one was). What he did know was that the Bourbon prince Louis Antoine, the Duke of Enghien, was living in the nearby German principality of Baden and had sworn to bring down both the French Revolution and Napoleon.

French troops arrested the Duke, and he was court-martialed that very night. This action violated the territory of a sovereign country, even though the Duke was a French citizen who was, as it happens, guilty of treason. He was accused of conspiring with British agents, was known to have fought in armies against his country, and had sworn to bring down the current government. The latter two actions alone constitute treason. Found guilty by a unanimous verdict of seven officers, the Duke was executed.

The courts of Europe were outraged, and many people still consider this episode a major black mark on Napoleon's career. His critics ignore the treasonous acts of the Duke and concentrate instead on the violation of Baden territory and the lack of credible evidence that the Duke was involved in any specific plot. On the latter, they certainly have a point; there was no evidence that Louis Antoine was involved in a specific plot to overthrow Napoleon.

The execution may have been a scandal to the courts of Europe (who, one suspects, would not have tolerated treason against *themselves*), but the French people took it in stride. More importantly, it sent the desired message to both royalists and Jacobins; neither group would ever again engage in a plot to kill Napoleon.

Even so, the plots against Napoleon's life emphasized the frailty of his rule. One bullet, and all he had worked to achieve might be lost forever. There was only one solution: dynasty.

Establishing an Empire

To establish a dynasty, Napoleon needed an heir to the throne. Throughout history, the traditional heir has been the eldest male son, but that wasn't necessarily the route that Napoleon would take. For starters, he didn't have a son! His eldest brother, Joseph, was a possibility, as would be offspring of his siblings. But he and Josephine were young and seemed likely to eventually produce a child.

Yes, I know. There's a nagging question in all of this. You're probably wondering, "How in the world would the people of France accept Napoleon, or anyone else, as emperor? After all, they just tossed out their monarchy and established a republic!"

The will of the people

The answer to that question is easier than you may imagine. Napoleon was already acting much like an emperor. In August 1802, the French people overwhelmingly voted to make him First Consul for Life with the power to name his heir. His "court" became a bit grander and his powers more centralized. Even diehard Revolutionaries had become convinced that a progressive Napoleon was far better than anyone else who was likely to come about.

Napoleon had other things going for him as well:

✔ He was wildly popular with the people.

✔ Everyone understood that whatever his title, he had risen to power based on his extraordinary talent and the will of the people.

✔ After taking power, each increase in his position was submitted for a vote of the people, and he got results that most politicians only dream about!

For my money, Napoleon was already set. Why bother trying to become emperor? Because some people feared that the power to name his heir might disappear should disaster strike.

Plus, by 1804, the people of France were ready to have him move to the next step. The Senate voted to propose the idea to the people, and the people, in turn, voted overwhelmingly in favor of the idea. Napoleon would be the new Charlemagne, Emperor of the French. Moreover, he would be given the right to adopt a male heir if he didn't produce one with Josephine. In one of those ironies of history, France would turn to an emperor to protect its Revolution!

Coronation

After the decision was made, planning the coronation became job one. The location was easy: Where better than the grand cathedral of Notre Dame? The famed artist Jacques-Louis David was commissioned to create imperial facades for the interior. Imperial symbols were chosen: the eagle for the empire itself, and the bee for Napoleon's personal family symbol. (The eagle tied the empire to ancient Rome, and people believed that the bee tied Napoleon to the sixth-century Frankish King Chilpéric.) Other symbols were used to promote images of Charlemagne, the last truly great emperor to whom the Pope had given the title Holy Roman Emperor.

Involving the Pope

And speaking of the Pope, one of the major controversies of the coronation regarded the ceremony itself. The French Revolution had pretty much tossed the Catholic Church out of France. Napoleon had worked hard to reintegrate the Church into society while maintaining a strict separation of church and state. More than a few Frenchmen would be displeased to see Pope Pius VII involved. Not only did they remember the Church's excesses in recent history, but they also understood that a Pope consecrating an emperor implies that the Pope is more powerful. (Charlemagne understood that and always regretted letting the Pope give him his title.)

On the other hand, most French were at least nominally Catholic, and the Pope's involvement might serve to give Napoleon's rule more legitimacy in the eyes of the other rulers of Europe. So the Pope was in, but not for the entire ceremony.

From the very beginning, it was understood that Napoleon would crown himself, thus avoiding Charlemagne's mistake. Napoleon's detractors like to say that he snatched the crown from the Pope, or that this was an act of unbelievable arrogance, but neither of those charges hold water. Napoleon was simply symbolizing that he was becoming emperor based on his own merits and the will of the people, not because of some religious consecration. The Pope knew about this move from the beginning and had no objection (not that it would have mattered).

The Pope did object to being present for the Imperial Oath, as that oath had Napoleon promising to uphold religious freedom. No problem. The Pope exited stage left prior to the administration of the oath.

Worrying Josephine

One person who did object to all this hoopla was Josephine. She understood that Napoleon's becoming emperor was all about providing an heir to the throne, something she had not yet done. The "fault" in this matter, whether Napoleon's or Josephine's, was not yet known, but she could see the writing on the wall.

Another issue regarding Josephine was the fact that in 1796, she and Napoleon had been married in a civil ceremony. This did not sit well with the Pope, who refused to consecrate her as empress. The about-to-become imperial couple solved that problem by having Napoleon's uncle, Cardinal Joseph Fesch, marry them in the church the night before the imperial ceremony.

Preparing for the big event

The rehearsals for the coronation were a real treat. Napoleon's sisters were jealous of each other, and all were jealous of Josephine. His sisters had already been complaining to Napoleon about their various titles, or lack of titles, in the imperial family, and they objected to having to carry Josephine's train. (I think Napoleon should have told them all to stay home, but Napoleon worked things out, more or less to their satisfaction.)

One very special person was missing from the ceremony. Napoleon's mother, Leticia, so despised Josephine that she refused to attend her son's coronation. Even so, Napoleon gave her the title *Madame Mère* (literally, "Madame Mother"), along with a bevy of servants and a pile of cash.

Becoming Emperor of the French

On December 2, 1804, massive crowds lined the streets of Paris. The imperial carriage went through the city, escorted by legions of mounted horsemen. Napoleon and Josephine, each wearing splendid coronation outfits (Napoleon's included a wreath crown like that of the Caesars), entered Notre Dame Cathedral. Soon thereafter, Napoleon was crowned Napoleon I, Emperor of the French (see Figure 20-1). Later, he would add "King of Italy" and "Protector of the Confederation of the Rhine" to his titles.

After placing the crown on his own head, Napoleon placed it on Josephine's, making her Empress of the French. It's hard to imagine things getting any better. Napoleon is said to have whispered into his brother Joseph's ear, "If only our father could see us now." Indeed, Carlo would have been proud. But he may also have echoed his wife Leticia's equally famous words (said sometime later), "If only this will all last."

Seeking a Dynasty

Napoleon's position as emperor established, he went to work continuing his reforms and winning his battles. But always in the background was the primary reason for becoming emperor to begin with: to provide an heir to the imperial throne and assure France — and the world — that, come what may, his legacy and his policies would continue.

Figure 20-1:
This very rare period engraving shows Napoleon crowning himself Emperor of the French.

In 1802, Josephine's daughter, Hortense, gave birth to a boy. The father (Hortense's husband) was Napoleon's brother Louis. This event appeared to solve the problem of succession, as Napoleon adopted the lad as his heir. For five years, all seemed well, and the issue of succession was seemingly safely behind them. Napoleon and Josephine ruled France and maintained a loving relationship (see Figure 20-2). But the boy died in 1807, moving the issue back to the front burner.

Figure 20-2:
These rare ivory plaques by Noël depict Napoleon and Josephine at the height of their imperial time together.

Goodbye, Josephine

By 1809, it was clear that the reason for the imperial couple's infertility was Josephine, not Napoleon. Napoleon had fathered an illegitimate child or two, most notably in 1809 with Marie Walewska (see Chapter 10). This fact, along with another foiled attempt on his life that year, caused Napoleon to give further, and more urgent, thought to the need for an heir.

Napoleon and Josephine had developed a loving and mutually supportive relationship. Napoleon's soldiers saw her as their good luck charm; indeed, the entire nation did. But Napoleon was determined to have an heir to the throne, even if it meant divorcing Josephine. It is difficult to say when he came to that conclusion, but in the fall of 1809, he finally got around to telling Josephine. It was a dreadful scene that resulted in Josephine fainting. (Well, maybe she fainted and maybe she didn't; it may have been an act of high drama!)

Napoleon felt that "France and my destiny" mandated the divorce, but he treated Josephine well. She got their home, Malmaison, as well as a palace in Paris and a château in Normandy. She retained her title of empress and, of course, kept her entire wardrobe. My wife is still jealous of her almost 300 pairs of shoes! He paid off her (surprise!) substantial debts and gave her a pension of 2 million francs a year. All of her homes were furnished in unbelievable style. She was, in short, an incredibly wealthy woman who would continue to play a role in French social and even political society. (See Figure 20-3 for an enduring image of Josephine as empress.)

Figure 20-3:
This 19th-century snuffbox shows the beautiful Josephine as empress.

Moreover, Napoleon took good care of her two children, who remained loyal both to their mother and to Napoleon. The divorce was made final in December 1809, but the two never lost their affection for each other and kept up communication until Josephine's death in 1814.

Hello, Marie Louise

The divorce taken care of, it was time for Napoleon to turn to a replacement. You and I may think that Marie Walewska would fit the bill. (I introduce her in Chapter 10.) After all, she and Napoleon were in love, and she already had a son by him. (And even if their illegitimate son couldn't become emperor, a future son would fill the dynasty bill.) But Napoleon was concerned about a possible scandal, and in any event Marie was (1) married to another man and (2) only of the minor nobility. Napoleon quite understandably wanted to use this marriage to gain him not only a fertile wife but a meaningful political alliance.

The person that Napoleon and his advisors most wanted to be Napoleon's new bride was the Russian Tsar Alexander's 15-year-old sister, Anna. The political implications of this marriage would be mind-boggling:

- ✔ France and Russia, already allies, would be sealed together by marriage, thus surrounding the rest of Continental Europe in a way that would be difficult to resist.

- ✔ A marriage of France and Russia might well lead to a general peace. Even Great Britain, France's staunchest enemy, might feel compelled to come to terms with France.

Alas, it wasn't to be. The tsar wasn't interested in *that* much solidarity with France. His family was still steaming over the execution of Louis Antoine, the Duke of Enghien, who was related to the tsar's family by marriage. The tsar hemmed and hawed and eventually told Napoleon no dice, at least until the young girl was 18. That answer didn't do wonders for Napoleon and Alexander's relationship, but Napoleon, ever the pragmatist, immediately looked at other options.

The only other real option was Archduchess Marie Louise, the 18-year-old daughter of Emperor Francis of Austria (see Figure 20-4). This marriage was almost as good as a marriage to the tsar's sister:

- ✔ The Hapsburg dynasty was the oldest and grandest in Europe; a tie to that family could finally give Napoleon legitimacy in the eyes of the old regimes that still saw him as a usurper.

- ✔ The ladies of that family were extremely prolific, a key element to consider.

- ✔ Finally, a look at a map of Europe in 1810 will show what a formidable force any alliance between the French and Austrian empires would be.

Figure 20-4:
A 19th-century miniature on ivory showing Marie Louise as empress.

Napoleon was convinced and sent word to an already supportive Austrian court. To them, it was a win-win situation. If Napoleon was to remain powerful for the foreseeable future, they may as well be on the winning side. And if he stumbled in Spain or elsewhere, Austria, at least, would be out of the line of fire and able to consider her options.

On March 11, 1810, Marshal Louis Alexandre Berthier stood in as proxy for Napoleon in a civil marriage ceremony in Vienna. The marriage took place during a massive round of parties, with each side seemingly happier about things than the other. (See Figure 20-5 for an image of the happy couple.)

Figure 20-5:
This gilt snuffbox was produced to celebrate the marriage of Napoleon and Marie Louise.

A few weeks later, a huge convoy escorted Marie Louise to Strasbourg. There, Napoleon's sister Caroline took charge, and a French honor guard fell into place, along with French attendants of every description. At Compiègne, Napoleon met his new wife in the rain at the gates of the city. That evening, they had a quiet dinner and then retired to the business of providing for an heir.

The Austrians and their emperor, Francis, gained much from the alliance. In addition to giving Francis numerous awards, including Officer of the Legion of Honor, Napoleon granted Austria what today we may call "most favored nation" status. Trade increased, loans materialized, and prisoners of war came home faster than normal. Napoleon was always generous to his friends or those whom he needed; Francis met both criteria.

On March 20, 1811, Marie Louise gave birth to Napoleon-François-Joseph-Charles. Don't worry, no one called him by that long name. He was known then, and is known now, by the title Napoleon immediately bestowed on him: the King of Rome. And if you still think that Napoleon was uncaring or completely obsessed with an heir come hell or high water, think again. The birth did not go well, and at one point the doctors informed Napoleon that they might have to choose between saving the child or the mother. "Save the mother," was Napoleon's immediate response. In the end, both mother and child were fine.

Napoleon's quest for a dynasty was now fulfilled. He had a political alliance bound by marriage, a son who was the grandson of the Austrian emperor, and an alliance with Russia and Prussia. Except for those pesky Brits and that little matter in Spain (see Chapter 12), everything seemed to be going Napoleon's way.

Part V

Influencing Nations: Diplomacy and Legacy

The 5th Wave   By Rich Tennant

"We call it a 'Napoleon' because all the ingredients were 'liberated' from other chefs' pantries."

In this part . . .

Much of Napoleonic history can be summed up as simply Napoleon versus Great Britain (or *England,* as I often prefer to call it, though why I insist on letting the Welsh and Scots off the hook is beyond me). The Brits (that would be the folks who live in Great Britain) just didn't seem willing to let Napoleon rule France, never mind all of the European continent. For a short time, though, it seemed that the two countries might actually work out their problems, and this part covers the promise and the failure of peace between these two great antagonists.

If relations with Great Britain didn't always work out, Napoleon had more success on the European continent and left a number of important legacies. Here, I have a look at Napoleon's contribution to a united Europe (partly deliberate, partly accidental) and the idea of religious freedom, especially for the Jews.

Chapter 21

Boney Times with the Brits

*W*e can view the Napoleonic period through many prisms. We can see it through the prism of the French Revolution, with its idealistic goals of liberty and equality (see Chapter 3). We can look at it in terms of the broad march toward democracy, which was speeded up by upheavals in the United States and France and pushed along by Napoleon's armies. In a similar vein, perhaps we could look at Napoleon's rule in terms of the inevitable replacement of the old order with the new — of a fragmented Europe constantly at war replaced by a modern Europe, united and at peace.

No matter how you view the Napoleonic period, one nagging factor that muddies the portrait of Napoleon's achievements is the conflict between Great Britain and France, between the Brits and *Boney* (as they liked to derisively call Napoleon — based, I suppose, on a play on his last name and the fact that in his early years he was quite skinny). Why?

✔ Ultimately, the British government prevented Napoleon from ruling France in peace.

✔ The British insisted on maintaining what they considered the appropriate balance of power, which was a major factor in keeping Europe at war for so many years.

✔ The British demonized Napoleon, harbored those who would seek his destruction, organized coalitions against him, and financed the resulting wars.

Clearly, Napoleon's ambition played a role in the conflict with England as well. We can only imagine what may have occurred if England and France could have made peace. Few nations influenced France more than Great

Britain, and their constant conflict influenced relations — both good and bad — between virtually all other nations of Europe.

In this chapter, I talk about relations between the Brits and Boney in general, and the Peace of Amiens in particular. I also touch on the one area that Napoleon thought was his ace in the hole: the economic embargo against Britain known as the *Continental System.* Finally, I discuss how Napoleon was demonized by his enemies, especially Great Britain.

Making One Great Effort at Peace

For much of the time that Napoleon was alive, relations between Great Britain and France were strained, to say the least. The two nations had a long history of antagonism, their common ancestry notwithstanding. (William the Conqueror, who famously invaded England in 1066 and gained power by winning the Battle of Hastings, *was,* after all, French. And someone once told me that the English language contains 10,000 French words!)

England had developed what we would say was a fairly enlightened form of government for the time. It had democratic aspects to its government (Parliament, for example, and the concept of *habeas corpus*) unknown elsewhere in Europe. The United States based much of its experiment in democracy on its British heritage.

The French Revolution added France to the short list of relatively enlightened European nations, and Napoleon continued and solidified many of the progressive ideas of the Revolution. Thus, it would make perfect sense if Great Britain and France had become the best of buddies. Great sense, perhaps, but it didn't quite work out that way.

Seizing a brief window of opportunity

Have you ever taken the lead in something, only to look around and find that you're all alone? Well, that's what happened to the British in 1801. After Napoleon defeated the Austrians and signed the Peace of Luneville (see Chapter 9), all of England's allies were at peace with Napoleon. The British people were not about to keep carrying on the fight alone, at least not then, so they put pressure on their government to seek peace. Pressure indeed. They forced Prime Minister William Pitt to leave the government (though admittedly more because Pitt supported Catholic emancipation in Ireland, an idea opposed by the king). They replaced Pitt with a government led by Henry Addington, who was willing to accommodate Napoleon.

Great Britain's policy had always been to seek a "balance of power" on the European continent. That means that Great Britain didn't want any one country to become too powerful. British money and military might, especially her navy, could take sides in Continental conflicts to assure that this balance was maintained.

Becoming weary of war

By 1801, Britain had some reason to fear Napoleonic France, but not enough to try to go it alone. France had expanded her borders and reached at least an uneasy peace with her neighbors, but perhaps that was as far as her reach would go. The British people were prepared to wait and see, and their government went along, however reluctantly. The British were tired of war, and without allies, British naval power alone would not be sufficient to defeat France.

The French, too, were anxious for peace. Napoleon had lost one of his major allies, Tsar Paul I of Russia, to assassination in March 1801. Then, in early April, the British fleet destroyed the Danish fleet at Copenhagen in a raid led by Admiral Horatio Nelson (see Chapter 11). With Russia no longer a dependable ally and with the Danish fleet gone, Napoleon had to abandon his long-standing idea of invading England.

Thus, neither power felt capable of dealing a death-blow to the other. Both would, in time, turn to economic warfare (which I discuss later in this chapter), but for the moment, peace seemed a possibility.

Napoleon had taken power in France with promises of military victory, peace, and prosperity. He had come through on the military victory part and was well on his way toward bringing prosperity to France. Peace, both domestic and international, now took center stage. All of Europe stood cheering on the sidelines: Everyone was sick of war.

Signing the Treaty of Amiens

Napoleon put out the first feelers for a possible peace treaty. After first one side and then the other seemed to reject the possibility of peace, both finally gave in to reality. In 1801, the two sides met in negotiations in the town of Amiens. France was represented by Napoleon's brother, Joseph. By October 1, the two sides reached a preliminary agreement, and the so-called Treaty of Amiens was ratified on March 25, 1802.

The Treaty of Amiens was a real coup for Napoleon and the French. The British were to leave Egypt and the island of Malta (which they had recently taken by force in order to put pressure on France), while the French were to give up pretty much nothing. Indeed, Great Britain recognized French control of the Netherlands; the west bank of the Rhine; and several territories in Italy, including Piedmont and Nice. Napoleon was required to give back the Papal States to the Pope and the Taranto peninsula to Naples, and he had to agree to Swiss neutrality.

What all sides gained, of course, was peace.

Celebrating "The Amazing Mr. Bonaparte"

All of Europe was abuzz over "The Amazing Mr. Bonaparte," who seemingly single-handedly had defeated powerful enemies, brought peace to the Continent, and created prosperity to France. As a result, Napoleon became an instant *cause celébre*. People from all over Europe, and especially from England, decided to include Paris in their vacation plans. They were anxious to gain a glimpse of the famous Bonaparte. (I can relate: Napoleon often causes me to include Paris in *my* travel plans as well!)

In Great Britain, and across all of Europe, fascination with Napoleon was reflected by the production and sale of prints, snuffboxes, miniatures, and bronzes of his image. Even British nobility were known to have such items (see Figures 21-1 and 21-2).

Figure 21-1:
Detail from an engraving of *Napoleone Buonaparte* done by Henry Richter, which is typical of images created during the Peace of Amiens.

Figure 21-2:
Detail
from an
engraving
by Hilaire
Le Dru,
Bonaparte,
published
in London
in 1801.
A rather
heroic
image, even
for the
time, to be
displayed in
England!

Reforming French institutions

Napoleon's star rose for good reason. Even before Amiens, Napoleon had been a whirlwind of action. Everything from cutting wasteful spending to weeding out corrupt judges had been on his agenda. A master of detail, he had been seemingly everywhere, doing everything:

- ✔ Safety on the highways? Hire more police.
- ✔ Not enough room for art treasures? Enlarge the Louvre.
- ✔ People out of work? Create jobs rebuilding Paris, improving transportation, improving water quality.

You name it, he did it. He was even contemplating the building of the Suez Canal, which he hoped to construct with Russian cooperation. There was also talk of a tunnel under the English Channel. Neither of these projects would be accomplished until the 20th century, but never let it be said that Napoleon didn't think big!

Napoleon had already started the process of reforming the economy, the law, and education (see Chapter 19). He had recently signed the Concordat of 1801 with the Pope (see Chapter 23), bringing to an end the single largest remaining source of domestic discord. Thus, Napoleon had fulfilled his promise to bring peace and prosperity on all fronts.

Achieving the height of popularity

The people of France rewarded him well for his efforts. First, he was named First Consul for ten years. But not long into that period of service, a national *plebiscite* (public vote) overwhelmingly supported the idea of him becoming First Consul for Life. That designation was awarded to him on August 2, 1802. Later that same week, the powers of his office were greatly expanded. At that point, he was very close to being the absolute ruler of France. When Napoleon turned 33 on August 15, he certainly had reason to celebrate! His popularity was at its peak, and all of France celebrated with him (see Figure 21-3).

Figure 21-3:
A snuffbox with a wax image of Napoleon as First Consul, signed by the noted goldsmith, medalist, and wax-modeler Joseph Anton Couriguer.

For a time, the Peace of Amiens seemed ideal. Trade increased, people and businesses prospered, travel was finally safe again, and no longer did nations sacrifice their youth and fortune to war. One critical demand of the French in peace negotiations had been a guarantee of open, or neutral, seas. Previously, the British had felt they had the right to board any ship or stop any shipment they wished. With the neutrality of the seas finally obtained, ships from all nations could bring trade goods to any other nation. Much like a modern-day free trade agreement, this arrangement led to a massive increase in trade. Businesses expanded, with many jobs filled by recently-released soldiers and sailors, no longer needed in a time of peace. Napoleon's public works program moved forward in leaps and bounds, all to the benefit of the French.

Failing Peace

If all this seems too good to be true, that's because it was. Both sides probably saw their agreement at Amiens less as a treaty than an armistice. Almost as soon as the ink was dry, the agreement began to go sour.

Refusing to abandon Malta

Great Britain was not pleased to have to leave Egypt, especially when she learned that the French forces there had been defeated by British soldiers and had themselves agreed to leave in August! Napoleon knew this in advance and pulled a fast one on the Brits. As a result, the Brits were even less happy to leave Malta, for fear their influence in the Mediterranean would be pretty much nonexistent (which was, of course, Napoleon's idea all along).

Even though the British had negotiated and ratified a treaty calling for them to leave Malta, they deliberately violated the treaty by refusing to leave. For a while they came up with various rather weak excuses, but in the end they simply said they were staying on the island. Needless to say, Napoleon — and much of Europe — was not pleased.

Making a last-ditch effort to negotiate

Napoleon did everything he could to avoid war while at the same time recognizing reality and expanding his army. He suggested having Russia control Malta, and the tsar offered to mediate the situation. No deal, said the British. Okay, in that case, how about Britain keeping Malta and France retaking the Taranto peninsula (the "heel" in the boot of Italy, which France had given to the Kingdom of Naples as part of the treaty)? Nope, that wouldn't do either, said the Brits, even though it would restore conditions in the area to their pre-treaty situation and thus protect British Mediterranean interests.

War was inevitable. Though the British government was divided and the debate spirited, the end result was never in real doubt. Before war was declared, Britain began to seize all French ships, an action in violation of international law. And on May 18, 1803, Great Britain declared war on France who, naturally enough, returned the favor a few days later. The War of the Third Coalition was about to begin (see Chapter 9).

The war would take a long time to get into full swing. Napoleon quickly seized the Taranto peninsula and took Hanover (a British holding on the Continent), as well as securing his positions elsewhere in Italy. More notably, he arrested all male British subjects in France between 18 and 60, declaring them prisoners of war. Many of them were British gentlemen on vacation — a vacation that was now to be extended for several years. (Of course, as gentlemen they were allowed to live on parole, and most lived fairly comfortably.)

Napoleon once again prepared for a possible invasion of England. But neither side was in a position to begin any real hostilities: France had an inadequate navy, and England had no allies.

Attempting Economic Embargo: The Continental System

In addition to traditional combat, England and France each engaged in economic warfare in an attempt to weaken the other. In 1806, Napoleon issued the Berlin Decrees, which instituted an economic blockade called the *Continental System.* This blockade was at least partially a response to Great Britain's embargo on all military shipments to France, a prohibition that opened the door to economic retaliation.

The idea of the Continental System was to cut off all commerce between Great Britain and Continental Europe. It was, in essence, Napoleon's attempt to use his land power to defeat England's sea power. To a point, it actually worked, as it did deprive Great Britain of some of its Continental trade.

But for the most part, the Continental System was a failure. The black market thrived: Even Josephine bought forbidden British goods! And Napoleon's brother, Louis, as King of Holland, was hard-pressed to deprive his merchant class of its critical trade with Great Britain. As Napoleon's brother, his official policy was to prohibit trade, but he somehow managed to ignore the sizable amount of smuggling that was going on throughout his kingdom. This behavior enraged Napoleon, who forced his own brother to abdicate the throne of Holland. Another relative, Napoleon's brother-in-law Joachim Murat, the King of Naples, was less than effective at enforcing the embargo as well.

Worse yet, the Continental System's need to control all of Europe's coastline led to Napoleon's invasion of Spain and Portugal (see Chapter 12). That invasion ultimately led to the British taking over the Iberian Peninsula and then marching into France herself. The action in Spain and Portugal was probably Napoleon's single biggest mistake.

Trying to force Russia to observe the Continental System was a real close second. Russian Tsar Alexander's desire to withdraw from the Continental System was one of the major reasons for the 1812 war between France and Russia, a war that was a disaster for Napoleon (see Chapter 13).

In short, Napoleon learned the hard way that

 ✔ It's just about impossible to seal off an entire continent.

 ✔ When it comes to trade, where there's a will, there's a way.

It's difficult to say exactly what the main cause of Napoleon's ultimate fall from power was. But for my money, the Continental System ranks high on the list. It was one of those "it seemed like a good idea at the time" deals, and it turned out to be a really lousy idea.

Demonizing Napoleon

In modern politics, opposing sides at least *pretend* to avoid personal attacks on their opponents (though, of course, they can't prevent their supporters from saying any number of nasty things). In the poisonous mood of the relations between France and England, no pretense of civility was made, especially by the British. British caricature artists and others did everything they could to make Napoleon, whom they liked to call *Boney,* into a monster. He was often referred to as the "Corsican Ogre," "the Usurper," or worse. His name was said to represent the sign of the devil. He was shown in hell, keeping company with rats, or even being roasted over a fire.

The personal attacks on Napoleon actually began as early as his 1796 campaign as a general in Italy, and they continued throughout his career. These attacks came mostly from England but also from other countries opposed to Napoleon, especially Germany.

The attacks infuriated Napoleon, who quite rightly took them very personally. He complained bitterly to the British government, especially during the Peace of Amiens. That government did take some limited action against some libelous writings of French nobles in exile, but it did little if anything to restrain writings of British poets or caricatures by British artists. Some of the more famous British caricature artists were James Gillray and Isaac and George Cruikshank. Collectors have recorded the existence of about 2,000 graphic attacks on Boney.

Napoleon tried to retaliate by encouraging French caricatures of the British, but these efforts generally fell a bit flat. Instead, the concentration was on developing positive imagery of Napoleon (see Chapter 24).

The constant barrage of negative, often very nasty, images of Napoleon produced in Britain had a significant influence on relations between the two countries. On the one hand, it was very difficult for Napoleon to take expressed British interest in peace very seriously when they were not calling a halt to these hateful images. (Remember, these images suggested, among other things, that Napoleon was a devil and Josephine was a whore. No wonder Napoleon was unhappy.) On the other hand, these images tended to whip up support among the British people for another war against France. After all, people may not have wanted to make war on Napoleon, the enlightened leader who was bringing reforms to his people. But against the Ogre of Corsica, the Great Thief of Europe? Bring it on!

Examples of early caricatures

Caricatures often jabbed at British politics, as well as at Napoleon. In 1803, for example, Gillray produced an image that shows Napoleon sailing across the English Channel while the British government awakes as if from a trance (see Figure 21-4). This cartoon was a jab at the peace elements of the government and was intended as a call to arms.

Figure 21-4:
In this caricature by Gillray, Napoleon's invasion of England brings a complacent government out of its trance.

Another caricature from 1803 by W. Holland shows Napoleon in a British castle and in big trouble (see Figure 21-5).

Figure 21-5:
Maybe
it was
caricatures
like this that
gave rise to
Napoleon's
image of
being short!

Examples of later caricatures

If caricature artists were active when Napoleon was at the height of his success, they had a field day when his fortunes began to decline. You can see one example of this in Figure 13-4 in Chapter 13; the British caricature shows Napoleon being defeated in Russia in 1812 by "General Winter." A year later, when Napoleon was defeated at the Battle of Leipzig (see Chapter 14), both British and German caricature artists went straight to work. Figure 21-6 is a German snuffbox that shows Napoleon as a nutcracker breaking his teeth on the "tough nut" of Leipzig. This image is one of the most famous to come out of the period.

There is an expression that a picture is worth a thousand words. Whether or not a picture is worth a thousand soldiers is quite another question, but there is no question that Napoleon's enemies used pictures as one of their weapons in their ongoing effort to destroy him. Did it make a difference? Perhaps not, but we can certainly be pleased to have the graphic remains of the effort.

Chapter 22

Creating a New United Europe

. . . .

In This Chapter

▶ Happy Italians and Poles

▶ Unhappy Germans

. . . .

*N*apoleon Bonaparte is often considered, if not the father of the European Union, at least one of its earliest advocates. There is little doubt that he laid much of the groundwork, both visionary and practical. Indeed, he even used the term *United States of Europe*.

Napoleon certainly envisioned a united Europe with

- ✔ One set of weights and measures

- ✔ One code of laws

- ✔ A unified transportation system of roads and canals

- ✔ Open borders

- ✔ A "European Market" trading system

- ✔ A common belief in the rights of man

- ✔ A common judiciary

- ✔ A common leader (him, of course)

Of course, Napoleon, like Alexander the Great, the Caesars, Charlemagne, and others before him, tried to create this united Europe through the force of arms, and to a very large extent he succeeded. When he gained control of an area, he promoted many of these ideals. And Napoleon certainly liked to compare himself to some of these earlier rulers, especially the Frankish emperor of the Holy Roman Empire, Charlemagne (see Figure 22-1).

Figure 22-1:
This period medallion shows Napoleon (wearing the laurel wreath crown of the Caesars) and Charlemagne together, a comparison encouraged by Napoleon.

Perhaps Napoleon's contribution to a united Europe can best be seen in terms of one of the unintended consequences of his campaigns: increased feelings of nationalism. While nationalistic feelings were often begun by Napoleonic policies that brought increased unity to an area (such as the Confederation of the Rhine or the Cisalpine Republic, which I discuss later in the chapter), those feelings often became stronger than any allegiance to the French Empire. This was especially true in Germany.

In this chapter, I briefly discuss the impact of nationalism in Italy, Germany, and Poland and its consequences for Napoleon and for the future of Europe. As we'll see, some folks were pleased with Napoleon's intervention. Others, not so much.

Promoting Italian Risorgimento

When it came to being a positive force for nationalistic unity, Napoleon was never better than he was in Italy. There, he is seen as an early proponent of Italian reunification, or *Risorgimento*. Italy had previously been unified by the growth of the Roman Empire, but after the empire's decline, Italy had disintegrated into a number of independent city-states. These states had often warred with each other and, especially in the north, had been influenced or controlled by other nations, especially Austria.

Making early moves toward unity

Napoleon was in many ways culturally Italian, as his native island of Corsica had long been controlled by Genoa and Italian was his native language (see Chapter 2). Very early in his career, Napoleon took a great interest in Italy, especially northern Italy, designing various plans for military action there. He finally got his chance to put his ideas into action when he embarked on his first Italian campaign in 1796 (see Chapter 6).

That campaign was successful, as Napoleon drove the Austrians out of northern Italy and defeated Austrian allies as well. In the ensuing Treaty of Campo Formio, Napoleon created two republics:

✔ The important Cisalpine Republic, which consisted of areas around the Po River in northern Italy, including the major city of Milan and several territories taken from the Venetians

✔ The smaller Ligurian Republic, which consisted of the Republic of Genoa and other areas

Both republics were given constitutions based on the French model, including the progressive guarantees of freedom and equality previously unknown to their citizens. Both republics gradually expanded and provided a level of independence and stability in the region, though admittedly under the influence and protection of Napoleonic France.

The Cisalpine Republic was renamed the Italian Republic in 1802, and Napoleon himself became its first president.

Creating a united kingdom

When Napoleon became Emperor of the French in 1804 (see Chapter 20), he wanted to secure his developing empire. He also wanted to promote greater unity — and loyalty to France — in northern Italy. To help in those goals, he combined the Italian Republic and the Ligurian Republic into one state, the Kingdom of Italy. This was a fairly large kingdom and was clearly going to be a part of Napoleon's empire. As such, it definitely rubbed the other nations of Europe, especially Austria and England, the wrong way. (It contributed toward Austria's participation in the Third Coalition against France, which I discuss in Chapter 9.)

European concerns notwithstanding, Napoleon was determined to go through with his plans for Italy. And when Napoleon was determined, well . . . ! He offered the crown of the new kingdom to his brother, Joseph. Not many people

could turn Napoleon down, but Joseph was one of them. He could see difficulties on the horizon and declined the honor. He really had no interest in
being Napoleon's puppet.

Without skipping a beat, Napoleon turned to Plan B, which involved having
himself crowned King of Italy. That is exactly what happened in Milan's cathedral on May 26, 1805. From that point on, Napoleon's title was Napoleon I,
Emperor of the French, King of Italy (see Figure 22-2).

Napoléon le Grand,
Empereur des français et Roi d'Italie.

Figure 22-2:
This period
engraving
shows
Napoleon
as Emperor
of the
French
and King of
Italy. His
weapons of
war are laid
aside, and
he sits on
the Throne
of Justice.

Napoleon may have been King of Italy, but he soon turned over administrative control to his stepson, Eugène de Beauharnais, to whom he gave the title
viceroy, or vice-king. Throughout the rest of Napoleon's career, the Italians
were generally loyal to him. Of course, not all Italians were pleased to have
traded Austrian dominance for French dominance, but little came of this
disenchantment.

As he had with the first two Italian republics he created, Napoleon provided
the Kingdom of Italy with a constitution and the French Civil Code, the *Code
Napoléon* (see Chapter 19). That code remains the basis of much of Italian
law today. Law books of the day would have the code in French on one page
with the Italian translation on the facing page.

The kingdom expanded considerably over time, gaining territory from Austria near the Adriatic in 1805 and some of the Papal States in 1808.

When Napoleon fell, the European powers tried to restore things to their pre-Napoleonic condition as much as possible. But the outline of Italian unity was firmly established and, in time, used as the basis for the creation of the modern Italian state. Today, the *Museo de la Risorgimento* (Museum of the Reunification) in Milan pays tribute to Napoleon's role in that process.

Establishing an Independent Poland

Poland had at one time been a significant central European nation, but it had the misfortune of being located between Austria, Prussia, and Russia. Each of these powers sought to expand, frequently at the expense of the Poles. By the Napoleonic period, Poland had been partitioned between the Russians and Prussians several times, to the point that she no longer even existed as an independent nation.

Poland did exist as a state of mind, however, and the Poles were anxious to find a way to return to their former status. They had been quite taken by the lofty ideals of the French Revolution (see Chapter 3) and soon came to see Napoleon as their potential liberator.

Creating the Grand Duchy of Warsaw

Napoleon was always glad to have the support of anyone, and as early as his first Italian campaign (see Chapter 6) he had welcomed Polish soldiers, most notably Polish *Lancers* (cavalrymen who carried lances), into his army. When his campaigns took him to Warsaw in 1806 (see Chapter 10), he was welcomed by the Poles as their liberator from the Prussians and the Russians, both of whom he was fighting at the time. The Poles welcomed him with open arms, in particular the open arms of Marie Walewska, whose long-term relationship with Napoleon I discuss in Chapter 10.

Napoleon gained more from Warsaw than a new lover. The Poles gave him thousands of soldiers and a loyalty that lasted to the end of his career. He, in turn, gave them at least part of what they wanted. With the Treaty of Tilsit in July 1807 (see Chapter 10), he took Prussia's portion of ancient Poland and created the Grand Duchy of Warsaw, a small nation of some 2.5 million people.

The Grand Duchy of Warsaw became in many ways a model for what a Napoleonic empire could look like. As with the Italians, Napoleon gave the Poles a constitution and the *Code Napoléon* for their legal system. He appointed the Saxon King Frederick Augustus as the Grand Duke (see Figure 22-3), and almost all the administrative positions were filled by Poles. Napoleon also freed the serfs, gave Jews the rights of full citizens, abolished slavery, and instituted other progressive reforms.

Figure 22-3:
This period
French
engraving
shows
Frederick
Augustus as
both King of
Saxony and
Duke of
Warsaw.

Yet, it must be said that the Grand Duchy was pretty much under the control of Napoleon. He made it a part of the Confederation of the Rhine (which I discuss in the upcoming section "Toward a Greater Germany") and of the Continental System (see Chapter 22). His desire to maintain good relations with Austria prevented him from restoring some of Austria's Polish territories to the Duchy.

The Poles had hoped for more but were grateful for what they got. Without question, they continued to hold out hope for a greater Poland, and when it didn't come they were naturally disappointed. Still, the Poles remained some of Napoleon's strongest supporters, second only, perhaps, to the French themselves. As with modern Italians, the Poles see Napoleon as a very positive force in their history.

Watching the Duchy dissolve

When Napoleon retreated from Russia in 1812 (see Chapter 13), it didn't take long for Russian Tsar Alexander I to grab the Grand Duchy of Warsaw for himself. He tried to pawn himself off as the "protector" of Poland, and many Poles hoped this would prove to be the case. However, they soon found themselves once again divided up between Russia, Austria, and Prussia.

Poles never gave up hope and participated in various uprisings later in the century, but it wouldn't be until the early 20th century that an independent Poland would reemerge. Today, it is a large and democratic member of the European Union.

Toward a Greater Germany

Unlike the Italians, Germans had no real history of unification prior to the Napoleonic period. What we know as modern-day Germany had long been a collection of small — sometimes *very* small — kingdoms and principalities. This collection had been brought under the umbrella of the Holy Roman Empire in 800 C.E. under the Emperor Charlemagne. That empire had withered away, and as Napoleon rose to power it consisted only of the German states under the control of the Holy Roman Emperor, who also happened to be the Emperor Francis of Austria.

Gaining control of German states

The Holy Roman Empire had lost most of its punch, and both Austria and Prussia eyed the German states for their soldiers and economic opportunities. The German states were also something of a buffer between Austria, Prussia, and France.

Napoleon was determined to bring the German states under his control, and after his victory over the Austrians and Russians in 1805 (see Chapter 9), he was in a position to do just that. In July 1806, Napoleon created the Confederation of the Rhine out of 16 principalities, most notably Bavaria, Saxony, Westphalia, Württemberg, Baden, and the Grand Duchy of Warsaw (which, of course, was not one of the German states).

This action brought the borders of the French Empire to those of Prussia and Austria. Prussia was also sandwiched between the western portions of the Confederation, namely Westphalia and Saxony, and the eastern portion, the Grand Duchy of Warsaw. This situation was the final straw for the Prussians, who declared war on Napoleon. With their defeat in 1807 (see Chapter 9), the way was clear for the Confederation to thrive.

Many of the tiny principalities were soon absorbed into a few of the larger ones. The Holy Roman Empire dissolved completely, and Francis gave up his title (while remaining Emperor of Austria). Napoleon encouraged the various principalities to adopt Napoleonic reforms, such as the *Code Napoléon,* but did not force them to be uniform in their approach. As a result, some of the states became quite progressive, while others adopted very few reforms. All participated in the Continental System (see Chapter 21), and all gave Napoleon soldiers for his various campaigns.

Promoting (unintended) nationalism

Bringing together the various German states had an unintended consequence: rising German nationalism. Very early on, many of the people in the Confederation began to resent their domination by France, but they did little to express their frustration.

Confederation states were required to provide soldiers for Napoleon's invasion of Russia in 1812 (see Chapter 13), and this they did, however reluctantly. But when the campaign turned into a retreat, their support for Napoleon began to waver. And when the retreat turned into a general withdrawal from the outer reaches of the French Empire back to France, one by one the Confederation states switched sides. The unkindest cut of all came at the Battle of Leipzig, when the Saxon army literally turned around and started firing on their (suddenly) former French allies (see Chapter 14).

After Napoleon's fall, the major European powers tried to return the situation in central Europe to its pre-Napoleonic status. However, German nationalism continued to grow, and the smaller Germanic states were never reinstated. Anti-French feeling continued to fuel German nationalism. By the middle of the century, much of northern Germany had unified. The Franco-Prussian war later in the 19th century solidified a united Germany, which continues to play a major role in European politics.

Short on Time, Long on Influence

Napoleon had always wanted to unite Europe under his control. This he did, but for a very short time. Of far greater importance was Napoleon's influence — intended or not — on the rise of nationalism in Italy, Poland, and Germany. The ultimate unification of these three areas went a very long way to create the Europe that we know today.

Historians love to speculate what would have happened if the Confederation of the Rhine had remained intact, or what would have happened if Napoleon had followed through on his promise to create a greater Poland. A few more years of unity, a chance to more fully adopt progressive reforms, and the history of Europe, so often a history of conflict and horror, may have been quite different.

Chapter 23

Religious Freedom and Jewish Liberation

. . . .

In This Chapter

▶ Signing the Concordat with the Pope

▶ Promoting Jewish freedom

. . . .

*O*f all the reforms instituted by Napoleon, perhaps none were more important than those involving religious freedom. To the modern western reader, religious freedom seems almost a given. But in Napoleonic France, not only was it not a given, it was a hard-fought victory.

For one thing, the Catholic Church, led by the Pope, was less interested in religious freedom than in restoring its prominence in France after the Revolution. To be blunt, the Church didn't want religious freedom; it wanted to restore its right to be the only recognized religion in France and in most of Europe.

On the other hand, the Revolutionaries were not at all interested in giving the Church, whose abuses were legend, so much as a camel's nose under the tent. The Revolution had been anticlerical in nature, and many in France were quite content to keep it that way. (Many of the peasants, however, wanted their old Church back.)

In the middle of all of this were the Jews. Long the targets of discrimination, they would discover in Napoleon not only a liberator of their current decidedly unliberated condition but a precursor of their eventual acquisition of a homeland in Israel.

In this chapter, I tell you how Napoleon brought religious peace to Europe, which included the return of the Catholic Church (with significant restrictions) and the establishment of freedom of religion throughout the French Empire.

Accommodating the Catholic Church

No question about it: The French Revolution (see Chapter 3) took place at least in part in reaction to the excesses of the Catholic Church. That religious institution, which had developed enormous wealth and power, had come to dominate most of central and southern Europe and had abused its status. Not at all interested in religious tolerance or freedom, it had instituted the Inquisition in Spain, torturing, jailing, and killing all with whom it disagreed. Jews, Muslims, and Protestants alike were in deep trouble.

The Inquisition didn't extend into the rest of Europe, but that was mainly because France, southern Germany, Italy, and much of the rest of Europe were already dominated by *the Church* (as it was generally known). Great Britain, northern Germany, Scandinavia, and a few other areas were dominated by Protestant sects, themselves less than tolerant of differing religious views.

Revolting against the Church

The French Revolution had pretty much removed the Catholic Church from its position of preeminent influence. Actually, it had pretty much removed the Church from France, replacing it with a sort of civil religion called "The Civil Constitution of the Clergy." The Church was allowed to continue to exist, but it was under strict governmental control.

The Church had long developed a reputation for being more interested in wealth than saving souls. Its higher clergy (bishops and the like) lived more like princes than representatives of a group that supposedly had taken vows of poverty. Moreover, the Church was quick to tell the common people how to lead their lives but not quick at all to work against those same people's oppression by the nobility. Even the local priests, called *cure* in French, were not safe from the people's wrath, as many of them had a reputation for ignoring vows of chastity, if not poverty.

It is really important to remember that the leaders of the French Revolution absolutely hated the Catholic Church. They killed priests and other clergy, sacked and destroyed many churches and cathedrals, and did all they could to drive religion out of France. They also confiscated most Church property and either kept it as property of the state or sold it to the highest bidder. Yet, many of the common people still wanted their religion and longed for the day that it was okay again to be a Catholic.

For its part, the Church did little to endear itself to the Revolution. It was a strong supporter of the Bourbon cause and worked to bring back the monarchy. It didn't support religious freedom and had no use at all for most of the other egalitarian ideals of the Revolution. In conservative, ultra-religious areas of France, Church leaders railed against the Revolution and supported counter-Revolutionary movements. Indeed, to some extent France was in danger of having a civil war between supporters of the Revolution and supporters of the Church.

Trying to ease civil strife

When Napoleon took control of France as First Consul in late 1799, he immediately understood that he governed a nation torn by many conflicts, not the least of which was the conflict over religion. Napoleon was essentially a nonbeliever and was probably somewhat bemused by all the fuss over who could pray to what god and in what manner.

But as a political leader, he clearly understood that he needed to find a way to bring a greater unity to France, including in the area of religion. No one wants to rule a deeply divided country. Besides, the Church was a bastion of *royalism* (support for the monarchy, another reason the leaders of the Revolution had little use for the Church), and he needed to diffuse that threat to his own rule. Shortly after his ascension to power, Napoleon began to seek ways to find an accommodation with the Pope and with religion in general.

Negotiating with the Pope

When Pope Pius VII was elected in the spring of 1800, Napoleon made immediate efforts to bring about some kind of rapprochement. He offered to bring the Church back to something like its previous (pre-Revolutionary) position of prominence if, in turn, the Pope would recognize the confiscation of Church property and the right of the state to control the Church as an institution.

The negotiations did not always go well. The Pope was not happy to have to bargain for what had once been his (or at least his Church's) and was not at all interested in Napoleon's initial offering. If he couldn't get his lands back, he wanted restitution. Napoleon wasn't about to face the political firestorm that would have ensued from a deal like that, so he suggested instead that the state pay the clergy's salaries. But the catch there was that the First Consul would have the right to nominate the clergy, who would then be invested by the Pope.

A major area of disagreement was the exact position of the Church in French society. Prior to the Revolution, the Catholic Church had been the official religion of France, and Pope Pius wanted Napoleon to restore that status. Like that was going to happen! Napoleon made it clear that he was quite happy to restore the Catholic Church as *one* of the religions of France but definitely not as *the* religion of France. Napoleon, unlike the Church, was a firm believer in freedom of religion.

The Pope soon learned that he was not dealing with just anyone and that Napoleon was negotiating from a position of strength. If the Pope wanted to get his religion back into France, it would happen pretty much on Napoleon's terms. After that was understood, negotiations moved along a bit better.

On August 15, 1801, Napoleon's 32nd birthday, the Pope signed an agreement known as *the Concordat.* This document allowed the Catholic Church to be *one* of the recognized religions in France but not *the* recognized religion, as the Pope had wanted. It gave Napoleon the power to appoint and pay clergy, with the Pope relegated to simply confirming them in their positions. Still, the Pope and his clergy were pretty pleased, for they were finally allowed back in France. Their pleasure was not shared by everyone, however.

Facing a backlash

Now, you may think that bringing back the Church while maintaining the rights of all other religions would be a wildly popular accomplishment. You'd be wrong.

Many of the Revolutionaries in and out of government were furious with Napoleon for signing the Concordat. Soldiers claimed that the agreement was an insult to the deaths of so many French who fought in the Revolution. Many leaders didn't want the Church back in France at all, for fear that the old excesses would soon reappear. And on the flip side, devout Catholics were not pleased at the restrictions that were placed on the Church under the agreement, or with the fact that Catholicism was only one of a number of religions recognized by the French government.

And royalists, who were the biggest losers in the deal, recognized that they had lost one of their strongest supporters. Catholics could hardly be expected to promote the demise of the very leader who had brought them back their religion.

Napoleon had a difficult time getting the Concordat through the legislative assemblies, dominated as they were by Revolutionaries. Some legislators tried to get major modifications, such as reducing the power of the Pope. But ultimately, they went along with the agreement.

Of all Napoleon's reforms, the Concordat was probably his least popular. Still, when the Catholic churches were reopened in April 1802, it had only been a month since the Treaty of Amiens, which held the promise of finally establishing peace between France and Great Britain (see Chapter 21). Napoleon had brought both internal and external peace to France in a short time, and for that, his popularity continued to soar to new and dizzying heights.

Promoting Jewish Freedom

The history of the Jews in Europe is an unhappy one. They suffered discrimination in every quarter and had been blamed for the Plague, economic depressions, famine, and pretty much everything else that ever went wrong.

The Catholic Church didn't exactly promote tolerance for other religions, especially Judaism. The Inquisition in Spain largely drove Jews out of that country. And the Crusades, nominally directed against Islam, often brought death and destruction to Jews as well. (Let's face it: Sometimes the Crusades degenerated into Christians killing Christians, all in the name of wealth rather than preserving the Holy Land.)

The French Revolution created little in the way of improvement for Jews. They were granted citizenship, but as a religious institution Judaism was considered pretty much on par with the Catholic Church. Synagogues were closed, and Judaism was treated with much the same disdain as Catholicism. France had a strong strain of anti-Semitism, and anyone who went up against that was in for a struggle.

Envisioning the Jewish state

From the very beginning, Napoleon promoted the liberation of the Jews. Throughout much of Europe in the 18th century, Jews had been forced to live in ghettos and even to wear yellow arm bands. In 1797, while in Ancona, Italy, Napoleon was made aware of this fact and was absolutely amazed. He quickly ordered that the arm bands be removed and that Jews be given the right to live wherever they wished. It was a policy that he would follow during all of his military campaigns throughout Europe. Many years later, in Poland, he closed the Warsaw ghetto in much the same way. Clearly, Napoleon saw discrimination against Jews as a direct affront to his firmly-held belief in equality, and he was determined to do something about it.

In 1798, Napoleon led an army that invaded Egypt (see Chapter 7). On his way there, he took over the island of Malta. When he discovered that Jews on that island had not been allowed to operate a synagogue, he issued an immediate order rectifying the situation.

After Malta, Napoleon gained control of Egypt and from there moved north into the Holy Land, which is modern-day Israel. He took with him a proclamation, dated April 20, 1799, that essentially declared that Palestine was to be a new Jewish homeland. Napoleon planned to issue this proclamation when he entered Jerusalem. Unfortunately for him, and for the Jews, he was stymied at the siege of Acre and never made it to Jerusalem.

Napoleon's campaign in the Holy Land resulted in his withdrawal to Egypt, and he never did issue the proclamation. The document still exists, however, and in 1947, David Ben Gurion used it as one of his justifications before the United Nations when he was seeking creation of the Jewish state of Israel.

Granting French Jews full citizenship

Napoleon did for French Jews what he did for Jews everywhere he went. The revision of the Civil Code, later called the *Code Napoléon* (see Chapter 19), granted religious freedom for everyone and paid particular attention to the Jews. Taking this stance against religious oppression was not an easy thing to do, given the strong political support for anti-Semitism. Indeed, over the years, Napoleon would have to continually work to see that his directives on the matter were carried out. He was determined to see that Jews were made full citizens, including having the right to freely practice their religion and participate in all aspects of social, economic and political society. But numerous newspapers and politicians routinely opposed him on this issue.

Determined in his objectives and frustrated by opposition, Napoleon decided to take a bold step. On May 30, 1806, Napoleon issued a decree calling for an assembly of Jewish leaders and rabbis to meet in Paris to discuss all issues related to Jews in France. This meeting was called a *Sanhedrin,* and it was designed in part to allow Jewish leaders to respond to the attacks being made against them. It was also called to signal once and for all Napoleon's support for full Jewish citizenship.

The Sanhedrin met at the City Hall in Paris on July 23, 1806. Every department of France as well as Northern Italy was represented by the 111 Jewish leaders. Napoleon announced the results of their deliberations and his support for their religious freedom on November 29, 1806. Jews were declared full citizens and Judaism made one of the three official religions of France, along with Protestantism and Catholicism.

The Sanhedrin convened again in February and March of 1807 to fine-tune the provisions of law granting Jewish independence.

Meeting opposition at home and abroad

Not surprisingly, Napoleon faced plenty of opposition to his move toward Jewish liberation. Not only did newspapers and political leaders oppose him, but so did some of his own generals and family members. His uncle, Cardinal Joseph Fesch, in particular, was convinced that these actions would lead to the end of the world.

No other leader in Europe supported Napoleon in his efforts. Tsar Alexander I of Russia was furious and made his feelings quite clear. Austria and England protested as well, accusing Napoleon of going against the natural order of things. It's hard to imagine such a backlash from such a reasonable policy, but backlash is exactly what Napoleon got.

That backlash was impossible to ignore, so in March 1808 Napoleon issued a decree that placed restrictions on Jewish freedom. This was an awful step backward, but it did cool down emotions a bit. Within a few months, the restrictions were pretty much removed in most of France, and by 1811 they were completely gone. Jews were finally full members of society, able to work, worship, and live as they wished.

Small wonder, then, that Napoleon is seen as a hero to many Jews today. Jews can credit him with helping to end the policies, if not the emotions, of institutionalized anti-Semitism in much of Europe.

Jews of Napoleon's time certainly recognized his importance to their status as a people. The period engraving shown in Figure 23-1 represents the gratitude Jews felt for Napoleon.

Figure 23-1: This period engraving shows Napoleon granting Jews their freedom through his decree of May 30, 1806 that called for a Sanhedrin, the first step toward full freedom.

NAPOLÉON LE GRAND,
rétablit le culte des Israélites, le 30 Mai 1806.

Part VI
The Part of Tens

In this part . . .

Travel is always fun, all the more so when you can visit a nice battlefield or three. In this part, I describe ten that you won't want to miss. What's nice about many of these sites is that they come complete with museum, interpretive center, local pub, and, most important of all, a gift shop.

I don't know about you, but I'd *love* to go back in history and give some advice to any number of historical figures. (Caesar: Under no circumstances are you to go to the Senate on the Ides of March! Listen to your wife: Stay home and paint the shrine.) Short of time travel, we can't really do that, of course. But history can be about pretending, so in this part I present just some of the advice I'd give Napoleon (who, if he had only listened to me, would still be emperor today!).

And to guide you in further exploration of the wonderful world of Napoleon, here, too, are some ideas about what resources to tap into next. Enjoy!

Chapter 24

Ten Interesting Battlefields to Visit

*I*n this book, I try to point out that Napoleon is far more than the sum of his battles. Still, it's hard not to see him in terms of his many victories (and a few defeats). For many people, standing on a field and imagining a magnificent charge of *heavy cuirassiers* (cavalrymen who wear steel breastplates and helmets) or the awful thunder of an artillery barrage is a big part of their fascination with history. If you're one of those people, Napoleon offers a virtual smorgasbord from which to choose. Not all battlefields are created equal, however, and in this chapter, I guide you to some of the most interesting.

Battlefields offer other opportunities besides the chance to imagine the events of war. They are often located near interesting cities or in beautiful countryside. They may lure you into a region or country you have not yet experienced and open the door to other enjoyments. In some cases, excellent interpretive centers or museums are close at hand. In other situations, local pubs or bistros may prove of greater interest. And for many of us, the ubiquitous gift or antique shops hold endless fascination. (My wife, Barbara, will tell you it's a battle to keep me out of them!) In short, battlefields offer something for everyone, so I encourage you to pack your bags and enjoy.

Waterloo (Belgium)

Fairly or not, Waterloo is the battle most associated with Napoleon (see Chapter 15). The battlefield is located a short drive south of Brussels. The battle of Waterloo was fought over a fairly wide area, and visitors can drive or walk to most of it. Highlights in the area include

- *Le Caillou,* which served as Napoleon's headquarters and is now a museum. A glass case containing the bones of a French soldier now lies where Napoleon had breakfast!

- The church of Saint-Joseph, which was used as an infirmary and is now a monument to the battle with almost 30 commemorative plaques.

- The Duke of Wellington's headquarters, now a museum as well.

- *Belle Alliance,* used as Napoleon's vantage point and made famous by the meeting there of Wellington and Gebhardt Lebrecht von Blücher.

- Hougoumont, where so many of Napoleon's troops were tied down.

- La Haie-Sainte, a critical farm in the center of the British defensive position that eventually fell to the French.

- Mont St. Jean, used as an infirmary.

- The Papelotte and La Haye farms, along with the Fichermont Chateau, which anchored Wellington's left flank and gave cover to the Prussians upon their entry to the battle.

- Countless small monuments and plaques located throughout the area.

A real lowlight of the visit is the Lion Mound, so called because this monstrosity has a large statue of a lion at its top. It ruins the area near the center of Wellington's lines, where some of the fiercest fighting took place, but there may be more postcards of the Lion Mound than anything else. On the plus side, if you climb the 226 steps to the top, you get a great view. And at its base is a must-see attraction: a panorama of the battlefield.

After the battlefield, a Napoleon brand beer at the nearby pub *Le Bivouac* may be in order, but not until you've checked out the many gift shops nearby.

Incidentally, if you didn't know better, you'd think that Napoleon won the battle. Statues of him outnumber statues of Wellington (to say nothing of Blücher) by a margin of at least ten to one.

Borodino (Russia)

There aren't many battles where both sides can rightly claim victory, but this may be one of them. Napoleon won the field and went to Moscow, but Mikhail Kutusov kept the Russian army in one piece (see Chapter 13).

Kutusov did something else as well. He insisted that the battlefield be maintained as a monument — the first in the world to be so designated.

Visitors can see the various *redoubts* and *fleches* (defensive earthwork structures) that were part of the defenses prepared by the Russians. The major positions held by Napoleon, Kutusov, and other leaders are clearly marked, and there are interpretive markers at various locations. A monument sits on top of the Great Redoubt, and countless others are located throughout the area. Don't miss the two monuments dedicated to the Russian and French soldiers, respectively. The museum is very well done and includes many artifacts from the battle, as well as interpretive material and a panorama with lights showing the positions of the different military units. The gift shop is outside and has limited material, but you can find some real bargains.

The drawback to Borodino is its location, which is near the small town of Mojaisk, about a two-hour drive from Moscow. Moscow offers additional sights related to the battle, including an excellent panorama, Kutusov's hut that served as his headquarters, excellent museums, and several monuments.

Obviously, there are many fine hotels and restaurants in Moscow, but if you want to feel you've stepped back in time, stay at the Hotel Metropol, just off Red Square and across from the Bolshoi opera house. This 100-year-old hotel must be one of the most elegant in Europe.

Austerlitz (Czech Republic)

The Battle of Austerlitz is generally considered Napoleon's greatest victory (see Chapter 9), and the battlefield is well worth a visit. It is located in the Czech Republic, east of the city of Brno, near the town of Slokov-Austerlitz. It's about a two-hour drive from Prague, one of Europe's greatest cities.

To tour this site, you need a car, as the battlefield is quite spread out. Unlike Borodino, not all of it is preserved on public land, but there is plenty to see. A real highlight is to stand on the Pratzen Heights and look out across the valley below. You can easily imagine the Russians' surprise to see the French coming up out of the fog, as well as the delight of those same French as they poured fire down on the hapless Austrians (see Chapter 9). There is a stone cross marking where Napoleon stood when he took the heights.

You can also drive to other important battle sites, monuments, and museums. Among the more interesting things to see are

- The Stanton, Napoleon's vantage point
- The 18th-century chateau where Napoleon stayed, now a museum
- The Peace Monument, located on the Pratzen Heights and constructed in the early 20th century

✔ A monument marking Kutusov's headquarters, near where the Russians were defeated

✔ The Posoritz Post House, which first served as the Russian General Peter Bagration's headquarters and then Napoleon's. Here, Napoleon began the peace talks that concluded later in the city now called Pressburg

✔ A monument marking Napoleon's headquarters on the morning of the battle, located on the Zuran Hill

You can find many accommodations in the area. I suggest the Stara Posta (the old post office) located just outside of Slokov-Austerlitz, but you can find many options in the village as well. And did I mention the antique shop?

Lodi (Italy)

The village of Lodi, (population about 40,000), dates to the Roman Empire and is very picturesque. Here, Napoleon claimed to have "found himself." While the action in Lodi was light compared to most battles, it was significant in the young general's development. On May 10, 1796, the French were on one side of the River Adda, and the Austrians on the other. To drive away the Austrians, the French attacked across a bridge (see Chapter 6).

The original bridge is no longer there, but much of the village looks just as it must have when General Bonaparte rode into town. It is easy to imagine the French soldiers in formation up and down the narrow streets, and if you ask the right person, you can go into the tower of the Church of the Madeleine that Napoleon used to direct the action.

Not surprisingly, there are a number of fine places to eat in Lodi, as well as an interesting church and several hotels. The city archives are full of interesting material related to the battle and subsequent French domination of the area. There is a commemorative plaque on a building just opposite the bridge, and others hang in several locations related to Napoleon's visit.

Aspern-Essling, Lobau Island, and Wagram (Austria)

After indecisive action at the Battle of Aspern-Essling on May 21 and 22, 1809, Napoleon withdrew to Lobau Island. On July 5 and 6, 1809, he broke out of the island and gained a great victory against the Austrians on essentially the same ground as the earlier battle, leading to their signing an armistice shortly thereafter (see Chapter 10).

At Aspern, you can see the 17th-century church used by Marshal André Masséna as an observation point. A commemorative plaque hangs there, and other monuments are nearby. In the villages of Aspern and Essling, you can see many buildings that were standing in 1809, and many of the battle sites are as open now as they were then.

The Island of Lobau has numerous walking paths, some with informational placards, and a small museum of the battle.

The battlefield of Wagram is quite spread out; you could easily spend more than one day seeing it. Numerous buildings from the time of the battle are still standing, and each one seems to have its own commemorative plaque. There are numerous monuments to soldiers and generals of both sides, some of which designate the precise location of various actions that took place.

Arcola (Italy)

Located a few miles southeast of Verona, Italy, the bridge at Arcola has entered the highest ranks of the Napoleonic legend. On November 15, 1796, Napoleon, seeing that his men were not advancing, grabbed a battle flag and led them across the bridge (see Chapter 6). For his effort, he accidentally was pushed into the river and had to be dragged out. But his bravery, and that of other generals, carried the day. Countless prints and other images promote this example of his early heroism.

The original bridge is gone, but its replacement is on pretty much the same spot. Near one end of the bridge, an obelisk erected in 1810 commemorates the event. In the town, a small chapel serves as a museum to the action.

Acre/Jaffa (Israel)

Napoleon's campaign in Egypt and the Holy Land (see Chapter 7) captures the imagination as much as any of his European adventures. Monuments and plaques are scattered throughout the region, but my favorite is the area around Jaffa and Acre (*Yafo* and *Akko* in Hebrew).

Jaffa has no battlefield to visit, but you can see the hospital where, in 1799, Napoleon visited his soldiers who had the plague. Just down the road at Acre, you can see the original walls of the town. Napoleon laid siege to the town from March 21 to May 20, 1799 but never took the city.

Thanks to the efforts of the Israeli Society for Napoleonic Research, there are numerous explanatory guideposts in key locations.

Eylau (Russia)

Also sometimes referred to as *Prussian-Eylau,* this battlefield of February 7 and 8, 1807 is located in and around the 14th-century town of Bagrationovsk in the area of Russia known as Kaliningrad. It is not the easiest place to get to, but the effort is worthwhile. In the town, there is a large statue of Russian General Peter Bagration. A fine museum sits nearby, as well as a cemetery that features a touching tribute to the unknown French and Russian soldiers buried there.

The various fields of battle are all around. Most notable is the church that served as Napoleon's headquarters and the grounds by the church where he was almost captured (see Chapter 10). The church survived by being converted into a refrigerator factory, and the original bishop's house is there as well. Just down the street, you can see the large open field where several major cavalry charges took place. Just outside of town near the Polish border, a large monument (erected in 1857) commemorates the battle and has bas relief busts of some of the generals. Some of the battlefield is located in neighboring Poland, but I advise you not to stray close to the border.

Friedland (Russia)

If you've made it to Eylau, then by all means go about 25 kilometers east to the town of Pravdinsk to see the battlefield of Friedland. This battle, which took place on June 14, 1807, was one of Napoleon's better victories (see Chapter 10). In the village, you can see a small museum, several monuments, and the house where Napoleon stayed. The best way to see the battlefield is to arrange to see it as Napoleon did, from the steeple of the local church. There, armed with a map, you can follow virtually all of the action.

There are no hotels in either small village, and few of the residents speak English. The Kaliningrad Hotel in the city of Kaliningrad offers decent accommodations and at least some English-speaking staff. Inquire there about getting a car, driver, and translator for what would be a full day trip to see these two sites, which are over an hour's drive from Kaliningrad.

Marengo (Italy)

Few battles have a greater role in the legend of Napoleon than that of Marengo, fought in Italy on June 14, 1800 (see Chapter 6). The site is located just outside the delightful village of Alessandria, about 80 kilometers east of

Turin. There are plenty of excellent places to stay and to eat and a few plaques related to the battle.

As you enter Marengo, visit the chateau located at the edge of town. There you will find a large statue of First Consul Bonaparte in the front yard. Notice the *trompe-l'oeil* ("fool the eye") façade of the building, which houses a nice museum. In the back, in a small park, is a fine statue of General Louis Charles Desaix, the real hero of the battle, who was fatally wounded in the action. Across the street is a column with an eagle commemorating the battle.

The battlefield is still largely open farmland, but little has been done to mark the area for tourists. A short drive from the column, toward Tortona, you find the farm that served as Napoleon's headquarters, complete with the mandatory commemorative plaque and, in this case, some cats that locals insist descended from some that were present for the battle!

Chapter 25

Ten Pieces of Advice for Napoleon

In This Chapter
▶ Political and military errors Napoleon shouldn't have made
▶ People he shouldn't have trusted
▶ Words of wisdom with the advantage of 200 years of 20/20 hindsight

I've often said that "If Napoleon had listened to me, he'd be emperor today." Many people fantasize about going back in history and meeting with someone famous. In this chapter, I get to live out that fantasy (sort of) and give Napoleon a piece of my mind. Whether or not he will listen, well, that is another story.

Get Rid of Talleyrand and Fouché

Charles Maurice de Talleyrand-Périgord served Napoleon in a variety of diplomatic posts, including foreign minister, while Joseph Fouché was minister of police. When you're trying to rule an empire, your staff should be there to support you, and not just when you're popular. But these two guys thought only of themselves (although Talleyrand was always claiming that he thought only of France).

When times were good, Talleyrand served Napoleon well, but times were not always good. Here are few reasons he was never named Employee of the Year:

✔ When Napoleon was in Egypt, Talleyrand was supposed to smooth things over with the Turks, but he somehow never got around to doing that. As a result, Napoleon had to fight the Turks as well as the local military forces. (For more on the Egyptian campaign, see Chapter 7.)

✔ As soon as he felt that Napoleon's star was no longer rising, Talleyrand had secret talks with the countries allied against Napoleon, as well as with the exiled royal family. When Napoleon abdicated in 1814, Talleyrand was behind the return of the monarchy, and he effectively prevented Napoleon's son and wife from taking over after Napoleon left.

✔ Tallyrand's final outrage against Napoleon was to convince the allies that they shouldn't trust Napoleon when he returned in 1815 but should instead go to war with him. Napoleon's son was briefly recognized as Napoleon II, but Talleyrand again successfully worked to restore the Bourbon monarchy.

Napoleon once referred to Talleyrand as excrement in a silk stocking, but he never took serious action against him. Big mistake.

Fouché wasn't much better. A strong supporter of Napoleon when he first rose to power, Fouché served as minister of police, becoming one of the most powerful men in the country. He helped eliminate Napoleon's enemies and built a network of informers that was loyal to Fouché first, Napoleon second. He was caught dealing with the exiled royals, but rather than being shot for treason, he was simply reassigned. His network intact, he continued to work behind the scenes for his own interests, including the accumulation of great wealth.

Fouché remained more or less loyal to Napoleon through Waterloo, but then he was instrumental in getting the legislative body to demand Napoleon's abdication rather than offering him its support.

Have Better Reconnaissance

As I explain in Chapter 17, Napoleon was a master of war and used modern tactics and organization that befuddled his opponents for many years. But he had some odd gaps in his approach to military issues. The strangest of these was the issue of reconnaissance. There are three classic examples of Napoleon's failure to use proper reconnaissance. Its proper use in all three would have led to a better result, and in one case (Russia), it may have staved off disaster.

Acre

At the siege of Acre (in the Middle East) in the spring of 1799, then-General Bonaparte was forced to attempt a frontal assault on the town. His soldiers managed to break through the wall, only to find an unexpected inner wall. Shocked and unprepared, they retreated, and the siege ultimately failed. Napoleon had some observation balloons with him but refused to use them. Had he done so, he would likely have had better success, because the aerial view from the balloons would have clearly revealed the inner fortifications. Instead, Acre prevented him from eliminating a formidable enemy and driving the British back into the sea. (See Chapter 7 for more on this campaign.)

Marengo

In the days leading up to the Battle of Marengo in Italy, which took place on June 14, 1800 (see Chapter 9), Napoleon was not completely aware of the size of the opposing Austrian force. As a result, he sent two full divisions off in different directions, reducing his force considerably. Unfortunately for him, the Austrians had marshaled their forces and now outnumbered the French by about 7,000 soldiers.

First Consul Bonaparte very nearly lost the ensuing battle. He won only because of Austrian incompetence and the fact that General Louis Charles Desaix's division heard the sound of the guns and hastened back to support Napoleon, arriving just in the nick of time. Napoleon could have avoided this near disaster by simply sending out adequate scouting parties of cavalry to determine the true strength of his opponents.

Leaving Moscow

As I discuss in Chapter 13, when Napoleon finally decided to leave Moscow in 1812, he had hoped to return by a route far to the south of the now-desolated route he took in to the city. His army was still in decent fighting shape, and the weather had not yet turned frigid.

Not far out of Moscow, he found his way blocked by the Russians. He defeated them in a skirmish, and they retreated behind a ridge. Convinced that he was facing a major Russian force, Napoleon reluctantly turned north, where he had to retrace his steps home through terrain that was colder and had been stripped bare of anything useful for survival.

Had a reconnaissance team been sent forward, it would have discovered that the Russians had melted away and that the coast was clear to the relatively resource-rich and warmer southern route. The withdrawal may still have been bad, but Napoleon's army would probably have survived in much greater shape and been able to stop further Russian advances. If so, the Russian campaign may not have had the far-reaching negative consequences ultimately paid by Napoleon and France.

Don't Depend on Your Siblings

Napoleon had seven siblings: four brothers and three sisters. Napoleon clearly expected that his brothers and sisters would help him in his career, and he ultimately gave them positions of power, prestige, and wealth. In the end, however, they were much more the burden than the blessing. This section offers the worst examples.

Ladies first:

- ✔ Caroline (1782–1839) was probably the worst offender. She married Joachim Murat, one of Napoleon's early companions who rose to the rank of marshal and later became King of Naples. Murat was a great cavalry leader, but while he was gone, Caroline got used to the life of luxury that came with her position. So much so that in 1814, when Austria and others were closing in on Napoleon, she coerced her probably all-too-willing husband to desert Napoleon and cut a deal to preserve their kingdom in Naples.

- ✔ Pauline (1780–1825) didn't engage in direct action against her brother, but her lifestyle left a great deal to be desired for the sister of an emperor! Living in Parisian luxury, she became known for her nude poses and sexual appetite. A drinking vessel was even molded from one of her breasts. Her scandalous behavior frustrated Napoleon, but Napoleon was joined in exile on Elba by only his mother and one sibling — Pauline.

Napoleon's brothers weren't much better:

- ✔ His elder brother Joseph (1768–1844) was well-meaning and probably would have made a decent King of Naples, which is what Napoleon originally made him. However, when Napoleon was seeking a king for Spain, he turned to a most reluctant Joseph. Naples was peaceful and relatively easy to rule. Not so Spain. Joseph had to deal with quarrelling French marshals, revolting peasants (yes, the peasants were, in fact, revolting!), and a fellow who later took on the title of Duke of Wellington who had a way of defeating the French armies that he faced. We can't blame all the problems in Spain on King Joseph, but Napoleon could have found someone far better to do the job.

  Later on, in 1814, when Joseph was in charge of the defense of Paris, his lack of leadership opened the door for the intrigues of Talleyrand (who I discuss earlier in the chapter) that would ultimately doom Napoleon.

- ✔ Napoleon's younger brother Louis (1778–1846) served Napoleon well in his earlier years, rising to the rank of general. Napoleon made him King of Holland in 1806, and it wasn't long before he and Napoleon were not seeing eye to eye. (For example, Louis felt that the Continental System would be quite harmful to his subjects and declined to implement it as firmly as Napoleon expected.) It seems Louis had the naïve idea that as king he could act independently of Napoleon. Wrong! Napoleon even married him off to Josephine's daughter, Hortense, but that marriage was unhappy and did Napoleon no good.

Forget the Continental System

Let's face it: From Napoleon's point of view, he could never win control of the European continent without defeating, or at least achieving a peace with,

Great Britain. The problem was, Napoleon had the best army, and the Brits had the best navy. Stalemate! The only way for Napoleon to win, as he saw it, was to have an economic blockade against the British: Keep them from trading with the Continent, and soon they'd be on their knees.

Unfortunately, Napoleon failed to notice that people on the Continent, including in France, needed (or certainly wanted) goods shipped by British ships. Heck, even his wife, Josephine, was known to get a few things from the black market.

The need to enforce the Continental System (as this blockade was called) led to the ultimately disastrous invasion of Spain and Portugal (see Chapter 12). And it was one of the main things that caused a split between Napoleon and Tsar Alexander I of Russia, leading to the disastrous invasion of Russia (see Chapter 13). Notice a trend here? Easy for me to say, but there had to be a better way.

Don't Marry Josephine

Now I'm in trouble. The romance between Napoleon and Josephine is the stuff of legend, compared to Romeo and Juliet. How dare I suggest they not get together!? Well, here's how. The marriage was based on a foundation of sand. Josephine was never what Napoleon thought she was. She had no money, she didn't love him, she wasn't faithful to him, she used her influence (and his name) to engage in military profiteering, she was a spendthrift who drove them to the brink of financial ruin — need any more reasons? (Okay, so my wife thinks I'm a hypocrite on that last one, given my own tendencies in that direction. What can I say?)

Napoleon was a brilliant young general with a great future in front of him when he married this impoverished older woman. He could likely have found someone with better connections and more wealth who could have helped him along in his career and been much more the loving wife that a young man needs.

Don't Divorce Josephine

Okay, I confess: I'm trying to have it both ways. But bear with me. After Napoleon and Josephine finally settled down to a reasonable married life as emperor and empress (well, that was a reasonable married life to them!), things actually began to work out rather well. They developed a strong mutual fondness for each other; the French people really grew to like them as ruling couple; other rulers, such as the tsar of Russia, were impressed by this charming, gracious, and outgoing empress; and the French army really seemed to see her as something of a lucky charm. In short, it was hard to imagine a better deal all the way around.

So what happened? Napoleon decided he had to have a son, and when Josephine proved unable to provide him one, he divorced her and married Marie Louise, the daughter of the Emperor of Austria. Napoleon and Marie Louise had a son, whom Napoleon adored, but frankly it was all downhill in Napoleon's career after that.

Napoleon never really stopped loving Josephine. Don't get me wrong: Napoleon and Marie Louise had a loving relationship. But she was an intellectual lightweight compared to Josephine, and the French never cared all that much for her. (After all, they had sent their previous king's Austrian wife, Marie Antoinette, to the guillotine.) And while Napoleon hoped his marriage into the Hapsburg family of Austria would gain him a steadfast ally, when Napoleon was down and out in 1814, guess who was among the first to desert him? If you guessed Austria, you have a good reason why Napoleon should have taken my advice.

Declare Victory in Moscow and Get Out of Town Quickly

In 1812, Napoleon invaded Russia, chasing the Russian army all the way to Borodino. After defeating them there, he occupied the holy city of Moscow. (The actual capital, containing Tsar Alexander, was St. Petersburg.) Russian partisans burned most of Moscow to the ground on the very day Napoleon entered the city, making it pretty clear that he would not be able to stay there for the winter. It also should've been clear, given the fact that the Russian army was still in pretty good shape and that Napoleon was deep into Mother Russia, that the tsar wasn't about to surrender or ask for peace terms. Winter was coming; it was time to go. Napoleon had won the only major battle of the campaign and all of the earlier skirmishes. He had taken Moscow. By traditional standards, he could declare victory and leave.

Instead, Napoleon sat around for week after week, waiting for a message from Tsar Alexander that would never come. After a five-week delay, he finally left. It was too late. Winter came early, and when Napoleon was forced to take the northern route back (see the "Leaving Moscow" section earlier in the chapter), his fate was sealed. Had he traveled four of those five weeks, all the scenes we see of the bitter Russian winter taking its toll on the French army would never have happened. Napoleon could have made an orderly withdrawal to Smolensk or some point further east and awaited further developments from a position of strength.

Declare Equal Rights for Women

By the standards of the day, Napoleon was pretty progressive. He promoted religious freedom, the notion of equality, and education, including for girls. There was only one area where, at least from today's point of view, he was lacking. He could have done more to promote the equality of women in France and, ultimately, throughout his empire. Had he done that, he would have gained the confidence of not only the women of France and Europe but of the liberals and revolutionaries who continued to hold him in some suspicion. Moreover, given his power and influence, he would have pushed the movement for the rights of women forward in a way that would have been difficult to oppose. It would have been another blow to the conservatism promoted by both the Church and royalists. It would even have gained him added support in Great Britain.

That said, I may be asking a bit much, even from a man as progressive as Napoleon. He was, after all, trying to pacify the Church and conservatives, as well as the liberals. Even the Jews, whose religious freedom he especially promoted (see Chapter 23), were not exactly at the forefront of feminism. As to the United States, the most progressive country of its day, it didn't allow women even to vote until 1920, almost 200 years after Napoleon lost power. Still, if Napoleon had taken this step, his legacy as the first great progressive force of modern Europe would have been assured, and the lives of women throughout Europe would have been improved.

Don't Become Emperor

Here I go again, getting in trouble with many friends in the field who will, among other things, point out that one of my books is entitled *Imperial Glory* and my house is full of stuff dealing with Napoleon as emperor. But the fact of the matter is that Napoleon never needed to be emperor, and it ultimately did him more harm than good.

When Napoleon was First Consul, he was given just about as much power as he had as emperor, including getting the position for life with the right to name his successor. But attempts on his life (see Chapter 20) led him to feel that he needed to solidify his position and perhaps gain favor with the ruling families of Europe by becoming "one of them." Nice idea, but it didn't work. He was never fully accepted by the other imperial and royal households, and his son was never allowed to rule.

Whatever Napoleon gained by his imperial trappings, his loss was far greater. He could no longer fully claim to be the son of the French Revolution, and it was really hard for a lot of people to see how a progressive reformer like First Consul Bonaparte could morph into Napoleon I, Emperor of the French, without losing a lot of his progressive ideas and images.

See Dr. James Verling on St. Helena

When Napoleon was sent in exile to the island of St. Helena (see Chapter 16), he was given a British doctor to attend to his, and his staff's, medical needs. That doctor, Barry O'Meara, eventually ran afoul of the governor of the island, Sir Hudson Lowe, and left. After that, the best doctor available on the island — the only actual physician — was an Irishman serving in the British military, Dr. James Verling. He was assigned by Sir Hudson Lowe to be Napoleon's doctor. Napoleon, however, was not interested in seeing anyone who was associated with Lowe (whom he saw as nothing more than a petty jailor), so he never saw Verling.

Verling did see Napoleon's subordinates. On Napoleon's behalf, they tried to hire Verling as more or less Napoleon's private physician, reporting only minimal information to Lowe and keeping medical information to himself. This confidentiality is what we may expect from a doctor today, but as a military officer that would have put Verling in a tough spot, so he declined.

Napoleon's health deteriorated, and in a few years he was dead. The cause of his death has been roundly debated. It seems likely, however, that if Napoleon had been under the expert care of Dr. Verling, whatever ailed him may very well have been detected and properly treated. If he was dying of cancer, he may at least have been made more comfortable. If he was dying of health issues related to the miserable climate, Dr. Verling may have been able to successfully lobby for a change of venue. Finally, if he were being poisoned, the chances of the symptoms being discovered and the poisoning ended were better with Dr. Verling than with anyone else on the island. In short, Dr. Verling was Napoleon's best chance to survive into old age and maybe, just maybe, get off the island. (To read more about Dr. Verling, you may consider my new book, *Napoleon and Dr. Verling on St. Helena* [Pen and Sword], which includes his complete journal regarding his relations with Napoleon.)

Chapter 26

Ten (Plus) Best Sources for Further Information

More books have been published about Napoleon than about any other person, probably in excess of 300,000 by now. I wouldn't doubt that he dominates Web sites and organizations as well. I can't even begin to summarize the myriad sources available, but in this chapter I at least point you toward a few in the English language that can get you started. The books all have bibliographies, and the Web sites have links.

Books and Periodicals

Following are my recommendations for some of the best items in print about Napoleon.

Reference books

Written by David Chandler and published by Macmillan in 1979 (and reissued in paperback by Wordsworth Military Library in 2001), *Dictionary of the Napoleonic Wars* is an excellent basic reference book on the subject. It has some 1,200 entries, all of which are cross-referenced. To go along with the text, Chandler included many illustrations and maps, as well as a timeline and a daily list of Napoleon's military movements.

I should point out that a healthy competition for *Dictionary* will come out in 2006 in the form of the *Encyclopedia of the French Revolutionary and Napoleonic Wars,* published by ABC-CLIO.

Biographies and Bulletins

Napoleon, written by Vincent Cronin and published by William Morrow in 1972, was issued in paperback by Harper Collins in 1995. Cronin's book is a classic to which I'm always pleased to return. It has a comprehensive overview and gives a well-rounded look at all aspects of Napoleon's life. Cronin paints a very personal, and sympathetic, portrait of Napoleon.

Two recent award-winning books are also worthy of consideration:

✔ Steven Englund's *Napoleon: A Political Life* (published by Scribner in 2004) has received favorable mention, though some reviewers say that it is a bit on the heavy side, at least for the Napoleonic novice. Englund provides extensive notes but no bibliography or graphics.

✔ Reviewers say that my own offering, *Napoleon's Road to Glory: Triumphs, Defeats and Immortality* (published by Brassey's in 2003), is easy to read and offers complete coverage. It includes extensive notes and a large section of works cited, as well as numerous graphics.

Imperial Glory: The Bulletins of Napoleon's Grande Armée, 1805–1814 was written by J. David Markham (hey, that's me!) and published by Greenhill in 2003. This book is the first-ever complete and accurate translation of Napoleon's Bulletins. In this book, you can read about Napoleon's military accomplishments, difficulties, and descriptions of his opponents.

Periodicals

First Empire: The International Magazine for the Napoleonic Enthusiast, Historian and Gamer is published in the United Kingdom by David Watkins. You can reach him by e-mail at dw@firstempire.net or visit the Web site www.firstempire.net.

First Empire includes a wide range of material, such as articles on Napoleonic history, historical sites, important museums and collections, games, book reviews, and news of Napoleonic events. It is lavishly illustrated in full color and always includes any necessary maps with its articles.

Organizations

If you're developing a serious interest in Napoleon, you have lots of company. In this section, I suggest ways you can get connected with people who share your fascination.

The Napoleonic Alliance

The Napoleonic Alliance is a general membership organization dedicated to the study of Napoleon and his times. It holds annual meetings that feature presentations by top scholars and amateur historians on a wide variety of Napoleonic topics.

Various social events and an opportunity to maintain what for some are life-long friendships make membership in this club well worthwhile. When possible, the conferences feature visits to places that have some connection to Napoleon. (This isn't always easy, given that Napoleon never actually *came* to the United States. But the organization visits public and private collections, sites related to relatives or others connected in some way to Napoleon, or simply interesting historical sites in the area.)

The Alliance also publishes a quarterly *Gazette* that features articles on Napoleonic topics, organizational news, book reviews, news of international events, and other material. The publication is well illustrated, though not in color.

You can visit the Alliance Web site at www.napoleonic-alliance.com. There, you will find articles on Napoleon and information on past and future conferences and tour opportunities. In the interest of full disclosure, I should say that for the past two years, I have served as president of the group, and I have also periodically served as editor-in-chief of the *Gazette*.

The Napoleonic Society of America

The Napoleonic Society of America (NSA) was the first such group to be formed, way back in 1983. The Napoleonic Alliance broke away from the NSA a few years ago, but the two groups have already held one joint conference, and plans are underway for more. They are likely to reunite in the future.

The NSA holds annual conferences, publishes a *Member's Bulletin,* and offers annual tours. Its Web site, www.napoleonic-society.com, offers various items for sale, in addition to the types of things offered on the Alliance site.

International Napoleonic Society

The International Napoleonic Society (INS) is not a membership group as such. It was formed by Canadian Ben Weider to promote the academic study of Napoleonic history. People who have made contributions to the field can be nominated as Fellows, and the group currently has in excess of 500 such Fellows around the world. The INS promotes Napoleonic scholarship through the use of literary awards, the prestigious *Legion of Merit,* and the organization of International Napoleonic Congresses. The INS Web site, `www.napoleonic society.com`, is available in French and English and is an excellent source of information on Napoleon.

You will be shocked — shocked! — to hear that I have long served as executive vice president and editor-in-chief for INS and am responsible for organizing the International Congresses.

Web Sites

If you aren't quite ready to join the ranks of the organizatons I mention in the previous section, or even if you're already a card-carrying member, visiting the following Web sites is a great way to feed your growing interest in Napoleon.

Napoleon Series

The Napoleon Series Web site (`www.napoleon-series.org`) is not affiliated with any organization. It is pretty much in a class by itself. The site says it has more than 8,500 articles, maps, illustrations, reviews, photographs, and charts. The Napoleon Series sponsors a literary contest, holds an annual fundraiser auction, and promotes Napoleonic activities worldwide. You can also join discussions on its Forum.

Napoleon Foundation

The Napoleon Foundation (`www.napoleon.org`) in France is dedicated to promoting Napoleonic knowledge of all types. This site, in both English and French, can keep you up to date on art exhibitions, auctions of Napoleonic memorabilia, recently published books (complete with reviews), and just about anything else you can imagine.

There are, of course, countless books and seemingly countless periodicals and Web sites that deal with Napoleon. It's easy — and fun — to start with the ones I mention here and then branch out to whatever you may enjoy.

Appendix A

Napoleonic Timeline

1769

15 August

Napoleon Bonaparte is born in Ajaccio, Corsica, which was transferred from Italian to French rule a year earlier.

1779

1 January

Napoleon and his brother Joseph enter school at Autun, France, mainly to learn French. Napoleon is 9 years old.

25 April

Napoleon enters Royal Military College at Brienne.

1784

15 September

Napoleon passes exams and is selected to attend the École Militaire in Paris. He begins studies on October 24.

1785

24 February

Napoleon's father, Carlo, dies.

September

At age 16, Napoleon graduates from military school and is commissioned as Second Lieutenant of Royal Artillery. He joins the La Fère Regiment at Valence.

1789

14 July

The fall of the Bastille signals the start of the French Revolution.

1792

20 June

Austria and Prussia (soon joined by England and others) form the First Coalition against France.

10 August

Napoleon witnesses the massacre of the Swiss Guards at the Tuileries by the Parisian mob. The monarchy soon falls, and the first French Republic is declared.

1793

21 January	King Louis XVI of France is executed.
31 May	The Reign of Terror in France begins.
September–December	Napoleon commands artillery and leads the French government's retaking of Toulon from royalists.
21 December	Napoleon, at age 24, is promoted to General of Brigade.

1794

28 July	Maximilien Robespierre is executed; the Reign of Terror ends.
9 August	Napoleon is arrested and jailed but is released in 11 days.

1795

Summer–Fall	Napoleon is stationed in Paris and meets Josephine.
22 August	The constitution of 1795 creates the Directory.
5 October	Napoleon puts down a royalist uprising and is soon promoted to general of division.

1796

2 March	Napoleon is appointed general in chief of the Army of Italy.
9 March	Napoleon marries Josephine.
4–22 April	Napoleon wins a series of stunning victories in Italy against Austrian occupiers and their allies.
10 May	Napoleon wins the Battle of Lodi in Italy.
15–17 November	Napoleon wins the Battle of Arcole in Italy.

1797

14 January	Napoleon wins the Battle of Rivoli in Italy.
17 October	The Treaty of Campo Formio between France and Austria is ratified.
5 December	Napoleon returns to Paris and is soon elected member of the National Institute of Sciences and Arts of France and appointed commander of the Army of England.

1798

19 May	Napoleon and his army leave for Egypt via Malta.
1 July	Napoleon captures Alexandria.
21 July	The French win the Battle of the Pyramids.
1 August	Admiral Nelson wins the Battle of the Nile against the French.
29 December	A Second Coalition against France is formed by Britain, Austria, and Russia.

1799

7 March	Napoleon takes Jaffa but is later stymied at Acre (in modern Israel).
25 July	Returning to Cairo, Napoleon defeats the Turks at Aboukir.
August–October	Napoleon leaves Egypt and returns to Paris a national hero.
9–10 November	Napoleon helps overthrow the Directory and becomes First Consul at age 30.

1800

13 February	The Bank of France is established.
15–23 May	Napoleon leads his army through the Alps to attack Austrians in Italy, beginning the second Italian campaign.
14 June	Napoleon wins the Battle of Marengo.
24 December	The incident of the "Infernal Machine": An attempt is made on Napoleon's life.

1801

9 February	The Peace of Luneville ends the War of the Second Coalition.
24 March	Russian Tsar Paul I is killed; Alexander I becomes tsar.
15 July	Napoleon signs the Concordat with the Pope.

1802

25 March	The Peace of Amiens between England and France is ratified.
1 August	Napoleon is named First Consul for Life.

1803

3 May	The United States buys the Louisiana Territory from France.
18 May	Great Britain declares war on France.

1804

21 March	The civil code is published, and the Duke of Enghien is executed.
18 May	The senate declares Napoleon Emperor of France.
19 May	The Legion of Honor is established.
2 December	Napoleon is crowned Emperor of the French.

1805

26 May	Napoleon is crowned King of Italy.
9 August	England, Austria, Russia, and Sweden form the Third Coalition against France.
17 October	"The unfortunate General Mack" surrenders at Ülm.
21 October	Admiral Nelson defeats the French and Spanish fleets at the Battle of Trafalgar but dies in the action.
2 December	Napoleon wins the Battle of Austerlitz over the Austrians and Russians.
26 December	The Treaty of Pressburg is ratified between France and Austria.

1806

12 July	The Confederation of the Rhine is created.
6 October	The Fourth Coalition against France is formed by Prussia, Russia, and England.
14 October	Napoleon defeats Prussia at Jena and Auerstädt.
21 November	Napoleon issues the Berlin Decrees, starting the Continental System.

1807

8 February	Russians and Prussians lose the Battle of Eylau.
14 June	Russians and Prussians lose the Battle of Friedland.
8 July	The Peace of Tilsit is made with Russia and Prussia; the Grand Duchy of Warsaw is soon created.
November	France invades Spain and Portugal.

1808

17 March	The Imperial University is created in Paris.
6 June	Napoleon's brother Joseph is made King of Spain.
15 July	Napoleon's brother-in-law Joachim Murat is made King of Naples and Sicily.
4 December	Napoleon enters Madrid and abolishes the Inquisition.

1809

9 April	Austria and England form the Fifth Coalition against France.
20–23 April	Napoleon defeats the Austrians at the Battles of Abensberg, Landshut, Eckmühl, and Ratisbon.
21 May	Napoleon is held off by Austrian Archduke Charles at the Battles of Aspern and Essling.
5–6 July	Napoleon defeats Charles at the Battle of Wagram.
16 December	Napoleon divorces Josephine.

1810

11 March	Napoleon marries Marie Louise of Austria by proxy in Vienna.

1811

20 March	Napoleon's son with Marie Louise, the King of Rome (Napoleon II), is born.

1812

24 June	Napoleon crosses the Niemen River to invade Russia.
July	Russia and England form the Sixth Coalition against France (and are later joined by Prussia, Austria, and others).
7 September	Napoleon defeats the Russians at the Battle of Borodino.
20 October	Napoleon leaves Moscow for Paris, arriving there on December 18th.

1813

26 August	Napoleon, now 44, wins the Battle of Dresden.
16–19 October	Napoleon is defeated at the Battle of Leipzig.

1814

January	France is invaded by Sixth Coalition allies.
10–13 February	Napoleon wins battles at Champaubert, Montmirail, Château-Thierry, and Vauchamp in France.
31 March	Allies enter Paris; a provisional government is formed.
6–11 April	Napoleon abdicates at Fontainebleau.
4 May	Napoleon becomes Emperor of Elba.
29 May	Josephine dies.

1815

1 March	Napoleon returns to France.
20 March	Napoleon enters Paris and the Hundred Days begins.
16 June	Napoleon defeats the Prussians at Ligny (Belgium).
18 June	Napoleon is defeated by the British and Prussians at Waterloo.
22 June	Napoleon abdicates again.
15 July	Napoleon surrenders to Captain Maitland of the *HMS Bellerophon*, hoping to retire in Great Britain.
15 October	Napoleon is sent into exile on St. Helena at age 46.

1821

5 May	Napoleon dies shortly before 6 p.m. at age 51.

1840

15 October	Napoleon's remains are exhumed for return to France.
15 December	Napoleon is interred in the *Hôtel des Invalides* in Paris.

Appendix B
Maps of Napoleonic Europe

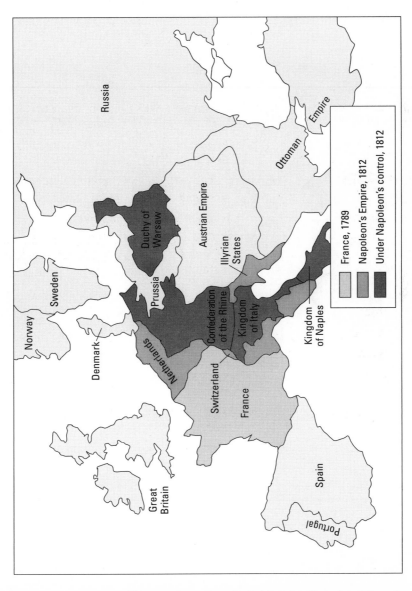

This map shows the extent of Napoleon's empire at its peak.

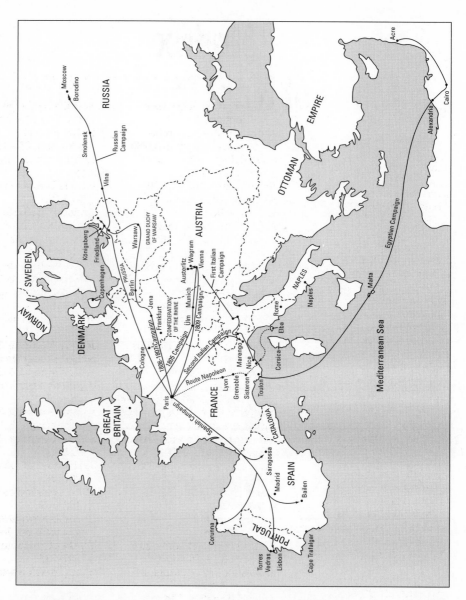

This map indicates the routes of Napoleon's military campaigns and the locations of key battle sites.

Index

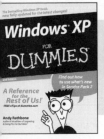

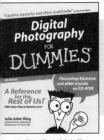

SPORTS, FITNESS, PARENTING, RELIGION & SPIRITUALITY

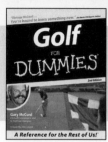

0-7645-5146-9

0-7645-5418-2

Also available:

- Adoption For Dummies
  0-7645-5488-3
- Basketball For Dummies
  0-7645-5248-1
- The Bible For Dummies
  0-7645-5296-1
- Buddhism For Dummies
  0-7645-5359-3
- Catholicism For Dummies
  0-7645-5391-7
- Hockey For Dummies
  0-7645-5228-7

- Judaism For Dummies
  0-7645-5299-6
- Martial Arts For Dummies
  0-7645-5358-5
- Pilates For Dummies
  0-7645-5397-6
- Religion For Dummies
  0-7645-5264-3
- Teaching Kids to Read For Dummies
  0-7645-4043-2
- Weight Training For Dummies
  0-7645-5168-X
- Yoga For Dummies
  0-7645-5117-5

TRAVEL

0-7645-5438-7

0-7645-5453-0

Also available:

- Alaska For Dummies
  0-7645-1761-9
- Arizona For Dummies
  0-7645-6938-4
- Cancún and the Yucatán For Dummies
  0-7645-2437-2
- Cruise Vacations For Dummies
  0-7645-6941-4
- Europe For Dummies
  0-7645-5456-5
- Ireland For Dummies
  0-7645-5455-7

- Las Vegas For Dummies
  0-7645-5448-4
- London For Dummies
  0-7645-4277-X
- New York City For Dummies
  0-7645-6945-7
- Paris For Dummies
  0-7645-5494-8
- RV Vacations For Dummies
  0-7645-5443-3
- Walt Disney World & Orlando For Dummie
  0-7645-6943-0

GRAPHICS, DESIGN & WEB DEVELOPMENT

0-7645-4345-8

0-7645-5589-8

Also available:

- Adobe Acrobat 6 PDF For Dummies
  0-7645-3760-1
- Building a Web Site For Dummies
  0-7645-7144-3
- Dreamweaver MX 2004 For Dummies
  0-7645-4342-3
- FrontPage 2003 For Dummies
  0-7645-3882-9
- HTML 4 For Dummies
  0-7645-1995-6
- Illustrator CS For Dummies
  0-7645-4084-X

- Macromedia Flash MX 2004 For Dummie
  0-7645-4358-X
- Photoshop 7 All-in-One Desk Reference For Dummies
  0-7645-1667-1
- Photoshop CS Timesaving Techniques For Dummies
  0-7645-6782-9
- PHP 5 For Dummies
  0-7645-4166-8
- PowerPoint 2003 For Dummies
  0-7645-3908-6
- QuarkXPress 6 For Dummies
  0-7645-2593-X

NETWORKING, SECURITY, PROGRAMMING & DATABASES

0-7645-6852-3

0-7645-5784-X

Also available:

- A+ Certification For Dummies
  0-7645-4187-0
- Access 2003 All-in-One Desk Reference For Dummies
  0-7645-3988-4
- Beginning Programming For Dummies
  0-7645-4997-9
- C For Dummies
  0-7645-7068-4
- Firewalls For Dummies
  0-7645-4048-3
- Home Networking For Dummies
  0-7645-42796

- Network Security For Dummies
  0-7645-1679-5
- Networking For Dummies
  0-7645-1677-9
- TCP/IP For Dummies
  0-7645-1760-0
- VBA For Dummies
  0-7645-3989-2
- Wireless All In-One Desk Reference For Dummies
  0-7645-7496-5
- Wireless Home Networking For Dummie
  0-7645-3910-8

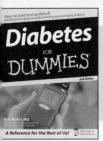

Diabetes
FOR DUMMIES

2nd Edition

A Reference for the Rest of Us!

0-7645-6820-5 *†

Low-Carb Dieting
FOR DUMMIES

A Reference for the Rest of Us!

0-7645-2566-2

Also available:
- Alzheimer's For Dummies
  0-7645-3899-3
- Asthma For Dummies
  0-7645-4233-8
- Controlling Cholesterol For Dummies
  0-7645-5440-9
- Depression For Dummies
  0-7645-3900-0
- Dieting For Dummies
  0-7645-4149-8
- Fertility For Dummies
  0-7645-2549-2

- Fibromyalgia For Dummies
  0-7645-5441-7
- Improving Your Memory For Dummies
  0-7645-5435-2
- Pregnancy For Dummies †
  0-7645-4483-7
- Quitting Smoking For Dummies
  0-7645-2629-4
- Relationships For Dummies
  0-7645-5384-4
- Thyroid For Dummies
  0-7645-5385-2

Speak Spanish — the fun and easy way!

Spanish
FOR DUMMIES

A Reference for the Rest of Us!

0-7645-5194-9

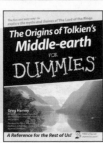

The Origins of Tolkien's Middle-earth
FOR DUMMIES

A Reference for the Rest of Us!

0-7645-4186-2

Also available:
- Algebra For Dummies
  0-7645-5325-9
- British History For Dummies
  0-7645-7021-8
- Calculus For Dummies
  0-7645-2498-4
- English Grammar For Dummies
  0-7645-5322-4
- Forensics For Dummies
  0-7645-5580-4
- The GMAT For Dummies
  0-7645-5251-1
- Inglés Para Dummies
  0-7645-5427-1

- Italian For Dummies
  0-7645-5196-5
- Latin For Dummies
  0-7645-5431-X
- Lewis & Clark For Dummies
  0-7645-2545-X
- Research Papers For Dummies
  0-7645-5426-3
- The SAT I For Dummies
  0-7645-7193-1
- Science Fair Projects For Dummies
  0-7645-5460-3
- U.S. History For Dummies
  0-7645-5249-X

Get smart @ dummies.com®

- **Find a full list of Dummies titles**
- **Look into loads of FREE on-site articles**
- **Sign up for FREE eTips e-mailed to you weekly**
- **See what other products carry the Dummies name**
- **Shop directly from the Dummies bookstore**
- **Enter to win new prizes every month!**

eparate Canadian edition also available
eparate U.K. edition also available

ilable wherever books are sold. For more information or to order direct: U.S. customers visit www.dummies.com or call 1-877-762-2974.
customers visit www.wileyeurope.com or call 0800 243407. Canadian customers visit www.wiley.ca or call 1-800-567-4797.